Abstracts *of* Early Kentucky Wills *and* Inventories

– 1780-1842 –

Copied from
Original and Recorded Wills and Inventories

By:
J. Estelle Stewart King

Southern Historical Press, Inc.
Greenville, South Carolina

This volume was reproduced from
An personal copy located in the
Publisher's private Library

All rights reserved. No part of this publication may be reproduced,
stored in a retrieval system, transmitted in any form, posted
on to the web in any form or by any means without
the prior written permission of the publisher.

Please direct all correspondence and orders to:

www.southernhistoricalpress.com
or
**SOUTHERN HISTORICAL PRESS, Inc.
PO BOX 1267
375 West Broad Street
Greenville, SC   29601
southernhistoricalpress@gmail.com**

Originally published: Beverly Hills, CA. 1933
ISBN #0-89308-747-5
All rights Reserved.
Printed in the United States of America

NOTE

In the Wills the first date given is the date of the instrument, the second date of probate. Few abbreviations have been used and these are obvious: Wit. - Witness, Bro. - Brother, Ex. - Executor and Executrix, Apprs. - Appraisers, Admr. - Administrator.

Where Indexes of Book B and C are given they will not be given in the General Index.

Some of these Wills have been presented in other publications but upon request they are included under one cover.

COUNTIES

INCLUDED IN THIS VOLUME

BARREN	Formed from Warren and Green Counties		1798
BOURBON	" " Fayette County		1785
BULLITT	" " Jefferson and Nelson Counties		1796
CALDWELL	Formed from Livingston County		1809
CHRISTIAN	" " Logan County		1796
CLARK	" " Fayette and Bourbon Counties		1792
CRITTENDEN	" " Livingston County		1842
DAVIESS	Formed from Ohio County		1815
FAYETTE	One of the first three counties formed		1780
FRANKLIN	Formed from Woodford, Mercer and Shelby Counties		1794
GARRARD	Formed from Mercer, Lincoln and Madison Counties		1796
HARDIN	Formed from Nelson County		1792
HARRISON	" " Bourbon and Scott Counties		1793
HENDERSON	" " Christian County		1798
HENRY	" " Shelby County		1798
HOPKINS	" " Henderson County		1806
JEFFERSON	One of the first three counties formed		1780
JESSAMINE	Formed from Fayette County		1798
KNOX	Formed from Lincoln County		1799
LINCOLN	One of the first three counties formed		1780
LIVINGSTON	Formed from Christian County		1798
LOGAN	" " Lincoln County		1792
MADISON	Formed from Lincoln County		1785
MC CRACKEN	" " Hickman County		1824
MERCER	" " Lincoln County		1785
MUHLENBERG	" " Logan and Christian Counties		1798
NELSON	Formed from Jefferson County		1784
NICHOLAS	" " Bourbon and Mason Counties		1799
OHIO	Formed from Hardin County		1798
SCOTT	Formed from Woodford County		1792
SHELBY	" " Jefferson County		1792
SPENCER	" " Nelson, Shelby and Bullitt County		1824
TODD	Formed from Logan and Christian Counties		1819
WARREN	Formed from Logan County		1796
WASHINGTON	" " Nelson County		1792
WOODFORD	" " Fayette County		1788

APPENDIX

```
GREEN . . . . Formed from Lincoln and Nelson Counties . . . . . . . 1793
HARRISON . . "         "  Bourbon and Scott Counties  . . . . . . . 1793
GALLATIN . . "         "  Franklin and Shelby Counties  . . . . . . 1799
```

BARREN COUNTY

BOOK A

ALFORD, HANSIL. Inventory. Oct. Court, 1807.

ASHBY, FRANCIS. Sept. 20, 1813. Oct. Court, 1813. Estate to Martha Cook. Ex: William Thompson. Wit: William Thompson, John Chambers.

AUSTIN, WILLIAM. Inventory. May 12, 1808.

BASS, PHILEMON. Dec. 17, 1814. Feb., 1815. Wife: Patsy. Sons: John, Talbert, William. Daus: Polly, Catharine, Elizabeth Helby (?). Ex: wife, Anderson Cockrill. Wit: John Elmore, Anderson Cockrill, Elizabeth Bass.

BAYLESS, JOSEPH. August 24, 1812. Dec. Court, 1813. Wife: Sarah. Children mentioned but not named. Ex: wife, Thomas Means, Samuel Billingsley (brothers-in-law).

BENNETT, WILLIAM. Sept. 24, 1806. Oct., 1806. Sons: Stephen, John. Wit: --- Daugerty, Isaac Bennett.

BERRY, AGUSTIN. Inventory. Feb., 1812. Apprs: James Campbell, Abraham Campbell, John Gatewood.

BISHOP, WILLIAM. July 26, 1811. ----Wife: Rebecca. Sons: Lowry, William, Cary, Beady, Joseph, John, Samuel. Daus: Clarisy McClain, Jane Malone, Betsy Bishop. Ex: son Lowry.

BLACK, JAMES. Inventory. July 16, 1801.

BLACK, JAMES, SR. July 31, 1801. Sept., 1802. Wife: Rachel. Sons: James, Robert, John. Daus: Ann, Margaret, Sarah Miller. Ex: wife, Edward Young. Wit: John Garnett, John Robertson, James Howell.

BOWLES, ANDERSON. April 25, 1811. ----Legatees: Gincy Bowles (sister), Sackeyriah Bowles (brother). Wit: Thos. Jonson, Jacky Bowles, Clarboun Bowles.

BOYD, JOHN. Inventory. Oct. 29, 1808. Apprs: Jacob Wilson, Samuel Williams, Obidiah Wade.

BREED, AVARY. Dec. 5, 1800. ----Estate to brothers and sisters. Ex: Nathan Breed (brother), Joseph Guist. Wit: David Hardin, William B. Gist, Christie Howard.

BRIDGES, JAMES. Dec. 7, 1802. Dec., 1802. Of Warren County, Ky. Wife: Nancy. Daus: Sooky, Elizabeth, Polly, Caty, Ana. Ex: Moses Bridges, Jonathan Cox. Wit: James Walker, Margaret Bridges.

BROOKS, JOHN, SR. Inventory. Oct., 1815. Apprs: Simeon Lewis, John Anderson, ----Anderson, Jas. Brooks, Admin.

BROWNING, WILLIAM. No date. Oct. Court, 1807. Wife: Elizabeth. Legatees: Chas. Browning, Thompson Browning, Robert Browning, Daniel Browning, Joseph Browning, Rebecca Browning, Nancy Comer, Mary Curtis, Elizabeth Browning, Ellender Browning (dau). Ex: wife, Charles Browning (son). Wit: Richard Condray, Jacob Condray, Daniel Browning.

BUSH, JOHN. Inventory. Jan. 4, 1814. Apprs: Alexander Davidson, John Renfre (?), Elmore Renfre (?), Isaac Ringe.

BYBEE, JAMES. May 3, 1813. July, 1815. Bros: Allen, Levi. Wit: William Anderson, David Woodson.

CARPENTER, SAMUEL. March 13, 1811. May, 1811. Wife: Caterner. Son: Samuel. Daus: Susannah Latimore, Margaret Orr, Sally Latimore, Elizabeth Short, Fanny Green. Ex: wife, Landman Short. Wit: John Brothers, Jacob Gooman, Sylvester Hall.

CHAMBERS, JOHN. Inventory. May, 1815. Apprs: Simeon Lewis, John Anderson, John Allen.

CLEMENTS, JAMES. Inventory. Feb. 17, 1817. Apprs: Benj. Buster, William Murphy, Joe Franklin.

COCHRAN, REUBEN. March 22, 1814. Jan. 1815. Legatees: Doses Barlow (?), Sukey Martin, Thos. Hinton (son of Richard Hinton). Wit: Lowman Short, Sion Short, John Cochran, Jr.

COLMAN, JOSEPH. Wife: Jane. Sons: Grief, Field, Philip. Daus: Betsy Kelley, Judy Cole. Wit: Ambrose Kenslow, Joseph Coleman, Joseph Ralston. August 3, 1808. Oct. 1809.

CONLEY, ISAAC. Nov. 11, 1815. Dec., 1816. Wife: Mary. Dau: Susannah Denton. Wit: R. P. Stumberger, Reuben Conlee, Levey Conlee.

COURTS, JOHN. Feb. 19, 1817. ----Wife: Fanny. Sons: Charles, William, Richard, John. Daus: Clara, Nancy, Amanda, Emily, Zerilda, Frances Bagsby, Kitty Ficklin, Polly Moss. Ex: wife, Bracton B. Winn, Robenson B. Beauchamp, Sylvanus Bagsby, Fredrick Moss. Wit: William Grey, Joseph Crockett.

CRAWFORD, DAVID. April 10, 1812. July, 1812. Wife: Polly. Sons: Jesse, James Fisher. Ex: wife, Samuel Douglas. Wit: George Douglas, Patrick Borseau.

CROW, JOHN. Inventory Sept. 14, 1804. Apprs: Atcher Craddock, Francis Lattimore, Andrew Walker.

DAVIDSON, ALEXANDER. June 15, 1811. August, 1817. Wife: Mary. Sons: Jesse, James, John, Alexander, Hezekiah, William, Elijah, Benjamin, Isaac, Abraham, Jacob, Asa, Ellis, Alin, Albert. Daus: Ann, Margaret, Elizabeth, Sarah, Rachel, one stepdaughter (not named). Ex: Alex. Davidson, Hezekiah Davidson, Benjamin Davidson (sons). Wit: George Murrel, William Trigg, William Depp. Clement Montage.

DODD, MARSHALL. Inventory. Nov. 2, 1816. Apprs: John Duff, James Leavel, Henry Carter.

DOWNING, JAMES. Inventory. Sept. 24, 1812. Apprs: James Campbell, Abraham Campbell, Charles Austin.

DUNHAM, MICHAEL. May 14, 1816. Nuncupative. Legatees: wife, children (not named), Newton Dunham. Proven by oath of John Dunham, Peter Dunham, James Bird.

EDWARDS, ALEXANDER. Inventory. Jan. 16, 1817. Apprs: James Jameson, Beverly Bradley, Jacob Maggart.

EMMERSON, JESSE. Inventory. April, 1810. Apprs: Henry Carter, John Duff, John Dodd.

EMMERSON, WILLIAM. May 2, 1812. ----Wife: Elizabeth. Son: John. Ex: wife, Zachariah Emmerson (brother). Wit: Thomas Winn, James Mathews, John Wheeler.

ESTIS, MARSHAL. Inventory. Nov. 14, 1810. Apprs: John Pool, William Leaper, James Reed.

FITZJERREL (FITZGERALD), WILLIAM. Inventory. Dec., 1813. Apprs: Simeon Lewis, Mathais Lair, John Black, John Allen.

FRIELY, CHRISTIAN. Nov. 16, 1810. Feb. 1811. Wife: Elizabeth. Sons: Nicholas, Edward, John, Adam, Jonathan, Samuel. Daus: Esther, Mary. Wit: Samuel Marrs, Thos. Wiley, Ezekiel Springer.

GADSBERRY, JAMES B. April 23, 1816. May, 1816. Sisters: Edith Gadsberry, Susan Gadsberry. Brothers: John Glazebrook, William Glazebrook (half-brothers). Mentions unborn infant of Anabelle G-----(illegible). Ex: Jordan Glazebrook (stepfather), Stephen Beauchamp (friend), Wit: Polly Glazebrook, Sally Trible, Lucy Cochran.

GALLOWAY, JAMES. Sept. 8, 1801. Jan., 1802. Wife: Elizabeth. Sons: William, John. Daus: Agnes Leaper, Elizabeth, Mary, Jane Rudy (or Reedy). Ex: wife, William Galloway, John Galloway (sons). Wit: Alex. Davidson, John Sanders, John Mayfield, Jr.

GENTRY, SAMUEL. Feb. 16, 1816. May Court, 1816. Wife: Sarah. Dau: Elizabeth. Son: Altha. Mentions other children but does not name them. Mention is made of his father's property in North Carolina. Ex: Gideon Mayfield, Benj. Adams, Wit: Nicholas Hauser, John Ingram, Elizabeth Brown.

GLAZEBROOK, JORDAN. Guardian of Gadsberry heirs.

GLAZEBROOK, RICHARD. March, 1816. April, 1816. Sis: Elizabeth Frances, Polly. Bros: James, John, William, Jourdan. Ex: John Glazebrook (bro.), John King (friend). Wit: Mathais Lain (Lair), Alex. Blair.

GREEN, S. Inventory. Nov. 22, 1815.

GRIDER, CHRISTOPHER. August 27, 1806. Nov., 1806. Wife: Nelly. Daus:

Nancy, Susannah, Ruth, Sally, Polly. Ex: wife, Jacob Grider, Sr. Wit: Solomon Dickerson, Daniel Wray, David Heady.

GRINSTEAD, JAMES. June 1, 1818. July, 1818. Of Albemarle Co., Va. Sons: James, William. "William to have money from Cornetts Estate". Ex: James Grinstead. Wit: Jesse Grinstead, John Grinstead.

GRINSTEAD, JESSE. Inventory. April, 1816. Apprs: Jourdan Glazebrook, Thomas Beauchamp, John Morrison.

HAMILTON, JOHN. July 30, 1801. July, 1802. Wife: Sarah. Daus: Jean, Eals (?). Sons: Jno., James, Robert. Ex: John Hamilton (son). Wit: George Keys, William Keys.

HAYS, JOSEPH. Inventory. August 1, 1816. Apprs: John Hamilton, James T. Tunstall, Buford Allen, Clabourn Hays.

HOLLODAY, JOHN. June 9, 1818. July, 1818. Wife: Eleanor. Legatees: Burrell Holloday (bro.), of Southampton Co., Va., James Neese (stepson), Robert Campbell, Alice (?) Craven. Ex: Philip Macy. Wit: James Nevill, Jeremiah Hovis, George Rogers, Joel Yancy.

HOWARD, OBIDIAH. March 1, 1804. Nov. Court, 1804. Wife: Priscilla. Children: Anna, other children mentioned but not named. Ex: William Howard, Stephen Howard (sons). Wit: Christopher Howard, Robert Kirby, John Lanham.

KERR, JAMES. Dec. 23, 1812. May Court, 1818. Sons: John R., William, David. Daus: Sarah Thompson, Polly Burch, Son-in-law: Benj. Buster. Ex: Clifton Redes. Wit: Samuel Murrel, Sr., Samuel Murrel, Jr., Samuel Jourden.

LEPENSBERRY, DAVID. Nov. 9, 1817. Nov., 1817. Wife: Lurana. Children: Thos. Hobbs, Marianna, Reuben, Regina, Ann Jane. Ex: Robert Lepensberry, William Lepensberry (bros.) Wit: Laban Jennings, John Lepensberry, Charles Drever.

LEWIS, PATRICK. April 4, 1810 ("Thirty-fifth year of American Independence"). July 16, 1810. Wife: not named. Sons: John, Lewis. Daus: Nancy King, Betsy, Mary. Ex: William Roark, Jonson Poe. Wit: William Curd, David Pursley, John Barr.

LOGSDON, THOMAS. April 18, 1818. May, 1818. Sons: John, Thomas. Dau: Mary White. Ex: John Logsdon (son). Wit: Philip Makey, Samuel Dodson, Job K. Logsdon.

MATTHEWS, JOHN. May 11, 1811. Jan. Court, 1812. Wife: Jenney. Sons: Pleasant, George, James, John. Daus: Nancy Mayfield, Betsy Welsh, Polly Mayfield, Sally Bush. Wit: Judith Pickett, Thomas Berry, Peggy Simeton, William T. Bush.

MC ADOE, JOHN. April 7, 1800. Jan. Court, 1802. Daus: Nancy Ralston, Martha Allen, Mary Moore, Roda Flipping. Sons: William, John. Ex: William Alleward, Thos. Flipping. Wit: Simeon Buford, William Buford, William Cann.

MONTAGE, CLEMENT. Inventory. August, 1813. Apprs: Alex. Blair, George Murrel, H. Trigg.

MURREL, JANETT. Jan. 30, 1804. Oct. 1814. Of County of Albemarle, Virginia. Sons: Samuel, George. Daus: Mary Page, Jenney Henderson. Mentions children of dau. Ann Hunter, children of dau. Milly Davenport. Ex: Samuel Murrel (son). Wit: Edmund Jewell, Hezekiah Jordan, Samuel Jordan.

POLK, MOSES. Inventory. Dec., 1815.

PREWETT, JOHN. -----July, 1818. Wife: Sarah. Sons: George, John. Daus: Sarah, Elizabeth. Ex: wife. Wit: Robert S. Thompson, Waddy Thompson, Cornelius Beazeley. Testators name is signed "John Pruate" but, indexed Prewett.

PULLIAM, BENJAMIN. Inventory. May 21, 1818. List of slaves and personal estate. Apprs: R. Daugherty, William Shirley.

RITTER, ABRAHAM. Dec. 30, 1805. April 1810. Wife: Margaret. Ex: wife, Joseph Ritter. Wit: John Kelly, Ralph Petty, John Ritter, Isaac Ritter.

ROSS, PHILEMON. Dec. 17, 1814. Feb. 1815. Wife: Patsy. Sons: John, Talbert, Warren, Isaac. Daus: Sally, Nancy, Metheldred (?). Ex: wife. Wit: John Elmore, Anderson Cockrill, Elizabeth Ross.

SAUNDERS, JESSE. Inventory. Dec. 30, 1813. Apprs: William Clark, William Depp, James Franklin.

SHIRLEY, JAMES. Inventory. Dec. 21, 1819.

SMITH, AMOS. Sept. 29, 1817. Oct. 1817. Wife: Nancy. Leg: Jno., Lydia, Nancy, Amos, and Synthianna Smith, Jency Walters Dau. of Henry Walters. Son: Jno. Ex: Philip Maxey, Richard Mumsford. Wit: Samuel Isaacs, Ransom, Amos and Jas. Fasinger.

SMITH, ISAAC. Inventory May 6, 1811. Wife: Sarah Hampton. Appr: Leonard Murry, Andrew Nuckols, Joseph Higdon.

SMITH, JEREMIAH. March 25, 1817. May, 1817. Wife: Diana. Child: Polly, Betsy Crouse, Amey Williams, Margaret, Suckey, Elsey, George. Ex: wife, Henry Simson, Esq. Wit: Williamson Davis, Robert Larks, Robert Barnett.

SMITH, WILLIAM. Sept. 8, 1801. Nov. 1801. Wife: Rachel. Children: Mary Jane, Messina. Wit: John Howe, John Smith. Ex: wife.

STOCKTON, DANIEL. April 24, 1800. Nov. 1800. Wife: Susana. Children: Newberry, Hugh, an unborn child. Wit: Robert Hill, Thomas Stockton. Ex: wife:

TADLOCK, JAMES. ----- -----Wife: Susan. Children: Elizabeth, Phebe, Sarah, John, Lewis, Urand, James. Ex: Robert Kirby, John Pinkley. Wit: Gabriel Murphy, Francis Gillihan.

TADLOCK, JOSHUA. July 12, 1805 ---- Wife: Nancy. Child.: Edward, Betsy, other children not named. Ex: J. M. Carrick. Wit: Thos. Wood, Daniel Browning, James McLain.

THACKER, BENJAMIN. Feb. 9, 1818. April Court, 1818. Wife: Nancy. Daus:

Delila, Sinthy, Henrietta, Martha. Sons: Abel, Allen R. Ex: Simeon Lewis. Wit: James Kirtley, John Kirtley.

TROTTER, JOHN. May 20, 1811. July, 1811. Wife: Chalia. Children: Polly, Elizabeth, William. Ex: wife, James Rice (friend). Wit: William Gray, William Mosby, Archibald Miller.

TUDER, HENRY. June 17, 1815. Nov. Court, 1816. Wife: Nancy. Sons: Abraham, Joel, John, Henry, Absalom. Daus: Nancy, Susanna, Phebe Enicks. Ex: John Tuder, Absalom Tuder (sons). Wit: Philip V. Young, Edmund Payne, Giles Kelly.

WAGGONER, JAMES. Inventory. May, 1811.

WAGGONER, RICHARD. Dec. 20, 1814. Jan. Court, 1818. Wife: Caty. Legatees: Beverly Bradley (son-in-law), Thos. Waggoner (son), Children of son James, dec'd. Ex: son Thomas, Thompson Crenshaw. Wit: George L. Cabaness, Alexander Mc Conless.

WHITE, GEORGE. May 29, 1809. July Court, 1809. Wife: Rutha. Son: Edmund. Dau.-in-law: Elizabeth Mc Daniel (stepdau.). Ex: wife, Edmund White (son). Wit: Thomas Dickenson, John Monroe, James Ritchey.

WHITE, HENRY. Feb. 28, 1802. August, 1810. Wife: Elizabeth. Daus: Susanna Jones, Martha Holloway, Polly Glazebrook, Rebecca White. Sons: Joseph, Simeon. Ex: wife, Joseph White, Simeon White (sons). Wit: Thos. Winn, Jr., Elijah Mitchell.

WILBORN, JAMES. Feb. 15, 1811. Aug., 1811. Wife: Esabel. Sons: Samuel, Joshua, other children not named. Mentions grandson but, does not name him. Ex: Samuel Wilborn, Joshua Wilborn (sons). Wit: Edward Barber, Gideon Wilborn.

WILLIAMS, BENJAMIN. Dec. 6, 1817. Jan. Court 1818. Wife: Winney. Daus: Nancy Bridges, Sally Williams, Polly Bridges, Elizabeth Tracy, Rachel Hawkins, Milly Ragland, Rebecka H------(illegible), Patsy Huckaby. Sons: James, William, John, David, Thomas, Richard. Wit: Richard Ragland, Jeremiah Bridges, Nathan Huckaby.

WILLIAMS, DANIEL. Oct. 7, 1800. July 1801. Wife: not named. Son: John. Wit: Jno. Martin, Mary Murry.

WILSON, JOHN. June 4, 1809. Nov. Court 1815. Wife: Elizabeth. Sons: Ezra, Sebert, Hosea. Daus: Nancy, Delilah, Sarah, Charity, Rhoady. Wit: ---- Daugherty. William Glover, John Franklin.

WROTON, NEHEMIAH. May 18, 1803. Oct., 1803. Ex: Sarah Wroton (wife). Wit: James Bratton, Fargus Johnston.

YOUNG, REUBEN. Aug. 24, 1815.

BARREN COUNTY

BOOK A

Index of Guardian Bonds, Inventories, Dowers and etc.

Allen, William

Bailey, Joseph
Berry, Ephiram
Black, Cortez
Burley, Thomas

Crews, James
Crenshaw, John

Hays, Thos.
Howman, Thomas
Hardwitch, James
Harris, Josiah
Hardy, Thomas
Hindman, Robert

James, Jamea
James, Samuel
Jones, James
Jenkins, James
Jewell, Chas.

Kirkham, John
Kinsloe, Conrod
Kelly, Samuel

Lloyd, Thomas
Leeper, Matthew
Lowe, Isaac
Lattimore, Francis

Lewis, William

Mc Murry, John
Mc Gill, James

Novil, Joseph

Pickett, Hannah
Pedige, Henry
Pickett, John
Polk, Moses
Peden, Francis

Ratliff, William
Renick, Samuel
Richardson, Dudley
Richardson, Holt
Rock, John
Ross, William
Ruckman
Ryan, Major

Sandusky, Andrew
Summers, John
Scott, George
Smith, Isaac
Sleaton, Dabney
Springer, John

Tinsley, Isaac

BOURBON CO.

BOOK A

ALLISON, CHARLES. Oct. 2, 1787. Dec. 1787. Wife: Jane. Sons: John, Alexander. Ex: Wife and John (son). Wit: Benjamin Harrison, Mary Allison.

ANDREAS, JACOB. March 1792. Sept. 25, 1795. Legatees: Elenor Brown, John Brown. Wit: Jas. Quinn, Luke Merryman, Keziah Reece.

BARTON, JOHN. ------1792. Oct. 1793. Wife: Martha. Sons: John, Moses, Charles, Elijah. Daus: Elizabeth, Lucy. Ex: Wife. Wit: Thomas Flemming, Samuel Flemming, Caines Brandon.

BROWN, ALEXANDER. Oct. 29, 1795. March 1796. Wife: Elizabeth. Sons: John, James. Daus: Nancy, Jane, Elizabeth. Ex:------ Wit:------.

BROWN, JAMES. Aug. 21, 1791. Jan. 1796. Wife: Rachel. Son: James. Dau: Katrina McCoy. Gr. sons: James McCoy, Samuel Brown. Ex: Wife, Samuel Henderson.

CLIFFORD, ROBERT. Feb. 13, 1791. July 1791. Estate to brother James Clifford, and sister Jane Clifford. Wit: James McCutcher, John Slute.

CONSTANT, CAPT. JOHN. Oct. 21, 1788. --------- Nuncupative. All estate to be divided between children (not named). Proved by oath of Mr. Van Swearengen. Wit: W. Abigail, Admin.

DOUGLAS, JOHN. Inventory. Aug. C.C.1793.

CUSHENBERRY, MOSES. Inventory. June 1792. Apprs: Daniel Durbin, A. Easten, James Kenny.

DOWDEN, JOHN. Inventory. Apr. 1791.

DUNLAP, JOHN. Feb. 2, 1791. Wife: Elizabeth. Dau: Smithia Kid, another daughter name not mentioned. Sister: Isabell Home and her son John. Ex: Wife, Thomas Dunlap (bro.). Wit: John Howe, William Dunlap, William Taylor.

FRANKLIN, ROBERT. Inventory. Apr. 30, 1791.

GALLOWAY, WILLIAM. Jan. 20, 1794. May 1794. Wife: Rebekah. Sons: George, James, Joseph, John. Daus: Mary, Ann, Rebeck. Ex: Wife, James Galloway (son). Wit: James and John Gollaway, Alex. Breckenridge.

GILBERTS, BARNEY. June C.C. 1790. Apprs: Jacob Lankston, John Burk.

GILLESPY, DANIEL. Inventory. Dec. 18, 1787.

GLASGOW, JNO. Aug. 15, 1794. Dec. 1794. Wife: Anna. Daus: Polly, Jenny, Bro: Nathaniel Glasgow. Wit: John, Alex, & Jas. Thompson.

GREEN, JOHN. Inventory. July 1792. Apprs: James Duncan, Thomas Kenndy, Joseph Kenndy.

HENDERSON? ALEX. Oct. 30, 1791. Oct. 1796. Sons: Robert, Samuel, James, Joseph, Alex., Daniel, David, George. Gr. sons: Alex. Henderson(son of John Henderson). Daus: Jane Beatty, Florence. Ex: Samuel Henderson and David Henderson. Wit: Samuel Henderson, Josiah McClure, Elizabeth Henderson.

HUMBLE, CONROD. Jan. 5, 1791.--------Wife: Hannah. Sons: Uriah, Noah, John Fitzwater(son-in-law), Richard Custer(son-in-law). Dau: Rachel. Ex: brother Michael, James Johnson(bro-in-law). Wit: David Wilson, John Wright, Moses Hecks.

JACOBY, FRANCIS LUCAS. May 7, 1788. July 5, 1788. Wife: Fredrica. Sons: Frank, Henry, Fredrick, Daniel, Jacob, Adam, John, Ralph Gladingsberg. Daus: Katrina Elizabeth Butler, Susanna, Becky. Ex: wife, John Grant, William Butler. Wit: John Grant, William Butler.

JAMESON, SAMUEL. Oct. 27, 1793. Dec. 1793. Wife: Rebekah. Legatees: Charles Jameson(eldest son of bro. William), Samuel Jameson (son of brother David),. Ex: James Kirkpatrick and Robert Finley. Wit: David Jameson, George Wilson, William Robinson.

JONES, JOHN. August 7, 1790. Dec. 1790. Wife: Susannah. Sons: John, Jacob, Benjamin. Daus: Christiana, Betsy, Susanna, Catharine. Ex: wife, Jacob Jones, (brother). Wit: Susan Keison, Christopher Keison, Henry Speaks, Jacob Creen.

JONES, SUSANNAH. June 15, 1791. Nuncupative. Mrs. Jones desires her oldest daughter to have her estate being she is lame and is not able to maintain herself. Proved by oath of Mary Swasick.

KINCAID, DAVID. Dec. C.C. 1795. Sons: David, Samuel, Thomas. Daus: Nancy, Elizabeth. Ex: David Kincaid (son). Wit: Michael Fisher, Joseph Petty.

LAIL, JOHN, July 2, 1793. -------Wife: Margaret. Legatees: John Lail(son), Catrenah Lail(daughter of Peter Lail), George Lail (son) and four children. Elizabeth F----(daughter), Mary L-------(illegible). Ex: wife, Casper Carsner, Andrew Simolt(?). Wit: Lewis Snell, Thomas Davis, C--- Brandon.

LAMY, JAMES. June 18, 1791. Oct. C.C. 1791. Legatees: Robert, Alexander (youngest brother), Patrick Gaffey, William Ardrey, William Nesbit and wife. "James Miller to have my velvet jacket and set-out coat." Mention is made of Pennsylvania money. Ex: John Ardrey, William Nesbit, James Egneu, Isaac Egneu. Wit: John Ryland.

LAUGHLIN, JAMES. March 4, 1791.--------. Son: George. Dau: Eales McLaughlin. Ex: D. Ealils, George Laughlin (son). Wit: Samuel White, John Weathernton, John Stevenson.

LEVENS, ANN. Dec. 4, 1793. March 1794. Sons: Henry Levens, Richard Levens, Nicholas Levens, James Levens. Daus: Patience Mash, Rebecca Solvey, Ann McCrary. Ex: James Leven (son).
Wit: William Sparks, William Wills.

LOGAN, WILLIAM. Inventory. Oct. C.C. 1790. Apprs: George and John Reading.

LYNE, EDMUND. Nov. 26, 1791. Dec. 1791. "Friend Harry Innes to execute will. Each slave in bondage under him shall be liberated." Wit: Thomas West., Richard W. Downing.

MASON, GEORGE. -----. Oct. 16, 1787. Who was shot by Indians at the lower Blue Licks in Bourbon Co. George Mason desires that Mr. Denit takes possession of all that belongs to him and sell enough to pay his just debts. Residue to James Taylor, son of Joseph Taylor of Fairfax Co., Va., near Alexdria, and to his brothers and sisters, to be equally divided among them except wearing apparel to be divided between Mrs. Johnson and his sister. Testator: Edward Lyne, William W. Flin.

MC CAN, JOHN. Sept. 21, 1795. -----. Wife: Nancy. Children: Mentioned but not named. Ex: Wife, Thomas Rule. Wit: John Rawlegh, William Kenneth.

MC CLURE, ANDREW. Aug. 15, 1793. Dec. C.C. 1793. Wife: Rebekah. Sons: James, Andrew. Daus: Ellinor, Polly. Two negroes, Isam and Doll, their freedom. Ex: Samuel McClure and John McClure (brothers). Wit: William Maxwell, William Craig, Alexander Martin.

Mc CLURE, WILLIAM. June 20, 1794. ----- Wife: Elizabeth. Daus: Lucy, Jain (or Fain), Alenor. Ex: John Mc Clue, and Samuel Wilson. Wit: Alexander Wright, Samuel Beard, John Kenny.

MC MILLTON, JAMES. Inventory. Apr. 9, 1791. Apprs: Robert Hutchison, John Strode, Sr.

MCNEY, AGNES. June 28, 1793. July C.C. 1793. Sons: John, Joseph, James. Daus: Isabella, Nancy, Sarah, Margaret. Wit: Samuel Blair, Robert Boyd, John McClanchan.

METHENY, THOMAS. Nov. 1793. Nov. 1793. Legatees: Ann, Sarah, (sisters), Thomas Slagle (Nephew). Ex: Father. Wit: John Neale, John Whitaker.

MOORE, JACOB. Sept. 6, 1790. Dec. C.C. 1790. Of Parish of Va., Co. of Bourbon. Legatees: Nancy Funk (sister), Elizabeth Alkire of the James Parish and County, Va. Wit: John Skire, John Edwards C.C.

MOORE, THOMAS. July 17, 1794. Aug. 1794. Wife: Mary. Sons: Thomas, John, Andrew, Peter, George, Fredrick, and unborn child. Wit: Christopher Shock, William Orr.

NORRIS, JOSEPH. Inventory. Aug. C.C. 1791. Apprs: John Wallace, Reuben------, Samuel Douglas.

OGIE, BENJAMIN. Inventory. Sept. 1791.

PATTON, WILLIAM. July 31, 1794. --------. Sons: John, Joseph, Thomas, William. Daus: Mary, Rosannah, Elizabeth. Ex: Joseph (son), Joseph McClintock (son-in-law).

PAYNE, JOSEPH. Jan. 3, 1796. ----- Wife: Peggy. Son: Thomas. Daus: Molly,

Betsy, Nancy, Aney. Ex: wife.

PEYTON, TIMOTHY. Sept. 5, 1782. ------. Wife: Sarah. Children: Sitha Ann, Ann Thorton, Francis, Elizabeth, Valentine Smallwood, and unborn child. Mentions bro. Valentine Peyton, and bro-in-law James Watson's child. Ex: wife, and James Matson, John Mc Millan. Wit: Jesse Davis, John Davis, George Jackson, Thomas Calvert.

READING, GEORGE. June 23, 1792. ------. (67 years of age.) Wearing apparel to son George. "Son John to have 400 acres of land which Simon Kenton entered and surveyed for me in my name lying on both sides of Flemming Creek, a branch of Blue-Lick." Mentions oldest son Samuel, and son George, and son William. Ex: George and John (sons). Wit: Benjamin Harrison, William Holliday, John Trimble.

REDMON, GEORGE. Dec. 31, 1789. Nov. 1796. Wife: Nancy. Sons: Thomas, Charles, George, William, John. Daus: Mary, Elizabeth, Margaret, Sarah. "Desires to be buried on the top of hill near peach nurcery (nursery) in Christian-like manner." Wit: John Cook, Samuel Cook.

SCONE, ROBERT. Nov. 9, 1808. Jan. 1809. Wife: Mary. Sons: Robert, James, Samuel. Dau: Polly. Gr.dau. Cinthy Berry Sloane, Rebecca Adams. Wit: Jane Champ. Book C.

SCONE, JOHN. Jan. 5, 1794. July 1794. Wife: Margaret. Sons: Thomas, Robert, John. Ex: wife, Bro. James. Wit: Samuel Slack, Thomas Scone, James Briton.

SCONE, THOMAS. Sept. 19, 1795. Oct. 1795. (Age 29 years). Wife: Isabel. Bros: Samuel, Robert. Each nephew to have a suit of clothes. Wit: Samuel Mc Dow, James Scone, James Bratton (Britton).

SHANHAN, DANIEL. Inventory. April 1792.

SHANKS, CHRISTIAN. --------. (probably 1787.) Inventory. Apprs: David Flickman, Thos. Mc Clanahan, Peter Vardman.

SMELZER, PETER. Oct. 21, 1795. Dec. 1795. Wife: Barbara. Estate not to be divided until youngest child, Jacob, becomes of age.

SMITH, JOHN. Feb. 2, 1794. July 1794. Wife: Catrina. Mentions William Mc Cann. Ex: James Ardrey, John Mitchell. Wit: Samuel Peyton, John Davidson, Stephen Peyton.

STROTHER, THOMAS. June 3, 1798. -----1798. Wife: Nelly. Legatees: Thomas Benson (son of William), William, Thomas, Peggy, Polly, Maria (Child of Thos. Mc Clanahan, Jr.). Ex: wife, Thos. Mc Clanahan, Jr.

THOMAS, JAMES. Aug. 30, 1794. April 1797. Wife: Sarah. Sons: David, James, Thos. Daus: Rebecca, Ann Jones. Wit: John Beggs, Conrod Custer.

THOMPSON, JOSEPH. Oct. 30, 1793. May, 1794. Wife: Jean. Estate to be divided when youngest son (John) reaches age of 21 years. Ex: wife, John Moore.

THURMAN, JOSHUA. Dec. 27, 1794. July 1795. To sister Mary Smith's daughter, land in Hanover Co. Va. Mentions brother John and son Thomas. Exr: John Thurman. Wit: John Jones, John Jones, Jr., Brazilla Endicott.

TODD, SAMUEL. Inventory. No dates. Apprs: Levi Todd, Robert Todd, Robert Parker.

TUCKER, EDWARD. Inventory. (Probably 1790) Apprs: James McClure, Isaac Huddell, Jacob Spears.

UNDERWOOD, REUBEN. Inventory. December, 1790.

WALLER, EDWARD. June 15, 1791. Jan. 1792. Wife Sally. Children: Mareann, Betsy, unborn child. Mother to have the property that may come from father's estate and lands in Stafford County, Virginia. Mentions brother Thomas Waller and several sisters. Exr: Col. John Edwards. In case of death of Col. Edwards then wife to be executrix. Wit: Alfred Ellis, Rachel Templen.

WARD, ISAAC. June 1, 1793. Nov. 1793. Wife Elizabeth. Sons: John, James and Isaac. Daughter Nancy. Exrs: wife, John Ward and James Ward.

WEAKLIN, WILLIAM COOK. Dec. 29, 1792. May 1793. Wife Mary. Sons: Bowles, Turner Rogers, Charley, William Canody. Daughter Betsy. Exrs: wife, son Bowles. Wit: Edmund Woolridge, James Jamison and William Hall.

WEBB, ADAM. Inventory. June 4, 1791. Apprs: John Strode, James Strode.

WEBB, JAMES. (Killed on last expedition against the Maume Indians) Nov. 20, 1790. Dec. C.C. 1790. Will was written at the house of Stephen Boyle where he resided. To Thomas Allen, an orphan child, a horse & bridle, to brother Benjamin, his clothes, to Stephen Ogden his crop. Wit: Master Ogden, Stephen Boyle, Robert Ellison.

WEST, JOHN. Nov. 23, 1791. Dec. 1791. Wife Rachel. Daughters: Sarah Eades, Margaret and Martha. Sons: John, Roger West. Extrx: wife. Wit: John Allen and Robert Eades.

WHITLEDGE, JOHN. Oct. 5, 1788. Nov. 1788. Wife, Alcey. Children: John, Susannah, Lina, Ursula, Thomas. Exr: Thomas Whitledge (brother).
Wit: Thomas Strother, Peggy Coppage, Nancy Metcalf.

WICKERSHAM, JOHN. March 19, 1791. Apprs: Reuben Rankin, James M. Graw, Samuel Douglas.

WILSON, JOHN. March 12, 1795. Oct. Court, 1795. Legatee: James Burns (son-in-law). Exr: David Wilson. Wit: John Beggs, Conrad Custer, John Hinkson.

WINN, OWEN. Inventory. Jan. County Court, 1792. John Edwards C.C.

YOUNG, SAMUEL. June 4, 1786. June, 1786. Legatee and executor, John Dawson. Wit: Benjamin Harrison, John Trimble, John Farlow.

BULLITT COUNTY

BOOK A

1799-----1824

ALLISON, ENOCH. Inventory. Nov. 21, 1814.

ALLISON RICHARD. April 5, 1808. Sept. 1808. Sons: Elisha, John, Enoch, David, Daus: Barbara, Lilly (hus. John Day), Eleanor (hus. Robert Richetts), Elizabeth (hus. Edward Archer), Gracy (hus. Harsh Tuel(?). Ex: Enoch Allison (son), Barbara Allison (dau.). Wit: Lemeck Sweargen, Landock Harris.

BAIRD, DAVID. Inventory. Oct. 1818.

BAYNE (BANE), THOMAS. June 6, 1822. Nov. 1822. Wife: Sarah. Sons: William, Walter, Henry, John. Daus: Rachel, Patsy, Elizabeth Walters, Sally Walters, Ann Walters. Son: Jesse. Gr.Child: children of dau. Polly (dec'd), and her husband Hendley Middleton. Ex: William Bayne, John Bayne (sons). Wit: John Hodgens, Philip Johnson, Greenberry Johnson.

BRASHEAR, NACY. Inventory. Nov. 21, 1821.

BRISCOE, SAMUEL. March 20, 1822. August 7, 1822. Wife: Nancy. Sons: Harrison, Nicholas. Dau: Ruth. Wit: Joel Harper, Francis Brady, Robert Patterson.

BROWN, JOHN. Feb. 6, 1817. April 1817. Estate to be equally divided between my children. Ex: Alex. Brown, Samuel Brown (sons).

BROWN, MARY. Nov. 7, 1817. April 3, 1820. Sons: Thomas, Nicholas. Gr.dau: Mary Brown. Ex: Thos. Brown, Nicholas Brown (sons). Wit: Henry Slaughter, Joseph Baughn, John Hall. (Mary Brown was the widow of John Brown).

BROWN, HUGH. Jan. 15, 1812. ----1815. Wife: Mary. Children mentioned but not named. 2 Gr.sons John and Hugh C------(illegible).

BRUSSELS, JOHN. Inventory. Oct. 1824. Admin: Sarah Buidusell.

CARPENTER, MARGARET. Sept. 13, 1820. Oct. 1820. Legatees: Rebecca Carpenter, wife of Michael Carpenter, Nicholas Bright, son of Abraham Bright. Ex: Abrm. Bright, Nathaniel Landers.

CARTMEL, NATHAN. Inventory. Jan. 7, 1805.

COLLINGS, SPENCER, SR. July 12, 1815. Nov. 4, 1821. Wife: Jane. Children mentioned: William, Spencer. Ex: William Collings, Sr. Wit: Jonathan Cox, Spencer Collings.

CORNELL, SOLOMON. August 8, 1812. July, 1812. Wife: Elizabeth. Sons: William, Solomon, Jacob. Daus: Sarah Rudd, Menebah Kiser (?), Charity Russell, Phebe, Polly. Gr.daus: Jane Cornell, Hannah Cornell. Ex: David Hall, Jesse, Drake. Wit: Elijah Wright, Sarah Harris.

CORNELL, SAMUEL. Sept. 12, 1817. Oct. 7, 1817. Wife: Nancy. Dau: Elizabeth. Sons: Samuel, William. Wit: John Withers, John Hall.

COPE, WILLIAM. April 27, 1808. July, 1808. Daus: Mary Wolf, Sarah Owen, Elizabeth Handsford, Hester Shelby, Emeline Ruby. Sons: Lawrence, William, Thomas. Ex: Harmon Greathouse, William Hill. Wit: John Overall, Caleb Wise, Richard Wise.

COPY, WILLIAM. May 22, 1812. July, 1815. Wife: Ann. Ex: wife. Wit: Caleb West, William Hilton.

COYLE (COILE), PATRICK. April 24, 1819. Nov. 1, 1819. Wife: Delilia. Child: Polly, James (infant), children of wife Delilia. Child: John, Lucinda Cam (chld. of first wife.) "To son John the old plantation and debts due me from Virginia". Ex: son John. Wit: H. Hambaugh, Samuel Brown, William Fidler.

CROW, SAMUEL. Dec. 6, 1819. Inventory. Apprs: William Watters, Jonathan Ricketts, George Gunterman.

CULVER, BENJAMIN. Sett. March 4, 1822.

DEATS, JOHN. Inventory. Oct. 13, 1821. Appr. Wm. Waters, Philip Grable.

DOOLEY, GEORGE. Inventory. July 5, 1819

DUVALL, DENNIS. Oct. 19, 1821. Dec. 2, 1822. Wife: Patty. Sons: Lewis, Dennis, Benj. Daus: Patsey, Margaret, Jane. Ex: Benjamin Duvall (son). Wit: Robert Samuel, James Hendrick.

DYSON, SAMUEL. Inventory. Sept. 1808.

EVERALL, WILLIAM. June 14, 1810. 1815. Wife: Ann. Dau: Catharine. Sons: John, William. Ex: wife, William Hilton. Wit: Nathaniel Saunders, Wm. Hilton.

FIELDS, HENRY. March 27, 1819. Oct. 1823. Wife: Suckey. Legatees: Polly Pharis, Elizabeth Stephens, Atrom (?) Fields, Lewis Fields, William Fontain Quinn (son of Arenors Quinn). "Son Henry to have land on which I now live, the balance of property to be divided among my daus. Lucinda, Nancy, Jane, Millord (?) Pharis, Harriet, Rolinda." Ex: wife, John Withers. Wit: Lewis Sale, John Withers, Jr., Wallie Withers.

FUQUAY, HENRY. Sale. Aug. 29, 1822.

GAMBLE, WILLIAM. Inventory. Sept. 1808.

GENTRY, MARTIN. Inventory. Nov., 1821. Apprs: Craven Peyton, Samuel Evans, Nathaniel Saunders.

GLENN, JOHN. Nov. 1, 1819. Nov., 1824. Wife: Ellener. Sons: John Westly, Glenn, William Owen Glenn, James Carpenter Glenn, Stepdau: Cithy Carpenter. Ex: wife. Wit: Jesse Wilson, J. Peacock, Nathaniel Canders.

GRIFFIN, JOHN. Inventory. May, 1815.

HALBERT, JAMES. June 14, 1820. July, 1821. Wife: Margaret. Sons: Humphrey, Marshall, James David. Ex: wife, George F. Pope. Wit: James Dozier, Joseph Huston. Margaret Halbert (wid. of James, dec'd. June 20, 1820) renounced claim under will, July 2, 1821. Wit: Joseph Huston.

HALL, SIMEON. March 29, 1821. Sept. 3, 1821. Wife: Nancy. Daus: Betsy, Sally, Nancy, Polly, Patsy. Sons: John, Simeon Porter. Ex: Clifton Hall (bro.), Austin Hall (nephew). Wit: John Hall, Charles Hall, John Pharis.

HALL, WILLIAM. Oct. 24, 1807. ----Wife: Hannah. Children: Austin, Piny Gentry, Juiah Rebua (?). Son-in-law Henry Gentry. Wit: Gideon Briston, James Briston, Nathaniel Briston.

HALL, DAVID. April 9, 1814. July, 1815. Wife: Rachel. Sons: William, Asa. Daus: Mary King, Nancy Porter, Barbary Gentry. Other legatees: F. Lovelace, Gr. son Asa Porter. Ex: Alex. King, Nicholas Gentry. Wit: Simon Hall, Albert Hubbard.

HARRIS, ZADOCK. Inventory. County Court, 1811.

HART, HENRY. -----July Court, 1815. Wife: Colby. Six children mentioned but not named.

HARDEMAN, JONATHAN. June 8, 1822. Sept. 2, 1822. Wife: Mary. Sons: Joseph, John, Jacob, Thomas, William, Squire. Daus: Elizabeth Hosidler, Sally. Ex: wife, Samuel Brown, James Clark, Joseph Hardeman. Wit: Jas. Clark, Christopher Ashbaugh.

JAMES, RICHARD. April 14, 1821. Dec. 1821. Wife: Elizabeth. Children: Anne Stalling, Richard, Elizabeth, Susan, John, Harriet. Ex: wife, Samuel Stallings. Wit: Richard James, Benj. Brashear.

JORDAN, JOHN. August 16, 1820. Nov. 5, 1821. Wife: Mary. Dau: Mary. Ex: wife. Wit: Samuel Brown, William Caldwell, Jas. Clark.

JONES, HENRY. Sales. Dec. 24, 1809.

KING, JOHN. Inventory. Oct. 17, 1822.

KING, WITHERS. June 1, 1816. Nov. 1818. Wife: Sarah. Sons: Seth, Alexander, Valentine, Nelson, John, William, Daniel. Daus: Polly, Levicey Caldwell, Fanny Neal. Gr.child: 7 child. of dau. Maria Ann Cunningham, Gr.son Elijah King, Sally King (dau. of John). Ex: Jno. King, Dabiel King (sons).

LEMASTER, JOHN. Inventory. August Court, 1807.

METZEL, FREDRICK. Dec. 20, 1818. July 5, 1819. Daus: Margaret Porter, Betsy Beale, Sina (Cinny). Ex: Samuel Brown. Wit: Henry Gentry, Moses Hough, Wm. Bateman, George Marshall, Jr.

MILES, NATHAN, SR. Oct. 1, 1816. Sept. 23, 1818. Wife: mentioned but not named. Daus: Polly Wills (Wells), Sally Simmons, Netty Wilcox, Elizabeth Simmons (hus. William Simmons), Sons: Walter, William (dec'd). Nathan, Richard, Moses. Ex: Richard Miles, Moses Miles (sons). Wit: James Pope, George Pope.

MORGAN, SAMUEL. Inventory. July, 1815. Admin: Rachel Morgan.

MUSGROVE, HENRY. Feb. 13, 1819. July 5, 1819. Wife: Rachel. Child: Rachel, Benjamin, other children not named. Ex: Henry Musgrove, Samuel Brown.

MYERS, JACOB. Oct. 2, 1796. Nov. 1802. Estate to brother Christian Myers and his children. Wit: John Ross, Enoch Burdette, Margaret Ellison. (This is the first will in Book "A".) Jacob Myers was from the County of Lincoln, Ky.

NAIN, WILLIAM. August 16, 1819. June, 1822. Wife: Polly. Daus: Cynthia Simmons, Elizabeth Glass, Rachel Nain, Nancy Nain, Lydia Robards. Sons: David, Thomas, Felix, Robert, Squire, John B. Ex: wife, John Duvall, Thos. Nain. Wit: William Caldwell, Joel Carpenter, John Thomason.

OVERALL, JOHN. Dec. 5, 1816. March 16, 1821. Estate to dau. Parstheny. Mentions daus. Fanny, Catherine, and sons Whitledge, Robert. Ex: Whitledge Overall (son), Benj. Irwin. Wit: Joseph Irwin, Benj. Irwin.

PAYNE, JOHN C. Jan. 15, 1820. April 3, 1820. Wife and children mentioned but not named. Ex: Newbern C. Wood (son-in-law). Wit: John Bull, John Alexander., N. C. Wood.

PEYTON, WILLIAM. Inventory. July 3, 1813. Admin: Mary Peyton (wife).

PITTINGER, MARY (widow of Edward Stone) Sett. Jan. 19, 1821. Apprs: Craven Peyton, Gideon Walker, Joseph Baird.

RAMON, ANDREW. May 20, 1812. 1815. Wife: Barbary. Sons: John, Nicholas, Jacob, William, Medlin. Daus: Mary Ash, Agnes Thompson, Sarah Thompson, Katharine Ramon. Ex: wife. Wit: John Gatton, James V. Gatton.

RICKETS, PETER AND MARY. Inventory. Nov. 13, 1818.

RICHARDS, GEORGE. Inventory. April, 1812.

ROBY, LAWERENCE. Sept. 2, 1813. Nov. 3, 1817. Wife: Catharine. Daus: Elizabeth Wilhoit, Polly Greenwell, Catharine, Susan, Patsy, Harriet. Sons: Samuel, William, Owen, Reason, John. Wit: Basil Gatton, Joseph Gatton, Sarah Weathers, Adolphus Roby.

ROGERS, EDWARD. Inventory. Nov. 1813. Admin: Elizabeth Rogers.

SHANKS, JACOB. Inventory. Sept. 6, 1819.

SHAIN, CHAS. AND WILLIAM. Settlement of accounts of Chas. and William Shain (dec'd.) Admin: Thomas Shain. Jan. 7, 1822.

SHANKS, ELIZABETH. Inventory. Nov. 10, 1821. Admin: Minton A. Shanks

SIMMONS, JESSE. Inventory. April, 1819.

SHEPHERD, ADAMS: April 7, 1819. Admin: Rachel Shepherd, Sarah Shepherd, Charlotte Shepherd, Julia Shepherd. Test: William Warren, John King.

SIMMONS, ROBERT. June 24, 1820. June, 1821. Wife: Catharine. Sons: James, Thomas, Elisha, Esau. Daus: Sarah Crenshaw, Susan Simmons. Wit: Joseph Greenwell, David Allison.

SIMMONS, THOMAS. Oct. 20, 1822. ------Wife: Sally. Ex: James Simmons (Brother). Wit: Casby Crenshaw, David Allison, Joseph Greenwell.

SIMMONS, WILLIAM, SR. August 29, 1822. Nov. 3, 1823. Wife: Elizabeth. Son: William. Dau: Cecelia Atwell. Ex: wife, Richard Simmons (brother). Wit: Mathew Wilson, Abraham Field.

SIMMONS, NOAH. Inventory. Jan., 1806.

SIMMONS, GRIFFITH. Inventory. Sept., 1808

STALLING, SAMUEL. April 1, 1822. Dec. 2, 1822. Wife: Sarah. Sons: Henry, John, Samuel, William, Thomas. Daus: Ann Bishop, Sarah Brashear. Ex: Samuel Stalling, Jr., Henry Stalling (sons). Wit: Richard James, Jacob Wells, Benjamin Brashear.

STRINGER, EDMUND, SR. April 5, 1821. June 4, 1821. Children: John, Richard, Thomas, Fanny Fidler, Franky Osburn, Susanna Paris, Nancy Griffin. Mentions children of dau. Betsy Fidler (dec'd.). Ex: John Stringer (son), John Paris. Wit: Austin Hall, 2 other names illegible.

STEEL, JONAH. Feb. 6, 1812. July, 1815. Wife: Arshi (?). Sons: James, Joseph, Dau: Mary.

TROUTMAN, MICHAEL. April 10, 1814. ----1815. Wife: Elizabeth. Children of wife Elizabeth: John, Peter, Leonard, Elizabeth. Children of first wife: Abraham, Isaac, Jacob, Rebecca Patterson, Mary Lemons, Margaret Lemone, Peggy Tombetson, Philip, also mentions heirs of dau. Caty (dec'd.). Ex: wife, Abraham Troutman, Philip Troutman (sons).

VAUGHN, RICHARD (RACHEL?). Inventory. Nov. Court, 1808.

BULLITT COUNTY

INDEX
BOOK B

1824---1833

Allison, Enoch
Allen, Thomas
Audd, Ann
Alexander, Fred. G.
Alexander, Abigail
Allen, Elizabeth
Allison, Isaac
Allen, Martin

Berkley, Hugh
Briscoe, Samuel
Brashears, Maresham
Bishop, Hy.
Beckwith, John
Brashear, Ignatus
Beckwith, John
Burditt, William
Burditt, Elizabeth
Briscoe, Edward (heirs)
Brashear, Benj.
Beckwith, Sarah
Blandsford, Walter
Blandsford, Mary E.
Burch, Eli.

Cameron, John
Carpenter, Joel
Caldwell, James
Carmell, James
Cartmell, H. C. M.
Chappell, Jesse
Chiseldein, Len (?), Sr.
Charles, Ezekiel
Chandler, William H.
Clevidence, Elizabeth
Cornwell, William
Crenshaw, Buford
Crandall, Thos.
Crenshaw, James
Crow, Elizabeth
Crutcher, John
Collings, Isaac

Deats, Michael
Deats, Catharine
Dodd, John
Drago, James

Dunn, John

Eden, John
Emmerson, Henson

Field, Henry
Forker, Mary
Fox, Philip
Froman, Susan

Gentry, Martin
Gentry, Nancy
Grace, Jacob
Glenn, John
Grant, William C.
Grafton, Nancy

Halbert, Joseph
Harris, Zedda
Hamilton, George
Hamilton, Samuel
Hart, Mary
Hardman, John
Hatfield, Jonah
Hedges, Joseph
Hedges, Nesley
Henson, Valendar
Hilton, Alex.
Hornbeck, Hiram
Hornbeck, Solomon
Hubbard, Eppa
Hugh, John

Irons, Agnes
Irwin, Thos.

James, Richard
Jones, Jesse
Jones, John
Johnson, Felix
Johnson, Ephiram

Kennett, Joshua
King, Henry
King, John
King, Polly
Kinneson, John

Lee, John
Lormor, Joseph

Masden, Benj.
Masden, James
Middleton, Thomas
Mc Caughey, Bart
Morrow, Will
Moore, Evans, Jr.
Moore, Geo. Washington
Moore, Louis
Mc Nutt, Thos.
Middleton, John

Nicholas, Joseph

Orms, John
Owen, Jno. S.
Owen, Sarah
Overall, Parthana
Overall, Whitledge
Overall, John

Pauley, Joseph
Price, Isaac
Pope, Benj.
Polly, James
Pope, Margaret
Percell, Isaac
Purcell, John

Quick, Dennis

Ralph, Thos.
Raymond, William
Reed, John
Rickett, Peter and Mary
Robards, Sevier
Rogers, Edwards
Robard, Granville
Roby, Lawerence
Roby, William, Jr.

Shanks, Elizabeth
Saunders, George
Shain, Chas. & Mary
Shawles, Jacob
Simmons, Wm., Jr.
Simmons, Levi
Simmons, Tabitha
Simmons, Thos.
Simmons, Will
Slack, Joseph
Smith, Peter
Snorden, Thos.

Stallings, Samuel
Stringer, Reuben
Stallings, John
Simmons, Nancy
Swearengen, Obidah
Saunders, Mary
Saunders, Thos.
Sliger, Lewis
Staples, Josiah
Simmons, Rhoda
Sands, Grace
Shawler, Mary
Stringer, Richard
Shain, Abel

Thurman, James
Thornberry, Samuel
Thomas, F. W.
Travis, James

Waters, William
Waters, Sarah
Welch, William
Wise, Richard
Wells, Richard
Webb, Agustine,
Wells, Thos.
Wells, Sarah
Wright, William
White, Brittain
Wright, William

Inventory of Alexander King.
Nov. 9, 1822. Bullitt County.

1 red cow
1 white cow
1 white face cow
1 red cow with white back
1 black cow, 1 black & white cow
1 white back heifer
1 black yearling
1 brindle yearling steer
1 black calf
1 brown horse
8 shoats
1 shovel plow, clevice, single tree
2 sprouting hoes, 2 broad hoes, 3 axes
2 set of gears
1 old drawing knife
1 hand saw, 2 augurs
1 grind stone
several old barrels
1 scythe & craddle
1 looming & warping bars
1 set of big spools & quill wheel
2 big sheels
2 pair of cotton cards
3 spinning wheels
1 old wheel & reel
2 old washing tubs
several buckets & Pails
1 side saddle
2 old saddles
3 bridles
1 large kettle
2 broken pots
2 ovens
1 set of chairs 1 doz. chairs
1 bureau
2 chests
1 large dining table
1 small table
1 kitchen table
1 rifle gun
1 old wedge
1 hammer
2 smoothing irons
1 churn
Sundry vessels

Books to the amount of $5.
2 large pewter dishes
7 pewyer plates
some spoons

1 set of Delf plates
1 set of cups & saucers
1 set of cups & saucers
1 tea pot & cream pot
1 tea pot
2 small dishes
8 bowls
1 large bowl
glass bottle
tea cannister
Candle snuffers
1 flax hackle
2 kegs
1 bed & bed stead
1 bed & bed stead
1 bed & bed stead
4 coverlets
3 quilts
counterpanes & quilts
geese
1 wheat fan
3 sheets
2 small trunks

CALDWELL COUNTY

BOOK A

1809 --- 1834

ANDERSON, CHARLES. Aug. 15, 1818. --------. Wife: Sally. Legatees: Alexander Anderson, John Anderson, Baily Anderson, Vincent Anderson.

ANDERSON, JAMES. May 24, 1815. --------. Nuncupative will. Legatees: Robt. Anderson, John Stevens, Martin Cantwell, Sarah Anderson, Jonah Anderson.

ARMSTRONG, JOHN. ------ ------ Wife: Anna. Sons: William, John, James. Dau: Betty. Ex: Brother William and John Hamilton. Wit: Brashear, Thomas and James Armstrong, Matthew Wilson.

ARMSTRONG, JOSEPH. ---- ----. Wife: Jane. Children: William, Abel, Lucinda, Hannah. Ex: Chris Armstrong. Wit: Drewery Smith, Edmund Franklin.

ARMSTRONG, MATHEW. Oct. 23, 1826. ----. Wife: Elizabeth. Sons: John, Mathew, William. Daus: Mary, Hannah, Elizabeth, Nancy, Mentty. Ex: Wife, and Wright Nichols. Wit: Reddick Nichols, Turner Carter.

ARMSTRONG, JOHN. Aug. 15, 1833. All to wife, Matilda. Test: Joshua Stallions.

ASHBY, STEPHEN. March 9, 1828. ----- Sons: Thomas, Robert, David. Daus: Mary Miller, Sarah. Gr. Chld: Malinda Miller, Dau. of Mary Miller, Gr.son John Ashley, son of Thos. Ashley, Gr.dau., Malinda Ashley, Dau. of Beady Ashley, Gr.dau. Susan, dau. of Robert Ashley. Ex: William Marrick and Braston Wall. Wit: John Wall, Chas. Jones, W. D.Davenport.

BAKER, BLAKE. April -- 1820. -----. Children: Thomas L., Blake, Polly Gregory, Christiana Baker, Freezie Baker; bro. John Baker. Ex: Wife, Christiana, John A. Phelps. Wit: James Bowland and Sharslin Garly.

BAKER, JAMES. May -- 1810. Inventory. Admin: Seth Baker, James Baker.

BALDWIN, WILLIAM. August 18, 1819. Inventory. James Morse. J.P.

BANNISTER, HUGH. August 1, 1829. Wife: Susannah. Mentions children but does not name them. Wit: James Bannister, John Timmons.

BEAR, THOMAS. Apr. 21, 1828. Inventory. Ex: Wife Elizabeth, John Barrell. Wit: Solomon Stanfield, Andrew Duncan, Ira Drewett.

BEARDEN, WIN. March 5, 1810. Inventory. Admin: John Bearden. Others named: John Bearden, Mourning Bearden.

BENNETT, COLEMAN. Dec'd. May 28, 1818. Inventory. Admin: John Scott, Wm. Chandler, J.P.

BIGHAM, JAMES. May 30, 1817. Inventory. Apprs: Michael Freeman, David Scott, John Algee, Andrew Dunn.

BOND, WILLIAM. Dec. -- 1813. Oct. 1825. Wife: Francis. Children: Winfrey, William, Thomas, Betsy Owens, Nancy, Charity Lacy, Polly Wolf, Judah Montgomery, Jane Weatherspoon, Frances Brooks, Willy Jackson. Ex: Winfrey Bond and William B. Bond. Wit: M. Phelps, N. Cravens, J.D. Cobb, Geo. Brown, Jos. Rucker.

BOWLAND, JAMES. Feb. 21, 1821. ------.Wife: Ricky. Children: Pheby, Elizabeth, Polly, Huldah, Sarah, John, James, Andrew. Other mentioned James Kilgore, son of Philip Kilgore. Ex: Wife Ricky and son John Bowland. Wit: John Gray, Isaac Gray, John Grasty.

BOYD, SAMUEL. Nov. 27, 1815. Inventory. Admin: Elizabeth Boyd. Apprs: William Norris, Jonah and Jesse Cobb.

BEAN, WILLIAM. Feb. 26, 1816. Inventory. Admin: Ann Bean, N. Casby J.P.

BRADBERN, WILLIAM C. Inventory. Apr. 22, 1820. Admin: Thomas Bradbern. Apprs: John Williams, Thos. Kemp, Abner W. Kemp J. P.

BROOKS, JESSE. Oct. 30, 1823. Nov. 18, 1823. Wife: Celia. Children mentioned but not named, brother-in-law, Wm. Johnston. Ex: Thos. Brooks, Jr., John Ogden. Wit: David Brooks, W. A. Phelps, J.P.

BROWN, ISAAC. Jan. 2, 1817. Inventory. Apprs: Edw. Robinson, William Armstrong, Logan Armstrong. Admin: Geo. Roberts

BURTON, WILLIAM. Feb. -- 1812. Inventory. Apprs: Banister Wade, Vincent Anderson, Thomas Anderson, Joseph Terry. H. H. Phelps C.C.

CAMPBELL, DAVID. Jan. 6, 1816. ------. Wife: Ann. Son: James. Other children, but not named. Wit: John B. Craig, Jane Craig, George Robinson, J.P.

CARRICK, JAMES. Sept. 10, 1812. Inventory. Admin: Margaret Carrick.

CARRICK, JOHN. Dec. 31, 1817. Dec. 25, 1820. Wife: Margaret. Sons: Stephenson, John, Samuel. Dau: Polly Price. Admin: Wife, Margaret, son John Carrick. Wit: Richard Newlin and Walter Duff.

CARTER, CHARLES. March 5, 1818. Apr. 1818. Apprs: James Hall, Mark Thornton, James Corlew, John Killian.

CARTWRIGHT, PETER. June 16, 1809. Feb. 5, 1810. Inventory. Admin: Wife, Christiana, son Rev. Peter Cartwright.

CATLETT, HANSON. June 4, 1824. Nov. 24, 1824. Wife: Minerva. Wit: E. Pennland, William Graham.

CLINTON, MATHEW. Feb. 3, 1832. ------. Mentions wife but does not name her. Children: William, Wesley T., others but not named. Ex: James Clinton Jr., Eleazer Smith, Jr.

COLE, JOHN. Dec. 19, 1812. Inventory. Apprs: John Carrick, Edward Maxwell, William Armstrong, David Campbell.

COLE, MARGARET. Fall of 1813. Inventory.

COBB, JOSIAH (or JOSEPH). Aug. 19, 1817. Inventory. Apprs: Hay Machen, Peter Purtle, James George.

COOPER, TRACY. May 3, 1834. May 19, 1834. Sons: Alexander, Francis H. Daus: Sally, Polly, Nancy, Margaret, Elizabeth, Jane, Martha Ford. Ex: Sons, Alexander and Francis.

CONYER, ROBT. I. Sept. 18, 1809. Inventory. Apprs: J. Mercer, Wash. Thompson, Charles Jones, William Leech.

CRUCE, ISAAC. March 20, 1814. -----. Wife: Jane. Children: James, Isabell, Elizabeth. Wit: F. Fowler, R. Cruce, Isaac Cruce.

DARRAW, WILLIAM. Aug. 18, 1834. Oct. 20, 1834. Wife: Polly. Children: Mentioned but not named. Wit: Stephen Carrick, John Rorer.

DAVIDSON, DAVID. Nov. 8, 1815. Inventory returned Nov. 18, 1815. Apprs: James Clinton, Joshua Clinton, David Caldwell. George Robinson J.P.

DAVIS, BROOK A. Feb. --1814. Inventory May 7, 1814. Admin: Sally Davis. Apprs: Bannister Wade, James Mc Caa, David Jones.

DEACON, JAMES. July 8, 1809. -----. Wife: Mary (dau. of Wm. Wilson). Legatees: James Deacon Scott, Benj. Hardin, James Reed (half bro.), Deacon Reed, Felix Dixon, Hardin Scott. Ex: Joshua Scott, Benj. Hardin. Wit: Wm. Armstrong, John Armstrong, H. Stewart.

DOBBINS, ALEXANDER. Sept. 18, 1809. Inventory. Apprs: J. Mercer, Wash. Thompson, Charles Jones, David Paret.

DOOM, JOHN. --------Wife: Polly. Sons: Isaac, Henry, Randolph, Jacob, Jesse, Willis (son of Mathew Dickersoh's wife, now living with Thomas Jones), stepchildren: Lavina Cross, Sally Cross, Joshua Cross. Ex: Sons Jacob and David Doom. Wit: Wm. Owens, Griffin Long, Jesse Glass.

DRAPER, THOMAS. May 3, 1825. Nov. 21, 1825. Wife: Mentioned but not named. Children: George, John, Robert, Katherine C. Mills, Lucinda Mallory, Sally Draper, Eliza Rucker, Virginia Draper. Gr.Dau. Sarah Groom. Ex: Sons John and Robert. Wit: Winfrey Bond, Enoch Bolling, James Wood.

DUNCAN, SAMUEL. Oct. 4, 1823. -----.Wife Sarah. Mentions brother and sister but does not name them. Ex: Brashel. Wit: Andrew Spillard, John Foley, Mason Foley.

EAST, JOEL. June 15, 1818. Inventory. Admin: Rebecca East.

FLINT, JOHN. Sept. 20, 1819. Nov. 23, 1819. Wife: Elizabeth. Children: Elizabeth, Bryant, Deborah, Margaret, Thomas, Hannah, Williams, John. Ex: Wife Elizabeth, Lewis Hamilton. Wit: Mercer Wadlington, Motley Gore.

FLOURNOY, DAVID. June 5, 1825. July 18, 1825. Wife: ----- Children: Samuel, Ann, Mildred, Thomas, Julia, Maria Louise, Prunette Roberts, Rebecca Bowles, Annie, Thomas. N.S. Dalham, C.C.

FOWLER, GEOFREY. Dec. 20, 1816. Feb. 1817. Wife: Clara. Legatees: Teremak,

James, John, Wiley, Bradford, Polly, Ida. Ex: Wife, Clara, son Joseph. Wit: Mercer Wadlington, John Craig, John Cockin.

FREEMAN, ALEXANDER. May 26, 1829. Dec. 21, 1829. Mentions Hardy F. Freeman, Henry Freeman. Wit: William Neeley.

FULK, OBIDIAH. Feb. 13, 1830. Apr. 19, 1830. Nuncupative. Wife: Elaine. Children not named. Wit: Henry Foulks, Stephen Newbery, David Bridges.

GARRETT, DAVID. July 14, 1825. Aug. 21, 1826. Wife: Jane. Sons: John, Jonas. Daus: Rhoda, James, Jesse, Polly, Susan. Ex: Wife Jane, Grace Grubs, James Cook. Wit: George Keslerson, Jr., Luke Nichols, George Mc-Colly.

GEORGE, ANDREW. July 1, 1816. May 25, 1818. Wife: Sarah. Mentions the child of dau. Rachel Thompson, other children not named. Ex: Wife, John George (son), John Kelf (son-in-law). Wit: William Bush, Alex. Smith, John Dilworth.

GEORGE, JOHN. Jan. 14, 1813. Inventory. Apprs: Josiah Cobb, William L. Norris, David Scott. Arthur Davis, J.P.

GILLIHAM, J. C. April 7, 1823. Oct. 1823. Wife: Betsy. Children not named. Ex: Wife Betsy. Wit: Mourning Roach.

GHOLSON, JACOB AND RICHARD. Feb. 23, 1818. Guardian bond. John B. Gholson appointed guardian for Jacob and Richard Gholson.

GILKEY, WILLIAM. May 21, 1810. Aug. 7, 1810. Children: Hannah, Barbara, Jemina, William, Anne, Thomas, John, Isaac. Gr.son Zephemiah. Son-in-law Chas. Frim. Ex: Samuel Greer. Wit: Thos. Greer, N. Thompson, J. Greer, Jr. (Thirty four years of American Independence.)

GILLIHAM, WILLIAM. July 30, 1811. Aug. 5, 1811. Wife: Mourning. Sons: Robert, Nerson, James. Daus: Elizabeth Leah, Margaret, Minerva, Orra. Ex: Jesse Greer. Wit: W. Bartin, Levi Greer, Jesse Greer.

GORDON, JOHN. May 11, 1815. Inventory. Apprs: A. H. Davis, Jepson R. Pemberton, Thomas Ruel.

GRAY, JESSE (?). Feb. 3, 1829. Inventory. Apprs: Vincent Anderson, Joe Fulks, James Brown.

GREGORY, JOHN. June 8, 1816. Inventory. Admin: Samuel Glenn. Apprs: Griffin Long, Josiah Chandler, William Chandler, James Henson.

GREER, JOHN. May 19, 1817. Inventory. Apprs: A. T. Jenkins, James Cunningham, Jona Shields.

GREER, JAMES. May 26, 1806. Aug. 1806. Wife: Elizabeth. Children: Jonathan, Isaac, William, Ruth, James. Ex: Wife Elizabeth. Wit: Isaac Greer, J. Mercer.

GRIFFITH, WELLS. Apr. 14, 1831. May 1832. Wife: Elizabeth. Sons: William, John, Hiram, Henry, Jeptha. Daus: Sally Burrus. Gr.dau. Phoebe. Ex: Wife

Elizabeth, son Jeptha. Wit: A. L. Pemberton.

HALL, CHARLES. Inventory. Apprs: James Hall, John Ramsey, William Ramsey.

HAMILTON, JOHN. May 27, 1830. Nov. 18, 1833. Wife: Martha. Son: John. Daus: Sarah Caldwell, Margaret Elder, Mary Miller, Ann Armstrong, Elizabeth Hamilton. Ex: John Miller and Frances Caldwell. Test: B. Caldwell, Thomas A. Caldwell.

HAMILTON, WILLIAM. July 21, 1811. Aug. 5, 1811. Wife: Elizabeth. Children: Anna Thomas, John Thomas, Samuel Thomas, James Dunn (these were probably Gr. children), Thomas Hamilton, James Hamilton, Lewis Hamilton, Sally Hamilton, Elizabeth Hamilton, and Nancy Hamilton. Ex: Wife Elizabeth, Edward Robinson. Wit: J. Stromat, William Sims, and John Durley.

HAMMOND, CHRISTOPHER. March 26, 1830. April 19, 1830. Sons: Benjamin, Martin, John, Joshua. Wit: Samuel Glenn and C. C. Cobb.

HANLEY, JESSE. July 23, 1812. Inventory. Admin: Providence Rose.

HARPER, MATTHEW. Apprs. appointed Apr. 1819. Admins: Gamel Gray, Moses Crow, Thomas Marsh.

HARRISON, JOHN. Nov. 3, 1815. Inventory. Apprs: Edward Robeson, John Story, William Mc Elroy. Admin: Nancy Harrison.

HARRIS, ROBERT. Sept. 17, 1821. Feb. 18, 1822. Wife: Mary. Son: Benjamin. Daus: Sophia, Dolly, Amanda, Narsissa Cooksey, Marcin Cook Harris (wife of Benj. Harris). Ex: Benj. Harris, Theophilus Cooksey.

HARRIS, WILLIAM. March 1, 1829. May 18, 1829. "All property to sister Maria T. Flournoy and two nieces, Rhoda, Laura Flournoy." Wit: James L. Dallam, C. W. Goodwin.

HAWORTH, JOHN. May 23, 1831. Aug. 16, 1831. Wife: Katherine. "To daus. Phebe and Amelia, land I bought of Justinian Cartwright. Test: Davis Dunniman, D. W. Goodwin and Howard Casedy.

HAYS, RICHARD. March 5, 1816. Apr. 5, 1816. Wife: Phebe. Daus: Loty, Catsey, Onely. Sons: Owens, John, Hammond, William, Levin, Othy. Ex: Phebe Hays and Thomas Kivil. Wit: Owen Hays, Joseph Moore.

HENSON, JOSEPH. Oct. 6, 1817. Inventory. Admin: Nancy Henson. Legatees: Wiley Wilfred Henson, four years of age.

HOLMAN, ABSALOM. June 1, 1829. May 18, 1829. Wife: not named. Children: Nancy, Mary, John, Elizabeth, Peline. Ex: Wife. Wit: John Holman, Samuel Musgrave, James Dallam.

HITE, JAMES. Nov. 28, 1818. Admin: Thomas, James Hite.

HOWELL, WILLIAM. August 21, 1817. Inventory. Apprs: Wm. Birdsong, John Holland, William Holland. Washington Thompson J.P.

HUGHES, JOHN. April 10, 1812. Oct. 5, 1812. Children: Elizabeth, Fanny,

John, Polly, Stanley, Sary Farmer, Elizabeth Bond. Wit: Mark Sullivan, William Cherto, Peter Pinacer.

HUGHES, JOHN. Dec. 25, 1822. April 29, 1830. Wife: Lillian. Sons: Jefferson, Pulaski. Ex: Henry Machen, John Jones. Wit: Wm. Johnson, Solomon Freer, Wm. Bond.

INGRAM, BENJAMIN. July 15, 1810. Nov. 5, 1810. Mentions wife but does not name her. Bro. John Ingram, William Darnall, son of William Darnall, Benj. Darnall, Sary Darnall, Benj. Benton, son of S. O. Benton are named as heirs. Ex: Joshua Saxon. Wit: Medes Saxon, Joshua Saxon, William Womax.

INGRAM, JOHN. Inventory. Dec. 13, 1816. Apprs. Vincent Anderson, Joseas Thelford (?), Joel Smith.

JENKINS, JESSE. Aug. 10, 1815. Aug. 16, 1824. Wife: Elizabeth. Daus: Stacy, Elizabeth. Ex: Wife Elizabeth. Wit: Levi Green, B. Mc Nabb.

JENNINGS, JOHN. ------- July 16, 1831. Children: Bailey, Doshey Wolf, James, Nancy Grubbs, Mirian Griffith, John, Winifred Herrel, Sarah Davis, Polly Griffith, Phoebe Bridges, David, Rebecca. Ex: John Jennings, Jr., Isaac Grubbs. Wit: George M. Class, J.B. Jennings.

JENNINGS, JAMES. Aug. 22, 1834. Oct. 21, 1834. Wife: Polly. Daus: Polly, Nancy. Sons: Garrat, Ned, John, Lewis, Isaac. Elizabeth and Anney, heirs of dau. Mehalay. Wit: William Howard and William Adams.

JONES, DAVID. Oct. 20, 1821. Jan. 28, 1822. Wife: Tabitha. Son: William, other children mentioned but not named. Ex: Wife, son William. Wit: Skaggs and William Jones.

JOHNSTON, MALINTHA. Sept. 7, 1813. Inventory. Apprs: John Craig, Elisha Walker, John Wilcox, Mercer Wadlington.

JONES, JOHN. Apr. 30, 1813. Inventory. Admin: Samuel Jones. Apprs: John Holman, William Asbest, John Weeks, J.P.

JONES, ANDREW. Dec'd. Jan. 5, 1815. Apprs: Elijah Bennett, Griffin Long, Peter Purtle, Samuel Glenn.

JONES, JOHN. Feb. 12, 1812. Inventory. Apprs: Isaac Mc Elroy, Elijah Bennett (?), John Jones, Stephen Bennett, William Mc Elroy. John Phelps C. C.

KANNON, KINSON. Inventory. June 2, 1810. Apprs: James Leech, Abraham (son), John Flint. J. Brown, J.P.

KEVIL, BENJAMIN. Inventory. Oct. 12, 1813. Apprs: H.-H. Davis, Jesse B. Pemberton, Richard Hays.

KILLAN, WILLIAM. May 4, 1829. Sons: William, Harris W. Daus: Modena. Wit: J. W. Marshal, Samuel Glenn, George Marshall.

KUKINDALE, JAMES. Inventory Dec. 1811. Feb. 1812. Apprs: Charles James,

Samuel Fowles, David Kilgore.

LACY, WILLIAM. Nov. 2, 1811. Dec. 2, 1811. Noncupative will. Wit: Patsy Lacy, George Burton, Joshua Saxon, Ulyses Saxon.

LAMAR, JOHN. March 4, 1817. April 28, 1818. Legatees: Sister Margaret, Solomon Lamar, Sarah Lewis. Wit: John and Mary Ross.

LAMAR, AMON. Dec. 10, 1830. May 16, 1831. Wife: Sarah. Mother. Wit: James Johnson, Polly Jenkins.

LANGSTON, JACOB. April 1, 1816. Inventory. Apprs: David Jarrell, William Owens, Henry Jones. Samuel Glenn, J.P.

LANGSTON, MARY. Inventory. March 5, 1819. Apprs: Joseph Chandler, Samuel Hammond, Samuel Glenn.

LAUGHTEN, -------- Inventory. Aug. 24, 1818. Apprs: John Weeks, Jesse Morgan, Thomas Simpson.

LEACH, JAMES P. Inventory. July 30, 1818. Apprs: Moses Clayton, William Vaughn, Stallard Scott.

LEECH, SARAH. Sept. 27, 1809. Jan. 1810. Sons: David, William, Joseph, James. Daus: Jane Vaughn, Eleanor Underwood, Susannah Lofter. Gr. children: John and Jean, dau. of Joseph. Wit: William Leech, James White, James Leech.

LEWIS, JOHN. Jan. 30, 1809. Jan. 1, 1810. Wife: Anna. Daus: Nancy Bruce, Mary Phelps, her children Mounring and Baylis Phelps; and Mary S. Hughes. Sons: Samuel, Thomas, Hugh. Ex: Mary S. Hugh, Samuel Lewis. Wit: Isaac Brown, Thomas Goodaker.

LIGGETT, ELIJAH. Feb. 26, 1813. Inventory. Apprs: Mark Thornton, Elijah Liggett, Aaron Compton, James Caraway, William Lofton, John Lyons.

LONG, GRIFFITH. March 9, 1810. April 28, 1817. Wife: Sally. Son: Phillip. Other children mentioned but not named. Ex: Samuel Glenn, Sally Long.

MARTIN, REUBEN. Inventory. Apr. 25, 1814. Apprs: Sam Witherow, John Volay, James Gregory.

MARTIN, JONAS. Inventory. Nov. 10, 1820. Apprs: William Owens, Robert Adams, Samuel Glenn.

MAXWELL, WILLIAM. Jan. 19, 1809. June 1809. Wife: Mary. Children: Jean, William, Elizabeth, Mary Lacky. Ex: Wife Mary. Wit: John David, Alexander Davidson.

MC CLURE, SAMUEL. Inventory. Nov. 14, 1814. Apprs: Chas. Anderson, John Henson, Conwell Smith.

MC DOWELL, GEORGE. Nov. 30, 1819. Dec. 27, 1819. Wife: Mary. Children: Nancy Ford, Fanny Willing, Catherine Spencer, Elizabeth Beigg (?), Polly

Camolile, Peggy, George, John, Daniel, William, Alexander. Ex: Wife Mary, son William. Wit: Gilbert Dodds, James Leach.

MC ELROY, JOHN. Inventory. April 26, 1815. Apprs: Arnold Jacob, Samuel Hammon, Edward Robinson, Samuel Glenn.

MC LEOD, RODERICK. Nov. 8, 1819. Nov. 29, 1819. Of Georgia. Sisters: Margaret Hall, Margarette Mc Leod, Sarah Mc Leod. Ex: Brother Alexander Mc Leod of Louisana.

MC VAY, JORDAN. July 18, 1826. Oct. 16, 1826. All to wife Celola. Wit: James M. Bompay, Andrew Hughes.

MILLER, JOSEPH. ----1815. Inventory. Apprs: James Morse, Samuel Smith, Samuel Black.

MITCHELSON, WILLIAM. Aug. 31, 1813. Nov. 22, 1819. Wife: Milly. Sons: Drewry, Edward, William. Gr.son, Eley Osborn. Ex: Wife Milly, William Satterfield, James F. Mitchelson, William Mitchelson. Wit: James Cook, Lewis Martin, J. Mercer.

MITCHELSON, EDWARD. April 15, 1821. Oct. 22, 1821. Wife: Nancy. Children: Zadock, Irena, Casander, Mary Evanline, Eley. Ex: Wife Nancy. Wit: I. Mercer, Joshua Osborn, F. Mitchelson.

MITCHELSON, EDWARD. Dec. 22, 1827. Feb. 1828. Wife: Fanny. Daus: Sarah Mc Carty, Clorinda Hutchinson, Elizabeth Mitchell, Polly Bearden (hus. Edward Bearden). Sons: Elijah. Ex: Wife Fanny, son-in-law William Mc-Carty. Wit: William Phelps.

MOORE, JOSEPH. Inventory. Dec. 1, 1820. Apprs: John Whitnel, Robert Whitnel.

MORSE, ELESEZAR. June 3, 1818. July 27, 1818. Children: Travis, Obedson (?), James, John, William, Jarrod, Lucy Bucy, Fanny Wofford, Ennice Bumpals. Ex: Sons Travis, Moses, Obedson, James. Wit: Ebenezer Morse, Spencer, John Colburn.

OLIVER, LEVI. Inventory. No date.

OGDEN, BENJAMIN. Nov. 8, 1834. Dec. 1834. Wife: Nancy. Children: Stephen, Mary Harpensing. Gr. son, Benjamin Harpensing, son of Asbury and Mary Harpensing.

ORR, ALEXANDER. Sept. 30, 1817. May 28, 1821. Wife: Martha. Daus: Polly, Nancy, Iolda, Peggy Craig, Martha Watson, Elizabeth, Jane Cooper. Sons: Alexander, Hugh, William. Ex: Son William, son-in-law John Craig. Wit: Jarrot Morse.

OSBORN, WILLIAM. June 4, 1816. Inventory. Admr: James Wadington.

PERKINS, STEPHENS. Oct. 19, 1822. Feb. 1830. Wife: Elizabeth. Children: Mary Strawmatt, William Perkins, Elizabeth Perkins, Thomas Perkins, Sarah Highland, Stephen Perkins, Jr. Ex: John Strawmatt, John Stone.

PERKINS, ADAMS. May 5, 1821. May 1824. Wife: Nancy. Son: Brock. Ex: Son Brook, William Johnes. Wit: Albert and Isabella Adamson.

PHILLEY, RODGER. Inventory. Jan. 24, 1816. Apprs: Solomon King, John Doom.

PRATT, EPHIRAM. Sept. 17, 1813. -----. Wife: Sarah. Dau: Hannah Pratt. Son: John. Ex: Wife Sarah. Wit: J. Whitnel, David Carly, Robt. C. Ritchey.

PRINCE, WILLIAM. June 7, 1808. Aug. 6, 1810. Wife Elizabeth. Children: Enoch, Reuben, Sally Connell, Polly, Della Ford, Nancy Wadlington, Elisha, Thomas, Rhoda, William, Frances, Betsy. Ex: wife Elizabeth, son Enogh, son-in-law E. Ford. Wit: William Mitchenson, Caleb Holcomb.

PRINCE, ELIZABETH. July 9, 1828. Aug. 9, 1828. 2 Gr. daus: Laura and Helen Prince. Wit: F. Mitchelson, Frazier E. Satterfield.

PRINCE, ENOCH. Dec. 1833. August 1834. Children: Parmecia Leiper, Martha Baldwin, Enoch Prince, John Prince.

PURTLE, MICHAEL. Jan. 7, 1820. May, 1820. Children: Jacob, Peter, Michael, Margaret Carmack, heirs of Martin Purtle.

PURTLE, MARGARET. Inventory. Feb. 18, 1815.

PUGH, JACOB. Inventory. July 27, 1815. Admr: Mary Pugh.

RAMA, JOHN. August 6, 1832. August 20, 1832. Gr. sons: Thomas, Martin, John Rama, heirs of James Rama.

REYNOLDS, EDWARDS. Inventory. No Date.

RITCHEY, ROBERTS. Oct. 2, 1826. Nov. 20, 1826. Wife: Elizabeth. Children: Elizabeth, Ann, Nancy Isabelle, Robert. Ex: Wife Elizabeth, Daniel Easley. Wit: James Black, F. W. Fowler.

ROBINSON, JAMES. Inventory. No Date. Admr: George Darby.

ROGERS, DREWRY. March 22, 1823. August 18, 1823. Wife: Francis. Son: William.

ROBERTSON, LAWSON. June 14, 1826. July 17, 1826. Wife and children mentioned but not named. Ex: Father. Wit: John Matlock, C. Ratliffe.

ROWLAND, LEWIS. June 2, 1834. Oct. 20, 1834. Wife: Rachel. Legatees: David and Henry Rowland, William Roach, Charles Jones, Mary Rowland, William Rowland.

RUCKER, JAMES. July 14, 1820. Oct. 1828. Wife: Susannah. Children not named.

SATTERFIELD, WILLIAM. Jan. 2, 1816. Nuncupative will. "Gloves to Elijah Satterfield. To brother Edward Satterfield, my hat; rest of estate to wife Polly." Wit: Thomas Hammond, Henry Jones.

SATTERFIELD, JAMES. Sept. 15, 1822. Oct. 1823. Wife: Polly. Daus: Amelia Chambers (wife of Thos. W. Chambers), Betsy Dunn. Son: Edward. Ex: Wife Polly, son Elijah. Wit: Will Landers, Elijah Shepman.

SAXON, ULYSIS. Inventory. No date. Apprs: William M. Darby, Adam Perkins.

SAXON, JOHN. ----1814. Inventory. Apprs: John Doom, Daniel Jarrett, Samuel Glenn.

SHAW, ANNER. Aug. 16, 1816. Daus: Mary Ann Dodd, Dorcas Shaw, Sons: John Shaw. Ex: Son Samuel Black, Dau. Dorcas Shaw. Wit: Hugh Kinkade, Samuel Black, Keturah Black.

SKINNER, AURELLA. Oct. 15, 1821. Oct. 22, 1821. Mother: Beulah Lyon. Dau: Beulah Lyon Skinner. Son: Fredrick H. Skinner. Ex: Brother Matt. Lyon, Jr. Wit: Ed Lyon, Lucy Galusha.

SKINNER, HENRY. June 10, 1819. July 26, 1819. Wife: Aurelia. Children: Beulia Lyon Skinner, Fredrick Skinner. Ex: Wife Aurelia, Mathew Lyon. Wit: Thomas Long, John Long, M. Lyon.

SMITH, JOHN. Feb. 16, 1816. April 22, 1816. Nuncupative. Sons: Reuben, John, Isaac, Hiram. Daus: Nancy, Rachel, Mary, Mitty, Betsy, Malinda. Wit: Abraham Stokes, John Brown.

SMITH, JOEL. May 17, 1824. Oct. 1824. Wife: Mary. Children: Thomas, Elizabeth Bell, Mary Laughlin, Sarah Hughlett, John Eart (?) who married dau. Rody, and his heirs.

SMITH, SAMUEL. May 15, 1823. Dec. 15, 1823. Wife Jean. Daus: Elrita, Betsy. Sons: Robert, John, Jesse. Ex: Wife Jean. Wit: James Davis, George F. Orr.

SMITH, WILLIAM. --------. Oct. 21, 1834. Wife: Rebecca. Children: John, Jane, Samuel, Polly, Elizabeth, Malinda, Robert, Martha. Wit: John Barnett, Logan Armstrong, Jesse A. Smith.

STANLEY, PERRY. Dec. 1814. Left Carolina for Kentucky. Inventory. Apprs: F. C. Sharp, H.W.Rocken.

STEPHENS, JOHN. ------.1813. Inventory. Admr: Elijah Stephens.

STEVENS, ELIJAH. May 2, 1834. Oct. 20, 1834. Wife: Elizabeth. Children: Edward, William, Elijah, Jesse, Herrington, Samuel, Zadock, Littleton, Lucretia, Ann. Ex: Wife Elizabeth, son Zadock. Wit: James Meek, F. Meek.

STEVENS, JOHN. Nov. 22, 1815. Inventory. Elizabeth Stevens, Sallie and Jesse Stevens. Apprs: William Buckyhn, Michael Cambell.

STEVENS, JOHN. Feb. 29, 1824. Aug. 16, 1824. Polly Stevens (widow of son Moses Stevens). After decease of Polly Gr. children to have property. Wit: Andrew Spilland, James Stephens, Elisha Smith.

STEVENSON, MATT. April 17, 1813. Oct. 20, 1815. Mentions wife and children but does not name them. Trustees: Joseph Alexander, Samuel Bleck.

STONE, JOHN. Nov. 23, 1815. Feb. 26, 1821. Wife: Sarah. Daus: Eliza Perkins (wife of Stephen), Susanna Morse (wife of Obidiah). Sons: William, John, Caleb. Ex: Friend and benefactor Solomon Stone. Wit: Elia Rankin, Jesse Rankin.

STRAWMATT, JOHN. April 26, 1813. Soldier in service of U.S. at Orleans. Sisters Sophia, Sallie. Bro. Brook. Three brothers and sisters mentioned but not named.

TANNER, JOHN. (Indexed as TAMIOR). June 20, 1812. Oct. 1812. Wife: Sally. Children: Rucker, Nancy, Polly, Tabitha, Joseph and one other that was illegible. Dinah Morton, Edward, Betsy, Sally, James, Milly Morton. Ex: Wife Sally, George Ruddell. Wit: Enoch Evans, George Jenkins.

TERRILL, ELI. (?). Nov. 15, 1815. Inventory. Apprs: M. Lyons, William Hammock(?).

THARP, JOHN. Feb. 10, 1827. Dec. 17, 1832. Wife: Polly. Children: Sons: Terry, John. Daus: Sally, Nancy, Rebecca, Elizabeth, Judah, Susanna, Polly, Caroline, Isabell; Nancy, dec'd., her children Woodson, Sally, Patty, William. Ex: Sons John, Terry. Wit: Ransford Smith, H. Hicks, John Barnett.

THOMAS, ZADOCK. May 13, 1829. Oct. 20, 1829. Wife: Sally. Children: Malinda, Louise Rhoda, Ranson, Fanny, Canda, William. Wit: Jeremiah Rucker, Charles Holowell, Thomas Rucker, Robert Boyd.

WADLINGTON, THOMAS. June 28, 1817. Inventory. Apprs: John Dobbin, Josiah Chandler, William Chandler, J.P.

WATSON, GEORGE. Dec. 20, 1819. Inventory. Apprs: Harmon Watson, Susanna Watson.

WHITNEL, JOSIAH. May 17, 1819. Inventory. Apprs: James McCakin, Micajah Bowen, A. A. Davis, A. H. Davis J.P.

WHITE, WILLIAM. No Date. Wife: Francis. Children: Sophia Wilcox, William, Thomas, James, Reuben, another dau. Wit: Thomas Thompson, James George, George Simons.

WILLIAMS, JESSE. May 3, 1817. Inventory. Apprs: James Moore, Anthony Laughlin.

WILLIAMS, ARTHUR. Jan. 6, 1813. Inventory. Apprs: Matt Stewart, Samuel Henry, John Holman, Brown, J.P.

WITHEROW, SAMUEL. Nov. 16, 1814. "All property to wife Elizabeth." Ex: Wife Wit: Phelps, James Smith, Edward Owen, James Finley.

YOUNG, DANIEL. -----. Jan. 1812. Children: Levick, William, Daniel, Polly, Franky, Emmy, Nancy, Betsy, Daniel. Ex: Abraham Boyd, David Barton. Wit: Samuel Fowler, Hardy and Fanny Fowler.

PETER CARTWRIGHT INVENTORY & C.

Pursuant to an order to as directed by the Worshipful Court of Caldwell County to view and appraise the property of Peter Cartwright, Deceased, the following is a return of the same together with the valuation thereof, towit:

1 Yellow mare and colt	$85.00
1 Brown mare and colt	65.00
1 Grey horse	32.50
1 Bay horse	45.00
1 Sorrelle horse	40.00
1 White heifer - 2 years old.	5.00
1 Steer - 1 year old	3.00
8 Head of sheep	12.00
28 Head of hogs	35.15
2 Feather beds	20.00
5 Bed quilts	16.00
2 Blankets 2 Sheets	10.50
4 Pillows and 1 bolster	6.00
2 Bedsteads & 2 Matts & under bed tick	4.00
1 Table	3.00
1 Chest	4.00
1 Glass box	1.00
1 Sugar Stand	.37½
1 8 gallon pot	2.50
1 Dutch oven and lid	1.50
1 Stew kettle and lid 2 pair hooks	1.50
5 Tin buckets	2.50
2 Pewter knives and forks	5.00
2 Queen ware	1.00
3 Vessels copper ware	1.50
1 Coffee Mill	1.00
1 Pair cotton cards	1.25
1 Smoothing iron	.75
1 Candlestick Snuffers & moler	.25
2 Books	.50
1 Slay and harness	.50
2 Gimlets	.12½
1 Reap hook	.50
A Parcel of spools and frame	.75
1 Grindstone	1.00
1 Hoe and axe	1.25
1 Bread tray	.37½
3 Barrels	1.00
Some pot tubes	.25
1 Shovel plough	1.75
1 Half shear plough	2.75
2 pair of Geer 1 double tree 1 clevis 1 bridle	2.75
1 Cotton Wheel	1.75
4 Chairs	1.50
4 Bells	1.37½
	$425.37½

9th of June 1809.

Signed: Peter Cartwright } Admr:
Christian Cartwright

CHRISTIAN COUNTY

BOOK A

1799 --- 1814

ADAMS ALEXANDER. March 17, 1805. July 1805. Wife: Isabella. Sons: William, Warren. Ex: Brother Matt Adams, Jacob Walker. Wit: Robert Irvine, Wm. Irvine, Andrew Miller.

ADAMS, JOHN. C. Inventory. Sept. 1812. Apprs: Mills Tandy, Benj. Douner, Daniel Fristol.

ALLON, JAMES. Inventory. May 30, 1812. Apprs: Alex. George, Adam Linn, Richard Bell.

ARMSTRONG, JOHN. July 19, 1813. Nov. 1813. Wife: Susanna. Sons: James Madison Armstrong. Ex: Joseph Whiteside. Wit: Isaac Clark, Frances Whitside.

BARNETT, JOSEPH. Dec. 13, 1798. March 1799. Wife: Mary Barnett, unborn child. Wit: Wm. Gibson, John Walker, Martin Mathis.

BARNETT, WILLIAM. Inventory. Nov. 6, 1801. Apprs: William Moore, Samuel Hodge (Hooge), Benj. Lacy, Isaac Stroud.

BARNS, CADER. June, 1812. -------. Wife: Winey. Sons-in-law: Andrew Collins, James Thomas, Richard Thomas. Son: Soloman. Dau: Milindy. Ex: William Carney, Elijah Whitney. Wit: Abraham Smith, Joseph Lawerence.

BLACK, HANS. March 10, 1806. Oct. 1807. Wife: Agnes Black. Sons: David, Thomas. Daus: Susanna Edwards, Ann Pyle, Sarah McAlroy (?), Elizabeth Brasere, Jean Pyle. Gr. son: Nicholas Pyle (son of Samuel Pyle). Ex: Wife Agnes, son Thomas Black. Wit: J. Gamble, Martha Gamble.

BROWN, HUDSON. Inventory Jan. 18, 1810.

BRIDGES, WALTER. April 14, 1806. Aug. 1806. Nuncupative. Wife: Name not given. Sons: John, William. Wit: William Driskel, Thomas Kennady.

BURDIN, JAMES. ------. Aug. 31, 1813. Wife: Sary. Son: John Larence (?). Daus: Patsy, Elizabeth Thomas, Polly, Sary. Wit: Abraham Boyd, Luke Thomas, Charles Linn.

CALVIN, JAMES. Feb. 21, 1803. July 1803. Wife: Susannah. Sons: Luke, Moses, Aron, Luther, William. Daus: Rachel Kennada, Elizabeth Hannah, Nancy James, Mary, Susannah, Sarah, Charity. Ex: Susannah Calvin, Jesse Brookes, Sr. Wit: John Routh, Isaac Stroud, Jole Calvin.

CAMERON, WILLIAM. Dec. 18, 1810. May 1811. Property to wife during widowhood, should she marry property to be sold and divided between her children. Wit: Archd. Mc Donald, Daniel Mc Illvan, Wm. Cameron, Joll Thompson, Jesse Thompson.

CAMPBELL, ANGUISH. Oct. 22, 1803. Inventory. Apprs: John Robinson, James Campbell, George Mc Cown.

CAMPBELL, JOHN B. May 21, 1812. Jan. 1815. Wife: Folly. Legatees: Real Estate from father to go to mother, Margaret Campbell, brother-in-law Robert Latham, brother Arthur's son, John. Enjoins wife to emancipate all her slaves. Ex: Wife, Robert Latham (brother-in-law). Wit: John G. Reynolds, Charles Coldwell. Wit: John Clark C.C.

CHESNUT, ALEXANDER. August 24, 1810. Admr: Sarah Chesnut.

COLLINS, WILLIAM. Inventory. ----1819. Apprs: Samuel Smith, Isaac Clark, Henry Clark.

COLEMAN, THADDEUS. Inventory. Sept. 16, 1811. Apprs: Samuel Moore, John Roberts, Anthony Sharp. Admr: Robert Coleman.

CRAVENS, James. Sumner County, State of Tenn. Nov. 25, 1797. July 1798. Wife: Mary Cravens. Mentions children but does not name them. Ex: John Craven of the State of Tenn., Robert Cravens of the State of Ky. Wit: Robert Hamilton, John Hodge.

COKER, SAMUEL. Jan. 26, 1817. March 1817. Legatees: William Coker (bro.), Samuel B. Coker Hall (nephew), son of Lewis Hall of Warren County. Ex: Bro. William Coker. Wit: Robert Colman, Henry S. Hunter, Samuel McFadden.

DAVIS, JAMES. Feb. 9, 1797. July 1797. Wife: Deborah Davis. Sons: William C. Davis, Abraham Miller Davis.. Daus: Botsy, Sally, Patty. Wit: Thomas Mc Murry, Abraham Miller.

DILLINGHAM, VACHEL. JR. May 7, 1803. July 1803. Wife: Polly. Son: Alfred David Smith Dillingham. Dau: Margaret Hester Dillingham: Ex: James Dillingham, Michael Dillingham. Wit: John Clark, Andrew Henry.

DILLINGHAM, VACHEL. Dec. 9, 1802. Feb. 1803. Wife: Hester. Sons: William, Joshua, James, Michael, Vachel. Daus: Stacy Babcock, Patience. Ex: Wife Hester, James, Michael Dillingham. Wit: Isaac Hargis, William Huntsman.

DIXON, JAMES. Oct. 27, 1808. May 1812. Sons: Hiram Dixon, James Dixon, David Wood (son-in-law). Gr.Son: James Brooks, (son of Margaret, my oldest daughter). Dau: Ann Wood, my youngest daughter. Ex: Hiram Dixon, David Wood, William Dixon. Wit: John Weldon, John Mitchell, John Gray.

DYER, BENJ. May 25, 1814. --- 1814. Wife: Elinor. Son: Albert G. Dyer. Stepsons: William, Robert Patton, sons of wife Wlinor Dyer. Brothers: John, Reuben, Mathew, Parker (?). Daus: Hannah Riddle, Esther Trumbo, Jane Dyer. Wit: John Taylor, William Martin.

DYER, JOHN. ---------. July 23, 1797. Wife: Elizabeth. Sons: John, James Hasur Mc Cager, Joseph, Abraham, Joel. Daus: Betsy, Mary Mc Cleud. Ex: Wife and son John. Wit: Thomas Wadlington, Reuben Loyalless.

HICKS, WILLIS. May 30, 1812. Aug. 1812. Wife: Elinor. Sons: Karr, Josiah, Willis, Mc Cay, Hamlin, Robert, John. Daughters not named. Ex: Wife Elinor, Robert, Karr, (sons). Wit: Absalom Hicks, Israel Robertson.

HUNTSMAN, WILLIAM. April 3, 1804. May 1804. Legatee: Betty Carter. Ex: John Roberts, Gilly Maddux. Wit: James Dillingham, Hannah Dillingham.

JONES, CADWALLEDER. Feb. 25, 1802. Apprs: Thomas Allmon, David Black, Edward Taylor.

JOHNSON, JAMES. Nov. 13, 1807 (?). Aug. 6, 1812. Wife: Mary. Daus: Jeany, Polly, Peggy, Sallie, Nancy, Martha. Sons: John, Simral. Ex: Wife, Mary, son Simral. Wit: Peter Ferguson, Joseph Shanklin.

KING, ROBERT. Aug. 28, 1807. Nov. 1807. Wife: Elizabeth. Sons: John, George. Daus: Isabel, Jane, Margaret, Elizabeth, Rebecah, Mary. Ex: Wife, Thomas Garvin, Joseph Shanklin. Wit: Young Ewing, Thomas Earle, Sally Garvin.

LAMPKIN, ROBERT. May 6, 1811. Inventory. Apprs: James Fruit, John Lockhart, Elijah Walker.

LACY, WILLIAM. Oct. 27, 1814. Nov. 1814. Wife: Elizabeth. Sons: Bartholomew, Philomen. Daus: Rhoda Edwards, Sally Weer. Four daughters mentioned but two named. Ex: sons Bartholomew, Philomen. Wit: Ben Lacy, Willian Husband.

LCOFFTUS, FRANCIS. Inventory Dec. 1801.

LEMARE, LUKE, (LEMAIR). May 19, 1798. Oct. 1798. Sons: John, William, James. Daus: Mary Montgomery, Naomai. Gr. Son: Alexander Lemare. Wit: Joshua Scott. Test: John Clark.

LYLE, BURGESS. Sept. 4, 1808. Feb. 1809. Wife: Judith. Mentions children but does not name them. Wit: Jacob Walton, Thomas Goode.

MARTIN, BAILEY. Oct. 7, 1813. ----- 1813. Wife: Elizabeth. Son: William. Mentions children but does not name them. Ex: Robert Graham, son William, Wife Elizabeth. Wit: James Smith, Charles Bradley, Henry Goren.

MC CARTY, FLORENCE. July 7, 1798. July 26, 1798. Legatee: William Biddle, also named Ex. Wit: James Squires, Roger Mc Daniel.

MC DONALD, JAMES. Jan. 14, 1814. Feb. 1814. Wife: Rachel. Sons: John, James, Isaac, Peter. Ex: Robert Means, Thomas Arbuckle. Wit: John Clark, John Means, Jonathan Bozarth.

MC DUFEE, DUNKIN. Dec. 13, 1808. March 1808. Legatees: Sister Catherine, Brother John, Nephews William, James Johnson. Wit: Malcolm Johnson, Catherine Johnson, John Johnson.

MC FARLAND, JAMES. Nov. 4, 1811. Nuncupative. Sons: Robert, Thomas. Wife name not given. Will proven by oath of Elizabeth Mc Farland, Nancy Mc Farland, Sally Porter. Jan. 1812. Test: John Reynolds.

MCFADIN, SHEPHERD. Inventory. Nov. 26, 1807. John Reynolds, C. C.

MC JUNKLIN, SAMUEL. April 25, 1808. June 9, 1809. Nuncupative. Indiana Territory, Knox County. Estate to son John. Wit: John Mc Donald, John Welkeay, Richard Stean.

MC MILLIN, WILLIAM. Nov. 9, 1810. Feb. 1811. Sons: Robert, Hugh, John, William. Daus: Elizabeth, Elinor, Easter. Ex: Thomas Garvin, William Mc Millin. Wit: Thomas Garvin, John Garvin.

MEANS, SAMUEL. Feb. 11, 1813. March 14, 1813. Wife: Mary. Sons: William B., Elijah, Robert, Young I. Ex: Bro. Robert Means, Wife Mary. Wit: Abner Bozarth, Noah Brunk, John Means.

MILLER, JOHN. April 19, 1814. June, 1814. Wife: Margaret. Dau: Jane. Sons: Alexaxander, John, Isaac, William, James, Josiah, Jesse, Samuel. Ex: Sons Isaac, William. Wit: Elijah Mc Crury, Mathew Bowyer, John Porkypee, John Bowyer.

MILLER, WILLIAM. ------. May 6, 1811. Gr.son: William Miller (son of Samuel Miller). Sons: Calurus, Samuel. Daus: Ann Boyd, Easter Roger, Martha Thomas. Ex: Daniel Benham. Wit: William Campbell, Ann Benham.

MILLER, WILLIAM. Dec. 7, 1811. Jan. 1812. Apprs. Ben Reeves, John Gilmore, Joseph Wear. Wit: John Reynolds.

MOSELY, JOSEPH. April 29, 1811. Oct. 29.------. Wife: Ann. Legatees: Molly Profit, Susanna Profit, her share to her daughters; Nacy Warrell Mosley, his share to his two sons, Fleming Mosley & Thomas Mosley; Jean Thomas (dau.) and her son Fields; James Mosley (son), John Mosley (son). Ex: Jesse Bland, Lewey Bland.

MYRIACK, RICHARD. Nov. 25, 1802. Inventory. Apprs: Peter Ferguson, Robert Adams, Mathew Logan.

PRATT, ZEPHENIAH. Dec. 17, 1808. Jan. 1813. Wife: Keziah. Daus: Elizabeth Griffen, Susan Owings, Nancy Reeder. Sons: John, William, Zepheniah. Daus: Mary, Sarah, Phebe, Heneretta, Patsy. Ex: William Gray, Moses Lasey. Wit: Jesse Brooks, Stephen Gray, Miles Gray.

READ, JOHN, SR., March 15, 1814. Nov. 1814. Wife: Margaret. Son: William Read. Daus: Margaret, Isabella, Jane Woods (wife of Joseph). Gr.son: John Read Wood. Sons: Alexander Read, John Read. Ex: Isham F. Woods, Alex. Read, John Cooper. Wit: John Carr, John Rogers.

REAGAN, DANIEL. Dec. 12, 1804. July 1805. Wife: Elizabeth. Children mentioned but not named. Ex: Wife, John E. Harrison, Jeremiah Reagan (father). Wit: John Campbell, Daniel Harrison.

RIGGS, TIMOTHY. May 3, 1805. May 1805. Inventory. Apprs: Peter Ferguson, Samuel Mc Faddin, John Man (?).

ROBERTS, JOSHUA. Jan. 25, 1816. Feb. 1816. Legatees: William Harland, Mary Harland (wife of William), Isabella (dau. of Wm. and Mary Harland), Arthus Mc Farland. Bros: James, Elijah, Joseph. Sisters: Franky Elliott, Nancy Mc Faddin. Ex: James Roberts, William Harland. Wit: Andrew Mc-Farland, John Stevenson, Sr., James Manning.

SHAW, WILLIAM. Feb. 19, 1814. March 1814. Wife: Ann. Sons: William, James, Samuel, Smith. Daus: Jane Stewart, Elizabeth Brittain, Martha Wilkey, Susannah Shaw, Ibby Shaw, Ann Shaw, my dau., with rest of above named children, one dollar each. William Stewart and James Wilkey to assist wife if needed. Wit: John Burgess, David Mc Clelland.

SHELLY, PHILLIP. Nov. 26, 1798. ----- 1800 (?). Son: William. Mentions wife and other children but does not name them. Wit: Thomas Lester, Thomas Wadlington. Wit: John Clark C.C.

THOMPSON, JOHN. Oct. 28, 1816. Dec. 1816. Wife: Sophia. Sons: Robert, James, John, Alex. Daus: Polly Mc Farlin, Jane Snoden, Sophia Thompson, Nancy Thompsin, Isabella Thompson. Ex: Wife, Sons Robert, James. Wit: Finis Ewing, Thomas Bryen, George Snoden.

THOMPSON, JOEL. March 15, 1810. Nov. 1814. Wife: Nancy Thompson, Samuel Goodwin. Admr: Robert Rogers. Wit: Archibald Mc Donald, Jesse Johnson, Robert Cain.

TREDWAY, AARON. Sept. 19, 1805. June 1814. Wife: Elenor. Daus: Nancy, Eleanor, Leanah, Jenny, Melinda. Wit: John Mabry, Isaac Cates.

WADLINGTON, THOMAS. Dec. 21, 1803. Inventory. Apprs: Geo. Pemberton, David Wood, Adam Lynn.

WADLINGTON, ELIZABETH. Nov. 29, 1809. -----1811. Son: Ferdinand. Dau: Marion Mills. Other children: Thomas Wadlington, Elizabeth Cooper, Sabre Brown. Wit: John Templeton, Absalom Bobo.

WEAR, JOSEPH. Dec. 12, 1811. ---------. Legatees: Bro. John Wear, Bro. John Wear's second son, William Wear; Bro. John Wear's sons, Joseph and James. Cousin James Wear, Mother Rebecca Goodtell. Ex: Brother John Wear. Wit: E. E. Goodtell, Rebecca Goodtell.

WILLBANKS, JOSEPH. Nov. 20, 1808. Wife: Judith. Sons: Willis, Daniel. Dau: Elizabeth Compton, Mary Ryan, Sarah Howard, Asinith Compton. Ex: Peter Ryan, Aaron Compton.

WISTER, FULGUM. Dec. 7, 1811. May 1814. Wife: Elizabeth. Sons: Daniel, John, William. Mentions daughter but does not name her. Ex: Wife, Elizabeth, Wiley Skinner, Jonathan Chandler. Wit: David Flanary, Elizabeth Wister.

YORK, JOHNSTON. Jan. 21, 1804. Inventory. Apprs: James Crabtree, Abner Robinson, James Campbell.

YOUNG, DAVID. April 11, 1817. May 1817. Wife: Phoebe. Legatees: Caleb Young, Anna S., Sarah King, Elizabeth Kanady, Phoebe Allison. Children of James Young, dec'd., Nathan Young, John Young, Polly Young, Gr.son, Elijah Young, son, John. Ex: Caleb Young. Wit: J. P. Finley, Benj. Johnson, Elizabeth Johnson.

CLARK COUNTY

BOOK A

1793---1809

ADAMS, JOHN. 1793. Bill of Sale.

ALDRIDGE, WILLIAM. Aug. 12, 1807. ------. Wife: Mary. Children: Nicholas, William, Mary Woosley, Rebecca Cook. Gr. Children: Sarah (dau. of Nicholas), Thomas Boulware (son of William), Sarah (dau. of William,)William, (son of William). Ex: David Hampton. Wit: Nathan Tucker, Archibald Cooper.

ALEXANDER, JOHN. ------. ------. Children: Andrew, Prudence Todd, Polly. Gr. child: Andrew, Alex. & Prudence Todd, Polly Alexander. Ex: Stephen Trigg, John Oldham. Wit: John Kelly, James Moore, Thomas Tribble.

ARNETT, ABIJAH. Inventory. July 15, 1799. Apprs: Josiah Jennings, James Dunkin, James McKee.

ARNETT, THOMAS. Inventory. May 1809. ------. James Forbes, Jonathan Bryan, C. R. Bradley, Aprs.

BAKER, ISAAC. Sept. 24, 1792. ------. (Of Bourbon Co., Ky.) Elizabeth Walker, Robert McFarley, Miriam Baker (Dau. of Bro. John). Ex: Bros. John and Joshua. Wit: Samuel Plummer, Robert Mc Donell, James Hulls.

BAKER, JOHN. March 11, 1803. Children: Joshua, John, Nancy, Marian, Elizabeth, Isaac Shelby, Cathbert Bullet. Ex: Sympson and Thomas Scott. Wit: John Ward, Thomas Hurdle.

BARNARD, WILLIAM. Inventory. January 22, 1803. Apprs: John Harris, John Berry.

BERRY, WILLIAM. Inventory. June 28, 1800. Apprs: D. Collins, Thomas Burris, John Young.

BLACKBURN, JOSEPH. Dec. 24, 1799. Inventory. Apprs: John Ward, John Hammer, John Ireland.

BLEDSOE, JOHN. Dec. 26, 1799. ------. Children: Elizabeth Adams, Sally, Thomas, William, John, (son-in-law); Lewis Bledsoe. Ex: Thomas Burris Sr., Dillard Collins. Wit: James Durmon, William Calloway, John Williams.

BODKIN, JAMES. Aug. 18, 1804. Wife: Dinah. Children: George, Thomas, William, James, Margaret Bensten, Sarah Barnor, Rachel Douglas, Betsy, Mary, Jinna, Ann Wise. Ex: Wife, son George. Wit: William Morris, Matt and John Patton.

BOONE, MARTHA. May 12, 1793. ------. Children: George, Joseph, Charity, Ell--, Jane Morgan, Macey Shell, Sarah Hunter. Ex: John Morgan, Jr.

BOX, JAMES. Sept. 21, 1806. ------. Step chld: Wm. Boyle and Prudy. Ex:

Wife, son Mina. Wit: David McGee, Joseph King.

BUNCH, ZACHARIAH. Aug. 26, 1794. ------. Wife: Sally. Children: William, Henry, Milly, Mourning, Anna, Lucy. Gr.son: James Cubbage. Ex: Wife, Elijah Summers. Wit: John Summers, Peter Dewit, Jr. and Sr.

BUSH, JOHN. Inventory. May 18, 1798. Apprs: R. Eubanks, Robert Clark, Robert Sanford, William Bush, Wiatt Bush. Admr: Mary Bush.

BUSH, WILLIAM. (CAPT. BILLY). "He was a friend and companion of Daniel Boone and others in the early settlement of Ky." Born July 25, 1746. Died July 25, 1815. Oct. 1817 there was a division of slaves among his children who were named as follows: William Tandy, Frances Giddings, Elkana, Cynthia, Susanna Morrow, Polly, Willis, Jane, Thomas. Wife: Frances (Burris) Bush. Book B.

BUSH, PHILIP. June 21, 1814. ------. Wife: Franky. Sons: John V., Robert, Thatcher. Daus: Nancy, Franky, Jane, Peggy, Sally, Polly. Ex: Wife, son John. Wit: John Ashburn, E. Bradford. Book B. P.438.

CAIN, HENRY. Inventory. December 23, 1803. Apprs: Daniel Ramsey, Joseph Stevens, Robert Richards, Ecton Smallwood, William Bush J.P.

CHEATHAM, ANN. Jan. 27, 1799. Dower. Apprs: John Baker, W. Sudduth, John Morgan.

CHEATHAM, JAMES. Oct. 12, 1795. ------. Wife: Ann. Children: James, Edmond, John, Polly, Olly. Ex: Thomas Dawson, Thomas Scott. Wit: William Knox, Joshua Stamfer, William Hill.

CHRISTY, JULIUS. Dec. 5, 1805. ------. Wife: Agatha. Children: John, Ambrose. Ex: Son Ambrose. Wit: Sarah Lay, Mary and Wm. Murphy.

CLARK, ROBERT. Dec. 13, 1806. ------. Wife: Betsy. Children: Patsy, Gest, Polly, Robert, Patterson, Susan Puckett. Bro. James, guardian for Robert. Ex: Wife, William Smith, James Clark. Wit: James Clark, Zachariah Field, Judith Campbell.

CLIFTON, DANIEL.--------. Killed by Indians April 2, 1794. Margaret Clifton. Wit: Samuel Downing, Enoch Smith.

COATS, MARY, M. March 1809. ------. Sister Ann Elgen, Walter Southland. Ex: Bro. John Southland. Wit: Thomas and John Constant.

CROSTHWAIT, AARON. Inventory. Dec. 13, 1798. Apprs: Joseph Dunman, James Palmer, John Ramsy.

CROSTHWAIT, AARON. Settlement. Marcy 31, 1804. James Taylow, James Simpson, Peter Flanigan.

CROSTHWAIT, JACOB. March 18, 1803. ------. Children: Samuel, Aaron, Brookman. John Ireland and his wife Elloner (widow of Aaron Crosthwait) Gr. Children: Elizabeth, Asa, Aaron Crosthwait. Ex: Elijah Crosthwait, John Coony. Wit: James Simpson, E. Spillman.

DANIEL, NANCY. Legacy. March 10, 1803. D. Hampton, James Quisenberry, Samuel Reed, David Hampton.

DANIEL, VIVION. June 21, 1802. ------. Wife: Nancy. Children: Peter, John, Margaret, Nancy Oldham, Jane. Friend Geo. Quisenberry who married dau. Jane. Dau. Frances Deal (3 chld: Elizabeth, Jenett, Daniel). Ex: D. Collins, Daniel Bullock. Wit: Robert, Isabelle and Samuel Steel.

DAVIS, SOLOMON. Inventory. July 10, 1801. Apprs: Thomas Pickett, Matt Anderson, Thomas Scott, Sarah Davis, Admr:

DAVENPORT, STEPHEN. Inventory. Dec. 22, 1802. Apprs: Jacob Marth, James Clark, John Rupard, William Hayne.

DOWNEY, MARTHA. Jan. 20, 1801. -----. Children: Samuel, William, Marian, Rebecka, Janst, Margaret, Elizabeth. Ex: Son Samuel and William. Wit: John Stevenson, Reason Bell.

EDMONSON, ARCHIBALD. Nov. 3, 1800. -----. Wife: Sidney or Lindy. Children: James, Thomas, Patsey, Suckee, Polly, Marjory, Debby. Ex: Wife, Aaron Lacklen. Wit: W. McMillan, Azariah Prather.

EMBREE, JACOB. Feb. 23, 1799. --------. All to brothers and sisters. Ex: Bros. William and Thomas. Wit: Michael Stoner, Joseph Embrae.

EMMETT, SARAH. --------. 2/3 to son-in-law John Gordon, 1/3 to Gr.dau. Anna Stone. Ex: John Gordon. Wit: Daniel Ramsey, William Kindrece, Amelea Daumes.

EUBANKS, THOMAS. Guardian Settlement. Oct. 31, 1803. Wit: Jacob Fishback, Willy Braffield, Willian N. Lane.

EVANS, RICHARD. Feb. 27, 1797. -----. Children: Mabrey, Mary Waddell, Elizabeth Stevenson, Susannah Waddell, James Evans, Anna Bell, Sarah Ev---. Wife: Mary. Wit: John and Robert Heels, Robert Walker.

FLORAH, WILLIAM. Inventory. March 1803. Ann Florah Admr:

FLYNN, M. Inventory March 9, 1807. Apprs: William Honey, Lusas Hood, Freeman Battershell.

GANES, W. Inventory. Sept. 1, 1809. Ex: William James, John Price. Apprs: Timothy Parish, John Martin.

GORDON, JOHN. July 18, 1803. -----. Wife: Judith. Children: Elizabeth, Mary, John, Lucy, Judity, William, Frances, Nancy, Benjamin. Ex: John and William Gordon. Wit: David and John Citley, Jacob Woodson.

HACKADAY, EDWARD. Oct. 1807. --------. Wife: Martha. Children: Betsy Irvine, Martha Shackleford, Isaac, Edmund. John. Ex: William Irvine, Isaac Hackaday. Wit: Robert Didlake.

HARRIS, THOMAS. March 9, 1793. -----. Wife: Mary. Children: Joshua, Caleb, four daus. not named. Ex: Wife, son Joshua. Wit: W. D. Ramsey, John M. Macklin, Wm. Bush.

HARROW, DANIEL. Aug. 12, 1795. ------. Children: William, Charles, James, Gr. son Daniel Hacket (Nelson and Elizabeth Hacket). Ex: James Gray, Samuel Harrow. Wit: William and T. Suddeth, Samuel Arnett.

HAZELRIGG, CHARLES. Oct. 19, 1795. ------. Eldest Bro. John, Nancy, Green and Fielding Clement, (Sarah Clement), Charles Oldfield (Sarah Huttin), Graham Nelson, (Elizabeth Nelson). Ex: Isaac Halbert, Graham Hazelrigg. Wit: George Winn, D. Daly, Thomas Winn.

HILL, JOHN. -------. Wife: Elizabeth. Children: John, William, Garland, Lucy. Son-in-law Josiah Ashley. Ex: Wife and son John. Wit: James Simpson, Peter Clapson.

HUKELL, HENRY. March 4, 1798. -----. Wife: Elizabeth. Children: James, Henry. Ex: Wife. Wit: Thomas Owen, Richard Hukel, Edward Roberts.

IRELAND, NELLY. Jan. 30, 1800. Dower. Wid. of Aaron Crostwait. Thomas Scott, Holly Crump, E. Calloway, James Flanigan.

JACOBS, CATHARINE. Nov. 1799. Dower. Widow of Henry. Wit: Matt Anderson, J. McCreery, John Skinner.

JONES, WILLIAM. May 18, 1809. -----. Wife: Polly. Children: Elijah, William, Lucy. Gr. Son Alex. Ex: Wife, son William. Wit: William Wayman, Jacob Fishback, Phebe Fishback.

JOHNSON, MARTHA. June 15, 1799. Dower. Formerly Martha Oliver. Wit: Jona, Morton, Jacob Crosthwait.

LEDGERWOOD, WILLIAM. May 7, 1792. Wife: Rebecca. Children: Samuel, James, Isabell, Margaret, Mary, Rebeccah. Ex: Samuel and James. Wit: James McWilliams, Robert McWilliams, Allen Neil.

LEWIS, ROBERT. Feb. 20, 1799. ------. Names John Lewis Martin, John Taylor Martin, Robert B. Martin, Sally Roland (Thomas R.), Polly Lewis (Jesse L.), Bro. Charles Lewis. Ex: Jacob Fishback, J. and James Martin. Wit: J. Martin, Thomas Martin, Matt Anderson.

LUSK, SAMUEL. Inventory. Nov. 1801. Apprs: Wiley Brassfield, James Young, William Young.

MARTIN, DAVID. Inventory. Jan. 1802. Apprs: Jonathan Morton, John Ramsey, William Redman, Sarah Martin (Admr.)

MC CAFFRIC, WILLIAM. Inventory. March 1793. Apprs: W. Suddeth, Arnold Hood, Levi Lockhart.

MC MURRY, SAMUEL. Inventory. May 1793. Apprs: Aziriah Martin, Josiah Hart, John Baker, William Craig.

MC CREARY, ROBERT. Inventory. Jan. 1796. Apprs: John Baker, John Morgan, John Strode.

MC CREARY, SAMUEL. Inventory. March 1796. Apprs: Josiah Hart, Wm. Craig.

MC DANIEL, WILLIAM. Inventory. Dec. 7, 1802. Apprs: James Young, Wm. Young, John Strode, Jr.

MC MILLIAN, JAMES. Jan. 22, 1796. -------. Children: Robert, James, Elizabeth, Mary. Ex: Eldest son, Robert. Wit: Jacob Armstrong, Elias Browning.

MC PHEETERS, JOHN. Oct. 23, 1795. -------. Wife: Elizabeth. Children: Charles, Sarah, Jenny. Ex: Wife, son Charles, James Crawford, William McPheeters. Wit: James Wardlow, James Ward, Jr., Martin Wardlow.

MORGAN, JESSE. Inventory. Jan. 6, 1796. Apprs: David Hampton, John Daley, Francis Cullam.

NOE, PETER. Jan. 16, 1802. -------. Wife: Mary. Children: James, Pryor, Sarah Tracey, Elizabeth Kincaid, Sable Tracey. Ex: Wife, James Noe. Wit: Samuel McKee, Paul Huls, James Clark.

O'HARROW, DANIEL. Inventory. June 28, 1796. Apprs: John Lockridge, James Wilson, William Yardley.

O'HARROW, PATRICK. July 1, 1795. -------. Sister Sarah. Nephew Patrick O'Harrow (son of John O'Harrow). Ex: Simon Adams, John O'Harrow. Wit: John Williams, Mary O'Harrow, Malcom Ward.

OLIVER, JOHN. Inventory. Apprs: Jonathan Morton, Radford McCargo, David Martin.

RAMSEY, DANIEL. July 23, 1806. ----. Wife: Rachel. Children not named. Ex: Wife, D. Hampton. Wit: Elizabeth Haggard, Alex. Anderson.

RAMSEY, NANCY. Nov. 28, 1797. Dower. Formerly Nancy Smith, Widow of Joseph Smith. Wit: Wm. Mater, D. Wilcox, Samuel Spurgin.

RAY, BENJAMIN. Inventory. Aug. 15, 1795. Apprs: George Miller, Philip Bush, A. Eubanks.

RICHARDSON, LANDIE. March 21, 1808. Wife: Betsy. Ex: Wife, Nathan Vier. Children not named. Wit: William and Polly Richardson.

RICHARDSON, ROBERT. Inventory. July 24, 1798. Apprs: Benjamin Taul, William Bullock, Micajah Clarke.

RICHARDSON, WILLIAM. Inventory. Nov. 1794. Apprs: Josias and William Bullock, John Burton, Jr.

RITCHIE, JANE. -----. May 1799. Children: Alex, George, Violette. Gr. sons, William and James Cardwell. Ex: William and James Cardwell. Wit: Fredrick Couchman, William McMillan.

RULON, NATHANIEL. Oct. 1794. Apprs: Nathaniel Sanders, Daniel O'Harrow, Jona Millholland.

SCOTT, BAPTIST. Dec. 5, 1801. -------. Wife: Nancy. Children: George, Elijah, Sarah (her son Levi), Elisha, Kesiah, Baptist. John Fauquor. Ex:

Wife: Dillard Collins, Edward Hockaday. Wit: Edward Summers, Nancy Stripling, Philip Ballard.

SMITH, JOSEPH. Nov. 28, 1795. ------. Wife: Nancy. Children mentioned but not named. Wit: Daniel Holmes, Enoch Smith, Mary E. Smith, Aaron Green.

STRODE, JOHN. April 1805. -----. Wife: Mary. Children: Molly, and others. Ex: John Strode, Thomas Lafferty. Wit: Maxmillen Bowen, John Warren.

STRODE, MARY. Oct. 17, 1805. Dower. Wid. of John. Wit: John Landen, George Hibbs.

SWANEY, DANIEL. May 24, 1799. -----. Wife: Sarah. Children: William, Mary, John, James, Samuel, Robert, Elizabeth, Cathen. Ex: Wife, son James. Wit: Daniel Scott, Paul Hoff, Richard Wharton.

SWINNEY, JAMES. Nov. 30, 1804. Apprs: George Shorp, Richard Warton.

TAYLOR, JONATHAN. Feb. 18, 1802. ------. Wife: not named. Nephew George. Son George. Ex: Sons George and William, Wife. Wit: Thomas Martin, Phebe Fishback, Hannah Tyler.

TINSLEY, DAVID. Inventory. April 25, 1798. Apprs: William Tinsley, Leonard Hill, Caleb Browning, R. Hickman.

TOWNSIN, JAMES. Dec. 1794. -----. Children: Rhoda, Garnet. Ex: Wife, Markham Ware. Wit: Peter Goosey, Caleb Ware, Benjamin Dunnwing, Samuel Carson.

WADDLE, GEORGE. Feb. 7, 1800. -----. Wife: Mary. Children: John, Daniel, George, William, Betsy, Nancy, Becky, Peggy, Susan, Mary Sarah. Ex: Wife, sons John and Daniel. Wit: John Baker, Peter Scholl.

WATSON, PATRICK. Inventory. April 8, 1801. Wit: William Watson, John McColl, Admr., George Taylor, F. Morton, L. Burbridge.

WHITE, JONA. Nov. 14, 1802. ------. Wife: Elizabeth. Children: Francis, William, Richard, Daniel, Elizabeth, Polly, Nanny. Ex: Wife. Wit: Andrew Hardy, Rawley Corbin, Moses Scott.

WILLS, FRANCIS. Inventory. Oct. 1796. Apprs: John Young, William Suddeth, William Craig.

WILLS, FREDRICK. Dec. 20, 1795. ------. Wife: Francis. Children: Sarah, Harrey, Richard, John, William, Derret. Ex: Sons John and Richard, son-in-law Tucker Hord. Wit: James Harris, W. Suddeth.

WILSON, JOSEPH. Inventory. Nov. 23, 1795.

WILSON, PEGGY. Jan. 1, 1802. Dower. From Hus. Joseph Smith. Wit: James Paoge, Jacob Coons, William Matire.

WINN, THOMAS. July 1796. Apprs: Wm. Johnson, John Horgin, Richard Holley.

WOOLMAN, JOHN. Inv. May 8, 1795. Wit: Jona. Martin, Chris. Martin, Philip Taylor.

CRITTENDEN COUNTY

BOOK A

1842 ---------

INDEX

Adams, Josiphine
Agee, Martha
Allen, B. J.
Allison, L.B.
Andrew, C. W.
Armstrong, M. E.
Arnold, Tabitha
Asher, William R.
Asher, William H.
Ashley, Berdine
Asbridge, Ellen.

Bailey, Mary
Barnett, Peter
Barnes, David
Barnes, Newsome
Baker, George C.
Baker, John M.
Barrett, William
Bagley, J.B.
Bell, Thomas
Bennett, Polly Ann
Bennett, Peter
Bennett, John
Beal, J. C.
Belt, Arthur
Bennett, Mary Jane
Belt, B. W.
Black, Daniel
Blue, J. W.
Blue, Jas. B.
Blue, Margaret
Brashear, A. J.
Brashear, M. L.
Brashear, Sarah A.
Brantlly, N.
Bristow, M.
Brantly, Fielding
Bradford, Thos.
Bradford, Kirby
Brashear, Elizabeth
Brice, John
Brooks, David.
Brown, John
Brown, Samuel
Bryan, David.

Cam, William, Sr.
Casper, Asa
Cain, Mary
Cameron, Thos.
Cardin, Mrs. Mary A.
Carter, Garland
Campbell, George R.
Cason, Henry
Carnahan, W. G.
Cardin, A. H.
Cardin, Silas
Clinton, James
Clement, Isham
Clinton, Peter
Clement, Sarah
Clark, Elinor
Clark, A. E.
Clark, John
Clement, William
Coffield, Isaac
Conditt, Susan
Conger, Elisha
Conger, Lemuel
Cobb, Thos. J.
Crider, Samuel
Crider, Stephen
Crider, William
Crider, A. A.
Crider, Cora Pierce
Crowley, T. J.
Crawford, Green
Crawford, Francis
Crayne, -----
Croft, Margaret

Dallins, Mrs. Mary J.
Damron, W.
Davidson, J. A.
Daugherty, Katharine
Dempsey, James
Dean, Alex.
Debor, Jesse W.
Dreeman, J. C.
Duncan, Rice H.
Duvall, James

Eberle, Mary E.
Edmonson, M. L.
Elder, John D.
Elder, Ben
Elder, George
Elder, J. C.
Elder, S. J.
Enoch, Benj.
Enoch, A. A.

Farley, Gatesfield
Flournoy, Thomas
Flournoy, W. E.
Fowler, R. M.
Fortts, R.
Ford, John M.
Fowler, James M.
Fowler, William
Fowler, Sallie
Foster, R. W.
Franklin, Jasper
Franks, John M.
Franklin, William A.
Franklin, C. E.
Franklin, Elijah
Franklin, John Louis

Hamby, Isaac
Hamby, Jesse
Hamby, S. P.
Handlin, Joseph
Hale, William
Haynes, M. B.
Hardin, John
Hawkin, Richd.
Haynes, Pernicea
Hawkins, John H.
Haynes, H. A.
Hatcher, James
Henry, J. S.
Henson, Mary
Hibbs, J. L.
Hill, J. W.
Hill, R. C.
Hill, James
Hillyard, George
Howard, William
Hoover, J. G.
Hodges, John
Highes, I.
Hughes, William
Hughes, H. H.
Hughes, Will
Hughes, James
Hunt, John

Huskins, Mary
Hughes, Lucinda

Jacobs, Frank
Jacobs, Amanda
Jackson, Sarah
Jackson, J. R.
James, Daniel
James, B. S.
James, G. S.
Jarrell, Sarah
Jennings, Ann E.
Johnson, James
Johnson, William
Jones, Daniel
Jones, B. M.
Jones, George

Kevil, J. B.
Kilpatrick, E. G.
Kirk, Fredrick
Kirk, John
Kirk, Fredrick
Koon, S.

Lacey, Jeremiah
Lamb, John
Lamb, Harvey
Lamb, J. M.
Lamb, L. H.
Lamb, Mrs. T. R. & Laurs
Lamb, J. Wilson
Lewis, W. A.
Leigh, Henry
Loftus, Sarah
Long, G. W.
Long, H. P.
Lucus, Robt. C.
Lucus, Sidney.

Marble, Sarah
Marble, William
Marshall, John R.
Martin,
Mayes, W. H.
Mc Cluckey, John
Mc Cheskney, John
Mc Collum ---
Mc Dowell, John
Mc Kinney, Vincent
Minner, Richd.
Miley, C. J.
Milam, Jas.
Morrow, Samuel
Morton, J.

Moore, R. L.
Moore, W. C.
Moore, John.?
Moore, George
Morgan, Andrew
Murray, William.

Nation, William B.
Nelson, J. T.
Newcom, William
Nunn, Thos.
Nunn, Ira.
Nunn, Samuel
Nunn, Mark

Oneal, J. H.
Owen, David
Owen, Mary

Palmer, Jane
Page, Wm.
Paris, J. L.
Paris, Arch
Paris, L. A.
Paris, Newton
Paris, Obidiah
Parish, Geo. W.
Peckins, A. J.
Perry, John
Perrin, B. G.
Peck, Matilda
Perkin, W. S.
Perry, Chas.
Perrin, Elizabeth
Pierce, C. J.
Porter, William H.

Ralph, John
Ralph, Mary
Ralston, Dell
Rease, Elisha
Reeves, Robt.
Rentfor, John
Reynold, Chas.
Redd. ----
Reed, Elizabeth
Rice, Edward
Rochester, Phoebe
Robertson, E. F.
Roberts, Evelyn Shelby
Rutter -------

Shaw, David
Shaw, Mrs. C. D.
Shelby, William.

Shearer, Jesse Willis
Smith, M.
Smith, Sarah
Smith, Samuel
Smith, Mahalia
Stephenson, David
Steel, David
Stevens, Mahalia
Stations, E. A.
Stone, Thos.
Stovall, W. W.
Stephenson, W. E.
Stallion, J. W.
Sullivan, H. L.

Tabor, John
Taylor, Timothy
Tackwell, M. J.
Thomason, Richd.
Threlkeld, R. S.
Tompkins, Henry
Towery, Margaret
Travis, Leonidas
Travis, Frances
Truett, Job
Trabue, Isaac
Trapnell, Phil.
Turk, Emeltom
Turley, Sanford

Ullman, Simon

Vaughn, David

Walker, Jas.
Walker, P. L.
Walker, Henry
Walker, R. N.
Walker, Andy
Wallace, William
Wallace, Thos.
Wallace, Arthur
Watson, A. P.
Watson, Henry
Watson, G. T.
Wheeler, J. H.
Wheeler, Jas.
Wheeler, Lydia
Wheeler, H. C.
Wheeler, Mrs. E. G.
Wilson, Robert
Wilson, Jeremiah
Wilson, John
Wilson, R.
Wilson, Simon

Witherspoon, Geo.
Williams, David
Williams, R. M.
Wring, S. L.
Wyatt, Shelby
Wright, Miller

Yandele, Sarah
Yates, R. H.
Yeakey, Henry
Yeakey, Harrison
Young, Stephen

DAVIESS COUNTY

BOOK A

1815 --- 1842

ADAMS, ELISHA. Jan. 12, 1842. Feb. 1842. Wife: Mildred. Legatees: Augustine Talbot, Thomas Poynter. Ex: Thomas Poynter. Wit: Henry Read, Augustine Talbot.

ALLIN, ROBERT. Sept. 12, 1812. Feb. 1818. Wife: Polly. Wit: Thomas Prity, Polly Prity, Benjamin Pate, William Allin.

ALLIN, WILLIAM. Nov. 22, 1827. Feb. 1828. Wife: Ann. Ex: John Johnson, John Huston. Wit: Benjamin Harris, Charles W. Taylor.

ANDERSON, DANGERFIELD. April 3, 1849. June 1851. Legatees: sister Eliza, and children. Ex: William Moorman. Wit: George W. Triplett, David Kenedy.

BAIRD, WILLIAM. Nov. 1, 1841. --- 1867. Children: Elizabeth, John, Wm., Fishes, Baird and five older ones not named. Sister Savilla. Ex: George Riley, Benjamin Rafferty. Wit: John McFarland, Edward T. White.

BANKS, C. P. Sept. 9, 1841. June 10, 1867. Wife: not named. Children: James, John, Mary Ann. Ex: wife. Wit: Samuel Catham, C. S. Mark.

BARKER, ELIZABETH. April 22, 1826. June 1826. Legatees: Elict Barker, Samuel and Anias, sons of Elict Barker.

BEAUCHAMP, ------. Jan. 11, 1833. May 1833. Wife: Sally. Children: Wm., Elizabeth, John, Sarah Ann Bartlett, Robert, Nancy Howard, Leah Biggs, Rebecka. Ex: Wm. Jett, George Moffett. Wit: W. T. Mason, George Moffett.

BELL, RICHARD. April 14, 1840. May 1840. Wife: not named. Dau: Elizabeth. Ex: Henry Head, Hillory Bell. Wit: Bryson Barnett, Wm. Head.

BINGHAM, THOMAS. July 2, 1837. Aug. 1837. Wife: Nancy. Children: Sally Kelly, Susan Lewis, Elizabeth Tribble. Gr.son: Thomas Bingham Kelly. Wit: Samuel Catham, E. S. Mark.

BRAND, JOHN B. June 16, 1851. July, 1851. Wife: Sary. Children: John W., Susan Jane, Samantha, Ayrean, Alvera. Wit: David Westerfield, John Mosely.

BRISTOW, JASPER. June 1, 1843. June 1, 1848. Wife: Rachel. Children: Benjamin, Briton, Annie, Samuel, Wm. T., Rachel, Hiram. Other his Elisha Johnson, Harriet Stoats, Elener Jones, James Hendricks. Wit: Wm. Crawford.

BUNN, NATHAN. Nov. 10, 1833. Dec. 1833. Wife: Elizabeth. Daus: Virginia, Sally. Ex: Wife Elizabeth. Wit: James Arnold, George Varda, Benjamin Harris.

BURTON, BASSETT. Sept. 1825. June 1867. Wife: Polly. Children: Creed,

Elisha, Lindsay, Hardee, Addison, Almyra, Catherine Burton. Ex: Wife Polly, Creed and Elisha Burton. Wit: Richard Lockhart, John E. Graves.

CARR, WILLIAM. March 31, 1853. June 1872. Wife: Mildred. Wit: J. P. Washburn, William Owen.

CASSIDY, JOSEPH G. No Date. Heirs: son Robert E., Brothers John B., Emmett, and heirs of William Poynter. Ex: John B. Cassidy, Thomas Poynter. Wit: Thomas Mc Creery, James Johnson.

CHILTON, JOSEPH. April 9, 1841. Aug. 23, 1842. Late of Faquier County, Va. Children: Lucy, Ann Johnston, Elizabeth Spillman, Juliet Keith, John A. Joseph O. Ex: Isham Keith. Wit: Chas. Chilton, Martin Brooke. (Probated in Fauquier Co., Va.)

CLAY, THOMAS. July 19, 1824. Jan. 1825. Wife: Mary. Sons: Facitus, Nester. Ex: Son Facitus. Wit: William Beall, G. Oberby (?), Seris Jones.

COMES, WILLIAM. May 8, 1834. Wife: Rachel. Children: Charles, Mary, Elizabeth, Felix, Benedict, William Peter, Trese Wallace. Ex: Felix Comes. Wit: Henry and Benjamin Read.

CONWAY, F. F. Sept. 1848. Oct. 1848. Wife: Betsy. Children not named. Ex: Wife. Wit: L. D. Conway, E. Bonner.

CRABTREE, ISAAC. Sept. 23, 1846. Feb. 1847. Wife: Sally. Daus: Eveline Pruden (Hus. Malon), Alcy Worthington, Julia Barnett, Emily Winstead, Caroline Crabtree, Sarah Crabtree, Elizabeth Crabtree. Ex: Eveline Pruden. Wit: Samuel Calhoun, C. C. Boswell, John Mc Farland.

CURRY, WILLIAM. March 25, 1847. Wife: Mary Jane. Children mentioned but not named. Wit: Daniel Williams, John R. Bryan, John R. Duncan.

DANIELS, JAMES W. June 9, 1838. August 1838. Legatees: Sister Margaret Morton's five children; brother Vivien, trustee for sister Mary Singleton, brothers Philip, John. Ex: Vivien Daniel, (bro.-in-law) Marin Duncan. Wit: Isaac Kenedy, James Weaver.

DAVIS, BAXTER: Sept. 1, 1839. Nov. 1839. Children: William, Thomas, Baxter, Ophelia Overall, Francis Young, Polly Ann Ramsay, Rachel Overall; children of sons James and John Davis, William Baxter, Mary, John, James Fletcher, and Gr. son Leondies Davis. Ex: Sons William, Thomas, Baxter. Wit: Obadiah Gordon, Isaac Hudson.

DAVIS, JACOB. Jan. 23, 1817. March 1817. Children: George, Jacob, Sally Mc Neer, Gr. son John Davis, son of Sally Mc Neers; Gr. dau. Mary Thrixton; dau. Druella Davis; sons Felix, Wilson. Wit: Benj., Archibald, John Johnson.

DICKEN, CHRISTOPHER. Dec. 31, 1841. ---1848. Heirs: Robert Dickens and Elizabeth Dicken, children of my brother Robert; brother Joseph. Ex: Ebenezer Cochran, Lucy Briggs. Wit: John Calhoun, Gardiner Fitts.

DULANY, ELIZA C. June 3, 1841. Dec. 1842. Children: Benjamin, Virginia, Nora (wife of Henry Gerves). Ex: son Benjamin, Henry Gerves.

FAITH, WILLIAM. July 27, 1840. Son: William. Other children not named. Wit: A. Jordan, John Mc Meeter, Samuel Harralson.

FENWICK, IGNATUS M. Aug. 28, 1832. Jan. 1835. Of Scott County, Ky. Wife:---- Daus: Lucy, Mary, Catherine. Other children not named. Ex: Wife. Wit: Anderson Taylor, James Combs, M.S. Dehoney.

FORD, RACHEL. March 3, 1838. Nov. 1839. Dau: Elizabeth Ford. Son: Spencer Ford. Wit: William Ford, Creed Burton.

GRIFFITH, JOSHUA. Sept. 13, 1839. Dec. 1845. Son: William R. Dau: Mary (hus. William Hansford), Gr. son Henry Griffith, son Remus, Dau. Ruth Cummings children. Ex: Son William, William Hansford. Wit: James Field, John Newton, Thomas Howard.

GRIFFITH, REMUS. April 11, 1843. Feb. 1846. Wife: Sally. Son: Henry. Daus: Ruth, Elizabeth, Lucinda Glover. Ex: Wife Sally, son Henry, Bro. William R. Wit: S. M. Wing, William Newton.

GRIFFITH, WILLIAM. July 13, 1848. March 1849. Children: William, Daniel, Clinton, Margaret (wife of son Henry). Wit: Philip Triplett.

HAGAN, SYLVESTER. Jan. 6, 1850. Feb. 1850. Wife Rachel. Son: Charles. Other children mentioned but not named. Ex: Wife Rachel, son Charles. Wit: E. C. Berry, Charles Miles.

HANNA, JAMES D. Dec. 25, 1833. -----. Wife: Name not given. Brother William.

HAWES, ALBERT G. March 1, 1849. ----. Wife: Adelle. Children mentioned but not named. Ex: Wife Adelle and brothers Hugh, Walker, Edward, Benjamin. Wit: R. W. Murray, W. Woolfolk.

HAYDEN, PHILIP. May 8, 1840. -----. Wife: Eliza. Children not named. Ex: Wife Eliza, Sylvertis Hayden. Wit: John R. Blanford, Urban Hayden, John Hayden.

HAYNES, WILLIAM. July 13, 1847. -------. Wife: Kitty. Children: Robert, Charles, Kitty. Ex: Brother Hardin Haynes, Creed Barton, Mason Pate. Wit: William Nickols, William Purnell.

HEAD, HENRY R. Oct. 1849. April 1850. Wife: Elizabeth. Children: William, Elizabeth, Celia, Franklin, Rigger, Ireland, Rebecca and to the heirs of his deceased children, Lucindy, Sarah. Ex: Sons William and Franklin. Wit: James C. Wells, Thomas C. Aud.

HIGDON, THOMAS. Oct. 20, 1846. Dec. 1846. Wife: Artemecea. Children and grand children but no names. Ex: Wife. Wit: Harrison Yewell, William R. Griffith, Moses Fuqua.

HORDS, GEORGE. Oct. 10, 1832. ------. Four children but names not given. Relatives: Thomas and Robert Hord. Ex: William Griffith, Dr. John Roberts.

HOWARD, GROVES. Aug. 4, 1847. Apr. 1847. Wife: Susan. Sons: Thomas, Oliver, and Benj. Brodie. Wit: Henry Howard, Mark Owen, Thomas Howard, Allen Howard.

HOWES, CLARA. Dec. 7, 1847. Dec. 1848. Ex: sons William and Benjamin Howes, Bro. Hugh Walker and wife Marie, Matilda Walker, Clara Roberts. Wit: Enoch Kendall, J. C. Whayne.

HOWES, RICHARD. Nov. 12, 1829. ----1867. Wife: Clara. Children: Samuel, Edwin, Susan, William, Benjamin, Aglett. Ex: Edwin, Benjamin, Samuel Albert(?). Wit: John Davies, Isaac Whayne, Willice Roberts, William Roberts.

HUSTON, JAMES. Aug. 10, 1831. Jan. 1843. John Huston, Jane Huston, Children. Wife: Mary. Ex: Wife Mary. Wit: James Bemis, James Tichner, John Orr.

HUSTON, MARY. Oct. 1, 1847. Dec. 1849. Widow of James. Children: John H. Huston, Mary Jane Hopkins. Gr. dau. Martha Hopkins. Ex: Son John, nephew Mark E. Huston. Wit: Abraham Houghton, Josiah Houghton, Mark E. Hasting.

HUSTON, WILLIAM. Nov. 12, 1831. ----. Wife: Susannah. Children: Benjamin, John. Dau: Ann Allin (wife of Wm. Allin), Lucy Johnson (wife of John Johnson). Ex: Wife Susannah, sons John and Benjamin. Wit: James Hillyar, Stephen Winston, J. Layton.

JACKSON, GEORGE. Nov. 5, 1838. Dec. 1838. Wife: Sarah. Children: Samuel, Christopher, Andrew, Washington, Joseph, Nancy and four other daus. Gr. Children: Ellen Horard, Sarah Jackson. Ex: Chris. Jackson. Wit: Lemuel Green, James Johnson, Powhattan Ellis.

JOHNSON, ARCHER. April 1845. Wife: Susan. Children: Archer, Samuel, George and others. Wit: Henry Wood, Samuel Loyd.

JOHNSON, JAMES. -----.1867. Nuncupative Will. Oath of John S. McFarland and Samuel Wing. Wife: Martha. Children: Cleopatra, children of daughter Nancy Clay. Ex: John W. Thompson.

KELLY, GEORGE. S. Dec. 9, 1847. ------. Wife: Jane. Children: Harriet, Polly, Mildred Leaman, Ruth Anderson, Jemina Hudson, Agnes Barnes, George, Talbott, Barnett, Elizabeth Bogarth, William. Wit: David Leman, Samuel Tanner, William R. Griffith.

KNOTT, MARY. Dec. 28, 1846. April 1847. Legatees: Mary Knott, Nancy Knott, Susan Knott, Bro. Joseph. (Leg. seem to have been sister-in-laws). Ex: William Bell. Wit: Thomas Head, J. H. Rodman.

MC CORMACK, JOHN. Sept. 19, 1850. Dec. 1850. Wife: Sarah. Son: Benjamin. Other children not named. Ex: Wife, son Benjamin. Wit: James Burton, John Lashbrook, F. W. Haynes.

MILLER, NANCY. Sept. 2, 1848. Oct. 1848. Legatees: Friends Dr. A. O. Ayers, Calvin Martin. Ex: Thomas Landrem, Rachel Tanner. Wit: Jacob Miller, N.A. Johnson.

MILLER, WILLIAM. Aug. 5, 1848. Aug. 1848. Wife: Susannah. Children: Emily, Frances, Ann Elmetz. Ex: Pleasant Miller, James Dawson, D. A. Miller.

MITCHELL, GIDEON. Jan. 3, 1848. Feb. 1848. Children: John M., Ranna Ann; children of dau. Canda. Wit: W. A. Johnson, Thomas Minton.

MONTGOMERY, T. F. Dec. 7, 1850. Wife: Mentioned but not named. Children: Athanaceus, John, Robert, Apalona, Joseph, Rachel, Lustis, Rebecca Watkin, Jane Warren, Margaret Head, Zacariah, who has gone to California; son-in-laws Henry Watkins, Alfred Warren, James D. Head. Wit: Thos. Head, John W. Compton.

NEWBOLT, GEORGE. May 5, 1843. Sept. 1843. Wife: Elizabeth. Children not named. Ex: Wife, Joseph Weaver, Harry Blair. Wit: Barna May, Ignatus Higdon.

PAYNE, CORNELIUS. Feb. 2, 1835. May 1835. Wife: Mary. Children: William, Eliza, Ann, John T., Edward W., Charles H. Wit: John Purnoll, H. Higdon, James Miley.

PETERSON, JOHN H. Jan. 27, 1834. June 1834. Prince George County, Va., Children: John, Maria H., Prentis. Ex: Wife, son John. Wit: N. B. Sturdivant.

PRIEST, HENRY. Sept. 27, 1845. ------. Mother-in-law: W. Whayne. Children mentioned but not named. Wit: Silas Moorman, James Johnson, Wm. H. Howard.

RILEY, CINTHIA. March 26, 1846. May 1846. Nuncupative will. Sister Elton Taylor and Mary Waniser. Wit: S. Humpreys, W. L. Crigler, John Donley.

SHOEMAKER, PRICE. No date. Wife: Cintha. Children: Louisa, Cintha, Capheconia, Martha, Samuel. Wit: Thomas Higdon, I. Higdon, R. Bryant.

SHUMATE, JOHN. June 2, 1841. Inventory.

SMATHERS, JAMES. Jan. 11, 1827. March 12, 1827. Wife: Elizabeth. Children: Asa, Archibald, John, Mary Ann. Ex: Wife and son John. Wit: William May, Jesse, Henry Bell.

STEVENS, WILLIAM C. No date. Children mentioned but not named. Wit: William Howard, E. S. Marks.

TAPSCOTT, WILLIAM. Dec. 27, 1823. ------. Wife: Nancy. Children: Henry, Nancy, Fanny Deland, Sally, Juliet. Ex: Wife and Phillip Triplett. Wit: James Rogers, J. Franklin, George Handley.

THOMASON, MARTHA. May 1850. Inventory.

TURPIN, WILLIAM. Dec. 22, 1824. Children: Sadlina, Lucy Nice, Polly Smitt, Thomas, Elizah Jane (dec'd); nephew Thomas Turpin. Ex: Sons William and Edwin, and John Gilliam. Wit: F. B. Dean, David N. Corday, Juliet Powers.

WHITE, HENRY. June 4, 1825. June 1826. Wife: Rebecca. Children: Thomas, Henry, Eliza, Ann, John, Franklin, Mary Francis, James. Son William appointed guardian for son John. Ex: Wife Rebecca. Wit: Samuel Seaton,

Thomas Moore, Thomas Vaught.

WHITE, REBECCA. Nov. 2, 1836. Nov. 1836. Children: Spotswood, Hewett, Mary F. White, James M. White, Margaret Fontaine. Ex: Richard Jett. Wit: John Duncan, William Mason.

WILLIAMS, ELISHA. Nov. 2, 1829. -----1867. Wife: Elizabeth. Dau: Elize and her three children Elecia, Elisha, Samuel. Test: Nathan Bunn, Levi Myers.

FAYETTE COUNTY

BOOK A

ADAMS, ALEXANDER. July 1805. Inventory. Apprs: Thomas Wallace, George Trotter, Jr., James Mc Coun.

BARKER, WATT. Inventory. May 14, 1804. Apprs: Simon Flickey, N. Barnes, Will Bobb.

BARTLETT, HENRY. July 25, 1792. Bro. John. Sisters: Elizabeth, Phebe, Polly, Sally, Franky. Wit: James Mc Crosky, Sucky Mc Crosky.

BEARD, SARAH. Sept. 30, 1805. Oct. 6, 1806. Gr. daus: Nancy Mc Gown, Sally Beard (dau. of Joseph), Sally Beard (dau. of William). Ex: William Beard, Joseph Beard (sons). Wit: W.F. Cosby, John Bryant, John Henderson.

BEASLEY, AUGUSTINE. Inventory. April 1808. Apprs: John Bryand, William Gibson, Elijah Poage.

BELL, JOHN. Inventory. Jan. 14, 1805. Apprs: John Parker, Evans Price, J. Robbs.

BOULEWARE, WILLIAM. March 29, 1799. Oct. 1803. Wife: Nettie. Sons: John, Jacob, William. Daus: Lucy Wortham, Frances Grub, Phebe Pemberton, Fanny. Ex: Wife, John Bouleware (son). Wit: Sarah Pemberton, Sally Noel, Alex. Noel.

BRADSHAW, JANE. June 13, 1804. April 1805. Son: Samuel. Daus: Isabella Burns, Sally Hoblet. Ex: John Graham. Wit: James Mc Dowell, Priscilla Goram, Frances Simpson.

BRECKENRIDGE. ------. April 1807. Inventory. Apprs: Robert Russell, John Richardson, William Moore.

BRIGHT, NICKOLAS. Aug. 4, 1804. ------. Second Wife: Rebecca. First Wife: Priscilla. Children: by Priscilla: George and Catharine. Ex: Maj. James Morrison, Samuel Ayers, George Young. Wit: Allon Magruder, Robert Holmes, C. Kiser.

BRUCE, GEORGE. Oct. 16, 1806. Nov. 1808. Wife: Temperance. Children: Warren, Pamelia, Polly Grant, Waddle, Benjamin. Ex: Wife, Samuel Blair, Leonard Young. Wit: James Gibson, Alex. Colbard.

BRYANT, MORGAN. Sept. 29, 1794. July 1804. Children: Rebecca, Morgan. Gr. son: Joseph Bryant, Gr. dau: Mary Bryant. Wife: Not named.

CADE, CHARLES. Inventory. August 25, 1806. Apprs: William Scott, Dennis Bradley, James Spurr.

CADE, CHARLES. May 17, 1803. July 1806. Wife: Catharine. Son: David and wife Lydia. Ex: Wife, James Whaley. Wit: Thomas Foster, John Hay, C.

Morgan, C. Grimes.

CALDWELL, ELIZABETH. Dower. Dec. 1800. James Mc Dowell, Henry Payne, David Logan.

CALDWELL, JOHN. -----1795. ----1799. Wife: Elizabeth. Dau: Polly. Rebecca, dau. of Mary Kelly. Bro. Samuel. Wit: John Cooper, John Mc Nair, Robert Pollock.

CAMPER, HENRY. Nov. 24, 1792. Jan. 1793. Wife: Name not given. Sons: William, Reuben, Henry. Daus: Nancy, Letty, Alcey. Ex: Wife, William Camper (son). Wit: William Triplett, Tillman Campers, Dinah Camper.

CARRY, ELINOR. Dower,----- 1805. Levi Todd Clk.

CHINN, MILLY. June 17, 1807. August 1808. Mother: Jane Tandy. John Allen and heirs. Ex: Asa Milyer. Wit: W. W. Tandy, David Castleman, Gabriel Tandy, W. D. Young.

CLAGGETT. ------. Inventory. Nov. 1805. Apprs: A. Young, John Jones, Arther Taul.

CLARK, JOHN. June 1806. July 1806. Wife: Catharine. Children: Polly, John, Charles, Alex., William, Jane, Mary. Ex: Wife, Samuel Blair, William Gibson. Wit: Robert Frazier, Elijah Mc Clenachan.

CLARKE, WILLIAM. Oct. 27, 1808. Dec. 1808. Sons: George, William, James. Son-in-law John Holmes and wife Fanny. Neghew Thos. Love Elliott. Wit: George Elliott, David Bell, Betsy Allon.

CROCKETT, WINDER. Jan. 18, 1800. ------1803. Wife: Ann. Son: Newbold. Daus: Betsy Earvin, Nancy Dingle, Lottie Hutchinson. Ex: Thos. Nutler, Robert Scott.

CURRY, NICKOLAS. Inventory. Oct. 1803. Apprs: James Whaley, Robert Marshall, Stephen Lay.

DAVIS, NATHANIEL. Inventory. May 13, 1805. Apprs: Walker Overton, William Downing, William Dunlap.

DINCHMON, JACOB. Inventory. Aug. 15, 1806. Apprs: Jacob Clair, Matthais Shyrock.

ELLIS, WILLIAM. Aug. 4, 1793. Wife: Aggee. Children: Susannah Clark, John, William, Thomas, Charles, Hezekiah, Phebe Mc Donald, Polly, Nancy, Betsy. Ex: Wife Aggee, Bro. John Ellis, sons William and John. Wit: William Ellis, Timothy Parrish, Benjamin Robinson.

ELLIS, WILLIAM. Dec. 5, 1805. Settlement. Robert Prewitt, Polson Hundley.

EPPERSON, RICHARD. Oct. 1806. -----. Wife and children not named. On oath Sally McNeil, Mary Baxter, Patsy Brink.

EPPERSON, SUSANNA. June 2, 1803. Nov. 1804. Sons: Francis, John. Wit: B. Abernathy, Chesley Epperson, Francis Epperson.

ERWIN, JACOB. July 30, 1806. Legatees: Dau. Jane Woods, Sis. Martha, Bro. William. Ex: John Bryan. Wit: Henry Payne, John Napper, Elizabeth Napper.

FENSTER, JOHN. Inventory. July 1808. Apprs: John Edminston, James Parrish, Jesse Bryant, William Stone, (Admr).

FERGUSON, JOSIAH. July 25, 1802. Apr. 1803. Children: Judity Wilson, Susannah Robert, Mary Duhamel, Jane Tomkin, Betsy, Nancy, Jonah, William, Joshua, Thomas, Catherine Jones. Wit: Thomas Clark, George Winn, Robert Marshall.

FRY, WILLIAM. March 28, 1796. May 1796. Wife: Rachel. Children: Rebecca, Elizabeth, Catherine, Jacob, Tom, Henry, Joseph. Ex: Wife, son Jacob. Wit: Obidiah Boone, Robert Migill, Peter Goodnight.

FULLERTON, WILLIAM. Aug. 12, 1801. Nov. 1805. Late of the Commonwealth of Pennsylvania. Estate divided among sisters. Ex: John Jordan, John Helm. Wit: Henry Clay, Thomas Wallace, Sam Brown.

GARDNER, ALEX. Inventory. Feb. 14, 1803. Apprs: Samuel Beeler, John McDowell, James Mc Dowell.

GILLESPIE, DAVID. Inventory. Dec. 23, 1803.

GILLESPIE, PATTY. Dower. Jan. 1804. H. Harrison, A. Montgomery, Thaddeus Dooling, E. Edminston.

GOODMAN, MARTIN. Settlement. Nov. 1, 1804. John Graves, Ezekiel Patterson, Moss Randolph.

GRANT, REBECCA. Inventory. Nov. 25, 1808. Apprs: William Moore, A. Brite, Samuel Caldwell.

GRANT, WILLIAM. Inventory. Aug. 1804. Apprs: A. Russell, Alberta Brite, William Moore, James Fisher.

GRAVES, THOMAS. Oct. 24, 1801. Dec. 1801. Wife: Isabel. Daus: Rosanna Randolph, Ann Hancock, Sally Graves, Mary Beeler, Siddy Graves, Isabel Graves. Sons: William, Bartlett, John. Ex: Bartlett Graves, John Graves (sons), Bartlett Collins. Wit: James Martin, William Dickey, Jeremiah Buckley.

GWYN, MORRIS. Jan. 3, 1798. April 16, 1803. Legatees: Morris Garnett (nephew), Eli Garnett, Lewis Garnett, William Garnett, Morris Garnett, Thomas Garnett, Phebe Garnett, Rebecca Garnett. Ex: William Hamilton. Wit: Anne Hamilton, Peggy Hamilton, James Hamilton.

HAMMOND, JAMES. Inventory. ----- 1783. Lewis Todd, C. C.

HAMMOND, JAMES. Settlement. Nov. 25, 1803.

HAMMOND, WINNIE. Aug. 17, 1804. Dower. H. Harrison, Leonard Young, W. Dudley.

HARRISON, HEZEKIAH. Aug. 2, 1806. ------. Wife: Jane. Daus: Nancy, Dulcima, Polly, Peggy. Sons: John, Dudley, Josiah, Jilson, Payne. Mentions mother, brothers Hosea, Hiram. Ex: wife, Henry Clay, John Pope, James Hughes, Jilson Payne, William Payne. Wit: John G. Harrison, Laurena Young, Ambrose Young.

HART, THOMAS. I, Thomas Hart, of Lexington, Kentucky, do make, ordain and publish the following as and for my last Will and Testament: I give and bequeath to my wife during her life the house and lot which I at present occupy in Lexington, also during the same period all my household and kitchen furniture and one hundred fifty pounds annually during her life, which sum I direct my executors (herein after named) to pay her quarterly. I also lend during her life the slaves Isham & Jenny, now in our possession, and direct my said executors to provide her by hiring one other good house servant during her life, all of which several provisions I intend and hereby declare to be in lieu and full satisfaction of all claims which my said wife might have upon my estate for dower or distribution.

I give and bequeath to each of my sons Nathaniel and John, the sum of one thousand pounds to be raised in six months after my death and to be put out on interest by my executors toward providing a fund to maintain them and to be paid over to them on their arrival at full age respectively. The interest accruing upon each legacy to be appropriated to the separate use of each of my said sons; and as a further provision for their maintenance I likewise direct my said executors to pay each of them one hundred pounds annually until they arrive respectfully at full age.

I appoint my son Thomas Hart guardian of my son John and empower my said son Thomas if he shall deem it for the interest of John to employ the said legacy of one thousand pounds to John in trade.

I relinquish to the Representatives of Samuel Price all claims of whatever description I have against them. I give and devise to my daughter Susannah Price the house and lot I purchased of John Jones in Lexington and also the sum of two hundred pounds to be paid her as soon as it can be raised with convenience, and I also direct my executors immediately upon my death to purchase two young negro women whom I give and bequeath to my said daughter.

I give and bequeath, besides the legacies aforesaid, to my son Thomas Hart, two hundred pounds; to children of my deceased daughter Elizabeth Pindell, two hundred pounds; to my son-in-law James Brown two hundred pounds; to my son-in-law Henry Clay two hundred pounds, to be paid to them or their representatives as soon as the situation of my estate will enable my executors.

I give to and invest in my executors the power of selling any of my lands not specially devised that they may think proper. I also give and invest in my said executors the power of making deed for any lands that I am or may be bound to convey and also settling by compromise, arbitration or otherwise any dispute that may exist in my lands.

All the rest and residue of my estate not before herein disposed of after payment of my just debts I give and bequeath to my children: Thomas Hart, Susannah Price, Anne Brown, Lucretia Clay, Nathaniel G. S. Hart, and John

Hart and children of my deceased daughter Elizabeth Pindell.

I hereby appoint my son Thomas Hart and my son-in-law Henry Clay, executors of this last Will and Testament, revoking and annulling all former and other wills by me heretofore made.

In Testimony whereof I have hereunto set my hand and affixed my seal this 31st day of August, 1807.

Signed:
Thomas Hart

Wit: John W. Hunt
Thos. C. Graves
Samuel Wilkinson

Signed and sealed and published in presence of.

Probated in Fayette County Court July 1808.

HENDERSON, JOHN. May 12, 1808. July 1808. Wife: Elizabeth. Children: Elizabeth Perkins, Jane. Ex: son-in-law Garnet Perkins, Isaac McIsaac. Wit: John Bouleware, Isaac McIsaac, Jr.

HIGGINS, JOEL. Inventory. Nov. 14, 1807. Apprs: Jesse Winn, Joseph Boonwell, James Nichols.

HILL JAMES. Sept. 22, 1808. ------. Wife: Margaret. Daus: Elizabeth (wife of James Henderson), Isabella, Polly. Sons: John, David, James, Fleming, William. Ex: wife, James Henderson. Wit: David Logan, James Harrison.

HILLOCK, HENRY. June 1800. -----. Legatees: James Hambleton Hillock, mother Sarah Hillock. Ex: Henry Marshall. Wit: Walter Karrick, Joshua Judd, Jonah Skelter.

HOLDER, SOHIA. Aug. 3, 1806. Oct. 1806. Sisters: Lydia, Fanny, Kitty Holder. Ex: Col. Richard Hickman, Maj. Robert Caldwell, John W. Holder, John Hart. Wit: John Holder, John Hart, Polly Hart.

HOLLEY, WILLIAM. April 6, 1803. -----. Wife: Henrietta. Children: Benjamin, Cinda Burton. Ex: son Benjamin. Wit: William Haley, James Weathiars.

HOLLYMAN, WILLIAM. Inventory. Oct. 1807. John D. Young.

HUFFORD, ANN. March 18, 1807. Oct. 1807. Children: Catherine, Adam, Susanna, Mary, Hannah, George, Elizabeth, Jacob, Barbara, Rebecca. Ex: John Burger, John Bastian. Wit: John Parker, John Collins, Joseph Craig.

HUNTER, GEORGE. May 17, 1804. Aug. 1804. Wife: Rachel. Children: George, Richard, Mary, Rachel, William, Elizabeth, Thomas. Gr.sons: George, James Hunter. Ex: wife, son Thomas. Wit: H. Harrison, Wm. Alexander, Charles Campbell.

JANUARY, PETER. May 10, 1802. Jan. 1805. Wife: Margaret. Children: Thomas, Mary Payne, Jennet Thurston, Derrick, Peter, James. Ex: son Thomas, son-in-law Daniel Payne. Wit: Adam Rankin, John Steel, E. Shorpe.

JENKINS, WILLIAM. Jan. 13, 1806. April 1806. Wife: Patty. Children: Sally, Patty, David. Ex: Wife. Wit: John Foley, Elijah Foley, William Foley.

JOHNSON, JOHN. Inventory. Feb. 1803. Apprs: Moses Patterson, John Graves, Robert Dilson.

KELLY, KATHARINE. Dec. 5, 1802. Apr. 1803. Widow of Samuel Kelly. Sons: William, Bobb, Samuel, John. Daus: Elizabeth Scott, Margarett, Rebecca, Sarah, Jane, Elinn (or Ann). Ex: Samuel Kelly, William Kelly (sons). Wit: Jane Dicks, Sarah O'Higgins.

KERSNER, CASPER. April 4, 1797. July 1797. Wife: Eve. Mother Margaret and children. Ex: Abraham Bowman, John Parker. Wit: John Ralston, Henry Kent, Levi Todd.

LAUGHLIN, PETER. June 8, 1802. Sept. 1802. Wife: Sarah. Sons: John Wilson, Benjamin. Daus: Margaret, Sarah, Isabel, Elizabeth (wife of John Forsthe). Gr.child: Sarah Forsythe, son of Peter L. Forsythe; John Wilson Laughlin's son Peter. Ex: John W. Laughlin, Benjamin Laughlin (sons). Wit: William Watson, Len Bradley, James Whaley.

LOWRY, JAMES. Feb. 2, 1795. Oct. 1796. Mother Melvin. Sister Mary Lowry. Bros. John, Melvin.

LOWRY, STEPHEN. March 1796. Oct. 1803. Wife: Kitty. Daus: Margaret, Mary, Sarah, Kitty. Sons: John, Abraham, Stephen, William.

LINGERFELTER, BERNARD. Inventory Oct. 29, 1805. Apprs: John Parker, James Robb, Evan Price.

LINGERFELTER, BERNARD. April 1, 1803. Aug. 1807. Wife: Barbara. Children: Catherine Cartle, Valentine, John, Jacob, George, Daniel, Maydoline. Son-in-law Fred Walls. Wit: Peter Gatewood, Jr., Richmond Dedman.

LUCAN, SUSANNAH. June 26, 1806. April 1808. Daus: Polly Moore, Nancy Cockrill. Ex: Chas. Lucas (son). Wit: James Whaley, Joseph Scraghan, Charles Givens.

MARSHALL, HENRY. May 17, 1806. July 1806. Wife: Catharine. Children: John, Polly. Children of bro. John Marshall. Ex: Henry Clay, John M. Boggs, George Trotter, Jr. George Haytel.

MARSHALL, JOHN. (Div.). Jan. 1804. Division of estate among widow and children.

MARSHALL, JOHN. July 6, 1803. Oct. 1803. Wife: Elizabeth. Children: Jane McCullah, James, Margaret, Sarah, Mary, Joseph. Ex: Wife, William Barbee, Robert Wilson. Wit: William Patterson, M. Randolph, John Lyle.

MASON, EDMOND. Jan. 16, 1805. May 1806. Cousin John Mason, Sr. Ex: John Mason. Wit: Daniel Hodge, Sally Mason.

MAZFIELD, GEORGE. Inventory. Apr. 15, 1805. Apprs: John Clark, William Gibson, Joshua Brown.

MC CANN, JAMES. Inventory. Nov. 1803. Apprs: James Eubanks, James Parrish, James Welsh.

MC CLELLAND, JOHN. Inventory. Nov. 1807. Apprs: Martin Wymore, Nathaniel Pettit.

MC CULLOUGH, PATRICK. Legatees: Jane Workman (niece), Margaret Workman, Agnes Drummond, Jane Mc Cullough, residents of Ireland. Ex: John Bradford, Andrew Holmes.

MC FARLAND, GEORGE. Settlement. 1804. Apprs: William Morton, Alex. Parker, James Morrison.

MC MURTY, JOSEPH. Dec. 11, 1800. Jan. 1801. Wife: Isabella. Children: James, John, William, Samuel, David, Levi, Nancy. Ex: William Hamilton, James Mc Dowell, John Mc Dowell. Wit: William Logan, John Gardner, John Hagerty.

MC NAIR, ----. Aug. 19, 1801. Dec. 1801. Wife: Jane. Sons: David, Robert, John. Daus: Polly, Elizabeth. Ex: Robert Patterson, Samuel Ayers, Alex. Parker. Wit: Levi Todd, John Rennick, Robert Hunter.

MEGONAN, ROBERT. May 15, 1804. -------. Wife: Not named. Wit: Thomas Bradley.

MILLER, WILLIAM. Settlement. 1790 - 1804. George Logan, Joseph Patterson.

MOFFITT, WALTER. Inventory. Dec. 20, 1805. John Bryant, Charles Megonan.

MONTGOMERY, JAMES, Capt. Inventory. Feb. 19, 1808. Apprs: Robert Prewitt, John Boyd, Charles Wicliff.

MORRIS, DANIEL. May 21, 1802. Dec. 1806. Wife: Ann. Children: David, John, William, Robert, Mary Hopkins, Roda Polke, Sarah Beauchamp. Ex: John, Robert Morris. Wit: William Lindsay, William Chambers.

MURPHY, NANCY. Inventory. Nov. 1803. William Gibson, Robert Poage, John McFranks.

NEALE, CHARLES. March 1, 1803. Oct. 1803. Wife: Ann. Children: Catherine Colbert, Polly, Gracy, Jane, Ann, Charles. Ex: wife, William Stone, Peyton Colbert.

NOE, RANDLE. Jan. 25, 1808. ---- 1808. Wife: Susannah. Children: Kesiah Roberts, Rebecca Money, Ann Bush, Hendrix, Lidia Fox, Margaret Fox, Landen, Daniel, Nancy Randall, Mary, Mariah, Jane, George, James, William, Susannah Boone. Wife: Elizabeth. Dau: Margaret. Bro. Alex. and William. Sister Mary and Margaret. Ex: James Noe, Obidiah Boon. (Wife Elizabeth, first wife).

NUTTELL, ELIJAH. Sept. 5, 1796. July 1803. Wife: Mary. Children: Sarah Rolling, Martha Demint, Mary Lamb, Elizabeth Palkner, Price, Thomas, Rebekah, Susannah, Nancy. Ex: wife, sons Thomas and Price. Wit: Henry Broek, Elijah Foley.

PARISH, JOHN. Dec. 30, 1806. -----. Wife: Patsey. Legatees: John Graves, sister Nancy Burbridge, bro. Timothy. Ex: Timothy Parish, John C. Graves.

PARISH, WILLIAM. July 15, 1808. Children: Benjamin, Jarrod, Milly Webster, Stephen, Ann Scantla. Gr.child: Rebecca, William, Linda, Jarrod Parish, Francis Scantlen. Ex: son Benjamin, James Arret. Wit: Joseph Dixon, Samuel Ayers.

PARKER, ELIZABETH. Dower. Aug. 1803. From estate of John Parker.

PARKER, JAMES. Feb. 19, 1797. Feb. 1803. Wife: Elizabeth, Dau: Margaret. Bros: William Parker, Alex. Parker. Sis: Mary, Margaret. Ex: Alex. Parker, John Coburn, John Bradford. Wit: Hugh Brent, Sr., H. Mc Illvan, John Calhoun.

PARKER, JOHN. Feb. 17, 1797. Feb. 1803. Wife: Christiana. Ex: Wife, Alex. Parker, John Bradford.

PARKER, MARGARET. Settlement. Oct. 23, 1797.

PARKER, ROBERT. March 4, 1800. April 1800. Wife: Elizabeth. Children not named. Nephew: Thomas Bradley. Ex: John Parher, Gen., Robert Todd, Thomas Bradley.

PAYNE, SANFORD. June 17, 1808. Aug. 1808. Wife: Ellen. Children: Hugh, Peggy Price, Sarah, Polly, Sally, Nancy, Sandford, Silas, Ellen, Liza. Ex: wife. Wit: Lewis E. Turner, Henry Payne, Sandford Payne.

POOL, THOMAS. Of Prince Anne Co., Va. Children: Seth, Anthony, Elizabeth Benthel, Rachel, Richard, William, Phillip, Ezekill, John, Samuel. Ex: wife, William Pool.

PRATHER, JEREMIAH. Sept. 9, 1806. Nov. 1807. Wife: Anna. Ex: Philip Brink, Robert Irwin.

RANKIN, JEREMIAH. Aug. 11, 1804. Oct. 1804. Wife and children not named except son John. Ex: bro. A. Rankin, bro-in-law William McClelland. Wit: Joseph Walker, M. Rankin.

REDMAN, BENJAMIN. Settlement. Mar. 1803. William Redman, Admr. Robert Wilson, Ezekill Patterson, Moses Patterson.

REYBURN, ADAM. July 21, 1797. April 1798. Wife: Elizabeth. Children: Elpsey, Adam, Thomas and others. Ex: William Dicky, son Joseph.

ROBINSON, DAVID. -----. -----. Legatees: Lands in Montgomery Co., Va. to Hibernian Soc. Philadelphia, bro. William, Gartsey Robinson (wid. of bro. John dec'd), Alex Montgomery, son of niece Elizabeth Montgomery; David Craig of Augusta Co. son of Rev. John Craig, three nephews: Robinson, David and Reynolds Leforce. Ex: Archibald Stuart, John Breckenridge, Frances Preston.

ROGERS, BIRD. Inventory. Oct. 12, 1801. Apprs: Jesse Winn, Bird Price, Pugh Price.

ROGERS, MARTHA. Dower. Oct. 12, 1801. Widow of Bird Rogers.

SAMPSON, SAMUEL. Jan. 18, 1803. -----. Wife: Catharine. Children: Not named. Mother Tamor. Ex: wife, John McDowell. Wit: Priscilla Goram, Jenny Cavins.

SIDMOR, MARTIN. -----. -----. James Smith, Lewis Ames, John Young.

SHAW, NOTHE. Inventory. Nov. 1803. Apprs: Peter Gatewood, Joseph Rutherford, Abraham Bowman.

SMITH, BENJAMIN. Oct. 12, 1797. June 12, 1798. Wife: Polly. Children: Clemon, land in Rockingham, Va., Anny and unborn child, nephew Benjamin Smith, Samuel Comer of Rockingham, Va. Ex: bro. William Smith, bro.-in-law Joseph Smith.

SMITH, GUY. June 19, 1780. May 1787. Of Granville North Carolina. Children: Sarah Coffee, Ann Vaughn, Elizabeth Mitchell, Guy, John, William. Ex: John Smith, John Young.

SPURR, RICHARD. May 7, 1790. June 1792. Wife: Franky. Sons: William, Richard, John, Daniel. Daus: Mary, Judith. Ex: Owen Winn, James Whaley. Wit: William Jenkins, Dennis Bradley, Elijah Holtsclaw.

STEELE, ANDREW. Sept. 12, 1793. Dec. 1794. Children: John, William, Margaret, Elizabeth, Vance, Jane, Priscilla, Brice. Ex: Rev. Samuel Shannon, Robert Patterson.

STUART, WILLIAM. Aug. 1803. Inventory. Apprs: I. Mc Cracken, James Vance, William Changers.

SUGGETT, JOHN. March 5, 1786. -----. Wife: Jemina. Daus: Catharine Merry, Elizabeth Smith, Jemina Johnson. "I give and bequeath to my son John Suggett all my wearing clothes except my brown colored coat and jacket, which I give to my friend William Tomlinson." Ex: wife, son John Suggett, William Cave. Wit: Robert Saunders, William Shortridge, Mary Shortridge.

TILFORD, JAMES. Inventory. Jan. 6, 1803. Apprs: Price Curd, Geo. Frazer, Alex. Black.

TODD, REV. JOHN. Feb. 10, 1792. Sept. 1793. Wife: Not named. Children: Sarah, John, Robert, Ann, Cousin Levi, Margaret. James Moore (hus. of Margaret), Rev. Daniel McCalla and wife Elizabeth (Todd), Dr. Andrew Todd and wife Mary. Ex: wife, Robert, Andrew Todd, son John. Wit: Turner Cath.

TODD, LEVI. Inventory. Oct. 27, 1807. Apprs: William Dunlap, George Hunt, Andrew F. Price.

TODD, MARY. Inventory. April 14, 1804. Apprs: Archibald McIlean Sr., Robert Todd.

VANCE, JOHN. Inventory. Feb. 2, 1805. Apprs: William Stone, Lewis Tumery, Henry Payne.

VANCE, JOSEPH. Jan. 5, 1807. -----. Wife: Jane. Children: William, Jean,

Gr. children: Elizabeth, Jean, Ann (child of Jean). Ex: Jane Vance, David Logan. Wit: Joseph Fleming, William Little, David Logan.

VALENDINGHAM, RICHARD. Settlement. 1804. James Valendingham, Admr.

VIVION, JOHN. May 24, 1789. April 1805. Wife: Martha. Children: Youngest son Flavel, dau. Franky, other children. Ex: wife, Philip Bush, John Vivion, Jr., Thacker Vivion. Wit: John Mc Guire, Benjamin Combs, Presley Anderson.

WARD, WILLIAM. July 22, 1795. --------. Son James, wife and other children not named. Ex: John Breckenridge, Col. William Ward, Capt. James. Wit: Mary Howard, John Greenup, Samuel Greenup.

WEBSTER, JOHN. Nov. 24, 1802. Aug. 1805. Wife: Ann. Children not named. Ex: Kelles Webster, John Webster.

WINN, GEORGE. Feb. 20, 1801. Aug. 1803. Wife: Lottie. Children: Thomas, Adam. Son-in-laws: Henry Cotton, Samuel Clay, I. Musick, Edw. Bradley, William Herndon, John Handley. Ex: wife, son-in-law John Hancock, Edmund Bullock.

WINN, L. Sept. 24, 1803. Apprs: William Davenport, Harry Mc Donald, Robert Marshall.

WINN, OLIVER. Sept. 8, 1805. Jan. 1806. Wife: Mary. Children: Sary Bogg, Susanna Spurr, Elizabeth Vallandigham, Polly King, John, Franky, Dorah Young, Nathaniel, Barbary. Gr.children: John and Jane King. Ex: wife, son John.

WHITESIDES, WILLIAM. Aug. 1, 1804. ------. Estate to bro. and sisters. Ex: John Whitesides, Henry Whitesides (bros.) Wit: John C. Graves, Thomas Ellis, John Whitesides, Sr.

WOODS, ANDREW. Sept. 2, 1806. ------. Wife: Jane. Children: Samuel, Margaret, Andrew, Sophia. Ex: Sons Samuel and Andrew. Wit: John Bowan, John Lyle.

YOUNG, GEORGE. Aug. 9, 1807. April 1808. Wife: Mary. Children not named. Gr.chld: George Bright, Kitty Bright. (chld. of Nickolas Bright). Ex: wife, Jacob Clain, John Sprinkle. Wit: William Todd, John Carty, Thomas Wallace.

YOUNG, JOHN. May 21, 1798. July 1798. Children: Polly Procter, her two children John, Charles; Ambrose, John, Jenny Harrison, Abner, Coleby. Ex: Abner Young, Ambrose Young. Wit: Eli Miller, John Price, Martha Holday.

YOUNG, WILLIAM. May 15, 1793. May 1803. Wife: Milly. Children: Minor, Judah Martin (hus. James Martin), Richard, Lettice, John, Patsey, Douglas. Ex: wife and bros. John and Leonard Young. Wit: Hezekiah Harrison, Polly Smith.

FAYETTE COUNTY

INDEX

BOOK B

Alexander, John
Allen, Benjamin
Applegate, Milton
Arthur, John
Ashley, Nathaniel
Atwood, Elizabeth

Bacon, William
Barr, Elizabeth
Bartholomew, Joseph
Bell, John
Bendlett, ----
Berryman, James
Bill, Daniel
Blair, Samuel
Blanton, Richard
Blest, Anthony
Boin, Elizabeth
Boyce, William
Bradbourne, Joseph
Breckenridge, John
Brown, Henry
Bullock, James

Caldwell, George
Campbell, Charles
Campbell, Robert
Carter, Job
Chinn, William
Clark, Joseph
Clark, William
Cockrell, John
Conner, Frances
Curry, John
Curry, Nicholas

Davis, ----
Davis, James H.
Davies, Ann
Dangerfield, William
Delisle, John

Edminston, J.
Ellis, William
Elrod, Robert
Estes, John

Fairs, Edmond
Ford, John
Franks, Elizabeth
Fry, Joseph
Frye, Jacob

Gillespie, David
Gilliam, Stark
Goodlow, Thomas
Grant, Rebecca
Grimes, Philip

Hardin, Charles
Harper, Peter
Harrison, Hezekiah
Hart, Nathaniel
Hart, Thomas
Hart, Thomas, Sr.
Hayden, Jeremiah
Henderson, David
Higgins, Az.
Holmes, Jonathan
Hunt, Robert

Johnson, Mathew
Jones, Asa
Jones, Hugh

Kay, John
Kirtley

Lay, Abraham
Legrand, John
Lewis, Thomas
Lowe, Charles

Parke, John
Parrish, William
Payne, David
Payne, Edward
Payne, Sandford
Payne, Silas
Pemberton, Walker
Perry, (heirs)
Peyatt, Salem
Pilcher, Joshua
Price, Christiana

Robinson, David
Rose, James
Ross, William
Runyon, J.H.
Ryman, Jacob

Shape, Richard
Shyrock, Christian
Smith, Benjamin
Smith, Dorcas
Smith, Jane
Smith, Mary
Spencer, Daniel
Steele, Richard
Stone, John

Tandy, William
Tatham, Charles
Taylor, Asa
Taylor, Ignatus
Teagarden, George
Thompson, James
Thompson, Parish
Tilford, Joseph
Todd, John
Tomlinson, Will
Tracy, Anthony
Turner, Catharine

Vance, James
Vance, Joseph
Vance, Robert
Vaughn, Lewis

Wallace, James
Webb, Charles
Welsh, Benjamin
Whitesides, John
Whitesides, William
Wingate, Cannon
Wood, Andrew

Young, George
Young, Richard
Young, Richard

FRANKLIN COUNTY

BOOK A

1795 -- 1810

ABBETT, JAMES. Sept. 17, 1804. Inventory. Apprs: Thomas Lewis, Eleazer Ellis, William Hall

ARBUCKLE, JOHN. Oct. 13, 1796. Feb. 21, 1797. Wife: Hannah. Dau: Betty. George Peyton. Wit: John David, Thomas Doughet.

ARBUCKLE, SAMUEL. Guardian for Elizabeth Arbuckle, Legatee to John Arbuckle, dec'd., Sept. 15, 1804. Wit: William Brayer, William Payne, Robert Blackwell.

ARNOLD, JAMES. March 5, 1810. Inventory. Apprs: Scott Brown, Anothy Crockett, Thomas Oliver (?), James Mitchell.

BEATTY, OTHO. March 17, 1804. Inventory. Apprs: P. Voorhees, Phil Bush, Bennet Pemberton, Daniel Weiger, C.C., Samuel Moxley, J.P.

BENNERS, ELIZABETH. Sept. 29, 1804. Aug. 1805. Dau: Ann Instone. Ex: Chris. Greenup. Wit: Thomas Lewis, James Witherow, John Stiles.

BLACK, JOHN. Nov. 26, 1806. Inventory. Apprs: Henry Miller, James Hatton, John Armstrong.

BLEDSOE, JAMES. Oct. 23, 1800. Nov. 25, 1800. Apprs: James Tate, William Smith, Robert Poindexter, Daniel Weisger, C.C.

BOULWARE, NICHLIN. Aug. 18, 1795. Sept. 15, 1795. Apprs: James Hayden, Simon Hancock, William Montgomery.

BOURN, ANDREW. May 1810. Inventory. Apprs: Henry Sheets, Ellis Lewis, William Mitchell, Samuel Mitchell,

BROWN, JOHN. ------. Sept. 25, 1805. Wife: Nancy. Sons: William, Daniel, Daus: Polly, Obedience. Bros: Jesse Brown, Daniel Brown. Wit: William Hickman, Moses Hickman, Richard Roberts. Apprs: William Ware, Edward Ware, Giles Samuel.

BROWN, SAMUEL. April 2, 1798. Dec. 1799. Wife: Mary. Legatees: Robert Brown Jamison. Ex: wife, Harry Innis, Daniel Weisger. Wit: John Raitton. Apprs: Otho Beatty, William Trigg, Isaac Gano, J.P.

BROWN, JANE. Nov. 2, 1807. Inventory. Apprs: William Boyd, John Reading, Robert Armstrong.

BYRON, HUGH. Dec. 1806. March 1807. Apprs: William Trigg, Nickolas Lafon, George Holloway, John Younger.

CARNES, PATRICK. Oct. 3, 1807. Inventory. Apprs: Edwin Moore, Timothy Moore, Robert Burchfield.

CARNEAL, THOMAS. June 26, 1811. Inventory. Apprs: Giles Samuel, George Brown, Daniel Brown.

CARSON, DAVID. Feb. 15, 1805. Inventory. Apprs: Samuel Moxley, Uriah Edwards, C. Farwick.

COLQUIT, SARAH. Feb. 15, 1796. June 22, 1796. Son: William. Dau: Sally Gibson. Children of dau. Ann Garnett, dec'd. Ex: Edmond Vaughn, John Brown, Ernest Martinie, John Brown. Wit: William Ware, William Ballard, Susannah Martinie. Apprs: William Ware, Edmund Ware, Richard Pemberton.

COOK, MARGARET. March 11, 1797. Feb. 1798. Children: Rachel Murphy, Bathsheba Dunn, Helen Bohannon, Rhoda Jamison, William, Seth, Margaret Hacket, Abraham, Uncie Miles. Gr.sons: William Cook, Seth Cook (sons of Jesse Cook, dec'd), Hosea Cook (son of Hosea Cook, dec'd.). Ex: sons William, Seth. Wit: John Lewis, John Miles, John Buckhannon. Apprs: James Porter, John Stephens, Henry Crutcher.

COLSON, JOHN. June 1, 1805. Inventory. Apprs: Langston Baker, John Richardson, John Younger.

COON, JOHN. April 10, 1819. Inventory. Admrs: William Jewell, John Ray, John Harrison.

COUCHMAN, JONATHAN. Nov. 15, 1798. Dec. 1798. Wife: Dicey, infant son. Other Legatees: Virgil Poe, Capt. William Fenwick. Ex: William Fenwick, William Manning. Wit: John M. Scott, James Benham, David Carson.

COULSON, JOHN. April 1807. Admr: William Trigg.

CRUTCHER, HENRY. Sept. 12, 1806. March 1807. Wife: Martha. Children: Joanna Sacra, Elizabeth Pemberton, Catharine Cook. Sons: Henry, Reuben, Isaac. Ex: William Cook, James Sacra, Jesse Brown. Wit: Will Samuel, James Porter, Achilles Sneed, D. Brown.

CRUTCHER, HENRY. March 1807. Inventory. Apprs: William Porter, John Smith, James Davis.

DODD, JOHN. Sept. 15, 1810. Inventory. Apprs: Jacob Stodghill, Jacob Bootz, Jeremiah West.

DUNCAN, BENJAMIN. Nov. 16, 1820. Inventory. Apprs: John Lillard, Ephiram Lillard, W. Hudgins.

EDGER, WILLIAM. May 1802. Sale. Apprs: Phil White, John Lightfoot, Robert Blackwell.

EDRINGTON, JOHN. May 16, 1808. Inventory. Apprs: Carter Blanton, W. Ware, Edmund Ware.

EDSON, JAMES. ------, -----. Inventory. Apprs: Edmund Vaughn, William Hall, W. Ware.

FENWICK, BELINDA. May 28, 1808. June 20, 1808. Dau: Elizabeth Culhoon. Sons: Ignatus, Joseph. Gr.sons: Enoch, Henry (sons of Joseph). Legatees:

Rev. Edward Fenwick, Right Hon. Dr. Carrol. Ex: son Ignatus. Wit: I. Tywman, John Scott, Sukey Wingate.

FOGG, JAMES. ------1802. ----1806. Dower. Eliza, widow of James Fogg, now Eliza Smith.

GANO, REV. JOHN. Dec. 29, 1798. Jan. 1805. Wife: Sarah. Sons: Daniel, Stephen, John, Isaac, Richard. Daus: Margaret, Sarah, Susannah. Ex: wife, Daniel Gano, Col. Baker Ewing, Gov. James Garrard. Wit: Turner Richardson, John Hunt, Margaret Hunt. Apprs: Daniel Peak, Morgan Bryan, John A. Mitchell, Thomas B. Warren.

GIBSON, HENRY. Jan. 20, 1801. Inventory. Apprs: James Ledgerwood, Mary Miller, James Hutton.

GRAHAM, JAMES. March 13, 1799. April 1799. Mentions wife and stepdaughter, Mary Canada. Children: Margaret, Ellender, John. Money due him in Lancaster, Pa. Ex: Jamey Tate, Henry Hockersmith. Wit: Thomas Settle, Gilbert Christian, Arthur Mc Gaughey. Apprs: Robert Holton, George Brown, Jesse Brown.

GRAHAM, FRANCIS. (Capt.) Dec. 1809. Inventory. Apprs: Hugh Innis, Thomas Church, Reuben Anderson.

GRAVES, WILLIAM. Aug. 7, 1804, Dec. 1805. Wife: Mary. Ex: wife, John Arnold, Jr., Wit: Thomas Withers, Scott Brown, Rebecca Withers.

GRESHAM, ABROSE. April 1810. Inventory. Apprs: Mathais Bush, Robert Armstrong, John Reading.

HALL, CABEL. August 18, 1810. Inventory. Apprs: Robert Brenham, William Samuels.

HARDIN, ENOS. ----. ----. Apprs: T. Brenham, Charles Taylor, Peter Saunders.

HARRIS, HANNAH. June 29, 1802. ------. Sons: John, Daus: Ann Innis, Elizabeth Todd, Sarah Smith, Mary Hanna, Rachel, Hanna. Ex: son John, Thomas Todd, Harry Innis (sons-in-law). Wit: Lewis Arnold, Ann Innis.

HAWKINS. -----. -----. Inventory. Apprs: William Boyd, John Williams, Charles Julian.

HEAD, BENJAMIN. March, 1809. Inventory. Apprs: Samuel Moxley, Clement Bell, William Samuels.

HEDD, BENJAMIN. Jan. 16, 1809. Inventory. Apprs: Samuel Moxley, Avery Brooks, Clint Bell.

HENSLEY, WILLIAM. Feb. 13, 1808. Inventory. Apprs: Walter Kennedy, David Egbert.

HICKLIN, -----. Dec. 1804. Inventory. Apprs: George Brown, Daniel Parks, Thomas Settle.

HOLLOWAY, CHARLES. -----. Jan. 17, 1803. Wife: Hannah. Mentions children but does not name them. Bro: George Holloway in Virginia. Ex: Jesse Vawter, Richard Shipp. Wit: John Graves, Hannah Musick, John Bell.

HOLLOWAY, CHARLES. August 15, 1803. Inventory. Apprs: Thomas Cox, John D. Graves, John Underwood.

HOLLOWAY, HANNAH. Dower. Apprs: John Head, Benjamin Head, and Sparker, Thomas Cox.

HOLTON, ROBERT. August, 1804. Inventory. Apprs: Henry Brock, Reuben Samuels, S. Mc Cracklen.

JAMES, ELIZABETH. May 17, 1810. Inventory. Apprs: John Hunter, John Yeatman, James Johnson.

JAMES, WILLIAM. Nov. 22, 1806. Inventory. Apprs: John Hunter, William Hall, Daniel Peak.

JACKSON, JOSHUA. April 20, 1804. Inventory. Apprs: Henry Brock, Nathaniel Saunders, Lewis Craig, Jr.

JACKSON, THOMAS. Jan. 29, 1797. Inventory. Apprs: Moses Milam, Elijah Hawkins, Robert White, William Mc Quade.

JOHNSON, WILLIAM. March 27, 1818.

JONES, LEVIN D. Nov. 21, 1798. Admr: Robert Miller.

KELBY, HENRY. Sept. 1820. Inventory. Apprs: Robert Blackwell, David Eggert, George Gordon.

LAWRENCE, SAMUEL. Aug. 30, 1811. Apprs: Moses Rutter, Russell Martin, William Bourn.

LLOYD, THOMAS. Aug. 10, 1792. Aug. 1795. Wife: Arminta Julianna. Dau: Mary Tate. Gr.dau. Martha Lloyd. Ex: wife, Nathaniel Saunders, William Montgomery.

LLOYD, THOMAS. Nov. 17, 1796. Apprs: John Edwards, George Brown, Jesse Brown.

LOFTUS, BURTON. June 20, 1805. Apprs: Reuben Samuel, John Samuel, Robert Fenwick.

LOGAN, JOHN. Dec. 19, 1807. Apprs: Peter Vorhees, Daniel Weisger.

LOWRY, THOMAS. Aug. 24, 1803. Nov. 1803. Legatees: Catharine Harris Shiell, Maria K. Innis. Ex: Harry Innis. Wit: John Morris, William Owen.

LYNNES, USLEY. Aug. 1808. Admr: Nel Lynn.

MAJOR, JOHN. Aug. 1, 1808. Apprs: Samuel Moxley, James Martin, Richard Price.

MARTIN, JAMES. Jan. 1812. Apprs: Wm. Garrard, Ezra Richmond, William Graham.

MARTIN, WILLIAM. Sept. 1819. George Smith Guardian of William Martin.

MARSHALL, WILLIAM. June 15, 1810. Apprs: John Hunt, John Phillips, James Mc Michel.

MASTIN, JOHN. June 26, 1810. Apprs: Giles Samuels, Daniel Brown, George Brown.

MC BRAYNE, WILLIAM. August 19, 1805. Ex: James Mc Brayne. Apprs: Will Payne, George Jordan, Phil White.

MC BRAYER, JAMES. "Gent". Aug. 2, 1800. Jan. 1801. Sons: William, James, Hugh, John, Andrew. Ex: son William, Samuel Mc Afee. Wit: Robert Blackwell, William Mc Brayer.

MC CALLISTER. ----. April 12, 1806. Apprs: John Russell, Ephiram Lillard, William Robinson.

MC CLURE, NANCY. Sept. 12, 1806. Settlement. Late Nancy Smith, on estate of George Smith.

MC DOWELL, JOHN. Dec. 23, 1809. Apprs: William Boyd, John Butler, Scott Brown.

MC GREW, WILLIAM. June 23, 1799. Widow Mary Mc Grew. Apprs: John Scott, Otho Beaty, Isaac E. Gaines.

MC KEE, PHOEBE. Feb. 12, 1808. Formerly Phoebe Baker. Allotment of dower.

MONTGOMERY, SAMUEL. June 1, 1797. Nov. 21, 1797. Sons: John, Joseph, Samuel. Test: Robert Montgomery, William Montgomery.

MOXLEY, C. April 18, 1820. Division of estate; widow Agnes. Children: Joshua, Kitty, William, Sally, Betsy, Jeptha.

MURRAY, WILLIAM. Of District of Villa Gayoso in Government of Natchez. Wife: Martha. Son: William. Dau: Anna Marian Rumsey. Property in Louisana to be unsold furing life of wife. James Mc Intyre sone of wife is not to live with his mother. Ex: William Dunbar, John Smith. Wit: Thomas Green, Everard Green, Roger Dixon, Bernard Isenhootz, William Smith. Probated in Philadelphia, March 1797. Franklin County, Ky. April 1707.

NELSON, WILLIAM. Sept. 18, 1820. Wit: Catharine Nelson, T. L. Baltzelt, George Baltzelt.

OWENS, WILLIAM. April 1819. Apprs: Daniel Weisger, William West, Hugh Innis.

PARKER, ROBERT. June 8, 1818. Division of estate. Guardian: Elizabeth R. Parker. Children: Roland & James.

PATTERSON, CHARLES. March 23, 1805. Apprs: Reuben Samuel, Henry Brooks,

Clement Bell.

PEMBERTON, RICHARD. Nov. 27, 1798. Apprs: William Payne, Richard Smart, Thomas Logan.

PEMBERTON, JANE. (now Jane Wilcox), March 15, 1805. Settlement. Apprs: Robert Blackwell, William Mc Brayner, Wm. Payne.

PERRY, JOHN. ----. Nov. 1796. Wife: Elizabeth. Children: Santford, Nancy, Robert. Ex: Robert Perry, Roderick Perry, John Rennick.

POINDEXTER, THOMAS. Jan. 15, 1796. July 1796. Sons: James, Robert, Richard, George. Dau: Elizabeth J. Cammack. Gr.child: Gabriel Thomas, Robert, James, Richard, George (children of dau. Lucy); Stithe, Nicholas, Francis, Garland Cosby (chld. of dau. Molly Cosby). Ex: sons Thomas, James, Garland Cosby. Wit: Joseph Adams, John Perry, Robert Perry.

POINDEXTER, THOMAS. Nov. 15, 1796. Daniel James, Admr.

POWERS, ROBERT. August 19, 1811. Apprs: Edmund Ware, Carter Blanton, John Jackson.

REED, THOMAS. May 14, 1808. (indexed Redd). Apprs: Richard Price, John Major, Sr., Richard Bouleware.

ROBINSON, ALEXANDER. Sept. 24, 1796. Nov. 15, 1796. Legatees: Mother, Martha, Isabel (daus. of sister Rachel Campbell), Polly Robinson (dau. of bro. Robert Robinson), Alexander Robinson (son of bro. John Robinson). Ex: bros. John, William. Wit: Robert Blackwell, Izabel Robinson.

ROBINSON, ALEXANDER. Dec. 20, 1796. Apprs: John Penny, James Jett, Robert Blackwell.

ROWZEE, PHIL. Aug. 15, 1808. Apprs: Reuben Samuel, John Castleman, Silas Douthitt.

SACREY, ISAAC. May 14, 1808. Apprs: Hugh Maclin, Francis Moss, William Letcher.

SAMUELS, PETER. Jan. 17, 1797. Apprs: William Ware, Edwin Ware, John Brown.

SAUNDERS, NATHANIEL. Dec. 2, 1807. Apprs: Reuben Samuels, Abraham.

SLAUGHTER, EDGECOMB. Apr. 21, 1791. Nov. 1799. Legatee: sister Martha Slaughter. Wit: Francis B. Slaughter, Philip Buckner, Pate Joyes.

SMITH, GEORGE. Oct. 27, 1800. Apprs: Randol Walker, John Lightfoot, George Jordan.

SMITH, ELIZABETH. Dec. 1805. formerly Elizabeth Fogg. Apprs: William Steel, Ross Railey, William Railey.

SNIDER, BOLTZELL. Nov. 19, 1810. Admr: Widow, Mary Catharine Snider. Apprs: Thomas Looflourrows, Allen Mc Cunley.

STEPHEN, DANIEL. Nov. 24, 1810. Apprs: Sparks Patrick Bryan, Marmaduke Beltz, Daniel Stephens.

THOMAS, EDMUND. Dec. 4, 1803. Dec. 1803. Wife: Ann. Mentions sons and daughters. Ex: Thomas Wallace, Henry Clay, Walter Chiles, George Madison, Thomas Todd. Wit: Isaac Gano, John Crutchfield, Barabas Mc Henry. Apprs: John J. Hunter, Phil Bush, Thomas Warren.

THOMPSON, HENRY. Feb. 1810. Apprs: Daniel Peak, James Gale, John Edwon.

TIPPING, EBENEZER. May 19, 1806. Admr: James Gale. Apprs: Nicholas Rupe, Moses Milam.

TRABUE, JOHN. Sept. 10, 1809. Apprs: Francis Ratliff, James Martin, Josiah Woodridge.

TRACY, JAMES. Feb. 19, 1810. Admr: Austin Bohannen.

TRACY, SAMUEL. Feb. 20, 1804. June 1805. Legatees: son John, dau. Polly Fought, Betsy Parant, James Tracy, Peggy Tracy. Ex: Thomas Quidy, James Smart, William Payne, Thomas Mc Cray. Wit: Thomas Quady, Thomas Parant, Daniel Weisger.

TUNSTALL, HENRY. June 18, 1810. Apprs: John Mitchell, Robert Brenham, William Gerrard.

TUNSTALL, THOMAS. Aug. 20, 1810. Apprs: Daniel Weisger, John D. Richardson, T. Cox.

WARD, ISAAC. Feb. 1811. Apprs: William Boyd, John Butler, Robert Armstrong.

WARE, REUBEN. May 1803. Apprs: Giles Samuels, Thomas Settle, Daniel Peak.

WARE, JAMES S. -----1790. Apr. 1796. Sons: James, William Edmund, John, Nicholas heirs. Dau: Clary Sale. Ex: sons James, William, Edmund. Wit: William Hickman, Thomas Sullinger.

WEBSTER, ANDREW. Sept. 16, 1805. Apprs: Reuben Samuels, Henry Brooks, John Long.

WILSON, JOHN. March 16, 1797. ----. Children: Nancy, Thomas, Sally, Mary Clark, John, Rachel. Ex: Thomas Gist. Feb. 1800, a codcil appoints son John Ex. Wit: Thomas Palmer, Robert Fenwick. Apprs: William Hensley, Ephiram Lillard.

WILSON, JEREMIAH. Aug. 1811. Guardian for Sarah Wilcox.

WILSON, THOMAS. Jan. 1800. Apprs: Thomas Logan, A. Crockett, Alex. Milam.

WINGATE, SMITH. Aug. 27, 1799. Apprs: Clement Bell, Andrew Williams, Thomas Bradley.

WOOLRIDGE, ROBERT. June 18, 1801. Apprs: Nathaniel Samuels, Giles Samuels, Baker Erwing.

ZOOK, DAVID. May 27, 1810. Apprs: Christie Greenup, John Younger, Isaac Holmes.

ZOOK, SOLOMON. May 29, 1810. Apprs: Chris Greenup, John Younger, Isaac Holmes

GARRARD COUNTY INDEX

BOOK B

1805 -- 1813

	Page
Adams, Feathergale. (Inventory)	201
Adams, Will (Will)	25
Alderson, Isaac (Will)	172
Alfords, Jacobs (Inventory)	111
Allens, Joshua (Inventory)	138
Arnold, Peggy (------)	39
Arnold, Reuben (Inventory)	184
Arnolds, ----- (Inventory)	145
Askins, Will (Will)	45
Backs, ----- (Inventory)	112
Ballingers, A. (Account)	33
Banks, Lynn (Settlement)	217
Barlow, ---- (Settlement)	221
Barlows, Henry (Sale)	84
Belles, ----- (Inventory)	75
Belles, Philip (Sale)	65
Bingamin, Henry (---)	199
Brassfield, Edward (Inventory)	69
Browns, John (Will)	167
Buckhanans, William (Will)	42
Burdetts, Fredrick (Will)	161
Burnsides, Walter (Inventory)	14

Coates, Elijah (Inventory) 17
Coats, ---- (Settlement) 23
Comeleys, David (Sale) 5
Compton, Zachariah (Will) 10

Downing, Rachel (Sale) 2
Draydens, James (Inventory) 6
Duggins, Daniel (Will) 2
Dunn, William (Inventory) 23

Englans, ----- (Will) .... --
English, Charles (Will) 6

Giles, ----- (Inventory) 15
Giles, Mary (Inventory) 7
Gooches, ---- (Inventory) 19
Grahams, Thomas (Inventory) 6

Hamp, Robert (Settlement) 23
Harris, Robert (Settlement) 3
Hays, ---- (Settlement) 22
Hendricks, Henry (Will) 24
Hiatt, ---- (Settlement) 14
Hiatt, (Abrms.) (Inventory) 2
Hogans, James (Account) 9
Holland, Joseph (Inventory) 1
Huffmans, ---- (Inventory) 4
Huffmans, Fredrick (Inventory) 2

Jackman, Hannah (Relinquishment) 5

Jackman, John (Will)	98
Jennings, Baylor (Inventory)	157
Lackey, Andrew (Inventory)	7
Lairs, ---- (Settlement)	228
Laros, ---- (Appraisement)	153
Lampton, William (Inventory)	135
Lear, William (Inventory)	47
Machlins, Dolly (Account)	109
Montgomerys, ---- (Inventory)	120
Morehead, Charles (Inventory)	121
Mullins, Samuel (Account)	94
Nolsons, Sarah (Will)	83
Nowlings, James (Inventory)	74
Pawling, William (Will)	35
Poors, Robin (Inventory)	143
Reeds, John (Will)	40
Smith, Sally (Inventory)	117
Stapp, Rachel (Inventory)	118
Steyer, Francis (Inventory)	8
Totten, John (Inventory)	10
Tungate(Tunget), Jeremiah (----)	36
Wallace, Micheal (----)	173
Wilie, John (Will)	72
Wilson, John (Inventory)	131

HARDIN COUNTY

BOOK A

1792 --- 1809

ASHCROFT, JEDIAH. Apr. 19, 1793. -----. Wife: Nancy. Sons: Jacob, John, Daniel. Daus: Nelly, Nanney. Ex: Nancy Ashcroft (wife). Wit: P. Philips, George Hamilton, John Odaniel.

BARNET, JOSEPH. Inventory. July 27, 1797. Appr: Robert Mosley, J. Craven, Chris. Jackson.

BEARD, JAMES. July 29, 1804. August 1804. Sons: Thomas, John P., Samuel, James, Joseph. Daus: Martha Bertiness, Mary Thalia. Ex: James Beard (son), Joseph Beard (son), James Miller, Samuel Miller. Wit: George Bertiness, John Hank, Samuel Miller.

BERRY, ENOCH. Nov. 13, 1807. Aug. 1808. Wife: Elizabeth. Sons: Benjamin, Samuel. Daus: Nancy, Peggy, Betsy. Ex: William Vertrees, Benjamin Berry. Wit: Tom Piety, Polly Piety.

BRADLEY, JAMES. Dec. 20, 1800. ------1805. Wife: Annie. Sons: John, Thomas, Elijah, William. Daus: Susanna, Mary Logsdon, Elenor Green, Sarah Greenwall, Katy, Rachel, Lucy, Rebekah. Ex: Elijah Bradley (son), Jacob Greenwall. Wit: Robert Hodgen, John Hodgen, Conrod Kaster, Richard Winchester.

BRASHEAR, NICHOLAS. Inventory. Oct. 5, 1803. Apprs: Thomas A. Coombs, Isaac Hodgens.

BRASHEAR, NICHOLAS. Inventory. Dec. 15, 1800. Apprs: Adam Coombs, John Thomas, Asa Kellam.

BRYAN, IGNATUS. Inventory. Nov. 22, 1803. Apprs: Jeremiah Parpoint, Josiah Anderson.

BURNS, ELINOR. Inventory. Mar. 25, 1800.

CALDHOON, HUGH. Inventory. May 27, 1809.

CARR, JOHN. Inventory. Jan. 22, 1803. Apprs: Jacob Enslow, George Howard, Nicholas Miller.

COATS, CATHARINE. Inventory. Nov. 26, 1806. Apprs: Thomas Pareman, Alex. Gilmore, Isaac Vertrees.

COOPER, JOB. Inventory. Nov. 19, 1804. Apprs: Isaac Finley, Edward Reed, Thomas Logsdon.

CRAFTON, JOSEPH. Inventory. Jan. 27, 1806. Apprs: Joseph Smith, Ralph Stovall.

CRAWFORD, ROBERT. Mar. 13, 1804. June, 1804. Wife mentioned but not named.

Dau: Mary. Gr.son: William Riley, John Riley. Ex: wife, Peter Carmick. Wit: Thomas Williams, Mary Carmick, Abraham Lucuss.

DODGE, JOSIAH. Inventory. August 10, 1804. Admr: Sarah Dodge, Thomas Mc Intire.

DOHERTY, RICHARD. Inventory. June 1809. Mention is made of Sarah Doherty. Apprs: John Henton, Thomas Clement, Sylvester Mack.

DORSEY, THOMAS. Mar. 24, 1790. Oct. 30, 1794. (Of Annrunsdel County, Maryland). Wife: Elizabeth. Children mentioned but not named: Ex: wife. Wit: Joe Dorsey, John Henry Dorsey, William Squire. "I request that my body be decently and privately enterred. My near relations and a few friends only being invited to attend my funeral at which I desire the funeral services of the Protestant Episcopal Church of which I am a member and it is my desire that no mourning be worn by my dear children other than black ribbons, hankerchiefs and gloves.

"As it pleased God to bestow upon me a liberal fortune which I have lately lost by my indiscretion and ill placed confidence and as a small amount can be saved out of the wreck of my fortune can not be placed in the hands of any person more truly prudent and frugal than my beloved wife and who as she divides her affections among her children will, I have no doubt, distribute equally among them anything that can be saved.

"I do give, devise and bequeath unto my wife and her heirs forever after payment and satisfaction of my just debts."

DYE, ISAAC. May 31, 1796. August 1796. Wife: Hannah. Sons: Isaac, James, Job. Daus: Sarah, Elenor, Milly, younger daus. not named. Ex: wife, Job Dye (son), Robert Hodgens. Wit: BonomShaw, Richard Winchester.

ELDER, JOSEPH. Inventory. Feb. 5, 1801. Apprs: James Brown, Daniel Viterow, Henry Buit.

ENLOW, MORDICA. Inventory. June 20, 1807. Apprs: James Smith, George Helm, N. Miller.

EWIN, JOHN. (Of Rockingham County, State of Virginia). Wife: Sally. Children: Henry, Wats, Jennetta, John. Mentions bro. Henry Ewin of Rockingham Co., Va., also mother Jane Ewin. Ex: wife, James Davis (bro-in-law), of Logan Co., Ky., George Bell (bro-in-law) of Hardin Co., Ky. Wit: Jacob Van Matra, Rebecca Van Matra, Joseph Van Matra.

FERGUSON, USHER. Inventory. July 2, 1805. Apprs: Richard Parish, Isaac Linden, Charles Sawyer.

FORELINES, JOHN. Inventory. March 20, 1814. Apprs: John Lucas, Adin Coombs, Edward Caroll.

FRAKES, HANNAH. Inventory. Oct. 1803. Apprs: Jacob Enslow, Nicholas Miller.

FRAKES, HENRY. ------. Oct. 19, 1804. Wife: Hannah. Son: Alexander. Ex: wife. Wit: Michael Hargow, Jacob Enlow, Randol Slack.

FRIEND, BANNER. Aug. 3, 1793. Dec. 24, 1793. Estate to sister Elizabeth Stuart and bro. Joseph Friend. Ex: Philip Phillips, George Hamilton, Wit: Isaac Hynes, Catharine Harris, Mary Yatslor.

GOODIN (GOODWIN), ABRAHAM. Inventory. Jan. 27, 1806. Apprs: Thompson Ashby, Markmor Shall, Sharp Spencer.

GOODIN, SAMUEL. Inventory. Jan. 1808. Admr: Samuel Goodin, Jr.

GRENEWALL, JOSEPH. Nov. 7, 1795. March 1799. Wife: Nelly. Sons: Ludwick, Joseph, John. Daus: Magdilene, Catharine, Susanah. Mentions children of son Michael. Ex: Nelly Grenewall (wife). Wit: James Nourse, Sarah Nourse.

GUM, JOHN. Inventory. Dec. 22, 1806.

HELM, BENJAMIN. Appointed Clerk of County Court March 25, 1800.

HINCH, JOSEPH. July 22, 1800. Orphan of George Hinch, bound to Isaac Larue to learn a trade.

HODGENS, ROBERT. Appointed Justice of County Court Nov. 25, 1800.

HOWELL, JACOB. Inventory. Aug. 21, 1802. Apprs: Francis Howell, Samuel Howell.

HUGHES, GEORGE. Inventory. Dec. 17, 1806.

JAGGERS, DANIEL. Nov. 16, 1807. Aug. 8, 1808. Wife: Hester. Sons: William, Nathan, Levi. Daus: Marthey Earters, Hannah Dancey, Nancy, Mary. Ex: wife, Jeremiah Jaggers, John Dancey. Wit: James Wilkinson, John Peebles.

KENNEDY, ROBERT. Inventory. Dec. 1803. Apprs: John Kennedy, Daniel Kennedy, Andrew Pairleigh.

KERMIKLE, PETER. Oct. 6, 1808. Nov. 1808. Estate to his children (no names). Ex: Abraham Lucas, Cornelius Lucas. Wit: James Mc Murty, Mary Craford.

KIMBERLIN, JACOB. Inventory. September 27, 1804. Apprs: James Young, Thomas Overall.

LARUE, JAMES. ------1798. Of Fredrick County, State of Virginia. Gives to his brother Jacob power of attorney.

LARUE, JOHN. Inventory. June 25, 1799. Admr: George Bell, Stephen Rawlings.

LARUE, PETER. -----. April 1798. Of County Hampshire, State of Va. Gives power of attorney to his brother Jacob who is a resident of Kentucky. Wit: Jacob Larue, James Larue, Isaac Larue, Samuel Larue, William Larue.

LUCAS, WILLIAM. June 8, 1803. Aug. 15, 1803. Wife: Caty. Sons: John, Abraham, other children mentioned but not named. Ex: Abraham Lucas (son),

Thomas Mc Intere.

KYKENDALL, JACOB. Dec. 26, 1803. May 1804. Wife: Mary. Sons: Henry, Jacob, John. Daus: Elizabeth, Rebecca. Ex: wife, Leven Deen, Thomas Deen. Wit: James Baird, Peter Bell, Mary Brown.

MAY, DAVID. Inventory. June 29, 1798. Apprs: Daniel Wade, Joseph Kirkpatrick, Isom Enlow (Enslow).

MC COMAS, NATHANIEL. Nuncupative will. Estate to bro. Mordecai's children. Proven by the oath's of Rhoda Gum, Peter Bell.

MC DOWELL, ROBERT. Jan. 4, 18--. Aug. 23, 1802. Legatees: Mother, bro. John Mc Dowell. Wit: James Wilson, John Wilson.

MC GOVERAN, CHARLES. Inventory. June 8, 1801. Apprs: Stephen Rawlings, S. Haycraft, Robert Huston. Admr: Elizabeth Mc Goveran.

MC INTERE, THOMAS. Inventory. Feb. 22, 1808. Apprs: William Brownfield, John Thomas.

MC KENSEY, ENOCH. ----1798. Nov. Court 1805. Wife: Rebekah. Ex: wife. Wit: Sally Williams, James Williams, Elizabeth Swan.

MC LAIN, JOHN. June 21, 1808. Aug. 1808. Legatee: Ann Strader. Wit: John Easter, Francis Strader.

MELINGER, WILLIAM. Inventory. July 7, 1798. Apprs: Timothy Coe, Hensby Reed, Philip Reed.

MILLER, CHRISTOPHER. Sept. 13, 1800. Sept. 23, 1805. Wife: Eloner. Sons: Henry, William, Philip. Heirs of dau. Nancy. Ex: Henry Miller, William Miller, Philip Miller (sons). Wit: Robert Hodgens, John Deremiah, A. Kellway.

MORRISON, DAVID. Oct. 28, 1800. Sworn in office of Coroner.

MORRISON, ISAAC. Nov. 28, 1798. March 1799. Wife: Phebe. Sons: Daniel, John. Dau: Sally Cook's three children, viz: Isaac Lewis Cook, Sally Cook, Phebe Cook. Ex: Daniel Morrison (son), James Morrison, James Nourse. Wit: Benjamin Frye, James Chambers, James Morrison.

PAIRPOINT (PEARPOINT), FRANCIS, JR. Inventory. Aug. 15, 1805.

PARETREE, JOHN. Oct. 19, 1806. Aug. 24, 1807. Legatee: Sarah Tucker. Wit: Alexander Lewis, William Hornback.

PAUL, JOHN. Inventory. Feb. 1805.

PEARPOINT (PAIRPOINT) FRANCIS, SR. July 20, 1805. Nov. 24, 1806. Gr.son: Charles Pearpoint. Ex: Mary Pearpoint (wife), Jeremiah Pearpoint (son). Wit: Michael Roll, Patience Anderson.

PEARPOINT, MARY. Inventory. Feb. 22, 1808. Apprs: Barton Robey, Josiah Anderson, John Kannady, William Jourdan.

PHEBUS, JOHN. Sept. 9, 1802. May Court 1804. Of Bullitt Co., Ky. Wife: Jemina. Ex: Wife. Children mentioned but not named in will, but other records give the names of children as follows: Polly, John, Samuel, Lewis, Jesse Fitzgerald (son-in-law), Michael Akers (son-in-law), Robert Martin(son-in-law). Wit: Samuel Hornback, James Westfall, Abraham Hornback.

PORTWOOD, PAGE. Inventory. July 11, 1808. Apprs: John Tharp, William Brooks.

PUTH, JACOB. Inventory. Sept. 23, 1805. Admr: James Brownfield.

RAWLINGS, EDWARD. No date, probably 1797. Wife: Rebeckah. Daus: Elizabeth Hart, Ann Hart, Lettis Rawlings, Rebeckah Rawlings. Ex: wife, Stephens Rawlings. Wit: Isaac Hynes, John Swank, Margaret Garrard.

REDMAN, THOMAS. Inventory. Aug. 24, 1799. Apprs: Richard Winchester, Joseph Kirkpatrick, Isam Enlow.

RICHARDSON, MARY AND ROBERT. Inventory. Sept. 1803. Apprs: Philip Rodgers, Jacob Lender, Peter Bodine.

STATOR, ADAM. Inventory. Sept. 16, 1802.

STUART, WILLIAM. Inventory. Oct. 28, 1795. Apprs: Samuel Watkin, Hannah Lincoln, Isaac Morrison.

SWEARINS, JOHN. Inventory. 1807. Admr: David Swearins.

THOMAS, HENRY. Inventory. Dec. 17, 1804.

TRUMAN, EDWARDS. Sept. 13, 1808. Feb. 13, 1809. Wife: Elizabeth. Sons: Henry, John, Walter. Daus: Nancy, Elizabeth. Wit: Tom Piety, Jesse Moreman, Shaderack Brown.

TRUNK, ABRAHAM. August 8, 1797. Nov. County Court, 1807. "Late of Jefferson County, Ky. Legatees: Daniel Trunk (bro.), Teny Trunk, Caty Trunk, Polly Trunk, Elizabeth Trunk (sisters). Brother and sisters "now residing in Virginia". Ex: Nathan Holeman. Wit: Ignatus Reyman, Ann Craven, Rebecca Barnet.

VANMETRE, JACOB. Nov. 11, 1798. Dec. Court 1798. Wife: Letty. Sons: Jacob, John, Isaac. Dau: Peggy. Gr.children: Catharine, Sarah, Letty, Elizabeth (heirs of son Abraham, dec'd.). Ex: Jacob Vanmetre, Isaac Vanmetre (sons), Samuel Haycraft. Wit: Robert Mosely, Chris Jackson, Madey Ann Todd.

VERTREES, JOHN. Nov. 8, 1802. Jan. 1803. Wife: Elizabeth. Sons: Joseph, John, Isaac, Jacob, Charles. Daus: Mary Mills, Sarah Rawlings. Gr.sons: William, James Allison. Step-children: Daniel and Rebecca McNeil. Ex: wife, sons Joseph, John. Wit: Charles Helm, Sally Helm, Henry Ewim.

WATTS, GEORGE. Jan. 5, 1808. July 1808. Wife: Prudence. Ex: wife, Christopher Dorty. Wit: Henry Ditto, William Ditoo. "Dear Wife: I take this opportunity to inform you that life is unserten and Death is serten. My will and desire is you should keep persesion of the plantation where you

now live on, during your widowhood. Pervided you should marry it is my
wish that you should have on-third of my estate. My daughter Polly should
have the sorrell mare and here oldest colt, saddle, bridle, bed, furniture.
All rest of my estate to be equally divided among all the rest of my children then left and the property then left to be sold at public sale next
July and on one years credit and the money not wanted in family to let
out on Intress."

WILLIAMS, JACOB. Inventory. ----25, 1804.

WINTEN, SAMUEL. Inventory. Aug. 25, 1794.

WITHERS, WILLIAM. July 29, 1809. Oct. Court 1809. Mentions former home
in Culpepper County, Va. Sons: William, Cain, John Parkinson, Hoard, Benjamin Lewis, Jiles Travis. Daus: Elizabeth Hoard Withers, Agnes Withers,
Nancy Grigsby (hus. Smith Grigsby), Susan Withers, Peggy Withers, Patsy
Withers. "Daughter Elizabeth to have silver spoons with letters E. K."
"My son Kene is spelt Cain, but it is understood Kene is his name although
spelt Cain." Ex: son William Withers, William Withers (my neighbor and
cozen". Wit: William Withers, John Ball, Hugh Lusk.

WYLEY, WALTER. Nov. 11, 1804. Jan. Court, 1805. Daus: Elizabeth Collett,
Casander, Willimina, Rachel, Mary, Susannah. "To Isaac Catlett my clothes".
Ex: Isaac Catlett. Wit: Joseph Smith, Joseph Crafton, Thomas Clemmens.

YOUNG, ADAM. Inventory. Sept. 12, 1806.

HARDIN COUNTY

BOOK B

INDEX

Arnett, Johathan
Atterberry, Richard

Brady, Morris
Bush, Christopher
Barlow, Michael
Bruce, Mary
Brown, Fredrick
Baird, James
Burris, Joseph

Caldhoon, Hugh
Cameron, Anguis
Chasteen, Lewis
Coombs, Samuel
Courts, Charles
Carter, Samuel
Cozart, William

Deavor, Henry
Dodson, William
Dougherty, Christopher
Dodge, Sophia

Ferguson, Asher
Ferguson, John
French, James

Gardner, Jonathan
Geoghans, Thomas
Gilliman, Thomas
Graham, Andrew
Gray, Joseph
Gorman, John
Groom, Samuel
Greenwall, Lewis
Guntryman -----

Hart, Joseph
Hart, Rachel
Harris, Samuel
Helen, Thomas
Hill, Thomas
Humphrey, John
Hunter, Robert
Hodgen, Robert

Jackson, John
Jones, Isaac

Joseph, Jonathan

Kennedy, Daniel
Kirkendall, Jacob

Larue Heirs
Larkins, William
Linder, Isaac

Mc Intire, Moses
Mc Intire, Thomas
Mc Cullum, William
Mc Lean, Leonard
Mc Daniel, Daniel
Mc Mahan, William
Miller, Peter
Miller, Alexander
Murphy, James

Nevitt, Joseph

Overall, Thompson

Pageit, Reuben
Pearpoint, Francis
Pearpoint, Francis, Sr.
Pearpoint, Mary
Potter, Daniel
Price, Richard

Read, John
Roof, Nicholas

Simmons, Benjamin
Stader, Anne
Sanders, Azariah
Skaggs, James
Stezer, Fredrick

Tull, Fredrick
Turner, Francis
Tharp, David

Watts, George
Waide, Horatio
West, Isaac
Withers, William
Wiseheart, George
William, John

Wiley, Thomas
Wooley, Hannah
Wood, Isaac
Wooley, William

HARDIN COUNTY

BOOK B

ATTABERRY, RICHARD. Oct. 4, 1808. -----. Wife: Rebekah. Ex: Richard Attaberry (son), Charles Attaberry. Wit: John Wright, Prudy Meeks, Robert Dorsey.

DAUGHERTY, CHRISTOPHER. Sept. 29, 1808. May Court 1811. Wife: Martha. Children mentioned but not named. Ex: Wife. Wit: John Daugherty, Jesse Daugherty, John Watts.

DEAVOR, HENRY. Sept. 21, 1806. April Court, 1812. Daus: Sarah Farmer, Margaret Hinton, Williettames Polk, Rachel Ash, May Hargas, Elizabeth Harras. Sons: Thomas, Steven, Benjamin. Gr.son: William Miles Deavor. Ex: Thomas Deavor (son). Wit: Thomas Ashley, Thomas Hargas, David Cradis.

MILLER, PETER. May 16, 1813. Oct. Court, 1813. Wife: Sarah. Sons: John, James, Robert, Samuel, Hiram, Peter. Daus: Nancy Duncan, Elizabeth Sayberd, Polly. Ex: not named. Wit: Denton Geoghegan, Achille Moreman, James Miller.

MC INTIRE, MOSES. Feb. 8, 1810. Aug. 1810. Wife: Mary. Sons: Nicholas Anderson, Charles M., Aaron James, Elijah, Moses. Dau: Mary. Ex: wife, John Churchill. Wit: Thomas Essex, Lewis Duffy, John Churchill.

GRAYHAM, ANDREW. June 26, 1810. July 9, 1810. Legatees: Corneliue McCarty, Laranna Mc Carty (wife of Corneliue, Thomas Mc Carty, Jr., Hardridge Mc Carty (son of Cornelius). Ex: Shadrack Brown, William Withers, John Ball, William Withers, Jr.

HODGENS, ROBERT. Feb. 1, 1810. -----. Wife: Sarah. Daus: Susannah Thomas, Margaret Vertrees, Phebe Larue, Sally Larue, Rebekah Keith, Elizabeth Hodgen, Polly Hodgen. Sons: Isaac, John, Samuel, James, Jacob, Jabe (?). Mentions heirs of Robert Hodgens, Jr. Wit: Jard Crutcher, Richard Winchester, Azual Lefollet.

REID, JOHN. July 8, 1811. July 15, 1811. Of Fredrick County, Maryland. Will was probated in Maryland. Wife: Ann. Sons: George Nelson, William Perry, John Alford, Joseph, Archibald, Thomas. Daus: Mary, Ester, Ann. Ex: wife.

BUSH, CHRISTOPHER. Feb. 24, 1812. Feb. 8, 1813. "In the name of God Amen I, Christopher Bush, of Hardin County and State of Kentucky calling to mind that all men must die and being desirous to provide for my loving wife and amply as my little property will admit of and also wishing to do equal justice between my children and conceiving that I have already given to all my children except Christopher and John, their full share of my estate both real and personal and being desirous that my two sons by name Christopher and John shall be secured in my estate equal to what I have given to the rest of my children who have left me, namely my sons, William, Samuel, Isaac, Elijah and my daughters, Hannah Radley, Rachel Smallwood, Sally Johnston. Do by these present make, ordain and publish this my last will and testament hereby revoking all other wills by me heretofore made or declared as my will.

"It is my will and desire that first all of my just debts be paid. It is then my will and desire that my loving wife, Hannah, have and fully enjoy unmolested for and during her natural life the plantation whereon I now live and all farming utensils and also all household and kitchen furniture, 2 horses or mares, the choice of all I have, and four cows her choice. It is my will and desire that my said wife hold, keep and enjoy them forever or give and dispose of them as she may think proper. It is further my will and desire that after the death of my said wife that the plantation and farming implements be equally divided between my two sons, namely Christopher and John, also all my stock and debts due me not heretofore disposed of after my just debts are paid.

"It is further my will and desire that all the balance of my land not heretofore given to my children be equally divided among all my children either by dividing the land or selling it and dividing the proceeds as they may agree. It is my further will and desire that my sons William, Samuel, Isaac, Elijah and my daughters Hannah Radley, Rachel Smallwood and Sally Johnston have $1. each paid out of the sale of the stock left to my sons Christopher and John or that Christopher and John do pay the above named William, Samuel, Isaac, Elijah, Hannah, Rachel and Sally their full share of my estate except there should be any land not heretofore disposed of and should there be any such land it is to be equally divided between my children.

"Lastly I do hereby ordain, nominate and appoint my loving wife executrix and my son Christopher executor of this my last Will and Testament. In witness hereof I have hereto set my hand and affixed my seal this 24th day of Feb. 1812.
                Christopher Bush

Test:
Ben Helms

HARRISON COUNTY

BOOK A

1793 -- 1814

AZBY, LINDSAY. March 12, 1816. Apr. 1816. Wife: Jane. Children: Nancy, Betsy, Polly, Sally, Son-in-law Robert Clifton. Ex: wife. Wit: James Mc Murty, David Mc Kee, Henry Seller.

BARNES, JOHN. Aug. 28, 1813. Dec. 1817. Wife: Hannah. Children: Abraham, John, Elizabeth, Rebecca, Anna. Ex: Charles Miller, Abraham B. Barnes. Wit: Robert Scott, William Gormany.

BEAVER, MICHAEL. March 5, 1811. March 1811. Wife: Christiana. Children: Michael, Abraham, Martha, Betsy Brummer Kelly, Barbary Coon, Nancy Armstrong, Matheas. Ex: wife, John Chinn. Wit: Piler Smieser, Joshua Lilly, William Curry, Jeremiah Morgan.

BLACKBURN, JAMES. Aug. 8, 1810. Dec. 1810. Wife: Jane. Children: Jean, William, Thomas, James, Ramkin. Ex: wife. Wit: Gavin Morrison, Thomas Rankin, Charles Kelso.

BLAIR, JOSEPH. Jan. 17, 1814. ------. Wife: Hannah. Children.-----. Ex: wife. Wit: James Wiglesworth, Richard King, Samuel Blair, Thomas Moore.

CALDWELL, JOSEPH. Feb. 10, 1810. Dec. 1810. Wife: Mary. Wit: Joseph Penn, John Williams, Jonas Hoffman, William Perrin.

CARTWILL, JOHN. Dec. 27, 1807. Feb. 1808. Wife: Susannah. Children: William, John, Thomas, Peggs, Elizabeth, Nancy, Mary, Martha, Jenny, Nelly. Ex: wife, Samuel------. Wit: William Ward, David Hawkins, Joseph Ward.

CHANDLER, SUSANNAH. Oct. 23, 1807. April 1817. Children: Henry, Sarah. Ex: Henry Chandler. Wit: John Crenshaw, Lewis Day, Nancy Day.

CLARK, JOHN. July 5, 1814. Aug. 1814. Children: William, Augustine. Son-in-law James Kelly. Wit: Joseph Taylor, T. M. Timberlake, Samuel Broadwell.

CLARKE, THOMAS. July 5, 1814. Aug. 1814. Children: John, Irvin, Peggy Mc Intire, Delia Price, Polly Boyd. Ex: John, Irvin, Peggy, Delia (chld.). Wit: Ben Warfield, John Frazier, Robinson Magee.

COLEMAN, HENRY. Nov. 14, 1807. April 1808. Wife: Mary. Children: Polly Green, Caty Miller, Lucy, Sallie, Peggy, Suckey, William, Edward. Son-in-laws William Moore, John Miller, Napoleon Coleman (son of William Coleman). Ex: William Moore, Thomas Moore, Edward Coleman. Wit: Joseph Boyd, Christopher Mc Cannico.

CROSSDALE, ABRAHAM. May 27, 1811. Nov. 1812. Wife: Margaret. Children: Ann, Abraham. Wit: David Holstead, John Cross, Richard Marsh, James Kelly, James Finley, G. W. Timberlake.

DESHA, MORGAN. Dec. 7, 1816. Oct. 1817. Wife: ----. Children: William,

Nancy, Nellie Gannon. Ex: Mr. Kilgore. Wit: W. W. Edmonson, James Agnew.

DIAL, EDWARD. June 27, 1796. Oct. 1796. Wife: Betsy. Children: Alex., William, Polly. Ex: John Stephens, John Massey. Wit: Edward Dyal, Jr., Alex. Dyal, James Curry, Simon Dyal.

DILLS, DAVIS. Oct. 15, 1806. Jan. 1807. Wife: Rachel (3rd wife). Children: John, Elijah, Jane. Ex: wife Jane, John Walton. Wit: John Miller, David Dills.

DRYDEN, DAVID. Nov. 14, 1803. Dec. 1803. Wife: Jean. Children: James, Peggy, Nancy, Patsy, Jenny, Ruhannah, Elizabeth. Ex: wife, James Stephenson. Wit: W. E. Boxwell, Nat Mc Clure.

DUNN, HUGH SMITH. Aug. 5, 1813. Oct. 1813. Children: Elizabeth Merchant, Archibald, Thomas. Son-in-law: Benjamin H. Hickman. Gr.sons: Eals and Hugh Smith Duncan Hickman. Mentioned Sarah Margaret Linginfelter, Mary Peck, Elisha Dunn. Ex: Benjamin Hickman, John Whittaker. Wit: Robert M. Duffer, John Whittaker.

DUNN, SAMUEL. Nov. 22, 1805. April 1806. Wife: Dorothy. Children: Ezeriah, Samuel Jr., Ann Massey, Mary Gossett, Abraham. Wit: Aquilla Perkins, William Douglas, James Woodson.

ECHETTE, SOPHIN. --------. Children: Valentine, Daniel, Sophia, Mc Cann. Gr.dau: Sally McCann, Betsy, Sallie. Ex: Nathaniel Glasgow, William Bayman, Samuel Lewis. Wit: Nathaniel Glasgow, William Bayman, Samuel Lewis.

ECKLER, JACOB. Aug. 24, 1798. Oct. 1798. Children: Ulrey, Mary, five sons, two dau. not named. Ex: Jacob Eckler, Francis Hostaters. Wit: Samuel Moore, George Ruppert.

ELLIS, WILLIAM. Aug. 14, 1812. May 1813. Wife: Lucy. Wit: John David, Ellis, Robert Ellis, John Mc Kinney, Lewis Hendrick.

FOWLER, JOHN. Aug. 7, 1812. April 1813. Estate in Virginia. Names sister Elizabeth, bro. William R. Wit: Miranda Lewis.

FINLEY, GEORGE. July 1818. May 19, 1819. Wife: Polly. Children: Jane, Polly. Wit: Benjamin Oversake, George Parmer, Polly Barry. Ex: wife, George Parmer.

GIVENS, JOHN. Aug. 3, 1818. Oct. 1818. Wife: Ruth. Children: Isabella, Letitia, Maria, George, Alex., James. Ex: wife, Alex Givens, Francis Grey. Wit: William Botkins, John Chinn.

HALL, JOSHUA. Sept. 24, 1812. May 1813. Wife: Sarah. Children: Rebecca Kuturah, Elizabeth Jones, Mary Kemper, John, Joshua, Thomas, Charles, William. Wit: William Vinard, John Thomas, James Furnish.

HAMBLETON, DAVID. Dec. 14, 1813. Apr. 1814. Wife: Mary. Children: William, Thomas, Alexander, Elijah, David, Elizabeth, Janey, Martha, Sally, Margaret, Nancy, Mary. Ex: wife, John Miller, John Mc Daniel, William E. Boswell. Wit: Will E. Boswell, Joseph Currey.

HAMILTON, THOMAS. Nov. 16, 1802. Oct. 1803. Wife:------. Children: David, John, William, James, Andrew. Ex: William E. Boswell. Wit: William E. Boswell, Joshua Mc Dowell.

HARDING, JOHN. Oct. 14, 1816. Nov. 1816. Wife: Harriet. Ex: wife, William Harding. Wit: Thomas Harding, Robert Mc Duffee, Braxton King.

HAWKIND, ALEX SMITH HANDLEY. Nov. 1, 1807. Dec. 1807. Wife: Nancy. Children: John, Milton, Alfred, Francis, Basil, Alexander, Thomas, Elender, Jane, Betsy Grubbs, Elizabeth Miller, Nancy Jackson. Ex: wife, Isaac Miller. Wit: Benjamin Hodges, Henry Edger.

HENRY, JOHN. ------. Jan. 1816. Children: Thomas, William, James, John, Nancy Northcutt, Betsy Dunn, Polly Dunn, Peggy Henry. Ex: William and James Henry. Wit: Will E. Boswell, Wilson Pickett.

HERREN, WILLIAM. Dec. 23, 1813. Jan. 1814. Wife: Anna. Children: George, Ezeriah, Samuel. Wit: Aquilla Perkins, Jonathan Marsh.

HOGG, MICHAEL. Nov. 2, 1814. Feb. 1815. Wife: Elizabeth. Children: Polly, Isabella, Nancy Cummins, Elizabeth, Thomas, David, Robert, Harvey. Ex: wife, son Thomas. Wit: Herbert Wells, George Payne, Alex. Douglas.

HOLIDAY, WILLIAM. Dec. 20, 1811. April 1812. Wife: Martha. Children: Jane, Rebecca, Nancy, Sarah Martin, William P., Joseph, James, Samuel. Ex: wife, John Patton. Wit: George Reading, Henry Edgar, William P. Holiday.

HOLLAND, WILLIAM. Aug. 4, 1813. May 1814. Wife: Amelia. Children: Anthony, Aaron, Uriah, Mary Greenup, Rachel Wilson, Polly Elliot, Rebecca, Lydia. Ex: sons Anthony and Uriah. Wit: Josiah Griffith, James Smith.

HUTCHERSON, MARY. Feb. 11, 1807. May 1807. Children: Mary Lewis Crosthwaite, Jane Stears Kinsler. Ex: Jacob Powers, Robert Mc Kitrick. Wit: William Stears, Robert Mc Kitrick, Ann Powers, Margaret Mc Kitrick.

HUTCHERSON, GEORGE. Dec. 24, 1813. Jan. 1815. Wife: Mary. Children: William, Sally Edwards, Polly Bennett. Gr.child: James Henry Hutcherson, Sally Hutcherson. Ex: William Hutcherson, Francis Edwards. Wit: Thomas Walden, David Williams, Jonathan Marsh.

JACKSON, JOSHUA. Sept. 4, 1813. April 1815. Children: Modica, Jack, Colby, Wingate, Joshua, Judith Hall, Phoebe Chopsher. Wit: Daniel Hall, Henry Hall, John Whitley.

JAMESON, GEORGE. Oct. 1799. Jan. 1800. Wife: Elinor. Children: James, Andrew, Nancy. Ex: wife, Squire Moore. Wit: John McClanahan, Francis Hiesler, Peter Price.

JONES, BENJAMIN. Oct. 19, 1795. Sept. 1796. Wife: Sarah. Children: Benjamin, John, Jonathan, Sarah Pursley, Rebecca, Mary C. Ex: Jesse Hume, John Darnaby. Wit: George Pursley, Betsy Cole.

JONES, URIAH. May 19, 1806. Jan. 1807. Wife: Mary. Ex: Wife, Robert Stevenson. Wit: John Morrow, James Mc Illvain.

KING, JOSEPH. Feb. 30, 1815. May 1815. Wife: Selia. Wit: Robert McDuffee, Braxton King, John Snodgrass.

KING, JOSHUA. June 7, 1802. Aug. 1802. Wife: Rachel. Ex: wife. Wit: Thomas Mullen, William Hall, Richard King.

KINKADE, JOHN. June 14, 1818. July 1818. Sister: Allis. Bros: Hugh, William, Nephew, John Kinkade. Ex: Hugh Kinkade, William Kinkade. Wit: Will E. Boswell, Joseph Carr.

LEMON, WILLIAM. ----. ----. Children: John, George. Wit: Josiah Whiteker, Andrew Barnett.

LOWRY, JEAN. Feb. 1, 1803. Jan. 1804. Children: William, Margaret, Jean, Robert, Robert's dau. Jean, William's dau. Jenny. Ex: son William. Wit: John and Joseph Craig.

MC DOWELL, JOHN. June 29, 1798. Aug. 1798. Wife: Catereen. Ex: wife. Wit: William Mc Farland, Esq., Robert Boyd, John Dance.

MC KETTRICK, ROBERT. March 13, 1795. July 1795. Children: John, Robert, William, James, Sarah, Esbell, Margaret. Land in Augusta Co., Va. Gr.dau. Jenny Guye. Son-in-law: William Metiare, John Wright, John Meglemmery, James Guye. Ex: sons John and Robert. Wit: John Hutcherson Sr., Moses McClure, William Schooler.

MC MILLIAN, HANNAH. March 8, 1809. April 1809. Children: John, James, Thomas. Gr.chld: John, Kenney, Thomas, Samuel, Hannah, James, (Chld. of John); Hannah, Mary, Betsy, Liday, (chld. of Thomas); Kenny, Thomas, Samuel, James, John, Hannah, (chld. of James). Ex: Joseph Ward, John Adams. Wit: George Smith, Benjamin Fry, Isaac Vaughn.

MC MILLIN, WILLIAM. June 4, 1817. July 1817. Bro: Kenady, Marshall, Andrew F., Samuel. Sister: Mary. Ex: Samuel Mc Millin. Wit: G. W. Timberlake, Charles Smith Jr.

MC MILLIN, SAMUEL. Aug. 15, 1816. ------. Wife: Easther. Children: William, Marshall, John, Andrew, Kenady, Samuel, Polly, Mary. Ex: wife, Andrew Mc Millin. Wit: Joseph Taylor, John Ward, William Lowry, A. F. Mc Millin.

MC NEESE, JOHN. Sept. 16, 1804. Nov. 19, 1804. Wife: Jean. Children: Alex, Abraham, Elizabeth Lemmon (hus. John), Ann Mc Connac (hus. John). Ex: Abraham Mc Neese, Alex Mc Neese. Wit: Josephus Perrin, Hugh Newell, John Berry.

MC KNUTT, ELIZABETH. March 24, 1815. April 1816. Children: Susannah Dickens, Sarah Cragg, Thomas, Samuel. Gr.dau: Betsy McKnutt Williams. Son-in-law: David Williams. Wit: Jonathan Marsh, John Berry, Samuel Williams.

MAHON, THOMAS. March 16, 1814. July 1840. Wife: Margaret. Children not mentioned. Ex: Benjamin Mills. Wit: Charles Smith, Edwin Anderson, John Jomdon.

MAIS, JOHN. May 15, 1805. Aug. 1805. Wife: named. Children: Jenny, Betsy, John, Thomas, Samuel, David, Annie Kirkpatrick. Wit: George Kirkpatrick,

William Stewart.

MASSEY, JOHN. Sept. 23, 1814. Oct. 1814. Children: Hugh, Betsy, Nancy, Delilah, Mary, Rebecca, John, William. Wit: Samuel Rogers, Charles McDaniels.

MILLER, HUGH. March 17, 1808. July 1808. Wife: Margaret. Children: Rebecca, Polly Mc Coy, Isaac, Elizabeth Anderson, Margaret Frazier, Jane, Ann Harrison, John, James, Alex. Bro: James. Wit: James Caldwell, George Frazier.

MINTER, DORCAS. Sept. 27, 1807. Dec. 1811. Children: James, William, Robert, Joseph, Dorcas Ardrey (hus. Wm. Ardrey). Ex: William Ardrey. Wit: Joseph Dodge, Daniel Duval.

MOORE, KISIAH. Oct. 20, 1815. Nov. 1816. Sister: Elizabeth. Boston, Benjamin, and James Moore also mentioned. Ex: Elizabeth and Benjamin Moore. Wit: Thomas Wolf, Benjamin Moore, Samuel Mc Millin

NEALE, BENJAMIN. Dec. 13, 1816. Feb. 1817. Wife: Dorcas. Children: Geo., James, William, Thomas, Benjamin, Jonathan, America. Mentions Gabriel, George, Reuben Anderson, Joseph Shropshire, Lattice Mc Daniel. Ex: Gabriel George, John Mc Daniel. Wit: John B. Tucker, Samuel Tucker, Alfred George.

NEELEY, BENJAMIN. March 12, 1797. May 1797. Children: William. Ex: John Mc Nees, William Arnold. Wit: Joshua Swinford, George Huffman, Hezekiah Doane.

NESBIT, SAMUEL. March 7, 1814. July 1814. Wife: Mary. Children: John, Robert. Daus., Samuel, James, William. Ex: wife and son William. Wit: W. Moore, A. Moore, Henry C. Moore.

PATTERSON, JAMES. March 2, 1811. May 1811. Bros: William, David, Robert. Sister: Polly. Ex: Robert Patterson. Wit: U. Stevenson, William Lawry, James Craig.

PENDLETON, HENRY. Nov. 19, 1801. Jan. 26, 1802. Wife: Agnes. Children: Elizabeth Hunter, Nancy C. Kennedy, Phillip, James, Edmond, (land on Potomac), Henry (lot, Hansackton, Md.), Son-in-law: David Hunter, John Kennedy. Ex: wife, son Philip, David Hunter, John Kennedy. Wit: Nicholas Orrick Pendleton, R. Pendall.

PHILLIPS, THOMAS. Aug. 25, 1817. Oct. 1817. Wife: Martha. Children: Moses, mentions others. Wit: Stephen Davis, William Blair.

PHILLIPS, WILLIAM. March 20, 1814. July 1814. Wife: Ellen. Children: Howard, Hyram, William, Warner, John, James, Austen, Polly, Ellen, Cordelia. Wit: James Coleman, James Robb.

PICKETT, JOHN. Aug. 22, 1808. Oct. 1808. Wife: Mary. Children: Richard, Thomas, George, John. Son-in-law: Nicholas Long, James Wilson, Littleton Robinson, Zachariah Wilson, Philip Samuels. Ex: George Pickett, William Brown. Wit: Edwin Reynolds, Robert Rankin, Gavin Morrison.

PORTER, CHARLES. April 4, 1818. July 1818. Wife: Sarah. Children: Catharine, Polly, Frances, Nancy, Malinda, Moody, Stanfield, Owing, Thomas, Lewis, Joseph, Shelton. Ex: John Smith. Wit: Charles Smith, Elijah Chinn.

POWELL, GEORGE. March 11, 1817. Aug. 1817. Wife: Margaret. Ex: wife, Jacob Keith. Wit: Arch Alexander, Thomas Brinson, Jacob Keith.

REID, JAMES. March 16, 1802. May 1802. Wife: Elizabeth. Ex: Wife, David Dryden. Wit: Benjamin Hamilton, James Mc Clure.

RILEY, WILLIAM. March 26, 1818. July 1818. Names wife, bro., Ninian Riley. Children. Ex: Ninian Riley, John Blair. Wit: Samuel Hine, James W. Riley.

RITTER, MICHAEL. March 16, 1812. May 1812. Wife: Mary. Children: Lewis, John, Susannah. Ex: Lewis Ritter, Thomas Dugan. Wit: Joshua Hall, Thomas Kemper, Jacob Martin.

ROZER, MICHAEL. -----. Oct. 1804. Wife: Caty. Children: John, Jacob, others not named. Ex: wife, son Jacob. Wit: William Turney, William Raymond, Peter Pope.

SCOTT, ARCHIBALD. May 1, 1798. March 1799. Wife: not named. Son-in-law: John Morgan, David Lawry, James Martin, Robert Thompson, Robert Russell. Ex: John Ellison, Robert Russell. Wit: William January, John Mc Grath, Polly Ellison.

SCOTT, JOHN. March 21, 1798. July 1798. Names Nancy Scott, Lida Scott, William Scott, Margaret Scott, Richard Schooler, Jacob Lockhart, Aaron Ashbrook, Hiram Scott, M. M. Baley.

SELLERS, JOHN. March 21, 1798. July 1798. Wife: Elizabeth. Children: Mary Elizabeth, Jane, Margaret, Sarah, John, Ruth, James. Ex: wife, John Adams, James Brown. Wit: William Adams, James Thompson.

SHERMAN, JOHN. Nov. 11, 1809. Dec. 1809. Children: William, Anna, Mary. Bro: Shadrack. Ex: Shadrack Sherman, Abraham Powell. Wit: Thomas Duncan, William Hutcherson, John Tucker.

SNEED, RICHARD. Aug. 19, 1806. April 1807. Wife: Patsy. Bro: Thomas. Ex: wife and bro. Thomas. Wit: William Adams, Larkin Price, James Adams.

STEADYCORN, LIMEN. Nov. 27, 1808. Dec. 1808. Wife: Rachel. Children: Samuel Ex: wife and John Shanly. Wit: James Galley, Samuel Endicott, Samuel Jamison.

STEPHENSON, JOHN. Oct. 26, 1800. Nov. 1801. Wife: Mary. John Minter mentioned. Wit: Samuel Mc Illvain, John Ermon.

STUART, WILLIAM. March 12, 1817. April 1817. Wife: Elizabeth. Children: Benjamin, Henry, William, Sally, Nancy, Jean Shields, Isabella Nisbit, Polly Anderson. Gr.sons: William Shields, William Nisbit, Jerimiah Nisbit. Ex: John Huddleson, Alex. Mc Daniel. Wit: Isham Tyree, George Kirkpatrick.

TURVEY, MARY. Dec. 11, 1815. Jan. 1816. Son: Braxton King. Wit: William Raymon, Robert McDuffee, John Heading.

TURVEY, WILLIAM. Sept. 26, 1807. Feb. 1808. Wife: Mary. Son: William. Ex: wife, Braxton King. Wit: Benjamin Hickman, William Raymond, Isaac Taylor, Zackus Key.

WATSON, JAMES SR. Sept. 9, 1816. July 1817. Children: Patrick, James, Daniel, Joseph, William, Elizabeth Blackburn, Peggy Jameson, Mary Ardry, Marth Linn. Dau-in-law: Nancy Watson. Ex: James and Patrick Watson. Wit: William Ashbury, Shadrack Hieatt.

YARNELL, I. (ISAAC?) April 8, 1809. July 9, 1809. Wife: Ann. Children: John, Samuel, Isaac, David, Sally, Philip, Christian, Jacob, Polly Simmons, Eliza. William Ralston, Jacob Coonrad also mentioned. Ex: Benjamin Hodge, S. P. Griffith. Wit: Thomas Hawkins, Leonard Stump.

ZUMMUTT, GEORGE. Sept. 24, 1815. Jan. 1816. Wife: Mary. Children: Philip, Christian, John, Jacob, Polly Simmons, Elizabeth Fry, Margaret Bever, Henry, Christina Snider. Gr.dau: Mary Louise. Ex: John Zummutt. Wit: Charles Smith, Jr., Austin Bradford, Jr., William Mosley.

HARRISON COUNTY

BOOK B

Adams, John
Anderson, John
Alexander, Wilson
Asbury, Henry
Ashcraft, Jacob

Bacon, Joseph
Bailey, Augustine
Bennett, William
Blair, Samuel
Brown, William

Carpenter, Daniel
Carr, Joseph
Casey, Archibald
Catherwood, Jane
Chambers, Josiah
Chinn, William
Cleveland, John
Cole, Leroy
Coleman, James
Craig, John

David, Jacob
Day, Lewis
Deck, Christian
Duncan, Joseph
Duncan, William
Dunn, I. J. W.
Durbin, Daniel

Eads, Boswell
Edgar, Henry
Ellis, Disey
English, William

Falconer, Richard
Fowler, James

George, Roland B.

Hall, John
Hannon, Margaret
Hanson, Sarah
Harcourt, Richard Sr.
Hawkins, Alexander
Hedger, Jonathan
Henderson, Fannie
Henderson, Richard
Henderson, William B.

Hind, John
Hinton, James
Hogg, Elizabeth
Holt, Jane Miranda
Holt, Thomas
Hudelson, William

Ingles, Joseph
Jones, Dumas
Jones, Evan
Juett, William

King, John
King, Richard
Kinman, William
Kirtley, Simeon T.

Lair, Anne
Lair, John
Lamme, Samuel
Lauderback, Andrew
Lewis, Alexander
Laughlin, John
Lyon, Humphrey

McLain, Arthur
McDaniel, Francis
McFarland, William
McLoney, Daniel
McMillin, Esther
McNees, Jane
Miller, Abraham
Miller, Elizabeth
Miller, Joseph Sr.
Miller, Kitty
Moore, Henry C.
Moore, Thomas
Morrison, David

Nesbitt, Jane
Neaves, Daniel
Neves, James
Night, Shadrack Sr.
Nisbit, Robert

Oder, James
Oliver, John

Patterson, Catherine
Patton, Joseph

Penn, Templeton S.
Pigg, Mouring
Pock, Philip

Ravencroft, Thomas
Redmon, Thomas
Roberts, Hugh
Rogers, John
Ruddle, Isaac

Shields, Archibald
Shropshires, James
Shurts, John
Smith, Chas. H.
Smith, John
Smith, John
Smith, John
Snell, Lewis
Snodgrass
Stewart, Robert
Swinford, Joshua

Taylor, John
Taylor, Joseph
Torry, Obadiah
Thornton, Anthony
Timberlake, Samuel
Toney, John
Tucker, Samuel
Turner, George

Vanderen, Jesse M.

Ward, John
Ward, Joseph
Whitson, James
Wiggins, Philip
Wigglesworth, James
Williams, Elizabeth
Wilson, David
Wilson, Hugh
Withers, Benjamin
Wood, James

An Inventory of David Rankins Estate.

		P.	S.			P.	Sh.
1	Cow	3	10	1	Bay horse	20	0
1	Cow	3		1	Sorrel horse	20	0
1	Cow	3	10	1	Negro woman (Milley)	80	0
1	Cow	2	15	1	Negro man (Harry)	20	0
1	Cow	3	00	1	Negro boy (Jerry)	25	0
1	Cow	3	5	21	head of sheep	10	10
1	Cow	2	15	1	grindstone		2
1	Heifer	2	15	1	tea kettle		7
1	Bull Yearling & heifer	2	5		Pewter & sundries	3	0
2	Heifers	4	0	1	pair of spoon moulds		
7	Calves	5	5		& 1 pair of wool cards		12
1	2 year old mare	8	0	5	crockery plates		2
1	mare	12	0	1	Lantern		3
1	2 year old mare	9	0	1	Bed stead & furniture	6	
1	Spring colt	4	10	1	" " "	10	
1	mare	5	0	1	" " "	12	
1	spring colt	6	0	1	Mans saddle	1	
1	loom		15	1	Chest	1	
	castings	1	15	1	Table		15
	Tongs & shovel		8	1	Looking glass & 1 sewer		15
1	Frying pan		6	1	Pr. of blow irons	1	10
1	Hand saw		2		Drawing gears & Tackling	1	7
1	Mattock & sundries		15	4	Gags	1	4
1	Pair of wool cards		3	1	Large Bible & hymn Book		10
1	Brass candle stick & still-			1	Gague & tubb		3
	yards		15	1	Steer	5	10
2	Pot trammels			8	Hogs	9	10
1	Hackle, 1 ax & spools		12	1	Hay stack	1	10
4	Reeds		4	1	Crib of corn	50	0
	Wooden ware		13	1	Oat stack	4	0
1	Pot & hooks		15		Old wagon iron	9	5
1	Whip saw	1	10	4	Shoats	1	4
1	Pair of pot hooks		2	11	Acres Fall grain	11	
1	Wooden wheel		10		Fodder house & blade stack	2	12
1	flax wheel		12		Geese	2	5
1	Riddle, 1 Reel & 1 barrel		6	1	Hand mill		10
					Breech bands, ironpot, iron chains & chest	1	14
						1105	19

Harrison County towit.
June 6th 1796
This inventory and Appraisement of the Estate of David Rankin, dec'd., was returned in upon Court and ordered to be recorded.
        Teste W. Moore C.H. C.

Hugh Miller
John Wall
George Frazier
        Appraisers.

HENDERSON COUNTY

BOOK A

1799 --- 1821

ANDERSON, TURNER. July 28, 1814. Feb. Court 1815. Sons: Western, John, D. Gr.child: children of Susan Rankin (dau.), mentions estate left by his child. grandfather John Daniel, also damages that may have to be paid Mary Fleming or her heirs. A bequest to friend Thomas Pleasants of Louisa Co., Va. Ex: Elijah King, Robert Church, Adam Rankin. Wit: James Ball, Benjamin Wall, Reuben Church.

ALVES, WALTER. Dec. 18, 1819. Dec. C. C. 1819. Wife: Amelia. Sons: James, Walter, William Johnston, Samuel, Haywood. Daus: Elizabeth Towles, Anne Henderson. Younger children not named. Estate is in North Carolina and Tennessee. Ex: wife, James Alves, Haywood Alves. Wit: Levi Jones, J. Fellows, G. Ormsby.

APPERSON, DAVID. Sept. 16, 1818. Jan. Court, 1819. "To friend James Wilson of Henderson, Ky., Samuel P. Campbell of Shawnee Town, Ill., to be in charge of my goods and property, money to be sent mother Martha Apperson, residing with son-in-law Clark Royster in Mecklinburg, Va."

BALDWIN, JOHN. Inventory. Jan. C. C. 1808. Apprs: John Mitchell, William Dyer, Peter Potter.

BARNETT, SAMUEL. Feb. 4, 1800. Division of estate to following heirs: Jacob Barnett, Humphrey Barnett, William Barnett, Joseph Barnett, Russell Hewett, James Gilliam.

BARNETT, SARAH. August 17, 1813. Nov. C. C. 1813. Sons: Joseph, Mark, Samuel. Daus: Sinthy Patten, Esther McAllister, Harriett Barnett. Ex: John Logan, Gen. Samuel Hopkins. Wit: George Sprinkle, John Slayden.

BENNETT, SARAH. April 16, 1816. ------. "After debts are paid by guardean, money left to be used to erect brick wall well constructed and sufficient to protect and inclose graves of deceased parents and relatives. What is left I bequeath to Uncle Charles Davis as a mite of compensation for the tenderness and affection which I have ever received as well from said uncle and guardean as the whole of his family." Other Legatees: Edward Bennett (bro.), and wife Ann, Mary Mc Bride. Ex: Uncle Charles Davis. Wit: Edward Davis, Mary Hamilton, John M. Hamilton.

BENNETT, SUSANNAH. Oct. 30, 1805. Nov. 1805. Daus: Elizabeth, Lucy, Sarah. Son: Edward. Children of Mary Mc Bride. Ex: Charles Davis. Wit: James M. Hamilton, Charles Davis, Robert Davis.

BELL, THOMAS. Sept. 1812. March 1813. Wife: Sarah. Children not named. Ex: wife, James Bell (bro.). Wit: W. Dixon, Henry Dixon, John Anderson.

BOOK, MICHAEL. Inventory. Jan. 10, 1817. Apprs: Presley Wigginton, Alexander Ramsey, Henry Dixon.

BRENT, INNIS. August 12, 1800. Sept. C. C. 1806. Wife: Catharine. Sons: George, Hugh, Julian. Dau: Caroline. Ex: Hugh Brent (of Bourbon Co. Ky.), Samuel Hopkins. Wit: Adam Rankin, John Holloway, Thomas Fowles.

CHANE, CYRUS. Inventory. April 25, 1801. Apprs: Henry Higgins, John Wagner, Baldwin Johnson.

CHEATHAM, JAMES (ALIAS JOHN LUTHERTAMD). Inventory. March, 1812.

CLAY, MASTERN. Dec. 29, 1801. June, 1807. Wife: Sarah. Sons: Thomas, James, Charles, Barnett, Mastern, Henry M. Daus: Elizabeth, Lucinda. Ex: William Williams (bro.-in-law), James Williams. Wit: Phil Barbour, George Brenkenary, John Rankin.

COOLY, THOMAS. Nov. 21, 1804. Dec. C. C. 1804. Wife: Susannah. Wit: Nathan Walden, Lewis Lamber, John Sprinkle.

DAVIS, JAMES. Oct. 7, 1800. Dec. 2, 1808. Wife: Patsy. Children not named. Ex: wife, James Davis (father). Thomas Morton. Wit: John Davis, Robert Davis, Harrison Davis.

DENNIS, THOMAS. March 24, 1808. April 4, 1808. Nuncupative. Wife: Polly. Children not named. Proven by the oath of Robert Agnew, William Frazier.

EASTWOOD, JOHN. ------. Nov. 30, 1807. Estate to son Abraham and wife (not named).

GALLOWAY, JOHN. Oct. 5, 1801. Nov. 1808. Wife: Franky. Sons: Pleasant, Zachariah, John, Obidiah, Daniel, Edward. Daus: Fanny, Christiana, Sarah Huddleton. Wit: Peter Evans, John Kiligan.

GARRARD, HENRY. Aug. 8, 1810. Inventory. Apprs: James Ball, N. C. Anderson, Johnson Faulkner.

GREEN, GABRIEL. Jan. 15, 1820. Feb. 1820. Wife: Sally. Sons: Richard Neale, John Ashton, Gabriel Grant, William. Daus: Amelia, Sally Boyle, Judith. Ex: wife, sons Richard Neals, John, Gabriel Grant, William. Wit: A. Green, G. Blackwell, George Neale.

GRIFFIN, WILLIAM. March 14, 1819. Nov. 1819. Wife: Mentioned but not named. "Estate of first wife has been distributed to oldest dau. Nancy. Children: Susannah, Joseph, Lucy, John, Anthony, Amelia, James (chld. of second wife). Ex: Hampton Jones, William Jones, Joshua Moss. Wit: Thos. Jones, Samuel Denton, Fountain Griffin.

HAMILTON, CHARLES. Nov. 19, 1804. Inventory. John Husband, John Hopkin.

HARDIN, ELIZABETH. Inventory. July 25, 1815. Apprs: Johnson Faulkner, John Hart, Henry Dixon.

HARKIN, MILES. Sept. 20, 1813. Nuncupative. At home of Elizabeth Reed. Legatees: Children of sister Nancy ------(last name illegible).

HART, ELIZABETH. Sept. 1, 1811. Nov. 1811. "My sons are all dear to me but they by the laws of North Carolina and Tennessee did share the lands of their deceased father in those two states to entire exclusion of my dear daughters, Rebecca Dixon, Susan Cowan, Mary Hillyer, Betsy Hart. Land which descended to me from son Nathaniel Hart to be sold and money disposed of as balance of my estate." Ex: Winn Dixon, Joseph Cowan. Wit: Craven Boswell, Robert Dixon, John Hart.

HART, JOHN. June 29, 1821. Oct. 1821. Wife: Patience. Sons: Thomas, John. Daus: Rody, Polly, Rebecca, Susannah Floyd, Nancy Fordon, Heziah Sugg, Lucy Ann Standley. Mentions legacy from bro. Lemuel Hart. Ex: Thomas Hart, John Hart (sons). Wit: John Mills, Richard Spencer.

HAYS, JOURDAN. Jan. 14, 1810. May C. C. 1810. Nuncupative. Estate to wife Prusey, except one feather bed to dau. Elisa Hays. Proved by the oath of James Parks, Rebekah Parks. Mentions bros. Bery, and Robert Hays.

HETH, WILLIAM. Sept. 11, 1819. May C. C. 1820. Wife: Elizabeth. Sons: William Henry, Andrew Thomas, John Thaddeus, Samuel Pleasant. Mention is made of a farm in Hampshire Co., Virginia, near town of Romney. Ex: Wife: Wit: Teliaferrio Howard, James W. Clay.

HIGGINSON, GEORGE. Oct. 25, 1820. Nov. 1820. Wife: Mary. Sons: George, Whitesides, Hinchliffe, Franklin, Jefferson Heull (?), Madison, Washington. Daus: Rebekah Grantham, Sarah Elizabeth. Ex: wife, William Williams, Hull Higginson (son). Wit: William Williams, ----- Newman.

HILL, JOHN. Feb. 4, 1817. Feb. C. C. 1817. Wife: Biddy. Daus: Suky Smith, Judy Clay, Elizabeth, Sally. Ex: wife. Wit: Ann Bennett, James Armstrong, Edward Bennett, Henry Towns.

HEBBS, CHRISTIAN BRITTINGHAM. Aug. 7, 1818. Dec. C. C. 1818. Sons: Tadlock Aydelott, Joshua, John Aydelott, Benjamin Aydelott. Daus: Ann Reed, Elizabeth Baird, Mary Mc Dowell, Leah Holland Smith. Ex: Maj. John Holloway, Capt. Daniel Smith. Wit: Elijah King, Alfred Williams.

HOOPER, WILLIAM. Inventory. Dec. 1809. Apprs: Aaron Higgins, Daniel McCernary, David Mathis.

HOPKINS, CATHARINE. Oct. 25, 1803. Nov. 1805. Legatees: Elizabeth Davis, Mary Holloway (sisters), Laurence Good Hopkins (nephew), Sarah Jones Hopkins (niece), Mary Catharine Hopkins (niece), Phillis (a negro woman to whom she gives her freedom). Wit: Ann Barbour, Mary Posey, Eliza Davis.

HOWELL, JELISON. Feb. C. C. 1803. Inventory. Apprs: Absalom Ashby, Vincent Fugate, William Howell.

HOUSLEY, THOMAS. -------. Nov. C.C. 1801. Nuncupative. Estate to Lelia Jones. Proved by the oath of Green Mossey, Sarah Mossey.

HUGHES, ROULAND. Inventory. August C. C. 1807.

HUSBAND, JOHN, SR. July 2, 1812. Aug. C.C. 1812. Wife: Sebilla. Son: John. Daus: Amy, Betty, Phoebe, Polly. Ex: wife, and her brother Frint. Wit: John Shaver, William F. Thompson.

HUSBAND, EMMA. Sept. 17, 1812. -------. "To daughter Mary Shaver and her six infant children: Herman, Peter, David, Eanny, Isaac, William. Ex: John Shaver. Wit: William Noble, James Frint.

INGRAHAM, WILLIAM. Inventory. Nov. Court, 1805. Apprs: John Hart, James Murray, Bennet Sandefer.

JOHNSON, BALDWIN. Nov. 10, 1807. Jan. 1809. Wife: Eliza. Sons: George, James, Daus: Margaret Scanlin, Hannah Verkenny, Sarah Higgins, Sukey Johnson, Elizabeth, Nancy. Other legatees: Children of John and Hannah Mc Kenney. Ex: wife, Aaron Higgins.

JOHNSON, ELIJAH. Inventory. Sept. 1809.

LAMBERT, JOEL. Oct. 20, 1815. Dec. C.C. 1815. Wife: Martha. Sons: Lewis, Evan, William, Joel, Jordan, Anthony, Samuel, Thomas. Ex: wife, Lewis Lambert (son). Wit: Evan Bennett, Betsy Bennett.

LASH, PETER, SR. Inventory. Aug. 10, 1810. Apprs: Isaac Sibley, Daniel Mc Cernay, James Morrison.

LAURENCE, ADAM, SR. July 21, 1800. Sept. 1800. Wife: Susannah. Sons: John, Adam, David, William, George, Joseph. Daus: Patience, Ruth Clap, Nanny Stretor, Polly Haynes, Susannah Sprinkle. Ex: Charles Davis, Anthony Bennett.

LEWIS, JOHN. August 25, 1801. Feb. C.C. 1802. Wife: Hannah. Wit: Benj. Berry, Martin Mathes, Daniel Mathes.

LYNN, DAVID. Sept. 7, 1817. ---- Wife: Elizabeth. Son: Andrew Robertson Lynn Dau: Martha. Son Andrew to act as guardian for younger children. Wit: J. Harvey, Nancy Huston, Nancy Sellers.

MASON, JOSEPH. March 29, 1799. July, 1799. Land in the Territory of the United States, north west of the River Ohio (Jefferson County) to Joseph Worthington. Nuncupative. Proved by the oath of John Carnahan, Rachel Thompson. Joseph Mason died on board a Kentucky boat near Pittsburg.

MARKS, JOHN. Sept. 24, 1816. Oct. 1821. Sons: John, Benjamin, Samuel, Jesse, Elisha. Daus: Rachel Marks, Martha Higginson, Margery Cruse. Gr. child: Ann Ginkins (dau.) children, Rachel Rankin. Sons-in-law: Owin Ginkins, Robert Rankin. Ex: sons. Wit: John Christian, Elly Linn, John Linn, Thomas K. Newman.

MAUM, JOHN. Inventory. March, 1808.

MC CLENDER, BENJAMIN. Inventory. March 1808. Admr: Sarah Mc Clender.

MC GREADY, JUDAH. Inventory. Feb. 1809. Apprs: John Husband, William Wardlaw, Joseph Fuquay.

PAINTER, WILLIAM. Settlement Dec. Court, 1818.

POINTER, JOSEPH. Nov. 7, 1812. Mar. 1813. Wife: Elizabeth. Ex: wife, Robert Terry, Obadiah Smith. Wit: Thomas Pointer, William Mc Clames, James B. Hopkins.

REED, LEWIS. July 13, 1813. Wife: Elizabeth. Sons: William, Samuel. Daus: Elizabeth, Mary, Evaline. Wit: D. Mc Bride, William Bowlin.

ROBESON, JOSEPH. Settlement. Nov. 1818.

SANDEFER, JAMES. April 24, 1804. Nov. 1807. Son: Bennet. Ex: Bennet Sandefer (son), Edwin Hopkins, J. Bills. Wit: John Sandefer, Ann Sandefer.

SCOTT, JAMES. Sept. 20, 1808. Nov. 1812. Sons: James, William, John, Abraham. Daus. Esther, Elinor. Ex: James Scott, Jr., William Stephens, David Stephens. Wit: Samuel F. Williams, David Stephens, Elizabeth Stephens.

SCOTT, JOHN. August 5, 1813. Jan. -----. Bros: James Scott, William Scott, Abraham Scott. Other Legatees: Polly Mc Cord, dau. of Abraham McCord, dec'd. Abraham Mc Cord's brother. Ex: three brothers. Wit: William Allen, John Allen, James Hillyer.

SIBLEY, JOHN. May 10, 1802. Oct. 1802. Nuncupative. Son: Enos Sibley. Proved by the oath of Isaac Sibley, Sarah Austin.

SLATER, JOHN. July 15, 1806. Nov. 1807. Estate to be sold and the proceeds sent to friend Margaret Riley in Kingdom of England. Lots to friends John Stapp and wife Martha. Ex: Gen. Samuel Hopkins. Wit: James C. Wardlaw.

SMITH, THOMAS. Inventory. June C.C. 1809. Apprs: Lazaarus Powells, Elias Turner, Joshua Hancock.

SPENCER, GEORGE. Inventory. Dec. C.C. 1812. Apprs: John Hart, Edmund Talbot, Robt. Church. Admr: Richard Spencer.

STANDLEY, JOHN. March 1809. Inventory. Apprs: John Denton, Hampton Jones, Henry Dickson.

STRAIN, THOMAS. Oct. 12, 1807. Jan. 1808. Wife: Jane. Sons: James, John, Eli, William, Isaac. Daus: Ann, Jene Galloway. Wx: Martin Cannado, John Galloway, Sr. Wit: John Cannado, Thomas Smith.

SUGGS, GEORGE A. Feb. 12, 1816. Admr: Patience Suggs, Willis Suggs.

VANHERK, JACOB. -----. -----. Admr: Jane Vankerk.

THOMPSON, JOHN. Inventory. Nov. C.C. 1800.

TOWNS, MARY. Jan. 27, 1818. Oct. C.C. 1821. Wife: Mary. Sons: Baxter D., Henry, John Ride, Alfred. Daus: Amelia Clay (hus. Chas.), Ann Bennett (hus. Edward), Elizabeth. Ex: Baxter Towns, Alfred Towns. Wit: Minrod Grigsby, J. Fellows, Obadiah Smith, James Wilson.

WEIR, BARALIEL. Inventory. Aug. 30, 1806. Apprs: Robert Robertson, William Stewart, John Leeper.

WOODWARD, PETER. No dates -----. Wife: Mary. Sons: Willis, William, Peter. Dau: Mary Frasiser. Mentions money owing from sale of land in North

Carolina. Ex: son Willis, Elijah King. Wit: William Sugg, John Frasier, William Frasier.

WILLINGHAM, THOMAS. Sept. 1819. Oct. C.C. 1819. "I lend to my companion Sussen called by some Susey Willingham and by others Susey Malden (Malin), children by her: Judy, Sophia, Susy, Jane Hurst, Jarrett, John, Isam, William, Nancy Mc Daniel, Polly Kilgore, Peggy. Ex: Companion Susey Willingham or Susey Malin, brother Jarrett, John Davis. Wit: Dokes Prowett, Thomas Kilgore, Zacharia Galloeway.

INVENTORY

AN INVENTORY OF THE ESTATE OF MR. ANTHONY BENNETT DECEASED.

```
One negro Man Dick ------------------------------  60.00.00
One   "    "   Abraham ---------------------------120.00.00
One   "    "   Sampson ---------------------------120.00.00
One   "    "   Peter -----------------------------  90.00.00
One   "    Woman Milly ---------------------------  30.00.00
One   "    "     Fanny ---------------------------  80.00.00
One   "    "     Fibby ---------------------------  90.00.00
One   "    "     Clara ---------------------------  90.00.00
One   "    "     Hannah --------------------------  64.00.00
One   "    "     Loleta --------------------------  60.00.00
One   "    "     Cinthi --------------------------  30.00.00
```

1 Bay horse
1 bay horse
1 sorrell
1 bay mare
1 sorrel mare
12 head of cattle
28 head of sheep
5 pounds of pewter
5 bears
5 bolsters
2 pillers
5 blankets
2 linsey and cotten bed quilts
5½ pairs of sheets
5 bedsteads and cords
1 dining table
1 chest 3 trunks and box
8 chairs
Table cloths
1 Old Bible, 2 Testaments
1 book entitled the Evidence of the Christian Religion
1 book Economy of Human Life
1 book Watts Hymns
7 old phamplets and spelling books
1 vol. of Kentucky Laws
1 Hennings Justice
1 Book Columbia Version
1 Gazateer and 3½ vols. of Smaclet Travels
1 Vol. Arrabian Nights Entertainment
1 vol. Right of Woman
1 vol. Roderick Randum
1 vol. Constant Lover
6 Queen china dishes
2½ doz. plates
2 dishes
10 pewter plates
9 pewter spoons
8 pewter tea spoons
2 or 3 pint bowls
1 small sugar

15 tea cups, 14 saucers 2 cream pots.
2 tea pots
½ doz. knives and forks
1 set of bench plains
1 cooper jointer
1 drawing knife
1 pair of nippers
3 shot moles
1 stone hammer
1 curry comb and brush
1 wood square
1 iron ladle
2 pewter pans
1 spindle and horn
1 stone Peek cutting knife & steel
1 Rifle Gun, shot pouch, bullet mould
1 looking glass
1 slate
2 pickling tubs
1 check reel 25 spools, 3 flax wheel,
    1 cotton
1 cane hackle
2 fat tubs
1 lock chain, 6 bridle bits, 13 horse shoes
3 clivises, 2 open rings
1 mans saddle & saddle bags
1 cut saw file and set
5 pair wagon gears
2 pack saddle and box
3 jack share ploughs
2 Dutch ovens
1 pair of pot hooks
1 washing tub
5 small piggins
2 grind stone
Quanty of hemp
27 heads of hogs in the woods
1 pair of smoothing irons

1 coffee pot
1 iron and spoon
5 hoes, 2 grubbing, 5 axes,
1 brand axe
4 augers, 1 chisel
1 handsaw, 2 handsaw, file,
1 gimlet
2 sheep shears
2 trowels
8 pounds of lead
2 pounds of steel
1 pewter candle moulds
1 copper jointer
2 shot guns
2 small stone jugs
1 pair of brass candle sticks
1 pair of snuffers
1 brush
1 10 gal. keg
1 5 gal. keg

1 churn
11 barrels & 2 hogsheads

7 pounds of old iron
3 reaping hooks
2 pare of stretchers
5 sturrup irons
2 bear share plough
1 wagon
1 10 gal. iron kettle
1 Cotton wheel
1 iron skillet
1 wash bowl
1 weaving loom
9 raw hides
Quanty of cotton
3 bells

March County Court, 1804.

HENDERSON COUNTY

INDEX

BOOK B

1821 --- 1840

Allen, Charles
Anderson, Littleberry

Barbour, Ambrose
Barnett, S. O.
Barnett, Joseph
Beverly, Robert & William
Bently, Edmund
Bently, William
Beckham, John
Bell, Thomas
Bethel, James, Sr.
Beger, Tobia
Brodhead, Daniel
Brown, Thomas
Butler, Dennis
Bugg, John
Burton, Edward

Cabell, Joseph
Cabell, Ann
Carrington, John D.
Clay, Susan
Cheatham, James
Cheatham, Daniel W.
Church, James
Church, R. Sr.
Collins, James
Coomes, J.
Crenshaw, Joseph
Crenshaw, Abner
Culverson, John

Davis, Charles
Davis, Baxter
Davis, John
Danforth, Timothy
Dennis, John
Dennis, Lurietta
Denton, Reuben
Dezern, Nathaniel
Dezern, Ann
Dosewell, Payton
Duncan, N. Jr.

Eachus, John
Eades, John E.

Eades, Joseph
Eades, John
Elam, Harmon
Elam, Williams S.

Falkner, J.
Falkner, Johnson
Farmer, James H.
Farmer, Henry A.
Fisher, Ann S.
Fisher, Mary Ann
Fowlkes, Jennings
Friley, Martin
Fuquay, John
Fuquay, Joseph

Galloway, Archibald
Galloway, Obidiah
Gaither, Horace
Garrard, Henry
Gill, Isaac
Gibson, William
Griffin, Daniel
Green, Agustin
Griffin, Anthony
Green, John
Green, Gabriel
Grant, Moses
Greathouse, Harmon
Grady, Leonard
Graves, John R.
Green, G. G.
Griffin, Abner
Gwatkins, James
Gwatkins, H. D.

Hancock, William
Hancock, Scarlet
Hancock, Harrison
Hancock, John
Harrison, John
Hancock, Clearcus
Harrison, Gabriel
Harrison, John
Hammond, Samuel W.
Hart, David
Hardy, Aaron

Hart, John
Hay, Rachel
Hay, Adam
Haynes, Samuel
Hazlewood, Dan.
Heth, W. H.
Hillyer, James
Hill, Francis
Hicks, Alex. G.
Hopkins, Edmund
Howard, C.
Holloway, John
Holmes, G.
Horsely, N. C.
Hughes, John
Hunter, M. S.
Hunter, John

Jennings, J.
Jones, Thomas
Jones, Hampton
Jones, Lucy
Jones, Ann
Johnson, Thomas J.
Jordan, Arch. T.
Junell, Andrew
Junell, Judith

Key, James

Langley, W. C.
Lambert, Lewis
Lambert, L.
Lester, Child.
Lester, Whitefields
Lilly, James M.
Lewis, Tjomas
Long, John
Lynne, Leon
Lynne, Henry
Lynne, James

Mc Cullagh, Samuel
Mc Callister, Aneas
Mc Callister, Mathew
Mc Cain, Eli
Mc Callister, Samuel
Mc Callister, Harriett
Mc Callister, Jane
Mc Cormick, Hugh
Mc Cormick, Sallie
Mc Canshan, George
Mc Clain, James
Mc Clure, John
Mc Mahan, James

Mc Mahan, Mary
Marks, John
Marks, Thomas
Mason, James B.
Maloney, Daniel
Moore, Elias
Moss, Terry
Murray, James
Muncaster, James C.

Negley, Elizabeth
Negley, Samuel F.
Nevell, John

Parker, Jonas
Perry, Tandy K.
Pew, John B.
Pittman, Yyre H.
Pointer, William.
Pointer, William.
Polette, James B.
Pool, Richard
Powell, Alfred
Powell, E. W.
Powell, Mary
Powell, Willoughby
Pruitt, Robert.

Randolph, Enoch
Rankin, A.
Rankin, Elizabeth
Ratleff, Wm. B.
Rawlett, Francis W.
Reed, Joshua A.
Robeson, Leon
Rudy, Henry
Ruggles, Nathanial F.
Russell, James

Sanner, Isaac
Sanner, Isaac
Savage, Jane
Schofield, James
Schofield, Louise
Selby, James
Sevier, Enoch
Smith, Daniel
Smith, Thomas
Smith, Robert
Spencer, Joel
Spotts, Samuel
Stott, Thomas
Strain, William
Streshley, Dennis

Talbott, Ben.
Talbott, John G.
Tate, Hugh
Terry, Robert
Towler, Luke
Towles, Thomas
Townes, Henry
Townes, Moody
Turner, Asa

Walden, Martin
Walker, Martha
Walker, Martha
Walker, Reuben
Walton, Elizabeth
Wardlow, William
Wardlow, James C.
Warfield, Richard

Webster, Harla
Williams, Burwells
Williams, William
Willingham, Jarrett
Willingham, Thomas
Wilson, Daniel
Williams, James
Williams, James
Wilson, James H.
Wilson, James (orphan)
Wilson, Elijah
Wilson, Susan
Wilson, Susan
Wilson, John
Wilson, John
Windsor, Newman
Woods, George
Woodward, Willie
Woodyear, L. W.

HENRY COUNTY

BOOK A

1800 -- 1812

ADMINE, GEORGE. July 2, 1804. Jan. C.C. 1805. Dau: Sally. Son: William. 2 daus. of son Michael. Other children mentioned but not named. Sarah (negro) to have her freedom. Ex: Henry Woolfolk, Henry Admine, Henry Warble. Wit: John Jones, Richard Woolfolk, Jr., Henry Warble (or Marble).

BASEY, THOMAS. Inventory. ----- 1810. Apprs: George Scott.

BRIGHT, TOBIAS. Inventory. Nov. 1801. Apprs: James Bright, Nicholas Smith, William Ford.

CANDOGRIFF, CHRISTOPHER. Inventory. May 1802.

CLARK, WILLIAM. Inventory. Feb. 1801

CLERM, PHILIP. Inventory. Feb. 9, 1801

CROSS, RICHARD. June 5, 1805. August C.C. 1805. Dau: Sarah Cross. Should dau. die negroes are to have their freedom. Ex: William Cross (father), Agnes Cross (mother). Wit: Samuel Mc Kinley, Thomas Lawson, Mary Cross.

DUNCAN, SAMUEL Inventory. June 1808. Apprs: David White, Sr., Jesse Ford.

DUPUY, MARY. Guardian of Washington and Polly Samuell, orphans of William Samuell. Aug. 18, 1806.

ELLISON, WILLIAM. Apr. 18, 1801. March 1803. Wife: Elizabeth. Children: Thomas, John, Gean, Margaret, Agnes. Ex: William Neal, Thomas Robertson, Elizabeth Ellison (wife). Wit: John Harris, Abraham Ball, Daniel Adams.

ERWIN, WILLIAM. Inventory. Feb. 12, 1801. Apprs: Jess Pringle, Nicholas Smith, Peter Kerlin.

ETHERON, JOHN. Inventory. August 1806.

FORD, WILLIAM. Inventory. March, 1805.

GOODE, REBECCA. Inventory. August 21, 1805. Apprs: Henry Bartlett, William Bartlett (sons-in-law). Children: Joel, Lemala, Richard.

GOODE, RICHARD. April 20, 1801. June C.C. 1801. Of Wythe County, Virginia. Wife: Rebecca. Children: Betty, Isan, Charles, Anna, Dice, Margaret, children of second wife Rebecca. Samuel, Richard, sons of first wife. Ex: wife, Peter Forde, John Jean.

GREEN, ISAAC. Inventory. Sept. 4, 1809. Admr: Caty Green.

GREEN, CATY. Inventory. Nov. 14, 1810. Admr: Abraham Wainscott.

HALL, DAVID. Nov. 22, 1805. Jan. C.C. 1807. Legatees: Samuel Hall (bro.),

Isaac Rees (friend), David Hall (father), mentions sisters but does not name them. Ex: James Hayden, Joseph Dupuy. Wit: Francis Hayden, Thomas Rees, Elizabeth Mitchell.

HARMON, MATHAIS. March 9, 1811. March C.C. 1812. Wife: Mary. Sons: John, Henry, George. Ex: Alexander Scott, George Miller. Wit: Charles Dorsey, Jr., Robert White, Robert League.

HENSLEY, FOSTER. Inventory. July 1812. Apprs: Reuben Gatewood, James Underwood, William Gatewood.

HILL, JOEL. Inventory. Jan. 4, 1809. Apprs: Reuben Pemberton, Abraham Frunk, Matthew Johnson, John Smith.

HILT, JOE. Inventory. Dec. 1808.

HUMBLE, MICHAEL. August 5, 1818. Sept. 1818. Wife: Peggy. Children: Fortunatus, Nancy, Patsy, Sally. Ex: Benjamin Whitson, James West. Book Two.

HUSTON, WILLIAM. Inventory. Oct. 16, 1804.

LAMAR, JAMES. Inventory. March 2, 1808. Apprs: Nathaniel Tracy, Jesse Ford.

MARSHALL, WILLIAM. Dec. 18, 1806. Dec. C.C. 1807. Wife: Mary Ann. Children: Lewis, George, William, Martin, Elizabeth Ballow, Mary Ann, Susanna, Jane. Ex: wife, sons Lewis, Martin. Wit: Jonathan Jones, Jesse Rice, John Ford.

MARSHALL, WILLIAM. Inventory. April 23, 1810. Admr: John Marshall.

MC CLELLAND, JOSEPH. June 19, 1810. Feb. C.C. 1811. Estate to wife Sarah. Ex: wife. Wit: John Wiley, James Chapman, James P------.

MC GUIRE, LAURANCE. April 3, 1804. June, 1808. Wife: not named. Children: Luke, Aaron, Abigail, Minerva. Wit: John Randall, William Wiley.

MEEK, JOHN. May 1, 1801. Dec. 1803. Wife: Margaret. Sons: Basel, John, Joshua. Daus: Sarah, Terah, Patience, Rachel, Tempey. Ex: wife, Jacob Meeks.

MOONEY, JAMES. Sept. 2, 1802. April 1804. Wife: Mentioned but not named. Dau: Mary Everton. Sons: William, Isaac, Joseph. Wit: James Pringle, Martha Smith.

MOONEY, SARAH. August 5, 1808. Nov. 1808. Daus: Mary, Nancy. Ex: dau. Mary. Wit: Joseph Young, Nathan Allen, Elijah Sutton.

MOORE, ANNE. Inventory. May 22, 1812.

NEVILLE, THOMAS. March 11, 1806. July 1806. Wife: Mary. Daus: Sally, Helen, Betsy, Mary, Kitty, Jency, Nancy. Sons: Thomas, Stewart, Robert, George. Ex: John Stewart, John Randall. Wit: Benjamin Perry, Joseph Montgomery.

PARKHURST, EZEKIEL. Jan. 10, 1801. August 6, 1801. Wife: Abiel. Ex: wife. Wit: Samuel Nelson, Nancy Nelson.

PERKINS, JOHN. Dec. 4, 1808. Feb. 1809. Children: Henry, Patsy Lawson, Samuel, John, Joseph, Jane, Polly. Wit: Samuel Young, George Hawkins.

RICE, WILLIAM. April 28, 1807. July 1807. Estate to brother John Rice. Ex: bro. John Rice. Wit: S. Hancock, Robert Samuells, John Sanders.

RICH, ISAIAH. Nov. 20, 1798. April 1800. Wife: Mary. Daus: Sally Edeman, Polly, Rebecca. Sons: John, Samuel, Isaiah, Amos. Ex: wife. Wit: Jesse Baker, Elizabeth Whicks, Samuel Brockman.

ROBERTS, PHILIP. Inventory. Oct. 9, 1802.

SAMUELL, WILLIAM, SR. Oct. 7, 1807. --------. Wife: Frances. Daus: Sarah Vaughn (late wife of Edmund Vaughn, Elizabeth Pemberton (wife of Henry P.), Fanny Goodwin, Agatha Bullard, Phebe Montjoy. Sons: Reuben, John, William. Gr.chld: Children of son William. Ex: wife, sons Reuben and John. Wit: John Rice, Josiah Durett.

SHACKLEFORD, FRANCIS. Sale. Dec. 30, 1807.

SHAW, RICHARD. Inventory. Dec. 7, 1799. Apprs: Robert Lawson, G. Calhoon.

SMITH, AGNES. Inventory. Oct. 1803.

SMITH, CHARLES. Inventory. Nov. 1803.

STUBB (STULL), WILLIAM. March 30, 1807. Admr: Jeremiah Farmer. James Miller made oath before J. P. that he heard William Stubb say he got 12 skins and acknowledged sending four bottles of whiskey.

THURSTON, CHARLES. Inventory. Feb. 13, 1809. Apprs: H. Duncan, J. Greathouse, Cuth. Bullock.

TUCKER, JOHN. Sale. Sept. 15, 1811. Admr: James Tucker.

WHITE, ARCHIBALD. Inventory. Oct. 1803. Admr: Dorcas Boone and hus. Edward.

HENRY COUNTY

BOOK B

Ball, Thomas
Batts, Thomas
Bartlett, Foster
Bawyer, Coonrod
Barnhall, Robert
Bartlett, Thomas
Bartlett, Jane
Bartlett, James
Baxter, Frances
Batts, Thomas
Bell, Richard
Bezley, Robert
Bergin, (guardian)
Bergin, George
Blackhammon, William
Bonta, Abraham
Bonta, Peter
Brown, Brazela
Britt, (Brite)
Brown, (sett)
Brown, Nathaniel
Bryon, Morgan
Bryans, (admr) (sett)
Brown, Nathaniel
Buckhanon

Cable, William
Chadwell, Nicholas
Clark, Aarm.
Clayton, (guardian)
Clark, Laurence
Colbert, Daniel

Douthet, Thomas
Duncan, James
Dupuy, Joseph
Duncan, William
Dupuy, John
Durrett, William

Edson, Edward
Ellison, Glavin
Estis, Joseph
Evans, John
Edwin, Joseph

Farley, Horest
Farmer, Jeremiah
Forbin, Robert

Forbis, Mary
Ford, Joseph

Galbreath, William
Gregg, Samuel

Harmon, John
Hayden, James
Hawkins, John
Hall, William
Hensley, Foster
Hitt, Elizabeth
Houston, Robert
Huston, Michael
Humble, Michael
Hughes, William
Humphries, Reuben

James, Daniel
Jones, Charles
Johnston, Rice

Irvin, Temperance

Kendle, David
Kiplants, John
Kindle, Peter
King, William
Kelly, William
Keiser, Frederick

Ladd, James
Little, Amos
Lowe, William
Lockhart, William

Mc Clane, John
Mc Dowell, William
Middleton
Mitchell, Margaret
Morgan, Mordecai
Morgan, Peter
Moodys, Blank
Mooly, John
Moore, William

Nichols, Abraham

Ogg, Thomas

Oliver, Prestley
Owen, Sally.

Parker, Harvey,
Partchurd, James
Piles, James
Prior, Samuel

Ransdell, Edward
Rees, Isaac
Rice, William
Robert, John
Robert, James
Runnolls, Jessie
Russell, John

Samuel, John
Samuel, Nancy
Sanford, Daniel
Sanders, Calvin
Scott, Elijah
Shepherd, William
Shieles, Alex.
Shackleford, William
Shannon, Robert
Smith, Margaret

Skidmore, William
Speers, Squire
Smith, Robert
Stewart, John

Taylor, Judith
Thompson, William
Thompson, Whitney
Thompson, Bethnel
Tucker, John
Turner, John

Vons, Peter

Waghe, Willis
Watkin, Evan
Weaver, John
Webb, William
Willis, William
Wilhoit, Isaac
Woodfield, (sett)
Woodens,
Woolridge, William
Woodson, Jesse
Wright, Francis
Wyman, Adams

HOPKINS COUNTY

BOOK A

1807 -- 1820

ADAMS, JAMES. Oct. 10, 1814. -----.1815. Wife: Agnes. Daus: Katy Bone, Polly Davis, Fanny. Sons: Andrew, Wilson, Matt, Robert, Alex, Jesse, James. Ex: sons Matt and James. Wit: John Adams, Thomas Adams, Wilson Adams.

ALEXANDER, WILLIAM. Nov. 10, 1814. ------. Wife: Agnes. Sons mentioned but not named. Ex: John Mathew. Wit: Eleanzer Alexander, Sr., Thomas Potter, Polly Alexander.

ANDERSON, ANDREW. August 13, 1817. Oct. 1817. Bro. Thomas, nephew Joseph, son of brother Thomas. Wife: sarah. Mother: Elizabeth Anderson. Ex: wife. Wit: Nancy and Thomas Browder.

ASHLEY, GEORGE. Jan. 7, 1817. April 1817. Wife: Alcey. Son: George. Daus: Belinda, Lelia Showmaker. Wit: Argyle Ashley, Beachly Jackson, Jesse Smith.

ASHLEY, ENNIS. Oct. 21, 1811. Stephen Ashley, Admr.

ASHLEY, ELENOR. Nov. 1811. Apprs: Stephen Ashley, Thomas Prayther, John Combs. Admr: Arggle Ashley, Robert Ashley.

ASHLEY, JEMINA, widow of Enos. Dower. Jan. 10, 1810. Apprs: Thomas Adam, Reuben Berry, George Tinnon.

ASHLEY, JANE. August 14, 1820. Widow of Henry Ashley. Children: Jane, Henry, Lettie, Thomas, Samuel, Tabitha, Patsy. Guardian: Wyatt Cox.

ASHLEY, A. Inventory. 1808. Apprs: George Ashley, Linn Brainon, Ben Slack, Enos Ashley.

BELL, ANDREW. Guardian for children of Benjamin Knox. ----1807. Polly Knox, wife of Benjamin Knox.

BERRY, EDWARD. Nov. 11, 1816. Inventory. Admr: Patsy Berry.

BOURLAND, WILLIAM. Jan. 2, 1800. Oct. 1807. Wife: Martha. Children mentioned but not named. Ex: Sam Browder, John Bourland.

BROWDER, HENRIETTA. Nov. 10, 1817. ------. Dower. Widow of Herbert. Apprs: Edmund Slaton, James Hicklin, Isham Browder.

BROWDER, THOMAS. Inventory. March 8, 1813. Widow, Rebecca. Apprs: Thomas Adams, Horatio Peacock, George Frigate.

CHRISTIAN, GILBERT. Aug. 6, 1812. Nov. 1812. Wife: Lucy. Children:Lucy, Gilbert, Patsy, Pamelia, Benjamin, Philemon, Richard. Ex: sons Benjamin, Philemon, Richard. Wit: E. Givens, William Owens.

CLARK, POLLY. 1813. Guardian for John Ruby.

CLARK, JOHN. April 1813. Inventory.

CLARK, EDWARD. Inventory. May 1818. Appraised Oct. 1818.

CROWLEY,. Inventory. 1814. Apprs: John Ashley, John Ramsey, R. Owens.

DOBYNS, EDWARD. Feb. 28, 1817. May 1817. Wife: Sarah. Children: Fidelia, Sally, Jensetta, Eliza, Edwards, Washington. Ex: wife. Wit: Thomas Halin, Lucy Jones.

DUNCAN, JESSE. Sept. 9, 1818. Dec. 1818. Children: Jane, Polly, William, Robert. Ex: son James.

EANS, MARY. July 5, 1819. Nov. 1820. Gr.children: (?), Edward Harris, George Harris, Elizabeth, Polly Harris, Charles Harris, Benjamin Harris, Rebecca, John. Ex: Asel Wier, William Wier, William Owen. Wit: James Thompson, Theodore F. Posy.

EARLE, ANNA. ----1812. Dower, widow of Baylis Earle. Apprs: George Ashley, John Harvey, Sam Woodrow.

EARLE, THOMAS. Dec. 31, 1813. Inventory. Apprs: Lemuel Harvey, Elias G. Smith, John Bone.

FOX, JAMES. June 22, 1811. -----. Children: Elizabeth, Titus, Allen. Ex: Sons. Wit: James Fox, Daniel Fox, Ebenenzer Bourland.

HALL, CALEB. Guardian to heirs of James Davis. James and Nancy Davic. Dec. 25, 1807.

HENDERSON, JOSEPH. May 1814. Inventory. Apprs: John Montgomery, Mathew Stephenson, William Martin, William Given.

HERALD, KEDAR. July 18, 1819. Oct. 1819. Children: Sally, Abner. Ex: Elenezer Givens, Robert Robertson. Wit: E. Givens, Thomas Givens.

HEWLETT, REBECCA. Jan. 30, 1819. Apprs: Thomas Adams, Horatio Peacock, James Foley, James White.

HOWELL heirs, Jalson Gibson, guardian. Oct. 1817. Apprs: William Ward, William Wilson

HOLLINGSWORTH, ROBERT. Inventory. Division of land, surveyed Sept. 14, 1808. Children: John, Robert, Joseph, James, Hannah, Elizabeth, Susannah, Hester.

HOWELL, WILLIAM. May 3, 1808. Inventory. Apprs: Reuben Berry, George Tinnon, Lewis Braiston.

JACKSON, JOSEPH. Nov. 13, 1813. Jan. 1814. Wife: Elizabeth. Sons: Isaiah, Jackson, Christopher, Nathan, John. Ex: Christopher Jackson, John Croft. Wit: Abel and Joshua Teague, Martin Croft.

KARR, JAMES. June 4, 1812. Inventory. Admr: William and Robert Karr.

KARR, ZILPAH. May 11, 1814. Dower. Widow of James. Apprs: Thomas Hill,

James Crabtree, John Malin.

KNOX, BENJAMIN. ----1816. Orphan of Benjamin Know, Sr., guardian appointed by the court.

LAFOON, MARK. May 6, 1806. Oct. 1809. Wife: Sally. Ex: John and Ebenezer Bourland. Wit: Noah Fox, Rutherford Lafoon.

LEEPER, JOHN. Jan. 1812. July 1812. Wife: Nancy. Sons: Samuel, James. Daus.: Capia, Rachel. Ex: sons James and Samuel. Wit: William Black, Mesheck Lewellyn, Samuel Giles.

LEE, GEORGE. ---- 1814. Inventory. Admr: Nickolas Anderson. Apprs: Solomon Silkwood, Peter Matthew, William Berry, Garton B. Maupin.

LINN, JOHN. March 15, 1810. May 1810. (Name is indexed as Simms). Wife: Anna Linn. Son: Starling Linn. Dau: Anna, three other children but names not given. Ex: John Mathews. Wit: John Edrington, John Wilson, James Mathews.

MENSER, DANIEL. August 28, 1810. Nov. 1810. Wife: -----. Children: Jonas Menser. Ex: Thomas Mc Caryl. Wit: John Mc Carol, Robert Holderberg.

MURPHY, STEPHENS. Feb. 15, 1810. -------. Wife: Hannah. Children: Polly, Charles, Stephen, John, Lydia, Sarah, Mitty, Eunice. Ex: wife.

NIXON, WILLIAM. Nov. 18, 1808. Nuncupative will. Legatees: Bro. Scarlet Nixon. Proved by oath of Martha Mosely and Annie Earle.

OLYNIN, JOHN. March 5, 1814. Inventory. Apprs: Lemuel Harvey, John Bone, Harbert Browder.

ORTON, EDWARD. Oct. 15, 1815. Jan. 1817. Wife: Anna. Sons: Robert, Thomas, William, Elijah. Daus: Rebecca, Patsy, Anna Nancy Hooker, Letty Campbell, Polly Adkerson. Ex: Samuel Woodson, Robert Orton. Wit: Argyle Ashley, Thomas Prather.

PARKER, DANIEL. -----1807. Inventory. Apprs: Robert W. Gary, Richard Dogge, Thomas Stokes.

RAMEY, WILLIAM. Aug. 13, 1814. Inventory. Apprs: Joseph Baker, Robert Adams, Robert Newton.

RICHARD, PHILEMON. Oct. 30, 1818. April 1819. Inv. Admr: Travers N. Hill. Apprs: M. Cargill, A. Ashley, Thomas Helm, Alex. Ashley.

ROSS, JOHN. March 23, 1817. Feb. 1819. Wife: Lydia. Children: Silas M. Ross, Patsy, Wiley, John, Sheldred, Thomas, Betsy Hopkins, Polly Roon, Sarah Clark, Peggy. Ex: Thomas Adams, Beckley Jackson. Wit: Robert Ashley, Argyle Ashley.

SHOEMATE, BENJAMIN. October 30, 1813. Inventory. Apprs: Jonathan Arledge, Henry Ashley, Samuel Short.

SISK, THOMAS. Aug. 9, 1814. Feb. 1816. Wife: Susannah. Dau: Liddy, Son:

Arey. Ex: Barnabas Lisk, Travers Hill. Wit: George Wright, Stephen Gray.

STOKES, CATHARINE. October 25, 1818. Feb. 1819. Gr.son: John Tinnons. Dau: Mariam Tinnon. Wit: Thomas Hooker, Sarah Hooker.

TINNONS, STEPHENS. June 18, 1813. Aug. 1813. Wife: Sarah. Lemuel Lafoon, Sinthia Lafoon, Mark Lafoon, Hanna Branon, Peter Ashley, Willis Liska. Mentions first wife's children: Tiebitha, Dosha. Wit: Argyle Ashley, Thomas Roberts.

WICKLIFFE, BENJAMIN. Dec. 1, 1817. Jan. 1818. Wife: Polly. Ex: wife, Daniel Mc Gary, William Oats. Wit: Bryan Oats, William Wilson, William Mc Lanathan.

WICKLIFFE, SARAH ANN. Feb. 14, 1820. William Wilson, guardian.

WHITESIDES, WILLIAM. Sept. 3, 1807. Oct. 1807. Legatees: brother John Whitesides, father mentioned but not named., Joseph Henderson's children, Samuel Whitesides. Wit: Joseph Nation, Thomas Parker.

WOODSON, SAMUEL, Appointed guardian for Thomas and John Berry, April 15, 1811.

JEFFERSON COUNTY

BOOK A

1784---1812

ABBOTT, RICHARD. April 6, 1795. June 9, 1795. Wife: Elizabeth. Sons: John, Gabriel. Daughters mentioned but not named.

ANDERS, VALENTINE. August 30, 1803. Oct. 3, 1803. Wife: Catharine. Brothers: Jacob, Fredrick, George, Nicholas. Sisters: Mary, Elizabeth, Esther, Catharine, Susanna. "Peter Bruner bound to me by his father, Joseph." Wit: Adam Hoke, Elias Malott.

APPLEGATE, THOMAS. Dec. 25, 1806. Oct. 8, 1808. Legatees: Samuel, Hezekiah, Benjamin, Tunis, Elijah, Elisha, Joanna, Elizabeth Baldwin. (children or grandchildren). Wit: Hiram Malott, Peter Miller, Fred Miller.

ASKEW, JAMES. Feb. 5, 1805. Dec. 7, 1807. Legatee: "A beloved friend with whom I live."

ASTURGUS, JAMES. July 14, 1792. Nov. 5, 1802. Wife: Margaret. Sons: John, James. Gr.children: Margaret Asturgus, daughter of son Peter(dec'd.), children of son M----(?),dec'd. Wit: Alex. Steele, Ben Johnson, Thomas Johnson.

BATE, SUSAN. Sept. 28, 1798. Oct. 19, 1801. Sons: John, James. Daus: Phillippi Lewellyn, Catharine Wagner. Grandchildren: Maria, Elizabeth and Susanna Lewellyn ; Catharine, James, Robert and Throckmorton Bate, children of son James.

BEARD, SARAH. Of Somerset County, Maryland. Oct. 13, 1795. Oct. 4, 1802. Sons: John, Charles, Thomas. Daus: Rachel Moore, Mary Beard

BERGEN, PETER. ------ Oct. 17, 1803. Nuncupative. Proved by the oath of Rachel Hall. Legatees: William Edwards (son of Richard Edwards).

BLANKERBUKER, JACOB. Jan. 2, 1801. ------Nuncupative. Legatees: wife and infant son Samuel.

BAIRD (BEARD), MARY. Sept. 28, 1789. Oct. 19, 1801. Sons: John, Samuel, Thomas, Robert, Joseph. Dau: Martha McClure (wife of Daniel). Gr.dau: Esther, daughter of son Robert. Wit: William McClure, George McClure.

BLACKFORD, ZEPHANIAH. May 20, 1782. April, 1784. Legatees: John Blackford (father), Reuben Blackford (brother), Yeats Conwell (friend), Baptist Society, nieces Hannah Ruth and Phebe (daus. of bro. Reuben). Mentions land entered in the name of Levi, William, Oliver, Joseph, Reuben, Isaac and Henry Blackford.

BEARD, CHARLES. -------- Oct. 4, 1802. Legatees: brothers Thomas and John, sisters Mary Beard, Rachel Moore (husband John Moore).

BOSTWICK, TRUMAN. Dec. 27, 1806. Jan. 13, 1812. Wife: Catharine. Son: Solomon, other children mentioned. Wit: Thomas Stewart, Edward Taylor, William Dougerty.

BRANHAM, DANIEL. March 15, 1810. May 11, 1812. Wife: Nancy. Dau: Patsy. Sons: Julius, Richard, Elijah. Mentions brother Richard, also George Bohannon as uncle of son Richard. Ex: Isaac Howe, George Sturgeon, George Bohannon. Wit: Robertson Vaughn, Richard Branham, Polly Branham.

BRASHEAR, WILLIAM, Sr. Sept. 26, 1789. Nov. 3, 1789. Son: Samuel Mason. Daus: Mary Ann, Elizabeth, other children but not named. Wit: Anthony Phelps Joshua Wheeler, Joseph Brashear, Edwin Phelps.

BRECKINRIDGE, ALEXANDER. May 16, 1797. June, 1801. Wife: Jenny. Sons: James Robert, Henry, Brown. Ex: wife, Robert Breckinridge (brother).

BRENDLINGER, CONROD. April 5, 1806. August 14, 1809. Wife: Mary Ann. Ex: John Balts, Wit: John Miller, Hezekiah Coats.

BRYAN, JOSEPH. Nov. 20, 1804. March 4, 1805. Sons: Joseph, John, Samuel. Daus: Martha Boon, Rebecca Boon, Mary Howard, Susannah Hind, Aylie Howard, Phoebe Forbes, Charity Davis, Elenor Adams. Grandchildren: Aylie, Noah, Jacob, Willet Adams.

CATLETT, ROBERT. Dec. 6, 1783. April, 1784. Of Fredrick County, Virginia. Legatee: brother Charles.

CECIL, THOMAS. Feb. 7, 1807. Nuncupative. Wife: Nancy. Wit: William Lampton, William Dougherty.

CHRISTIAN, JOHN. Of Fayette County, Ky. August 1800. April 9, 1801. Legatees: Sam Brown, Leonard Fleming (cousin), Ann Fleming (of Virginia), Elizabeth Dickerson and husband, other sisters mentioned. Slaves to have their liberty at his death. Ex: Alex. Bullitt, Dr. Walter Warfield, John Pope. Wit: Mary Howard, Mary Parker.

CHRISTIAN, WILLIAM. March 15, 1786. May 1786. Wife: Anne. Daus: Priscilla Bullitt (hus. Alex. Scott Bullitt), Sarah Winston Churchill, Elizabeth, Ann, Dorthea. Son: John. Ex: Alex. S. Bullitt, James M. Cowles, John Brown.

CLARL, JOHN. Jan. 7, 1797. June 6, 1797. Legatee: Richard Taylor.

CLARK, JOHN. July 24, 1799. Oct. 1, 1799. Sons: Jonathan, William, John, George Rogers, Edmund, Tolin (dec'd.). Sons-in-law: Owen Gwathney, William Crogham, Richard Anderson, Charles Thruston. Grandsons: John O'Fallon, Ben O'Fallon. Ex: Ben Sebastian. Wit: John Hughes, Mastor G. Clark, Robert Moore.

WILL OF JOHN CLARK

IN THE NAME OF GOD AMEN. I, John Clark of Jefferson County, State of Kentucky, being at present in a weak and low state of health but at the same time perfectly in my senses and considering the uncertainty of life do think proper to make my last Will and Testament which I do in the following manner:

First, I direct all my just debts to be paid and satisfied as shall hereafter be mentioned and then dispose of remainder of my estate in following manner:

I give and bequeath to my son Jonathan and his heirs and asigns forever all the estate both real and personal now in his possession.

I bequeath to my son William and two grandsons John and Benjamin O'Fallon and to their heirs and asigns forever to be equally divided between them - share and share alike - 3000 acres of land which I claim under an entry on a Treasury Warrant No. 7926 made in the surveyors office of Fayette County on the 29th day of March 1783, which land has been surveyed and for which a patent hath been issued in my name.

I give and bequeath to my son Edmund and to his heirs and asigns forever 1000 acres of land situate, lying and being on the waters of the east fork of the Miami River which I claim under an entry on part of a military land warrant No. 307 made in the office of the surveyor for the Continental line on the 16th day of August 1787, also 1000 acres of same which I claim under entry on part of the aforesaid warrant No. 307, made in the office of the aforesaid surveyor for the Continental line of the 17th day of August 1787.

These entries are made in the name of Tolin Clark, decd., and my son Jonathan, the heir at law hath relinquished in my favor his rights thereto, also three negroes to wit: Peter, Venus's child, Seippo and Daphny, children of Rose, also the sum of money which my son Jonathan advanced to him agreeable to my request.

I give and bequeath to my son George Rogers and to his heirs and asigns forever one negro man named Levi and one negro woman named Venice with her present and future increases except Peter.

I give and bequeath unto my son-in-law Owen Gwathing and his heirs and asigns forever all the estate both real and personal now in his possession, also 1000 acres of land situate and lying on the waters of Poag Creek in the County of Logan, for which land I have a deed made by my son Jonathan, dated on the 24th of October 1796.

I give and bequeath to my son-in-law William Crogham and to his heirs and asigns forever one negroe woman named Chastian, also all her five children together with her future increase, which negroes are now in possession of said Crogham.

I give and bequeath to my son-in-law Richard Anderson and to his heirs and asigns forever one negroe woman named Kate, also one other named Phebe, also all children of said negroes with their future increase, which negroes are now in possession of said Anderson.

I give and bequeath to son-in-law Chas. M. Thruston and his heirs and asigns forever four hundred acres of land situate and lying in County of Shelby on waters of Clear Creek, being of the settlement part of my tract of my tract of fourteen hundred acres of land, also one negroe woman named Angella and her children, together with her future increase, which negroes are now in possession of said Thruston. I do give unto said Thruston all monies due from him to me.

I give and bequeath unto my son William and to his heirs and asigns forever the tract of land whereon I now live, together with the appurtenances thereunto belonging. Towit: my stock of horses, cattle, sheep and hogs, my Stoll and all my plantation utensils, the whole of my household and kitchen furniture, also the whole of the debts due me on Bonds, notes or Book accounts, except the money due me from my son-in-law Charles M. Thruston.

I also give to my son William one negro man named York and wife Rose and their two children, Nancy and Juba, also three old negroes, Jane, Cupid and Harry. I also give to son William the whole of my lands in the Elinose grant which said lands are deeded to my son George Rogers Clark. It is my will that my said son William shall pay all my just debts and also that he shall pay unto my two grandsons, John and Benjamin O'Fallon, when they shall be of age the following sums of money; towit: to John O'Fallon one hundred pounds, to Benjamin O'Fallon fifty pounds, all these debts and payments are to be made by son William out of legacy which I leave him.

I give and bequeath to my two grandsons, John and Benjamin O'Fallon, to them and their heirs forever four negroes, towit: Ben and Priscilla and their increase, also Esther with her future increase, which negroes are to be disposed of at the discretion of my executors to be hereafter named for the benefit of said John and Benjamin O'Fallon until they shall come of age at which time negroes are to be equally divided between them and delivered into their possession.

I do hereby appoint my son Jonathan, son George Rogers, son William, sons-in-law Richard Anderson, William Croghan, Charles Thruston and friend Benjamin Sebastian executors to this my last Will and Testament and I do hereby revoke all former wills heretofore made by me and declaring this to be my last Will and Testament. I have signed and affixed my seal this 24th day of July, 1799.

                 John Clark.

Signed Sealed & Published by
the testator John Clark as and
for his last Will & Testament in
presence of us who signed our names
in his presence and in presence of
each other.
    John Hughes
    Robert K. Moore
    Mastor G. Clark
Probated Oct. I, 1799.

CORNELIUS,WILLIAM. Nov.21,1800. Jan.19,1801. Wife: Catharine. Son:Daniel, should he die estate to John Philips and George Hawks.Ex: Thomas Johnson, William Johnson. Wit: James Carmolle,Samuel Reaugh,Philip Smith.

COVERTON,PRISCILLA(indexed as Covington).Dec. 4,1811. Dec.9,1811.Sons: Philip,Abel. Dau: Matilda. Gr.dau: Priscilla,dau. of son Philip. Wit:Fred Edwards,Joseph Edwards,John Whips.

COWAN,JOHN. August 23, 1807.Sept.,1807. Wife: Mary. Sons: John,William, James.Daus: Elizabeth,Margaret.

CRAWFORD, DAVID. Dec. 14, 1801. Codcil March 14,1802. Sept.20,1802. Sons: David,Reuben, Nathan,Charles,John. Daus: Sally Cooke, Elizabeth Davis, Nancy Jones. Wife not named. Ex: Chas. Taliaferric,David Warwick. Wit: John Pryor,William Pryor.

CUMMINS,WILLIAM.Sept.17,1795. Dec.6,1796.Wife: name given as Mary and Margaret. Dau: Mary,Jenny. SonS: William,John,Henry,Moses,Ebenezer. Wit: Robert Mc Intire,Joseph Shaw,George Pomeroy.

DANLEY,WILLIAM.Dec.12,1812. June 14,1813. Died at Vincennes,Ind. Legatees: Elias Dorsey Lawerence,Edward Brown,George Whips,Jr.,Corbin N. Dorsey, Ben Lawerence. Proved by the oath of W.F. Query.

DENNY,JAMES. April I, 1806.Sept. 10, 1808. Wife: Nancy. Sons: Edward,James. Daus: Polly,Synthia. Ex: Richard Dickinson. Wit: William and Patrick Taggart.

DORSEY,EDWARD. May 2,1804. Nov.5,1804. Daus: Anne(Polly),Matilda,Patience Luckett. Sons:Elias,Leaven Lawerence,Benjamin. Wife: Susanna. Wit: Ben Lawerence,Leaven Lawerence, Willia Hord.

EARKINSON,ELIZABETH. Jan. 15,1789. June 2, 1789. Daus: Ruth, Elizabeth, Rebecca,Nancy,Caty. Son: Ben. Wit: Richard Waters, Stephen Richardson, David Morgan.

ELLIOTT,JAMES.August 20, 1792. March 5, 1793. Legatees: John(nephew),son of bro.William,John(nephew),son of bro. Daniel,Robert Campbell. Ex: John Campbell,Henry Reed, James Moore. Wit: William Rhoades,Michael Dillion, William Beard,Daniel Scott, Chas. Scott.

FLEMING,MARTHA. Sept.9,1801.June 1801. Sons: Ben Rodman,James Rodman,John Samuel,Alex., Hugh Rodman. Daus: Jenny Rodman. Gr.children:William Pope Rodman(son of Thomas),Martha and William Rodman(child.of son John),Amy Rodman,William(son of Hugh). Wit: Joseph Ogslesby,Mary Rodman.

FLOYD,JOHN.-------March 4,1794.Wife:Jenny.Sons: William,Preston,George,unborn child.Dau: Mourning.Bros: Isham, Charles, Robert. Mentions father and youngest son of Robert Davis. Wit:William Pope.

FULLINWEIDER,PETER.Oct.22,1790. Dec.1790.Wife: Caty.Children: Henry,Elizabeth and unborn child. Ex: Jacob Fullinweider(bro).Wit: Martin Daniel, Eleanor Cooper.

GATEWOOD,JOHN. Feb.10,1795.July 7,1795. Sons:Fleming,James,Fullinton, John,Fielding. Daus: Catharine, Ann, Alsey, Clara,Sarah,Judith,Frances, Penelope. Ex: Abraham Hite. Wit: Ed Jones,John Brown,Samuel Bochin.

GALLOWAY,GEORGE. May 1,1785. March 6,1800. Sons: William,John, Joseph. Daus: Mary Jenkins(hus.Launcelott Jenkins),Margaret Pomeroy(hus. George Pomeroy).

GEIGER,GEORGE.Feb.22,1812. August 10,1812.Mother Elizabeth Geiger.Brother John.Ex: Dan Felter, John Edwards. Wit: Fred Geiger,Jacob Geiger, Jeremiah Gillman.

GOBAN, JOSEPH.(GODINS).Dec.22,1790. Feb.1,1791. Wife:Liddy. Mentions three sons.Wit: John Bobin,Paul Spears,Thomas Mc Clain.

GREGG,JOHN.Oct.25, 1791.Feb.1792.Wife: Ann.Children:Margaret,Lydia, Mary, David. Wit: John Perkins,James Ferguson.

GRANDY,GEORGE,SR.Sept.11,1783.April,1784.(First will recorded in Jefferson County).Wife: Elizabeth. Sons: Robert Samuel, Charles Felix,John,George. Dau: Polly.

HARRYMAN,CHARLES. June 15,1798.Nov.3, 1806.Wife: Hannah.Sons: Job,Josiah, David, Elijah,Charles. Daus:Mary,Rebecca,Elizabeth. Wit: Robert Ward,Drusilla Hodges, Catharine Lock.

HALL,WILLIAM.May 23,1801.June,1801. Legatees: John Brown and wife.

HARDING,HENRY. Oct.12, 1796.Nov.1,1796.Wife: Rebecca. Sons: Henry,John Wilmouth.Daus: Cathy,Sara.Ex: Moses Keykendall,Jonathan Nixon.Wit: Joseph Keller, John Netherland.

HAWKES,JOHN.Sept.2,1790. Dec. 7,1790. Wife: Catharine. Ex: Philip Smith, Thomas Minter. Wit: Thomas Mc Clain,Adam Mong, Thomas Minter.

HAWKINS,DAVID. August 5, 1786. Nov.7,1786.Wife: Alice. Sons: David,Henry, William,Thomas.Daus: Catharine, Sarah,Eleanor,Ann,Mary,Rebecca. Wit:Peter Lovell, John Mc Mahan, Joseph Enlow.

HITE,ABRAHAM.March 20,1787. Feb.20, 1790. Wife: Rebecca. Sons: Isaac,Abrm., Joseph. Other legatees: John and William Hite,sons of bro. Joseph;Hannah Van Meter and son Thomas. Mentions that his father ,Joseph Hite,has a law suit pending against Lord Fairfax. Wit: Vincent Williams, Alex. Doran, Isaac Van Meter,Thomas Neal,Daniel Ashby,John Bateman.

HITE,ISAAC.Feb.8,1794. March 4,1794. Wife: Harriett. Daus: Rebecca Van Meter Hite, Elizabeth Rigby Hite, Son: Jacob.Ex: Robert Brecenridge,Richard C.Henderson,Abraham Hite(bro.). it: Joseph Hite,Anderson Levington,Samuel Green, William Fitzgerald,Timothy Condit.

HITE,REBECCA.April 21,1809.June 12,1809. Sons: Abraham,Joseph, Jacob.Other legatees: Jacob Hite(son of Isaac), Isaac Hite(son of Harriet Bridgeford).

HODGE,WILLIAM.June 7, 1804. July 23, 1804. Wife: Peggy. Other legatee:Mrs. Bosque. Ex: Gabriel J. Johnson,Harry Duncan.

HOKE, ANDREW. Sept. 23, 1790. Jan. 4, 1800. Wife: Barbara. Sons: Jack, Peter, Leonard. Daus: Elizabeth(wife of John Pottorf), Barbara Myers(wife of Jacob), Clara Miller(wife of John Miller of Baltimore). Ex: sons Adam, Peter, Jacob.

HOLEMAN, NICHOLAS. March 14, 1791. June 1, 1791. Daus. of mother-in-law: Nancy, Sarah, Patsy, Jane Holeman. Ex: Zachariah Fisher. Wit: James Fisher, Samuel Fisher, George Holeman.

HOLLIS, WILLIAM. May 24, 1806. June 13, 1808. Wife: Nancy. Ex: Isaac Whayne, R. Slaughter, Maidis.

HOLT, JOHN. August 26, 1804. April 1805. Chld: Ben, Sarah McLahlan, Isaac, John, Mary, Nancy, Rebecca. Ex: Robert Tyler, Keener Seaton. Wit: James Anderson, George Hoke, Roby Maidis.

HUNTER, JOSEPH. -----. Nov. 4, 1794. Legatees: William and Asahel Linn, sons Joseph, Joshua, Archer. Wit: John Pope, James Stewart, Thomas Long.

HUME, JOHN. May 2, 1798. Oct. 4, 1802. Wife: Jean. Dau: Sarah Sturgeon and son John Hume Sturgeon. Plantation to Chris Young, if his wife dies plantation to go to her sons Peter and John. Children of dau. Mary Soverains to have two hundred pounds. Ex: Thomas Sturgeon, Robert Breckinridge.

JOHNSTON, DOROTHY. April 27, 1792. June 5, 1792. Sons: Robert, General, John. Daus: Polly Harrison, Nancy C. Johnston, other children mentioned. Ex: John Harrison, Michael Lacassagne.

JOHNSTON, PETER. July 31, 1793. August 5, 1793. Bros: James to have seventy five acres in Fredrick County, Maryland, mentions bro. Jacob. Wit: Abraham Decker, John Martin.

JOHNSTON, WILLIAM. Sept. 18, 1794. March 6, 1798. Wife: Betsy. Son: James Chew Johnston. Ex: Ben Sebastian, Thomas McMunn.

JONES, CHRIS. April 5, 1802. Nuncupative. Children: James, Robert, Mary, other children mentioned. Wit: James McCasland, James Farnsley.

JOYES, PATRICK. May 24, 1806. July 8, 1806. Wife: Nancy. Children mentioned but not named. Wit: Ludlow Clark, Truman Bostick.

KIRBY, SAMUEL. March 27, 1795. ------ Legatees: Miss Nancy Earickson, Nelly (dau.), James (son). Wit: Michael Lacassagne, Reuben Eastin, G.J. Johnston,

KENNISON, STEPHEN. ------May 11, 1813. "Starting on a campaign may never return." Mentions his father, sisters Eliza and Nancy, bro. James, nephews John Rice and Joseph Plasters, Sally Ann Rice. Ex: Abner Fields, James Earkinson. Wit: Gabriel Fields, James Farnley, William Earkinson. (Stephen Kennison's name was signed in German)

LEATHERMAN, CHRISTIAN. August 16, 1786. Sept. 6, 1786. Sons: John, Daniel, Samuel, Peter, David. Wife: Julianna. Ex: Christian Leatherman (father). Wit: William Pope, William Payne, Asabel Linn.

LEMEN, ROBERT. Sept. 10, 1786. Feb. 7, 1792. Parents: Robert and Isabella Lemen. Bro: Samuel. Sisters: Lucy Newland, Isabella Cox. Niece: Jean Stevenson. Ex: Jacob Newland.

LACASSAGNE, MICHAEL. July 9, 1796. Oct. 1797. Legatees: Mrs. Elizabeth Mc Clell and, Robt. Moore, John Walker,Sr., James Beauvis, Jenny Lacassagne (sister), John Cox, Cornelius Beatty, Stephen Ormsby, John Thruston, two mulatto children Charles and Lucy to have their freedom at twenty five years of age. Ex: Stephen Ormsby, Robert K. Moore, Cornelius Beatty, James Beauvis, John Thruston, John Thompson, Ben Sebastian.

LEATHERMAN, MICHAEL. July 8, 1812. August 10, 1812. Nuncupative. Wife and unborn child to have estate, if they die brothers Jacob and John to have property. Proved by oath of Peter Shrote, George Fredrick, John Miller.

LINN, WILLIAM. July 8, 1780. April 3, 1781. Wife: Letitia. Daus: Ann, Rachel, Theodatia, Lannie(?). Sons: William, Asabel, Ben. John and Josey Linn children of Rachel. If daus. Theodotia and Lannie (?) return from the Indians they are to have one thousand acres of land, but if they do not return the land to be divided among my sons. Friends James and Samuel Kibbie, John and Ben Earkinson to have twelve hundred acres below the mouth of the Miama. Wit: Charles Locke, Sanford Edwards.

LITER, HARRIS. Jan. 8, 1810. March 12, 1810. Wife: Elizabeth. Daus: Barbara, Sarah, Magdalene Berts (wife of Amos Berts). Sons: Jonas, Jonathan, Henry, John Beatty (former son-in-law). Wit: James Bates, William Booth.

LUCKETT, JOHN. Dec. 30, 1804. Jan. 7, 1805. Bros: William, Philip, Samuel, Craven. Sister Eliza Luckett.

MI MICHAEL, JAMES. DEC. -1804.--1805. Wife: Eleanor. Son: John. Wit: George Pomeroy, Joseph Dunbar, Nicholas Buckner.

MC MANNIS, JOHN. July 18, 1804. Oct. 2, 1804. Wife: Ann. Sons: John, George, James. Stepchildren: Ruth Williamson, George Williamson, Moses Williamson. Ex: William Welch. Wit: Thomas Stafford, George Bishop, Richard Mills.

MARDEN, ROWLEY. April 5, 1803. Feb. 6, 1814. Wife: Elizabeth. Sons: Rowley, Nathan, Abner, William. Dau: Lucy, Linney. Ex: William Chambers. Wit: Francis Slaughter, William Poulter, Jacob Fine.

MERRIWETHER, DAVID. Dec. 4, 1794. August 4, 1795. Wife: Mary. Children: Henry, others not named. Ex: William and James Merriwether. Wit: Mary Merriwether, Jasper Anderson.

MERRIWETHER, PATTY. Oct. 14, 1801. Oct. 28, 1801. Daus: Ann Hughes, Polly Merriwether, dec'd., Elizabeth,dec'd., Mildred Mitchell,dec'd. Sons: Valentine, William. Wit: Robert K. Moore, C.Prince.

MERRIWETHER, WILLIAM. Oct. 20,1790. Feb. 1,1791. Wife: Patty. Sons: William, Valentine,David. Sons-in-law: James Merriwether, John Hughes. Wit: John Clark, George Clark, A. Churchill, Henry Churchill.

131

MOORE, JAMES FRANCIS. July 18, 1807. Jan. 10, 1810. Wife: Elizabeth. Dau: Elizabeth Pendergrass (wife of Jesse Pendergrass and dau. of first wife), Cassandra Miller, Zeruah Jones. Sons: Hector, Nimrod. Son-in-law: John Jones. Wit: J.H. Davis, Ann Davis, Worden Pope, Levi Tyler.

MORGAN, DAVID. August 6, 1792. May 6, 1794. Wife: Elizabeth. Wit: James Palton, Samuel Kirby, Evan Williams.

MORGAN, ELIZABETH. Dec. 22, 1801. Jan. 7, 1802. Legatees: Morgan Morgan and David Morgan (nephews of late husband), Elizabeth Emmons, Peggy Tyson (sisters-in-law), Mary Stinson and Sidney Dougherty (sisters), Ben Tyson, James Prather, Worden Pope, children of bro. James McConnell (James, William, Francis, Mary, Betsy, Peggy), children of bro. William McConnel(James, Robert, William, Patsy, Mary Rankin McConnell, children of sister Sidney Dougherty (John, James, Peggy), Thomas Stinson (son of sister Mary Stinson). Wit: John Collin.

MYRTLE (MIRTLE), JOHN. July 27, 1801.---- Wife: Phebe. Mentions children but does not name them.

NEAL, DR. JOHN. Feb. 5, 1809. Sept. 11, 1809. Share of fathers estate to be divided among sisters Matilda, Sarah Ann. Library of medical and historical books to be kept for brother William. Ex: Richard Taylor, Martin Brengman.

OGLESBY, RICHARD. August 17, 1798. Nov. 5, 1799. Wife: Nancy. Children: Jesse Washington, Fredrick Ware, Matilda, Richard, Woodford, Rachel, Jacob, Willis. Ex: Joseph Oglesby, Nancy Oglesby.

OLDHAM, WILLIAM. Sept. 13, 1791. Dec. 6, 1791. Wife: Penelope. Children: John, Richard, Abigail, William. Ex: Richard Henderson, Richard Taylor.

PAUL, PETER. August 3, 1784. Nov. 1784. Wife: Eunice. Son: John.

PARISH, JOHN. June 5, 1803. Dec. 3, 1804. Wife: Easter. Daus: Nelly Holt, Becky Mason, Leah Costen, Sarah Dickinson, Charlotte Reed. Sons: Richard, Hezekiah. Gr.son: James Holt. Wit: James Moore, Charles Sherman.

PARSLEY, GEORGE. Oct. 27, 1804. Nov. 6, 1804. Dau: Susannah, other mentioned but not named. Wit: William Hawthorne, John Wallace, William E. Wells.

PENN, CLOE. July 2, 1812. May 10, 1813. Negro Nell to be free, money to be put in trust to provide for her when she is old. Ex: James Blain, James Moore, Rachel Moore.

PERRY, NOBLE. Nuncupative. August 14, 1809. ----1809. Wit: Andrew Hite, William Dougherty, John Bain, Jacob Getz.

PRINCE, SILVANIUS. April 26, 1808. July 11, 1808. Wife: Ann. Sons: John, Thomas, William, Edward, Albertus. Dau: Ann Allison, Nieces: Ann and Catharine Earickson. Mary Ross, Rebecca Wells (daus. Of son Edward), Ex: William Ellison. Wit: Edward Jones, Nicholas Stoner, R. Kendall, Thomas Prince.

QUARTERMOUS, JAMES. April 28, 1803. March 13, 1809. Wife: Elizabeth. Children: Elisha, Thomas, Nancy, James, Rhoda Saunders. Wit: John Moore, James Robb, Learn Cooper.

REAGER, JACOB. March 15, 1790. June 18, 1790. Wife: Elizabeth. Stepdaus: Nancy and Sally Colgahoon. "My four children, Henry, Maria, Sally, Jacob". Ex: Col. Richard Anderson, Major William Croghan.

REED, HENRY. Nov. 7, 1793. April 1794. Legatees: Eleanor Elliott, Martha Patten, Elizabeth Wise, James Reed (of Denny Co., Ireland), son James, son Robert, son Henry. Ex: George Wallace of Pittsburg, Andrew Kennedy. Wit: Thomas Baggs, Bartholomew M. Shane, Joseph McNutt.

RHODES, WILLIAM. No dates. Estate to wife Sarah. Wit: James Patton, Sam Vail, John Blanchard.

SEATON, RODHAM. Jan. 4, 1804. Dec. 2, 1805. Wife: Mary. Son: Thomas G., Kenner, other children not named. Daus: Sarah, Bettie K. Ex: Reuben Smith, John Asher. Wit: James Mundle, Kenner Seaton, Andrew Mundle.

SHAKER, CHRIS. Nov. 8, 1802. Oct. 3, 1803. Wife: Elizabeth. Children: George, Katie. Wit: Adam Shreader, Jacob Shreader, Jonathan Thomas.

SIMES, SIMEON. March 11, 1813. May 10, 1813. Wife: Elizabeth. Children: Germain, Rachel, Sally, Rosetto, one unborn. Ex: Isaac Whayne. Wit: A. Slaughter, Walker Pruitt, William Dubberly.

SLAUGHTER, CADWALLADER. Jan. 27, 1798. March 6, 1798. Sons: Ed Pressley, Francis R. Sons-in-law: Chas. Moorehead, John Churchill. Wit: Benoit Dement, William Sullivan, Daniel Donohoe.

STEWART, JOHN. Sept. 25, 1805. Nov. 4, 1805. Wife: Elizabeth. Sons: Isaac, James, Willis, John. Wit: John Miller, John Kelley.

STEWART, STEPHEN. ---May 11, 1812. Children: James H., Priscilla, Cincha. Wit: James Stewart, William Goodwin.

STUART, JAMES. Sept. 16, 1791. Feb. 7, 1792. "Entering a campaign against the Indians in defense of our country." Legatee: Thomas Richey, beloved friend. Wit: William Prince, David Standiford.

STROUD, JOSEPH. Feb. 27, 1813. March 1813. Wife: Polly. Wit: G. J. Johnson, Francis Moss.

TAYLOR, JAMES. Sept. 3, 1807. June 13, 1808. Sons: John Gibson, James. Daus: Elizabeth Pendleton, Mary Barbour, Ann Crutchfield. Bros: Edward, Francis, William. Wit: Richard Barbour, Richard Taylor.

TERMENT, HUGH. Of Caroline Co., Va. May 10, 1798. August 7, 1798. Bro. Washington to have land in Kentucky. Sisters Lucy, Sally, Dolly Ellis and mother to have remainder of estate. Wit: Presley Thornton, Rice Parker, Richard Taylor, Colby H. Taylor, Anderson Watkins.

THRUSTON, JOHN. Jan. 15, 1802. March 1, 1802. Wife: Elizabeth. Daus:

Elizabeth Taylor, Catharine, Fanny, Mary January (hus. Thomas January). Sons: Thomas Whitting, Charles, Alfred, Louis, Algeano (?). Other legatees: Charles Cary, bro. Buckner Thruston. Ex: Alex. S. Bullitt, Buckner Thruston, Edmund Taylor. Wit: Fort Cosby, John Collins, John Fipps, Rowland Fipps.

TODD, SAMUEL. Jan. 17, 1810. Dec. 1812. Wife: Jean. Son: John. Sons-in-law: John Craig, Thomas Crawford. Wit: Enoch Magruder, John Stonestreet, William Edwards.

TRANT, PHILIP. Oct. 9, 1784. Feb. 1785. Estate to John Moylan of Philadelphia. Ex: Richard Anderson, Patrick Joyes. Wit: William Johnston, Walter Davis, William Orr.

TULLY, CHARLES. ------March 6, 1787. Wife and children mentioned, but not named. Ex: Alex. Breckenridge, John Tully, Jr. Wit: William Floyd, James Floyd.

TURPIN, RICHARD. August 11, 1787. Brother Henry to have all property in North and South Carolina. Bro. Thomas and Jeremiah (bro) have the remainder in Virginia. Wit: George Shepherd, Peter Shepherd.

VAUGHN, ANDREW, Jr. August 16, 1784. Nov. 1784. All estate to father Andrew Vaughn.

WATKINS, BENJAMIN. Oct. 20, 1799. April 1800. Wife: Drusilla. Daus Elizabeth Ford, Sarah Shaw, Jane. Son: William. Ex: Jesse Ford. Wit: John Care, John Huckleberry.

WATSON, WILLIAM. July 31, 1789. Feb. 1, 1791. Estate to mother Eran Watson, of New Castle Co., Delaware. Mentions brother Thomas Watson and sister Margaret Watson. Ex: Jacob Newland. Wit: William Shannon, Samuel Shannon.

WATTS, JAMES. April 3, 1795. May 5, 1795. Legatees: bro. John, nephew James Lowery. Ex: Evan Evans. John Porter. Wit: G. J. Johnson, Robt. George, John Irwin, Stephen Blackwell.

WELLS, WILLIAM. Of Ft. Wayne, Indian Territory. Dec. 17, 1810. Dec. 14, 1812. Estate to wife and five children. Children by former wife: Anna, Rebecca, William, Wayne, Polly. Son Samuel Geiger Wells by my present wife. Ex: Samuel and Yelverton Wells (bros.).

WHITLOCK, CAPT. NATHANIEL BACON. Died Dec. 12, 1809. Jan. 6, 1810. Brother George to have property including the care of his son George. Proved by the oath of David Wade, Levi Taylor.

WRIGHT, SAMUEL. Dec. 30, 1811. June 8, 1812. Wife: Poggy. Children by first wife: Sally, Harvey, William, Richard, Zephaniah. Mentions two sons by present wife. Other children: Nancy, Peggy, Robert.

WOODBERRY, JOHN. Feb. 13, 1787. August 11, 1787. In the First American Regiment under Capt. David Segler. All my pay to Patrick Mackerson. Wit: Stephen Richard, Robert George.

YENOWINE, LEONARD. Dec. 26, 1806. March 2, 1807. Wife: Margaret. Sons: John, Peter, Jacob, George, Leonard, Fredrick. Daus: Betsy, Christina, Margaret, Madlena. Wit: John Evinger, Herman Evinger.

JESSAMINE COUNTY

BOOK A

1798 -- 1813

ALLISON, PETER. June 4, 1802. Sons: John, Thomas. Daus: Nancy, Polly, Campbell, Esthers Weathers. Gr.sons: John Weathers, Peter Campbell. Ex: John Campbell, Peter Weathers. Wit: John Lowery, George Smith, Wilson Hunt.

BARNET, JOHN. Inventory. June 1811. Apprs: Abner Young, Morgan Brown, John Greenwood, John Young.

BARR, ZACARIAH. April 1, 1812. Wife: Sarah. Sons: John, George. Dau: Agnes Buford. Ex: wife, sons John, George. Wit: Nathaniel Harris, Richard Dennis, Peter Poindexter.

BENNETT, REYNOLD. Inventory. Apprs: John Mc Kinney, James Overstreet, William Mc Cormell.

BOUREN (BOURNE), REUBEN. March 31, 1807. June 1807. Wife: not named. Son: Joseph. Daus: five, but not named. Ex: Samuel Price, Elijah Bourne. Wit: Daniel Bourne, William Bourne, Benjamin Scott.

BOURNE, FRANCES. June 2, 1803. Sept. 1807. Wife: Not named. Sons: William, Ambrose, Abner, John, Daniel, David. Daus: Lucy Lowen, Agnes Hudson, Tabitha White, Fanny Young. Gr.dau: Tabitha White. Ex: sons John, Daniel. Wit: Armistead Reed, James Reed, Samuel Reed.

BRUSTER, JAMES. Aug. 15, 1807. --------. Wife: Elinor. Son: James. Daus: Elinor Dunn, Sally Ervin, Jenny Ervin, Agnes Alexander, Polly Dunn. Gr. children: children of dau. Peggy Carr. Ex: William Allexander, Nathaniel Dunn. Wit: James Doak, Thomas Browning, Joseph Doak.

CARNS, JAMES. Dec. 22, 1800. Apr. 1801. Estate to friend John Flicklin. Ex: John Flicklin. Wit: Lawerence J. Daly, Robert Sherwood, Alfred Williams.

CHILES, JOHN. Jan. 4, 1813. Wife: Elizabeth. Sons: Henry, David, Daniel, Garland. Daus: Ann Stone, Elizabeth Gates, Susanna Hightower, Sally, Sophia Gates, Lucinda Gates. Ex: wife, Richard Hightower, Elijah Gates. Wit: John Metcalf, George Walker.

CLAY, SAMUEL. Inventory. Jan. 31, 1807. Apprs: John Blakely, Sr., Robert Shankland, Charles Duncan.

CLOSE, JOHN. Inventory Sept. 18, 1809. Apprs: Peter Poindexter, Zachariah Barr, Samuel Marrs.

COGER, MICHAEL. Feb. 19, 1801. Sept. 1801. Wife: Mary. Sons: James, Thomas, Michael. Daus: Elizabeth (wife of Matt. Anderson), Mary (wife of Elijah Cartmill). Ex: Joseph Crockett, Elijah Cartmill, John Barkly. Wit: Joseph Crockett, Bennett Henderson, John Mc Knight.

CUNNINGHAM, WALTER. June 7, 1807. ------. Wife: Jean. Son: John. Daus: Jean, Isabella, Mary Lowry (wife of Robert Lowrey),. Gr.dau: Sarah Larmine. Ex: wife, William Drake, Robert Lowery, John Cunningham (son). Wit: David Steel, Jr., Enoch Chambers, Samuel Steel.

DAVENPORT, JAMES, (JONAS). April 5, 1802. Aug. 1802. Wife: Alice. Sons: Samuel, William. Daus: Polly, Nancy, Elizabeth. Ex: wife, George Walker. Wit: John Carrol, Thomas Fletcher, George Walker.

DICKERSON, MARTIN. July 21, 1810. --------. Sons: David, Lewis, George, William, Fountain. Daus: Fanny Mc Clure, Nancy Jackson (hus. David), Polly. Ex: --------. Wit: William Mc Dowell, John Thomas.

DILLIN, THOMAS. July 27, 1796. Sept. 1803. Sons: Stewart, Squire. Daus: Margaret, Jane, Nancy, Sarah, Elizabeth, Mary Mc Cabe, Ezabelle, (wife). Ex: Charles West, John Mc Kinney. Wit: Frances Dallam, John Cutright, M. Wealch.

DUNN, JAMES. Nov. 6, 1806. Feb. 1808. Wife: Martha. Sons: James, Nathaniel, Alexander. Daus: Jean Spears, Elinor Dunn (widow of son Samuel). Gr. children: John Carson, Alexander Carson, Jenny Carson, Henry Doak, Martha Woods, Jean Spears. Ex: Nathaniel Dunn (son), Joseph Wood. Wit: William Garnett, James Garnett.

EDMOND, WILLIAM. Sept. 21, 1806. Nov. 1808. Legatees: sister's children: Mary Mc Milley (?), Rebecca. Bro. Samuel Edmon's children: Rebecca, Polly, Jincy, John. Bro. Robert. Ex: James Edmon (bro.), Hugh Scott. Wit: Ephiram January, John Young, Joseph Woods.

EMPSON, CORNELIUS. May 27, 1808. Aug. 1808. Wife: Hannah. Sons: John, Cornelius, Richard, Thomas. Daus: Elizabeth, Rachel, Sarah Stephens, Polly Mc Donald, Margaret Bryan. Ex: wife, Nathaniel Harris. Wit: Abraham Copell, Sr., Abraham Copell, Jr., James Risk.

FOSTER, JOHN. April 25, 1808. June 1808. Wife: Leanah. Sons: Pleasant, David, William. Ex: William Moore, William Organ. Wit: Robert Miner, David Speen, Robert Calterson.

FROST, EZEKIEL. Inventory. March 1810. Apprs: James Lockett, Shadrack Moore, William Sallie.

FULKERSON, ABRAHAM. April 6, 1806. Feb. 1813. Wife: Ann. Sons: Abraham, Ford, William, stepson Stonestreet. Daus: Sally Sutton, Nolly Smith, Betsy Speed. Ex: sons Abraham, William.

GATES, CHISLEY. Apr. 4, 1800. Oct. 1800. Wife: Susannah. Daus: Sally, Sophia, Lucinda. Son: James. Ex: wife, Elijah Gates (brother).

GATEWOOD, AGUSTINE. March 18, 1802. May 1802. Wife: Betsy. Daus: Fanny, Elizabeth, Mary. Son: Richard. Ex: wife, John Castleman (son-in-law). Wit: William Pollard, Edmund Bryan, David Oliver.

GATEWOOD, THOMAS. Inventory. August 23, 1811. Apprs: Jacob Sandusky, Nathaniel Evans, Ephiram Sandusky.

GILBERT, AGULLA (AQUILLA). Dec. 20, 1806. Feb. 1807. Sons: Isaac, Charles, Michael, Benjamin, Samuel. Daus: Elizabeth, Martha. Ex: Michael Gilbert, Benjamin Nickolson, Benjamin Gilbert. Wit: Ezekiel Gilbert, John Metcalf.

GILMORE, JOHN. June 16, 1807. Aug. 1807. Sisters: Martha (wife of Josiah Burton), Elizabeth (wife of Robert Simpson), Sarah (wife of Andrew McCampbell), Jane Farley, Elina Mc Campbell (wife of James Mc Campbell). Nephews: John Burton, John Mc Campbell. Ex: James Mc Campbell, Samuel Mc Campbell.

GILMORE, ELIZABETH. Sept. 19, 1804. Dec. 1805. Sons: John. Daus: Genet Gilmore, Susannah Gilmore, Elinor Mc Campbell, Elizabeth Simpson, Martha Burton. Ex: James Wallace (bro.), John Gilmore (son). Wit: Samuel Mc Dowell, Abraham Cassel, John Rusk.

GRAY, PATRICK. Aug. 14, 1812. March 1813. Wife: Margaret. Sons: Hardin, Lee, David. Daus: Magdaline, Margaret. Gr.children: Sarah Gray, dau. of son David. Ex: wife, sons David, William. Wit: James Baxter, James McKinney.

GRIFFIN, JASPER. Inventory March 1810. Apprs: James Higginbotham, Samuel Johnson.

HEYDON, JOHN. June 27, 1801. -----. -----. Wife: Lucy. Sons: William, Jeremiah, Elijah, Noah, Lewis. Daus: Susannah, Sarah Thomas, Betsy Brown, Thirza Nelson, Lucy Salee, Polly Heydon. Ex: William Heydon(son), Abraham Bowman, George Smith.

HOOVER, DAVID. April 14, 1813. Nuncupative. Wife: Elizabeth. Bros: Moore Hoover, Jonas Hoover. Ex: wife, Andrew Hoover, Henry Hoover,Jr. Wit: Andrew Hoover, Barberry Hoover.

HOWARD, SPENCER. Inventory March 24, 1800. Apprs: John Miller, John Kellar, Gabriel Madison.

HULSE, DANIEL. Sept. 11, 1804. May 1805. Wife: Dinah. Sons: Allanson, George. Dau: Diedania. Ex: wife, Walter Kerr.

HUNTER, HENRY. Oct. 15, 1810. Jan. 1811. Wife: Sarah. Sons: Nathan, Henry. Children by first wife not to share estate. Children of first wife: William, Charles, Peggy Bartlett. Ex: Samuel Hunter. Wit: Jacob Hunter, Philip Roberts.

JOHNSON, JAMES. Dec. 7, 1808. Wife: Sarah. Legatees: Sylas Johnson (bro.), Samuel Muldrone, John Muldrone (bros.-in-law), Robert Johnson (bro.). Ex: John E. Rogers, George Walker. Wit: William Walker, George Walker.

LACEFIELD, PETER. Inventory. March 1807. Apprs: Richard Lapon, Randol Walker, William Hayden.

LOCKHART, JAMES. Aug. 1, 1804. Nov. 1804. Son: Silas. Daus: Elizabeth, Rebecca, Sarah. Ex: James Johnson, James Dunwidie, Roger Patton. Wit: James Johnson, Zadock Cannon, John Eakin.

LOGAN, ARCHIBALD. Guardian for infant son of Samuel Davenport, March 1808.

LOWERY, NATHANIEL. June 2, 1810. Aug. 1810. Wife: Mary. Sons: John, Gersham, Thomas, William. Ex: wife, Peter Higbee, Gersham Lowery. Wit: Benjamin Webber, Ashford Hardy.

MC DOWELL CALEB. Inventory April 29, 1811. Admr: Eliza Mc Dowell.

MC ELHANEY, JAMES. August 11, 1801. Wife: Ann.

MC KINNEY, JOHN. Settlement. Nov. 1, 1811.

MINOR, THOMAS. Inventory. August 1812. Apprs: Samuel Johnson, Jasper Griffin.

MOORE, SHADRACK. July 1812. Nov. 1812. Sons: Job, Shadrack, Jeremiah. Daus: Polly, Peggy, Jency, Nancy Young (decd). Wife: Rebecca. Ex: Archibald Lofton, John Mosely.

MORRISON, WILLIAM. Inventory Nov. 1808.

MURRAIN, ALEXANDER. Sept. 29, 1808. -------. Daus: Martha, Polly, Judith Elizabeth, Catharine. Son: William. Ex: William Lewis, Thomas Lewis, James Curd. Wit: Nathaniel Harris, Peter Pollock, Patrick Noonan.

NETHERLAND, POWHATAN. Feb. 23, 1813. Nov. 1813. Legatees: father, mother, Benjamin, John (bros.), Patsy, Mary Ann (sisters). Ex: John Metcalf. Wit: John Kersey, Hervey Ball.

PATTON, ROGER. Nov. 10, 1811. Feb. 1812. Sons: Benjamin, Thomas, William, John, Martin. Daus: Margaret, Sarah, Elizabeth, Mary Ann, Easter Patton (wife of John Patton). Ex: John Perry, Hugh Anderson, Benjamin Patton. Wit: John Eakin, William Simpson, Benjamin Gilbert.

PIGMAN, CHARLES. Inventory. Sept. 1802. Apprs: William Price, William Morrison, Joseph Hoover.

PREWITT, JOSEPH. Jan. 30, 1808. Feb. 1808. Wife: Polly. Sons: Joel, Moses. Daus: Betsy Talbot, Nancy Rice, Peggy Howard, Judy. Ex: Robert Prewitt, Bird Prewitt, William Prewitt, Joel Prewitt, George Walker. Wit: Thomas Caldwell, James Erving, Mary Price.

PRICE, -------. Inventory Oct. 1808. Apprs: A. Logan, Robert Shanklin, William Hughes.

RAINS, JOHN. Inventory. August 28, 1811. Apprs: Richard Hightower, Francis Lowery (?), Benjamin Gilbert.

RYLAND, JOSEPH. Inventory. Dec. 2, 1811. Admr: Rosey Ryland.

SCOTT, JOHN. -------, -------. Legatees: Hannah Scott (mother), Sally Holmes, Nancy Gailey (sisters), Hugh Scott (brother), Simpson Scott (nephew, son of William Scott). Ex: Hugh Scott (bro.), Hugh Holmes, Thomas Scott (uncle).

STEEL, DAVID. Nov. 3, 1812. -------. Wife: Mary. Sons: David, Samuel.

Daus: Polly, Nancy. Ex: ------. Wit: Robert Lowery (?), Thomas Rice, Mary Lowery (?).

SMITH, ELIZABETH. June 1, 1807. Nov. 1808. "My dear children as I am just leaving the world this is my last desire that what little belongs to me may be disposed of (Viz): my negro girl Brady and my beds and beddings and cloathes to my trusty and deserving granddaughter Ann Dallam. My negro boy to my dear Harrold Dallam. I can write no more. I am in misery. Your affestionate mother, Elizabeth Smith."

SMITH, GEORGE. Jan. 1809. March 1810. Wife: not named. Son: Philip, other children but not named. Ex: William Hughes, John Mosely. Wit: Richard Lafon, Thomas Hayden.

SMITH, ISAAC. Jan. 4, 1806. Feb. 1807. Wife: Polly. Children mentioned but not named. Ex: Jacob Todhunter, Abraham Venable. Wit: Isaac Thomas, George Armstrong, Robert Crews.

SPEARS, ROBERT. Inventory. Sept. 1806. Apprs: John Mc Kinney, Samuel Rice, John Howel.

STONESTREET, JOHN. March 1, 1803. --------. Wife: Ann. Sons: John, James. Dau: Nelly Darnaby. Ex: wife, Robert Campbell. Wit: John Lowery, Levy Walker, Thomas Butler.

TAPP, LATANI. March 1806. Inventory. Apprs: Richard Young, Abraham Venable. Admr: Lewis Tapp

TAYLOR, DAVID. Dec. 31, 1801. Feb. 1802. Legatees: John Taylor, Joseph Taylor (bros.), sisters unnamed. Ex: John Brunneley (bro.-in-law).

TEMPLEMORE, WILLIAM. Feb. 1806. Inventory. Apprs: C.W. Mc Dowell, Pat Gray, John Eakin.

TURNER, WILLIAM. May 16, 1807. June 1807. Wife: Action. Sons: Starling, Peter, James. Ex: sons Starling, Peter.

WALKER, COURTNEY. Feb. 7, 1804. March 1804. Legatees: Helen Call, Margaret Temple (sisters), Susannah Aldridge (niece), Andrew Walker (bro.) Jacob Walker (nephew, son of David Walker). Ex: George Walker (bro.). Wit: James Harris, David Walker, Jr.

WALKER, GEORGE, SR. Dec. 22, 1798. March 1800. Wife: Priscilla. Sons: David, Benjamin, Jacob, William, George. Dau: Nancy. Ex: William Walker, George Walker (sons). Wit: David Evans, George Walker, Robert Spears.

WEBBER, CHARLES. June 17, 1799. ----- 1799. Legatees: William, Philip, Archer (bros.). Ex: James Owen, Robert Cochran (?). Wit: R. Brashear, Jacob Rice, Peter Akin.

WEST, CHARLES. Jan. 1, 1803. Nov. 1812. Wife: Susannah. Daus: Philadelphia Summers, Janey Curd, Patsy Prewitt. Sons: Richard, John, Charles, Thomas, Clark. Ex: wife, Richard West (son).

WILKERSON, PETER. Inventory. April 2, 1801. Apprs: Francis Miller, Samuel Walters.

WILSON, ISAAC. Inventory. August 11, 1801. Apprs: Thomas Steel, John Hunter.

WILLIAM, JAMES. June 20, 1803. -------. Wife: Ann. Son: James. Daus: Nancy Walker, Frances Fisher. Gr.son: Matthew, William, Gr.dau: Sally. Wit: -- George Walker, John Perry, M. Bourne. Ex:

WILLIAMSON, THOMAS. Oct. 31, 1800. April 1801. Wife: Elizabeth. Children but not named. Ex: wife, her father (not named), her bro. Thomas. Wit: John Walters, Samuel Walters, John Suffrett.

WILLIS, SHEROD. March 3, 1806. June 1806. Wife: Mary Ann. Daus: Elizabeth, Jane, other children but not named. Ex: wife, John Ellenbaugh, John Hunter. Wit: Joseph Hemphill, Joseph Dickerson.

ZIMMERMAN, FREDRICK. Inventory. Sept. 25, 1805. Apprs: William Sheave, John Barry, John Barnett.

KNOX COUNTY

BOOK A

1801 - 1842

ANDERSON, JAMES C. Sept. 15, 1837, Oct. Court 1837. Legatees: Jas. W. Anderson, Catharine Anderson, Sinthha Aldridge, mother. Wit: Sam F. Miller and William Dezier.

ANDERSON, WILLIAM. April 1, 1827, Jan. Court, 1828. Wife: Elizabeth. Sons: John, Ambrose, William, Bradley, James. Daus: Cynthia, Lucinda, Marinda, Eliza, Jane, Susanna Herren. Ex: Eliz. Anderson, Ambrose Anderson. Wit: Ezekiel L. Jones, Nicholas Tresper, Armsted Prawitt.

ARTHUR, THOMAS. May 17, 1828. Oct. Court 1833. Son: Ambrose. Son-in-law Robert Gregory and wife Milly. Other legatees: negroes, Mary, Lucy, Jack. Ex: Ambrose Arthur. Wit: James Save, Lyne S. Kenningham, Wm. Baker,Sr., Benj. Gregory, Blaggrove Hopper, Matthais W. Cain, Coleman Rice. The children of Thos. Arthur not mentioned in will were: Jeanna McSpadden, Elizabeth Leash, Mary Baker, Sally Goodin, Susannah Stewart, Thos. Arthur,Jr.

BALLINGER, EASTHAM. Inventory. Feb. 13, 1806.

BARTON, SUSANNAH. Oct. 16, 1837. Oct. Court, 1838. Dau: Catharine Barton. Wit: Henry Barton,Jr., Peter Helton,Jr.

BARTON, WILLIAM. Inventory. August Court, 1840.

BLACK, JOHN. Inventory. May Court, 1822.

BLAKE, JOHN. Inventory. Sept. Court, 1810.

BARBER, JOHN. Inventory. Jan. Court, 1837.

CAIN, PETER. March 25, 1814. May 2, 1814. Wife: Cathren. Sons: Daniel, Jesse. Dau: Susannah. Ex: wife. Wit: Peter Engle, Jas. Parsons, Jno. Engle.

CAMPBELL, ALEX. August 10, 1810. Sept. Court, 1810. Legatees: Nathan Shelly, Elizabeth Shelly, Jacob Herman, Alex. Campbell (son of Jas. Campbell),Jas. Campbell, Wm. Campbell, Sam Campbell, Jeremiah Campbell, Eliz. Campbell, Jasper Campbell, Jne. Campbell, Alex. Campbell (son of Jne. Campbell), Suy Campbell, Catharin Campbell, Wm. Campbell, Nancy Campbell, Sam Shelly. (The relationship not mentioned.) Wit: Jas. Card, Brooks Smith, - Smith.

CAMPBELL, ARTHUR. May 3, 1810. Sept. 2, 1811. (A citizen of the state of Va., now at times a resident in the state of Ky.) Wife: Margaret. Sons: William John B., Charles Lewis, Arthur Lee, James, David. Daus: Elizabeth, Margaret, Mary Beard, Jane B., Martha C., Ann Agusta. Gr.children: Arthur Beard, Margaret Beard. Nephew: David Campbell. Ex: Jno. B. Campbell, Arthur L. Campbell, Isaac Sawyer, Chas. Campbell, David Campbell. Wit: Martin Beaty.

CAMPBELL, JAMES H. Feb. 23,1814. Nov. Court, 1815. Ex: bro. David H. Campbell. Wit: William Proffitt, Uriah Allison, William Beard.

CATHER, EDWARD. Feb. 1814. Aug. Court, 1814. Wife: Elizabeth. Sons: Edward, William. Daus: Peggy Moore. Gr.children: Isaac, Lewis, Edward and Elizabeth Sullan. Ex: Eliz. and Wm. Cather, Major James McNeil.

CATCHING, SAYMORE. Inventory. October Court, 1833.

CHESNUT, JOHN. March 21, 1805. May 5, 1805. Wife: Patience. Sons: John, Jacob, Abraham, Benjamin. Daus: Ann, Nancy. Ex: sons Abraham, Benjamin. Wit: Jonath McNeil.

CHICH, JOHN. Inventory. August Court, 1835.

COBB, ROBERT. ----Sept. 1834. Legatees: Radford Cobb, Isabell Cobb, mentions brother and sister but does not name them. Wit: Wm. Cunningham, John Aikman, Isaac Hide, Perry Manpin.

COBB, AMBROSE. Inventory. August Court, 1827.

COX, AMOS. Inventory. January Court, 1839.

COX, WILLIAM. Inventory. Oct. 27, 1801.

CRAIG, JOSEPH. Inventory. February Court, 1814.

CUMSTALK, JOSEPH. Sept. 14, 1801. May 3, 1802. Wife: Elizabeth. Sons: William, Joseph, Isaac. Daus: Susannah, Mary, Ann, Sarah, Elizabeth. Gr.child: Sarah. Ex: Elizabeth Cumstalk, Leonard Claiborne Shoemaker. Wit: John Cummin, John Slaughter, Sarah Slaughter.

DAVIS, RICHARD. April 19, 1815. Sept. 4, 1815. Wife: Elizabeth. Son: Preston. Son-in-law Joseph Belew and his children by dau. Polly. Dillian Asher, Jno. McNeil, Wm. Sims, Jas. Sims (sons-in-law). Daus: Nancy Asher, Patsy McNeil, Sarah, Betsy Sims, Susan Sims. Wit: Andrew and George Craig.

DELANEY, WILLIAM. Jan. 24, 1815. Feb. 6, 1815. Sons: James, William. Daus: Betsy, Jane. Elbert Howard and wife (relationship not stated). Ex: James McNEIL, Wm. McKee. Wit: Jona. McNeil, Benj. Tuggle, Eulias Howard.

DICKEY, THOMAS. Inventory. January Court, 1842.

DICKINSON, ISAAC. No dates.

DIZNEY, ELIJAH. Inventory. Inventory. October Court, 1835.

DUGGER, JAMES. Inventory. Sept. Court, 1814.

EARLY, WILLIAM. Inventory. January Court, 1814.

EDWARD, WILLIAM. Inventory. July Court, 1830.

ELLIOTT, ELIZABETH. Inventory. March Court, 1814.

ENGLE, PETER. Inventory. June 10, 1840.

ENGLE, GEORGE, Sr. May 24, 1822. June 1826. Wife: Elizabeth. Other legatee: Joel Vannoy. Ex: wife, son Peter. Wit: Joseph Eve, Ramon Warfield, Harrison Warfield. (Children but names not given)

FARRIS, JAMES. Inventory. Sept. Court, 1821.

FOLEY, MOSES. Oct.25, 1823. June 1824. Wife: Rachel. Sons: Martin, Hugh. Ten other children by a former marriage, names not given. Ex: Randolph Adams, Thos. Foley (son). Wit: H.G. Miller, Wm. W. Mitchell, Asal Elliott.

GOODEN, BENJAMIN. Inventory. January Court, 1828.

GREGORY, THOS. Jan.20, 1828. May 1828. Wife: Jeriah. Children: Ryal, Mackiah, Frances, Wright, Peggy, Joanna. Other legatees: Stephen & Elizabeth Meper, Fletcher Carnes, Nimrod Brackett. Ex: Jno. & Robt. Gregory. Wit: Austin Hagard, Jno. Tucker. (Will also recorded in Monroe Co., Tenn.)

HAYNES, JOSEPH. Dec. 31, 1822. June 1823. Wife: Dorcas. Sons: Richard, Jas., Ephiram. Daus: Eliz., Sally, Polly. Ex: Reuben and John Hendrickson. Wit: Thos. McClure, Jas. Templeton, Emmy Templeton.

HENDRICKSON, EZEKIEL. Inventory. August Court, 1810.

HERNDON, JOHN W. May 16, 1836. July 1836. Wife: Susan. Ex: wife, Greenfield Adams.

HOPPER, BLAGGROVE. March 4, 1831. May 1831. Wife: Rhoda. Daus: Polly, Nancy Ramtutler, Sally Vannoy, Dorcas Neill, Elizabeth Vannoy, Betsy. Sons: John, Joseph, William, Harris H. Gr.children: Anderson and Eliza Vannoy. Ex: Richardson Herndon. Wit: R. Herndon, Samuel Hutson, Lyne S. Kinningham.

HORN, CHRISTOPHER. July 27, 1832. May 1838. Wife: Betsy. Heirs of first wife, names not given. Sons: Isaac, Stewart, Thomas, Abraham. Ex: wife. Wit: Jas. F. Ballingul, William McGowand.

JOHNSON, DANIEL. Jan. 12, 1803. Aug.1, 1803. Sons: Joseph, James, David, Daniel, Isaac. Daus: Elizabeth Bundy, Hannah Ingram. Ex: James Johnson. Wit: Alex. Stewart, John Arthur, Priscilla Arthur.

JOHNSON, DANIEL. Dec.6, 1820. Jan. 1821. Wife: Rachol. Ex: wife. Wit: R. Herndon, Philip Coffelt, Landy Roy.

KEMPER, ELIAS. Aug. 20, 1835. Jan. 1836. Wife: Mary Ann. Sons: Archibald, William. Son-inlaw: Gabon Moore. Dau: Susan Kemper. Ex: wife, William Barton. Wit: Alexander Butler, James L. Woods.

LAMBERT, HUGH. Inventory. May Court, 1822.

LEE, NANCY. Nov. 8, 1841. C. 1841. Legatees: Ferraby Johnson, Nancy Cox, James Lee, Hannah Rose, George Lee, William Johnson, Isaac Johnson, Gabe Cox, Port Lee. Wit: P. B. Hopper, William Black.

LEWIS, JOHN. Inventory. June 1821.

LEWIS, WILSON. Inventory. Sept. Court, 1808.

MASSEY, JOSEPH. Inventory. March Court, 1815.

McLAURINE, JOSEPH. (Certified copy of Will of Joseph McLaurine of Cumberland Co., Va.) Wife: Susannah. Son: Albert. Ex: James McLaurine, Bartholomew Tuchart, John Hatcher. Wit: Joseph Jenkins, John and Elizabeth Hatcher.

McNEILL, JONATHAN. Nov. 21, 1823. Jan. 1824. Wife: Jean. Daus: Betsy Pitman, Jane McNeill, Polly Robinson, Patsy Farris, Pheba Howard. Sons: Thomas, Jonathan, James, John, Joseph. Ex: James and Jonathan McNeill.

MEPER, SAMUEL. Inventory. December 1837.

MILLER, JANE. Dec. 3, 1829. May 1830. Legatees: William Miller, Elijah Disney, Elisha Payne, Rachel Payne, David Miller, Elisha Payne's wife. Wit: Jeffrey Champlin, Rachel Cobb, Amy Garland.

MILLER, WASHINGTON. Inventory. November Court, 1813.

MILLS, ANOTHY. Inventory. Dec. Court, 1833.

MUNCY, WILLIAM. Inventory. September Court, 1808.

OWENS, EDWARD. Feb. 27, 1835. Dec. 1838. Wife: Nancy. Daus: Patsey, Polly, Sally, Connorty. Sons: John, William, George Bush, Thomas, Richard, Newton, Edward, Washington Bush, John Bush, William Owens (son of Jno. Owens), Edward Owens Cumstalk (son of Coleman Cumstalk). Ex: Nicholas Trosper. Wit: John Higgins, William Trosper.

PARMAN, GILES. Oct. 24, 1832. Jan. 1832. Wife: Pheba. Legatees: Mary Cathrine Mackey's children. David Curtis. Gr.son: William P. Black. Sons: Emanuel, Joseph, Giles, Jr., Jacob. Daus: Rachel Henderson, Elizabeth Girdner, Susannah Dunn, Frethia, Masse Black. Ex: Fredrick Cox, Frethia Parman. Wit: John Cox, William Floyd, Stephen Floyd.

PARKER, JAMES. Inventory. Sept. Court, 1821.

PHELPS, WILLIAM. March 22, 1821. May 1821. Sister: Jane Haynes. Ex: Richard Ballingul, Jane Haynes. Wit: James Ballingul, Wesley M. Garrett, J. Parson.

PITMAN, RICHARD. Inventory. August Court, 1814.

PITMAN, THOMAS. Inventory. August Court, 1814.

POGUE, JOHN. Sept. 14, 1840. Oct. 1840. Legatees: Martha T. (illegitimate child of Martha A. Tuggle. Ex: James H. Pogue, A.E. Pogue. Wit: Silas Woodson, Sam F. Miller.

POPE, THOMAS, Sr. Dec. 3, 1833. July 1834. Wife: Patsy. Sons: James, Lorenzo, Fielding, Thomas, Smith, William. Daus: Jane Tuggle, Nancy Woods, Mahala Pogue, Elizabeth Pope, heirs of dau. Catherine Jamison (dec'd.), heirs of Polly Johnson (dec'd.). Ex: James H. Pogue, Lorenzo and Smith Pope. Wit: Richard Tuggle, John Patton.

PRICHARD, THOMAS. Inventory. February Court, 1815.

RAINS, HENRY. Inventory. April Court, 1838.

RAY, NICHOLAS. Inventory. December Court, 1841.

RENFRO, JAMES. Jan. 15, 1833. August 1835. Wife: Dorcas. Daus: China Ward, Jermia Wallins, Ruth Gibson, Inda Renfro, Mary Moss, Jane, Charity Hogan, Theodosha Herndon, Olvis Johnson. Sons: William, James. Ex: William and James Renfro. Wit: James Love, Joseph Eve.

ROSS, HUGH. Inventory. Feb. Court 1835.

STEWART, ALEXANDER. Jan. 22, 1835. April 1835. Wife: Cathrine. Daus: Peggy Edwards, Ann Alsup, Euphenia Culton, Polly Wyatt, Elizabeth Walker. Sons: William, Isaac. Ex: Isaac Stewart. Wit: Wade N. Woodson, Anderson Stewart, Nelson Stewart.

STEWART, CHARLES. Inventory. November Court, 1809. Admr: Susannah Stewart, Ambrose Arthur.

SUMNER, LURENA. July 23, 1821. Dec. 1821. Son: John Sumner. Dau: Denzetta Sumner. Wit: John Y. Criswell, John Green.

TAYLOR, JESSE. Nov. 26, 1839, Dec. 1839. Wife: Lucretia. Other legatees: William Barton's infant daughter. Ex: Evan Jones, John Patton. Wit: Sam F. Miller, Asal Elliott.

TUGGLE, JAMES. Jan. 15, 1838. Jan. 1838. Wife: Nancy. Sons: James, Thomas, Thomas, Spencer, John, Jesse, Smith. Daus: Mary Tuggle, Martha Smith, Elizabeth Ballinger, Susan Pope. Ex: Spencer, John and Richardson Tuggle. Wit: Henry Pope, John Patton.

TUGGLE, THOMAS. Dec. 8, 1834. Feb. 1835. Daus: Sally and Mahala McNeill. Sons: Richardson, William, James, Benjamin, Henry,dec'd. Ex: Richardson Tuggle, John Patton.

WARD, THOMPSON. August 26, 1841. Oct. 1842. Wife: Samantha. Dau: Lavina. other legatee: Blakely Logan (relationship not given). Ex: Frank Ballinger. Wit: Sam F. Miller, Cornelius G. Faris.

WHITE, WILLIAM. Inventory. November Court, 1013.

WILSON, DAVID. Dec. 17, 1830. April 1831. Wife: Mary. Daus: Ellen Huff, Margaret Branton, Diana Kersilles. Sons: David, George S., John, Peter. Gr.daus: Diana Smith, America Wilson, Diana Wilson. Ex: Peter Wilson. Wit: Joseph Prichard, David Wilson.

WOODS, JOHN. April 8, 1836. Jan. 1837. Wife: China. Sons: James, Samuel, William, Nelson, John. Daus: Mary Burch, Charity. Ex: James and Samuel Kemper. Wit: James Renfro, Jane Renfro.

WYATT, Samuel. Inventory. August Court, 1835.

LINCOLN COUNTY

BOOK A

1781--1790

BALL, EDWARD. Sept. 29, 1788. Oct. 21, 1788. Wife: not named. Sons: William, Shadrack. Dau: Elizabeth. Ex: wife, son William. Wit: Joseph Helm, William Marshall, David White.

BERRY, JAMES. March 10, 1781. Jan. 15, 1782. Wife: Christina. Children: Elizabeth, unborn child, John Wilson (stepson). Ex: wife, Ebenezer Miller, John Smith.

BERRY, JOHN. August 10, 1789. July 20, 1790. Wife: Hannah. Sons: James, William, Joseph, John. Daus: Betsy, Polly, Hannah, Sally, Peggy, Jane. Ex: wife. Wit: James Piggott, James Kerr, Isaac Fallis.

BOWDERY, SAMUEL. May 1, 1790. Dec. 21, 1790. Wife: Elizabeth. Daus: Jemiah, Martha (youngest daus.). Ex: wife, son James. Wit: Francis Cutting, John Bailey.

BOWMAN, JOHN. Feb. 5, 1784. August 17, 1784. Wife: Elizabeth. Legatees: son John, bros. Abraham and Isaac, sisters Mary Stephens, Elizabeth Ruddle, Sarah Wright, Regina Durley, Rebecca Brinker. Ex: wife, bros. Abraham and Isaac. Wit: Joseph Love, James Cox, Richard Foley, Wilson Maddox.

BULGER, EDWARD. August 21, 1782. Jan. 21, 1783. Legatees: brother Daniel Bulger, Abrm. James, Capt. John Smith, Jonathan Drake, Thomas Guess. Wit: John Reed, Henry French, William Crow.

CARPENTER, JOHN. Nov. 10, 1784. Feb. 15, 1785. Wife: Elizabeth. Son: George. Daus: Mary, Margaret. Bros: Adam, George. Ex: wife, Conrod Carpenter, Adam Carpenter. Wit: James Coppedge, John Liter, Isaac Shelby.

CASSEY, JOHN. April 28, 1790. July 20, 1790. Wife: Margaret. Sons: James, Mathew. Dau: Agnes. Ex: Hugh Logan. Wit: John Magill, Hannah Barry, Esther Daugherty.

CHAPMAN, EDWARD. July 26, 1788. Sept. 16, 1788. Wife: not named. Sons: Edward, William, Lewis. Dau: Sally. Wit: Isaac Farris, Benjamin Talbert, Jerrusha Lovas, Daniel Chapman.

DUNCAN, ANDREW. March 25, 1784. Feb. 21, 1786. Legatees: Andrew Buchanan (son of sis. Eliz.), Andrew Craig (son of sis. Mary Craig), Jenny McKenney (sis. Jean's dau.). Ex: William Emiston, John McKenney. Wit: John Edmiston, Robert Harreld, John Buchanan.

FLOYD, DAVID. Sept. 12, 1787. Dec. 16, 1788. Wife: Sarah. Sons: Benjamin, George, John, David. Daus: Mary, Grace. Gr.dau: Mary Singleton (dau. of Sally Singleton, dec'd. Ex: sons Benjamin, John, George. Wit: John Bryant, Robert Singleton.

FROMAN, PAUL. April 28, 1783. May 20, 1783. Wife: Elizabeth. Sons: Paul,

Jacob. Daus: mentioned but not named. Ex: son Jacob. Wit: John Woolman, Christian Samet.

GILLAS, WILLIAM. April 2, 1783. April 21, 1784. Legatees: bro. Thomas and son William, Edward and Elizabeth Cathers. Wit: Jno. Jameson, Jas. Scott.

GORDON, JAMES. Nov. 16, 1784. July 19, 1785. Wife and children but not named. Ex: wife, Martin Nall, Edward Darnaby. Wit: Edmund Ware, Henry Ware.

HANNAH(HANNA), ALEX. July 21, 1785. Sept. 21, 1790. Wife: Isabell. Elizabeth Wylie, Jean Moffett, Margaret Galbreath (sisters). Bro: John Hanna. Ex: wife, Robt. Moffett. Wit: James Davis, Hugh Galbreath, Robt. Moore.

HARLAN, SILAS. Jan. 7, 1780. Jan. 22, 1783. Bros: Elijah, James, Jehu. Ex: bro. James. Wit: Jere. Briscoe, Charles Farguson, Jacob Harlan.

HART, NATHANIEL. June 27, 1782. Jan. 22, 1783. Wife: Sarah. Children: Simpson, Nathaniel, Keziah Thompson, John, Mary, Ann, Cumberland, Chinai, Thomas, unborn child. Ex: Thomas, David Hart (bros.). Wit: William Calk, Nicholas George, Nicholas Anderson. Inventory. July 20, 1784. Apprs: William Hay, Higgason Grubb, Haille Talbot.
"The late Capt. Nathaniel Hart of Woodford Co., thus wrote in 1840: I went with my mother, in Jan., 1783, to Logan's station (Lincoln Co.) to prove my father's will. He had fallen in the preceding July. Twenty armed men were of the party. Twenty three widows were in attendance upon the court to obtain letters of administration on the estates of their husbands, who had been killed during the past year. This is exclusive of the much larger number who were killed leaving no estate which required administration."
(Collins History)

HICKS, WILLIAM. Aug. 14, 1780. May 15, 1781. Wife: Agnes. Children: sons John, William, others not named. Ex: wife, Wm. Cleery. Wit: Jas. Davis, William Young, Sam'l Gordon.

LANKFORD, JOSEPH. Sept. 1, 1783. July 20, 1785. Wife: -- Children: Joseph, Sarah, others not named. Ex: wife, James Brown. Wit: Jas. Curry, Daniel Brown, Edward Taylor.

LINDSAY, JOSEPH. July 11, 1782. Jan. 21, 1783. Wife: Ann. Sons: Joseph, Fuller. Ex: wife, bro. William. Wit: John Kennedy, John Ray.

LOGAN, JAMES. May 23, 1787. July 15, 1788. Wife: Martha. Sons: James, Matthew, Hugh, David, Jonathan, Charles, Robert. Dau: Martha. Wit: Alex. Gaston, William Main, Mary Gaston.

McBRIDE, WILLIAM. Oct. 3, 1781. Jan. 21, 1783? Wife: Martha. Sons: William, Lapsley. Daus: Sarah, Martha, Elizabeth, Mary. Ex: wife, Jas. Davis.

McMURTY, JOHN. July 7, 1780. Feb., 1782. Wife: Mary. Sons: William, James, Sam'l. Wit: John Hutton, James Hutton, William McMurty.

MONTGOMERY, JOHN. May 15, 1789. March 16, 1790. Wife: Mary. Sons: Joseph, James, William, Thomas, Sam'l, Robt. Ex: sons James, William, Sam'l. Wit: John Montgomery, Nathaniel Evans, Sam'l. Montgomery.

POTTS, JOHN. Oct. 9, 1783. June 21, 1785. Wife: Naomi. Son: David. Dau: Sarah Burke. Gr.son: John Potts. Ex: son David, Thomas Harbison, William Shaw.

Radcliffe, Charles. Nov. 13, 1780. Feb. 20, 1781. Wife: not named. Legatees: 3 children, but not named. Ex: Daniel Radcliff. Wit: Azor Ross, Thomas Moore, Joseph Scott.

SHIELL, HUGH. August 24, 1782. Nov. 15, 1785. Wife: Ann. Dau: Catharine Harris Shiells. Ex: wife. Wit: George Muter, Mary Faunt Lee Roy, Thomas Lorie.

SLAIDE, STEPHEN. Feb. 26, 1789. April 21, 1789. Wife: Ann. Daus: Margaret and Mary. Ex: wife, William Walton. Wit: Andy Oliver, Joseph Horn.

SMITH, HENRY. Dec. 9, 1788. Sept. 15, 1789. Wife: Margaret. Sons: Henry, Liberty, Henry Garrot (stepson). Daus: Elizabeth, Seday Duff, Close Doal Smith, Sarah St. T -----(?). Ex: Samuel Taylor, Edmund Smith, Christopher Smith. Wit: John Bryant, George Douglas, Ezekiel Lacefield.

STEWART, WILLIAM. August 20, 1781. Jan. 21, 1783. Legatees: father, sisters Mary and Hannah. Ex: James Hunter, James Smith, William McBride. Wit: Clough Overton, Ebenezer, T. McBride.

SWAN, JOHN. July 12, 1780. Feb. 18, 1783. Wife: not named. Sons: John, Joel, Thomas. Daus: Elizabeth, Kittie (Letty ?). Ex: wife, Richard Swan, Jacob Van Matroe. Wit: Mary Hunter, Rebecca Rowling, Margaret Haycraft.

WILLIAMS, GILES. Nov. 28, 1787. June 17, 1788. Wife: Sarah. Daus: Sarah, Nancy, Lizzie. Ex: John Jones, George Smith. Wit: William Hamilton, Philip Thurman, John Fields.

YOAKUM, MATHIAS. Jan. 29, 1780. Feb. 18, 1783. Wife: Eleanor. Son: George Yoakum. Nephew: George Yoakum. Ex: wife, George Yoakum. Wit: William Walton, Peter Deyerle, Peter Heaney.

LINCOLN COUNTY INVENTORIES.

BOOK "A"

Adams James. August 8, 1785.
Arnold Mark. Oct. 20, 1785.

Ball Edward. March 9, 1789.
Berry James. Jan. 22, 1783.
Bowman John. Oct. 20, 1785.
Boughman Henry. June 2, 1783.
Bryen William. Oct. 1, 1781.
Bugler Edward. April 5, 1783.

Carpenter Adam. Feb. 15, 1785.
Carpenter John. Nov. 15, 1785.
Chapman Dianah. Nov. 14, 1785.
Chapman George. Dec., 1784.
Collins Aaron. June, 1789.
Crutchfield James. July, 1788.

Daniel Walker. Feb. 20, 1787.
Daniel Walker. Nov. 25, 1789.
Duncan Andrew. March 21, 1786.

Felan James. Feb. 14, 1784.
Fisher James. Feb. 14, 1784.
Floyd David. July 21, 1789.
French John. Jan. 18, 1791.
Froman Paul. March 27, 1784.

Garnett Anthony. April 17, 1784.
Gibson John. July 17, 1781.
Gillis William. June 15, 1784.
Goodnight Michael. May 21, 1783.
Gordon James. Oct. 18, 1785.

Hart Sarah. March 10, 1786.
Hart Cornelias. Feb. 10, 1785.
Hart Nathaniel. May 25, 1784.
Harlan Silas. June 14, 1783.
Hawkin Daniel. Feb. 18, 1783.
Henry John. Sept. 13, 1783.

Jack Samuel. Jan. 11, 1783.
Jackman Adam. Feb. 18, 1783.
Johnson Chris. April 19, 1783.

Kennedy John. Jan. 22, 1783.

Langford Joseph. Aug. 25, 1786.
Lindsay Joseph. March 20, 1783.
Lover John. March 4, 1789.

McAfee William. April 17, 1781.
McBride Frances. Aug. 12, 1790.
McBride William. June 27, 1783.
McCallister George. July 20, 1790.
McGrincy John. August 12, 1790.
McKinnley Andrew. April 17, 1790.
Miller Andrew. Aug. 28, 1784.
Miller Henry. April 5, 1783.
Miller John. July 17, 1781.
Mitchell John. June 21, 1785.
Montgomery John. July 17, 1781.
Montgomery William. July 17, 1781.
Montgomery Walker. July 1, 1790.
Moore Samuel. July 20, 1785.

Overton Clough. May 20, 1783.

Potts John. June 3, 1786.
Patterson Benj. Oct. 18, 1785.
Price Benj. June 20, 1786.

Robertson James. Jan. 23, 1784.
Rose Lewis. March 29, 1783.
Rutherford John. April 18, 1789.

Sherley Michael. Feb. 15, 1785.
Shiells Hugh. Feb. 23, 1785.
Slade Stephen. May 2, 1789.
Smith James. July 13, 1783.
Smith Henry. Oct. 30, 1789.
Stewart William. March 19, 1783.
Swan John. June 17, 1783.

Tansten Chris. April 19, 1783.

Williams Gillis. July 1, 1788.
Wilson John. March 16, 1784.
Wornel Richard. July 16, 1790.
Wright James. Feb. 18, 1783.

LIVINGSTON COUNTY

BOOK A

1799 --- 1818

ADAMS, JACOB. Feb. 19, 1815. May 1815. Wife: Elizabeth. Dau: Furnethy Turner. Ex: wife, Hugh Golleher. Wit: James Williams, Elizabeth Martin Golleher.

ANDERSON, ANDREW. Feb. 29, 1816. Nov. 1816. Wife: Rhoda(?). Dau: Sinthy. Sons: Thomas, Richard, Andrew. Wit: James Mitchell.

BERRY, SOLOMON. ------. July 21, 1818. Wife: Isabella. Children: mentioned but not named. Ex: Willis Champion, Henry Burgess. Wit: John Hardin, Samuel Ramages.

COFFUTH, BENJAMIN. May 3, 1816. ---- 1816. Wife: mentioned but not named. Ex: wife, Xpher Haynes. Wit: John Geshen, John Champion.

CRUSE, STEPHEN. July 5, 1816. August 1816. Children: Washington, Elizabeth Eliza. Ex: Richard Cruse, James Duff. Wit: James Johnson, W. Stewart.

DEAL, JOHN. Dec. 20, 1805. Feb. 1806. Estate to father and sister(not named). Wit: Alexander Anderson, A. James.

DOBBINS, HUGH. March 6, 1815. May 1815. Legatees: Nancy and Elizabeth Dobbins (sisters), Archer Farley, John Dobbin's children. Wit: E. Walton, Quincy Henten.

DUVAL, ELISHA. Feb. 20, 1817. April 1817. Estate to wife and children but does not name them. Wit: James Mitchell, W. Stewart.

FOWLER, STEPHENSON. Jan. 19, 1816. ------. Wife and children mentioned but not named. Ex: wife. Wit: Xypher Haynes, John Philips, W. Stewart.

GRIFFITH, WILLIAM. May 6, 1809. Feb. 1811. Mother: Jane Payne. Sister: Margaret Griffith. Other Legatees: James Hollurn, Joseph Hollurn, Thomas Payne(half bro.), Patty Baker(half sister). "To William Griffith of Ohio State, land in Virginia." Son of Edy Harris. Ex: James Ritchey, Washington Stewart. Wit: John Cole, Jeremiah Walker.

HALL, DAVID. Nov. 9, 1801. March 1802. Wife: not named. Sons: John, Hugh. Ex: wife. Wit: William Dobbins, John Conway, Valentine Conway.

HIGGINS, HENRY. August 28, 1811. Oct. 1814. Wife: Polly. Son: Henry. Dau: Kitty Davenport. Other Legatees: heirs of Aaron Higgins and his widow Sarah, Ann Harris, William Higgins(brother). Ex: wife, James Morrison, Daniel McEnney. Wit: James Morrison, Daniel McEnney.

INGRAM, JAMES. Oct. 4, 1806. April 1807. Wife: Caty. Children: mentioned but not named. Ex: Benjamin Ingram(son), Samuel Burton(son-in-law). Wit: Moses Ingram, Falton East.

JARRETT, WILLIAM. Feb. 14, 1814. August 1815. Daus: Rebekah Allison, Susannah Jenkins, Elinor Henthon, heirs of Ann Hardin(dau.). Sons: John, Thomas, Daniel. Ex: John Jarrett, Thomas Jarrett (sons). Wit: Samuel Glenn, John Scott, William Owens.

KAW, MARGARET. Dec. 2, 1805. May 1806. Sons: James, William, John, Robert. Daus: Polly Johnson, Elenor Hicks, Margaret Dunn, Sarah Briscoe, Nancy Karr. Ex: William Karr(son). Wit: Mary Smith, Jane Hardin, Thomas Johnson, Elizabeth Long.

KILGORE, BENJAMIN. March 22, 1802. Dec. 1802. Sons: James, Jonathan, John, William, David, Hugh, Samuel. Daus: Jane Adair, Elizabeth Wood, Isabel Greer, Polly Kilgore. Wit: Jonathan Greer, William Gilkey, Z. B. Hobert.

KILLOUGH, ALLEN. July 3, 1814. Feb. 1815. Wife: Margaret. Sons: John, Samuel. Dau: Sarah Holmes. Wit: D. Killough, James Taylor.

LEWIS, LILBOURNE. April 9, 1812. May 1812. Legatees: Charles L. Lewis (father), Martha, Lucy and Nancy Lewis (sisters). Ex: father, Rev. Wm. Woods, Samuel Harkins, James McCawley. "Rocky Hill, April 9, 1812. Mr. James Cawley: I have fallen a victim to my beloved but cruel Letetia. I die in hopes of being united to my other wife in heaven. Take care of this Will and come here that we may be decently buried. N.B. With this enclosure myself and brother request to be enterred in the same coffin and same grave." "Rocky Hill, April 10, 1812. My beloved but cruel Letitia: Receive this as a pledge of my forgiveness to your connection. The day of Judgement is to come, I owe you no malice but die on account of your absence and my dear little son James. Adieu, my love."

LEWIS, RANDOLPH. Jan. 16, 1811. Feb. 1811. Wife: Mary. Sons: Charles, Howel, Tucker, Robert, Warner. Daus: Mary, Lucy, Susannah. Ex: Charles L. Lewis, Henry Williams, Mary A. Lewis, Lilburne Lewis. Wit: Charles A. Lewis, A. Persons, Martha C. Lewis.

LOFTON, SAMUEL. June 17, 1804. Jan. C. C. 1808. Wife: Sarah. Sons: Thomas, Samuel, James, John. Daus: Peggy, Elizabeth. Ex: John G. Lofton, Samuel Lofton, Jr. (sons), William E. Phillips (son-in-law). Wit: Joseph Hamilton, James Hamilton.

LOWRY, JOHN. April 1799. July 1800. Wife: Mary. Ex: Jonathan Ramsay. Wit: Samuel Lampkin, Thomas Patterson.

LUSK, JAMES. Sept. 24, 1803. Oct. C. C. 1803. Wife: Sary. Ex: John Reed, Gershorn Clemens. Wit: Joseph Ylie, Robert Lusk.

MASTERS, JOHN. April 21, 1812. August 1812. Wife: Delilia. Daus: Rachel, Ruthy. Ex: wife, Richard Masters. Wit: William Smith, John Roberts, John Killough.

MILES(MILLS), RICHARD. July 2, 1803. Oct. 1803. Wife: Jane. Children: Charles, another child but not named. Ex: Charles Miles(son), Edward Lacy (father-in-law). Wit: Charles Miles, Edward Lacy.

MILLER, MARY. March 20, 1802. June 1802. Sons: Charles, John, Stephen. Ex: James Deacon, Joshua Scott. Wit: Joseph Reed, James Miller, Alexander

Maxwell.

MONTGOMERY, JOHN. Nov. 29, 1808. -----. Wife: Merney. Children: mentioned but not named. Ex: wife, Richard Merner, Arthur Love. Wit: Porter Kirk, Andrew Love, William Wood.

PERKINS, BENJAMIN. Jan. 3, 1806. August 1806. Wife: Saner. Children: Issac, John, others not named. Ex: wife, William Perkins. Wit: James Kirkpatrick, William Perkins.

PIRTLE, MARTIN. June 24, 1806. Oct. 1806. Wife: Peggy. Ex: wife. Wit: Nathaniel Danner, Samuel Pirtle, John Dennis.

PORTER, THOMAS. May 15, 1818. May C. C. 1818. Wife: Coneant. Sons: Berry, Charles. Gr.children: Mary Ann McDaniel, Thomas McDaniel, Oabel McDaniel, Bend McDaniel. Ex: wife, David Davis, Berry Porter. Wit: David Davis.

ROWLAND, REUBEN. Jan. 4, 1806. July 1806. Wife: Anna. Sons: Lewis, John B., Henry, Reuben Jr., Micajah. Daus: Mary Bush, Lydia. Wit: James Smith, James Miller, George Gordon.

RUTTERS, JAMES. Feb. 10, 1814. Dec. 1814. Daus: Peggy Ray, Sally Rice, Polly Phillips, Lettis Lewis, Elizabeth Rogers. Gr.son: James Lewis. Sons: James, William, Edmund. Ex: sons Edmund, James and William. Wit: Henry Delaney, Rhoda Delaney.

SADLER, GEORGE. Oct. 15, 1801. August 1802. Legatees: George Sadler, son of Richard(brother), Deborah Bell's(sister) two daus: Mary, Elizabeth, their father William Bell, Esther Lacy's(sister) two daus: Sarah, Bethat, Joshua Lacy(nephew), Robert Lacy(son of Edward), James Dodd.(son of Jane Dodd), James Miles(son of William). Ex: Edward Lacy and son William Lacy. Wit: Edward Lacy, Richard Miller, George V. Lusk.

WILSON, JAMES. Oct. 15, 1811. Nov. 1811. Wife and children mentioned but not named. Ex: John Dobbin, Hugh Dobbin. Wit: Nancy Dobbin, Susannah Dobbin.

WOOD, WILLIAM. Oct. 21, 1818. Dec. 1818. Dau: Lusana Puckett. Son: Micajah. Other children mentioned but not named. Ex: son Micajah. Wit: A. McAlister. Polly Rice, Berry Hodge.

WOOD, WILLIAM. Sept. 20, 1806. April 1807. Wife: Anne. Mentions four children but only names Spencer. Ex: wife, John McClough, John Spencer.

WOOD, ROBERT. Dec. 6, 1805. August 1806. Wife: Mary. Children: not named. Wit: William Prince, Ben Kevil, William Mitcheson.

SCOTT, JAMES. June 10, 1810. Nov. 1811. Wife: Agnes. Children: James, Joseph, heirs of Sally Bridges. Ex: wife, son James Scott. Wit: Joseph and Margaret Reed.

SCOTT, JOSEPH. March 31, 1817. May 1817. Wife: Sarah. Children: mentioned but not named. Wit: James Killough, Joshua Perkins, Nathan Bennett.

SELLARS, MATHEW. Dec. 20, 1807. Jan. 1808. Wife: Ann. Sons: John, Mathew,

Samuel. Daus: Salomy Travis, Ann Galloway, Rhoda Taylor, Mary. Ex: Rhoda Taylor, Ann Galloway. Wit: Samuel Harris, D. Jarrell.

SHELBY, WILLIAM. July 3, 1817. August 1817. Wife: Sarah. Daus: Sarah, Polly Elizabeth. Sons: William, Laurence, Andrew, Moses, Aaron, Thomas. Ex: Moses Shelby, Aaron Shelby(sons). Wit: William Stewart, Henry Heel(?).

SHIELDS, PAGE. Nov. 30, 1815. Feb. 1816. Legatee: John Mitchell. Wit: James Mitchell, James Trimble, John Mitchell.

SPINK, JAMES. May 31, 1806. July 1808. Wife: Sally. Son: John. Daus: Nancy Miller, Molly Watson, Sally Watson. Ex: wife, John Spink(son), Samuel Watson. Wit: J. E. Pound, W. W. Hammond, Elizabeth Pound.

STEWART, AYRES. Dec. 20, 1812. Jan. 1813. Wife: Tinsey. Two sons mentioned but not named. Ex: James Johnson, Washington Stewart. Wit: Thomas Freyer, Milton Stewart.

STEWART, HUMPHREY. April 25, 1812. July 1812. Wife: Susannah. Son: John. Dau: Elizabeth Trimble. Gr.son: Walker Trimble. Ex: Edward Lacey Jr., Richard Mennet. Wit: Andrew Lane, John Young, James Akin.

TERRY, THOMAS. March 31, 1823. June 1823. Wife: Nancy. Daus: Nancy, Sally Coleman. Sons: Champion, John, Thomas. Ex: wife, son Champion. Wit: William Grey, Presby Grey.

WADLINGTON, JAMES. -----. March C. C. 1800. Wife: Margaret. Sons: Thomas, James, Mercer, William, Warner. Dau: Jane Gary. Ex: Thomas Wadlington Sr. Wit: William Prince, Isaac Grubbs, Ben Kevil.

LOGAN COUNTY

BOOK A

1792 --- 1812

ALLEN, REUBEN. March 5, 1812. May 12, 1812. Wife: Elizabeth. Sons: Roland, Benjamin, James. Daus: Franky, Drusilla, Anney, Charity. Son-in-law: John Keys, hus. of dau. Franky. Gr.son: William, son of James. Ex: Roland Allen, James Allen (sons). Wit: Beverly Allen, James Mitchell, Henry Wells.

ANDERSON, THOMAS. March 4, 1800. -------. Wife: Margaret. Sons: William, James, Henry, Samuel. Dau: Rachel. Ex: William Anderson, James Anderson,(sons). Wit: Andrew Boyd, Amis Balch, Andrew Bay.

BAILEY, JOHN. Sept. 1809. Inventory.

BAKER, ROBERT. Feb. 14, 1809. May 1809. Wife: Sarah. Sons: Robert, John, Royal, Samuel. Daus: Betsy Dudley, Polly Clanton, Nancy Hallum. Gr. chld: Patsy, Sally, Joseph, Robert Payne(chld. of dau. Polly Clanton). Son-in-law: William Baker. Ex: John and Royal Baker(sons). Wit: Michael Finley, Philip James.

BARNETT, WILLIAM. Oct. 6, 1799. ---- 1799. Wife: Martha. Son: Thomas, other children mentioned but not named. Ex: wife, Archibald Felts. Wit: John Barnett, Mary Barnett.

BARNETT, WILLIAM. June 29, 1804. --------. Sons: Adam, Thomas, Fields. Dau: one dau. mentioned but not named. Ex: wife, James Curry Barnett. Wit: Thomas Barnett, John Barnett, S. W. Shannon.

BARTON, JAMES. March 24, 1804. ------. Wife: Mary. Children: Barbary Smith, Stephen, William, other children mentioned but not named.

BARTON, JAMES. August 17, 1804. ------. Legatees: Nancy Barton, Molly Barton.

BEARD, BERZILLA. Dec. 12, 1800. Dec. 1800. Nuncupative. Estate to wife, Mary, youngest son, not named, and gr.son, James Call. Proven by oath of Mary Ham, Vachel Avins.

BELL, JOHN. Oct. 27, 1802. Nov. 1802. (From Virginia) Children: Susannah (now Susannah Steel), Rachel, Eleanor, John.

BERNARD, MARY. April 17, 1807. ---- 1811. Leaves estate to mother Henningham Bernard. Mention is made of late father, John, and late brother, William. There is a copy of the will of John Bernard of Buckingham, Va., recorded with the will of the testator but it is illegible. Ex: Henningham Bernard(mother)

BILLINGSBY, SAMUEL. May 25, 1804. Inventory.

BOWIE, PATSY. Dec. 12, 1799. ------. Legatees: Else(sister), Rease(brother), Patsy Bowden(niece), Jesse Bowden. Wit: Charles Slocum, Ann Motley, August Arrington.

BOYD, DANIEL. Oct. 10, 1797. -----. Wife: Ruth. Sons: John, Matthew(two youngest sons). Daus: Janey Boyd, Frances Boyd. Gr.dau: Elizabeth Boyd. Ex: Edward Richey, Ralph Fleming(friends). Wit: Robert and Chatham Ewing.

BROWN, JOHN. Sept. 9, 1800. -----. Wife: mentioned but not named. Sons: James, John. Daus: Mary Prewitt, (others not named) Ex: John Prewitt, Samuel McCracken, Henry Mauzy. Wit: John Hanna, Henry Mauzy, Samuel McCracken.

CONNER, WILLIAM. March 4, 1807. Division of estate.

COOK, JOHN. Oct. 24, 1806. Nov. 1806. Wife: Mary. Children: mentioned but not named. Ex: wife, Benjamin McReynolds. Wit: George Caldwell, Sally McReynolds, Hugh Porter, David Porter.

ELY, ELI. Jan. 13, 1806. -----. Wife: Sally. Children: Micheal, Betsy, Sally, Jesse, Thetus(?). Ex: Edward Ely(brother), Reuben Browning. Wit: Thomas Blanchard, Martha Ely, Allen Acock.

EWING, JOHN. Sept. 20, 1803. -----. Wife: Martha. Sons: Samuel, Finnis, Rubartus, John. Dau: Lokey B. Ewing. Ex: wife, Reuben and Chatham Ewing (brothers). Wit: Finnis and George Ewing.

EWING, WILLIAM. June 1, 1799. Nov. 1799. Wife: Florence. Sons: James, William, Samuel. Daus: Peggy, Betsy. Wit: John Hay, John Rise, ---- Thompson.

GRAVES, FREDRICK. April 13, 1807. Inventory.

JONES, JUDSON. Sept. 14, 1803. Nov. 1803. Estate in Montgomery County, State of Maryland, to brothers and sisters, viz: Benjamin, Richard, Henry, Edward, Joseph, Oratio, Jacob, Walter, Elizabeth Bell(wife of Carlton Bell), Sarah Magruder(wife of John B. Magruder). Ex: Walter Jones(brother). Wit: James Wilson, Philip Latham, William Whitaker.

LANG, NIMROD. March 15, 1813.

LANGSTON, RAGLAND. Oct. 15, 1816. Nov. 17, 1816. Wife: Dicey. Mentions father Joseph Langston. Children: Polly Townsend, Agnes, Joseph John Langston, Ragland Morton Langston, Mangham Ephiram Langston, Aviana, Jackson Perry Carel Langston, Sukey Cromwell Langston(?). Ex: John Langston(bro.), Spencer Curd, Jonathan Smith. Wit: Walter Jones, Spencer Curd, Sterling Barnes.

LATHAM, DICKEY. Feb. 29, 1805. Oct. 1805. Sons: James, Philip, Robert, John. Daus: Fanny Slaughter, Lucy Morehead, Betsy Rollins, Polly. Gr.dau: Betsy Morehead. Ex: wife, son John. Wit: Ninian Edwards, Elizabeth Berry, Horace Merry.

LOCKHART, DAVID. Nov. 16, 1814. Dec. 1814. Wife: Avery. Children: not named. Wit: P. L. Pritchett, John Bush.

LODGE, MATHEWS. Nov. 15, 1807. -----. Estate in trust for brother, Brook Lodge, and sister, Joannah Lodge. Father to act as trustee. Wit: Robert McCabe, James Myles.

McCOOMBS, JESSE. Oct. 20, 1812. June 1814. Wife: Sally. Sons: Jesse, John. Daus: Mary, Elizabeth. "Rest of estate to Society of Shakers". Ex: son John, Samuel G. Whyte. Wit: William Johns, B. D. Price.

McINTOSH, -----. Inventory. Feb. 1816.

McKNOWN, LAURENCE. Oct. 6, 1806. -----. Wife: Hannah. Children: mentioned but not named except Sipio. Ex: Col. Sam Caldwell. Wit: Sam Wilson, Samuel Ashmore, William Ashmore.

McLEAN, EPHIRAM. Jan. 19, 1813. Feb. 15, 1813. Wife: Elizabeth. Children: John and others not named. Ex: wife, James Wilson, Tucker Baylor, Jacob W. Walker. Wit: F. G. Baylor, Chatham Ewing, Green Rice.

McLEAN, SUSAN. April 29, 1812. May 1812. Sons: Ephiriam, Robert Allison. Dau: Susan Howard McLean. Ex: son Ephiram, Samuel Wilson. Wit: John and Elizabeth McLean.

McPHERSON, GEORGE. Dec. 2, 1811. Dec. 1811. Estate to sons Murdock and Evan. " Should any of my other children come to America they are to be given their share of my estate ". Ex: son Evan. Wit: Neil McPhaill, John Potter.

McREYNOLD, JAMES. July 19, 1803. Inventory.

McREYNOLD, ROBERT. Dec. 1803. Inventory.

MILLER, RANDLE. May 14, 1810. Nov. 19, 1810. Wife: Elizabeth. Children: Elizabeth(youngest child), others not named. Ex: John Miller, W. Taylor. Wit: Wright Taylor, John Miller, Henry Miller.

MITCHELL, GEORGE. May 16, 1796. -----. Wife: Jenny. Children: mentioned but not named. Ex: John Lend, Rowland Madison. Wit: Sam McFadin, Randolph Binks, Samuel McNeel.

PORTER, -----. Jan. Court 1815. Settlement.

RAGSDALE, SALLY. Nov. 16, 1816. Inventory.

REED, JAMES. Dec. Court 1803.

RICE, JAMES. Nov. 1810. Inventory.

ROBERTS, LINA. Jan. 24, 1814. -----. Estate to brother Alfred Roberts' son, Baylor Roberts. Ex: Beavenger Roberts(brother). Wit: Thomas Townsend, Samuel Davis, Boas Roberst.

ROLLINS, JAMES. ---- 24, 1810. Inventory.

STEPHENSON, THOMAS. April 1806. Inventory.

SUMMERS, ROBERT. Oct. 11, 1797. -----. Wife: Mary. Children: mentioned but not named. Ex: wife, William Hay, John Hay. Wit: William Ewing, Daniel Hay, Joshua Talbot.

WARD, JOHN. March 25, 1811. August 19, 1811. Wife: Mary. Sons: Jeremiah, John, James, William, Thomas, Lewis. Daus: Sally, Polly, Peggy, Lucy, Nancy. Ex: John McDowel, Jeremiah Ward.

WARD, MICHAEL. June 20, 1814. Nuncupative. Wife: Mary. Sons: Jonathan, Jesse, Philip. Daus: Nancy Rowland, Milley, Jenney. Proven by oath of Robert Scott, Jacob M. Wood.

WARFIELD, ANN. May 20, 1820. Inventory.

WATSON, JOHN. August 1815. Inventory.

WEST, JAMES. Nov. 1808. Inventory.

WHITAKER, THOMAS. Dec. 1809. Inventory. Mentions Mark Whitaker, Henry Whitaker.

WHITE, JOHN. Nov. 1803. Inventory.

WHITSETTE, WILLIAM, Sr. March 15, 1805. -----. Wife: Ellen. Sons: James, William. Daus: Sally Porter, Peggy Blakey, Ellen Ewing. Gr.children: William Blakey(son of George and Peggy Blakey), William Whitsette(son of James Whitsette), William Ewing(son of Reuben and Ellen Ewing). Ex: wife, Reuben Ewing, William Whitsette. Wit: Reuben Ewing, Chatham Ewing.

WHYTE, ISAAC. April 5, 1814. June 1814. Wife: Polly. Sons: Daniel, Thornton, Benjamin, Samuel. Dau: Polly. Ex: wife, Samuel Whyte.

WILCOX, JOSIAH. Oct. 16, 1813. -----. Wife: Eleanor. Sons: Charles Granderson Wilcox, Nathan Miles Wilcox. Ex: John Breathitt. Wit: Smith Hansbrough, G. A. Martin, James Allnutt.

WILKINS(WILKINSON), JOEL. July 26, 1807. August 1807. (Late of Prince George County, Virginia) Brother, Watt(Wiatt). Father, Fredrick Wilkins. Ex: brother Wiett, John Cross.

LOGAN COUNTY

BOOK A

INDEX OF GUARDIAN SETTLEMENTS, INVENTORIES, DOWERS ETC.

Acock, John
Allen, Beverly A.
Ashley, ----

Browning, Isaac
Brien, James
Bradford, Samuel
Britt, William

Edwards, Penelope

Ferguson, William
Fisher, William
Fleming, Hannah
Fleming, Ralph
Foster, John
Frizzle, William

Gilbert, William
Gorham, Thomas
Green, John

Hannah, David
Hambrick, H.
Hampton, Thomas
Henderson, Thomas
Herndon, James
Hendry, William
Hinton, John
Hew, Levi
Howard, James
Hunter, James

Ingram, William

Johnston, John
Johnson, Nathan
Johnson, William
Jones, Aaron

Kennedy, John
Knott, Z.

Mays, James
Moore, Jesse

Orndoff, John

Phelps, Burgess
Philips, William

Ragsdale, Fredrick
Reed, Isaac
Renshaw, William

Simpson, Jonathan
Sonelson, Stephen
Stanley, Jonathan
Strader, Conred

Talkington, Elizabeth
Tayler, William
Temple, Stephen
Thompson, Thomas
Tilghman, Stephen
Travis, Benjamin
Travis, Thomas

MADISON COUNTY

BOOK A

1785 -- 1806

ANDERSON, SAMUEL. Dec. 10, 1804. April 7, 1806. Sisters: Mary Maxwell, Ann Gass, Mary Campbell, Becky Morrison and niece Betsy. Bro. William A., Isaac, James. Ex: Bro. James. Wit: William Briscoe, David Maxwell.

BLACK, JAMES. Inventory. Nov. 1790.

BLOCKLEY, JOHN. Inventory. May 25, 1790. Apprs: Isaac Muse, Joel Hill, Wills Cook.

BLYTHE, WILLIAM. July 18, 1795. Aug. 1800. Wife: Amy. Children: James and step son David Martin. Ex: Robert Rodez, Jacob Patton.

BRIDGES, GEORGE. (of Fayette Co). Sept. 7, 1790. July 3, 1792. "To niece Betsy Fox, dau. of half bro. Samuel Fox, a late emigrant from Hanover Co., Va. To Niece Rebecca Farthing, dau. of half sister Ann Farthing of James City Co., Va. Niece Betsy Piggott, dau. of sister Mary Piggott of City of Williamsburg. Bro. Isham Bridges. Ex: Isham Bridges. N.B. "The annexed was wrote by my own hand if any dispute should arise I hope the hand writing can be proved without much trouble should I not return from camp. I expect to go on the 10 inst. Tis my desire this may be over without being proved or recorded till fall 1791."

BROOKS, ROBERT. July 26, 1793. Estate taken charge of by court at request of creditors.

BURGIN, ISAAC. March 10, 1794. March 1794. Wife: Mary. Children: Nancy and others mentioned but not named. Wife and Dennis Burgin Ex:. Wit: Leaven Gray, Charles Burgin. Apprs: Edward Carpenter, Oct. 7, 1794.

BURNET, ROLAND. Sept. 13, 1789. March 2, 1790. Of Madison Co., Commonwealth of Va.). Wife: Margaret. Estate to wife and children not named. Ex: Cornelius Maupinee, John Miller. Wit: Daniel Mc Guire, William Chinault, Charles Colley, Peter Bush.

CAMPBELL, THOMAS. May 17, 1796. Oct. 1796. Wife: Eleanor. Children not named. Ex: Bro. John. Wit: John Campbell, George Moore, Ben Hall.

CHAFFERY, CHARLES. Inventory Feb. 1787. Apprs: James Robinson, William Miller, James Adams.

CHIZUM, JAMES. March 8, 1795. -----. Niece Sarah K. Williams. "To William Hogans, Bench Plains and Bed plain and my best hat and striped Nankeen coat. To Sohia Strawhen, one new chart that is not quite finished. To John Wheeler, one leaden cullard coat, two of my best shirts, a pair of boot buckles. Rest of estate to mother and children of bro. John Williams, viz: Thomas, John, Isaac, Betsy, Rosy, and Samuel Williams and niece Mary Chambers. Sister Martha Dosey and dau. Delia. Ex: John Sappington, John Wheeler. Wit: Thomas Trvis, Thomas Strawhen, John Caperton.

CLOYD, SAMUEL. Feb. 20, 1789. May 5, 1795. Of Montgomery Co., Va. Wife: Elizabeth. Nenyan Cloyd and son Thomas mentioned. Ex: wife, Joseph Cloyd. Wit: G. , James and Thomas Cloyd.

COCHRAN, JAMES. Jan. 25, 1806. Feb. 1806. Wife: Jane. Children: Samuel and others not named. Ex: wife and son Samuel. Wit: John Snoddy, John Cochran, John Mills.

COFFEY, NEBUZARADAN. Oct. 1796. March 1797. Wife: not named. Children: Joel, Sary, Polly, Fieldan, Betsy, Ruth, Sail, Mas Hays. Wit: William Allen, C. Coffey, Marthy Coffey.

COLLIER, JAMES. Sr. Dec. 22, 1804. Jan. 1805. Nuncupative. Committed to writing by James Collier, Jr. Money deposited with Joseph Ellison for benefit of children and admr. of estate. Proved by oath of John Collier, Jr. and Sr.

COULTER, JAMES. April 30, 1806. July 7, 1806. Wife: Alcey. Children: James, Isabella Jackson, Elizabeth, Aubrey, Sally, Polly. Ex: wife, William Miller. Wit: James Talbott, Arch Woods, James Bratton.

CREATH, WILLIAM. ---------. Children: William, Sarah, Jean, Robert, children of son William. Children of George Fordam. Ex: wife and son William. Wit: Alex. Marshay, John Snoddy.

DEVER, WILLIAM. Sept. 13, 1802. Oct. 4, 1802. Wife: Janes. To bro. and sisters James, Samuel, Nathan, Amos, Rebekah and Peggy. Ex: wife, Joseph Kennedy, Andrew Harris. Wit: Alex. Mc Mullen, William Roberson, Margaret Roberson.

DONALDSON, ANDREW. Dec. 21, 1802. April 1803. Wife: Christiana. Children: Robert, Andrew, Rachel. Wit: John. Kincaid, James Mc Williams, William Donaldson.

DOZIER, JAMES. Oct. 21, 1790. May 3, 1791. Wife: Martha. Children: Zachariah, Elizabeth Davis, (gr.dau. Rebekah Davis), and Rebekah Scott and her son James, Sarah Montgomery and her son Thomas, Susannah Crews (hus. Elijah Crews), Leonard, James, Thomas, John, Gr.son John Cash. Ex: sons Leonard and Zachariah. Wit: Aaron Lewis, Benjamin South, Wildon South.

DUNCAN, BENJAMIN. Nov. 3, 1796. Dec. 6, 1796. Wife: Elizabeth. Children: John, Samuel, Benjamin, Elizabeth Arnot. "To son John new suit of clothes, Great Coat, short coat, Jacket and Overhalls. Wit: John Black, Alex. Macky Alex. Garton.

ELLETT, ROBERT. April 6, 1802. Feb. 1806. Wife: Elizabeth. Bonds due him in old Virginia for plantation. Children: James, Amey, Agnes, Rebecca, Margaret, David, Polly. Gr.dau: Polly, dau. of Margaret. Ex: John Snoddy. Wit: Robert Caldwell, John Kincaid, William Douglas.

ESTILL, MARY ANN. June 7, 1801. -----. 1806. Children: Sarah, James, Samuel, Wallace, William, Isaac, Abigail and John Woods her hus. Wit: Peter Wood, Susannah Shelton.

FARRIS, MICHAEL. Oct. 27, 1799. Dec. 1799. Wife: Fabey. Children: Dudley,

George, Thomas and others. Ex: wife, John Snoddy. Wit: James Moore, William and Robert Creath.

FARTHING, EDWARD. Nov. 2, 1803. May 1806. Wife: Margaret. Children: Dudley, John, Gydiah. Ex: wife. Wit: Jonathan Kidwell, Thomas Stucker, Vincent Kidwell.

FLETCHER, WILLIAM. May 12, 1790. Aug. 7, 1792. Wife: Wenifred. Children: John, James, Robert, William, Mary, Betsy, Sally. Wit: Will Orear, William Calk, James French.

FORD, PETER. March 4, 1798. Oct. 5, 1801. Wife: Sarah. Children: Daniel, Joel, Jacob. (land in Buckingham Co., Va.), Ruth, Ann, Judith, Sally, Laban. Step Children: Polly and Samuel Stone. "To dau. Polly if she is recovered from the Indians". Ex: wife and sons Daniel and Joel.

FOWLER, MATHEW. Feb. 6, 1802. May 4, 1802. Wife: Nancy. Children: Richard, Mathew, John, Edward. Military claim to be divided among sons Edward, Richard, John. Wit: William Martin, Edward Logsdun.

GASS, DAVID. April 14, 1806. May 5, 1806. Wife: Sarah. Children: Susannah Harris, John, William, James, Mary Black, Thomas Margaret Mitchell. Son-in-law John Mitchell. Gr.son James Mitchell. Ex: wife, sons John and James. Wit: Richard Gentry, John Reed.

GREEN, STEPHEN. July 7, 1801. April 5, 1802. Wife: Jemima. Children: Martin, William, Rudah Finney, Susannah, Sarah, Stephen. Stephen (dec'd) left three small children. Ex: Martin Green, William Green. Wit: Humphrey Jones, Jemimah Allen, George Moon.

HAMILTON, WILLIAM. June 28, 1800. Aug. 3, 1800. Children: Patrick, Mary, Isabella, Easter, Carline. Ex: William Tucker, Samuel Tucker, Hamilton Tucker. Wit: George Tucker, John Campbell.

HARRIS, CHRISTOPHER. Feb. 13, 1791. March 1794. Children: Dabney, Sarah Martin, Robert, Mourning Jones, Christopher, Mary Jones. Ex: (1st part of will) Foster Jones, Christopher Harris. (2nd part of Will) Wife, son Overton, John, Benjamin, William, Barnabec, (land in Albermarle Co., Va.), James, Samuel. Other children: Jane Gentry, Margaret Harris, Isabel Harris. Ex: wife, John Sappington, John Harris. Wit: Hartley Sappington, Ruth Sappington.

HART, WILLIAM. Dec. 10, 1804. Jan. 4, 1805. Wife: Nancy. Children: John, Henry, Jesse, Anne. Ex: Peter Todd, Daniel Mc Guire.

HAWKINS, NATHAN. Jan. 14, 1794. Nov. 4, 1794. Wife: Catharine. Children: Elizabeth Level, Mary Stephenson, Nancy Schooler, Marcy Barnet, Nicholas, Nathan, Simon. Ex: wife. Wit: Leven Cole, John Bone, Thomas Bone, James Purtin.

HAY, WILLIAM. March 15, 1790. April 7, 1790. Wife: Sarah. Children: Betsy South, Roland, Jones, Dacia, Kezia, William, Fauna, Celia Thania. Ex: son Roland, John South, Richard Tunstall. Wit: William Jones, William Hollands, John Bush.

IRVIN, DAVID. April 3, 1801. Oct. 1805. Wife: Jane. Children: Mary, Elizabeth, Magdalin, Anna, William, Sarah, Jane, Robert, Frances, Margaret, Amelia Stephen, Polly, Daniel, Christopher (dec'd.). Wit: M. D. Harden, Eliza Patric, John Hochraay.

JOHNSON, BARN. May 18, 1798. July 1798. Wife: Jane. Children: Barnabas, Robert, William, "Cather Kinder dau. of my dau. Jane Kinder and hus. George Kinder". Wit: William M. Mc Guire, Peter Kinder, Daniel M. Mullins.

KINCAID, JOHN. July 9, 1792. March 1793. Wife: mentioned but not named. "To sons John and James land in Washington Co., Va. on Clinch River where I once lived." Youngest sons David and Moore. Daus: Ruth, Jean. Son-in-law William Baird. John and Sarah Barksdel. Gr.sons: John (son of James Kincair), Joseph Jameson (son of Samuel). Ex: wife, son John. Wit: Alex. Mackey, Andrew Kincaid.

KINCAID, JOHN. March 17, 1804. April 2, 1804. Wife: Agnes. Children: Agnes, Andrew, Joseph, Elizabeth, John, James, Jean, Sarah. Ex: wife, Udley Campbell, John Garvin, Thomas Edmiston. Wit: Udley Campbell, John Edmiston.

KAVANAUGH, CHARLES. Oct. 13, 1795. Oct. 4, 1796. Legatees: James Mills Moors, Charles Cavanough Moore and Elizabeth Moore. (children of James). A law suit pending in Culpetter Co., Va. Ex: William and Charles Kavanough. Peter Wood. Wife: Ann. Heirs of son Phillemon Kavanaugh (dec'd): Mary, William, Charles, Joel, Sarah Ann. Wit: Will Irvine, William Fox, James Hackaday.

LOWRY, JAMES. Oct. 23, 1802. Dec. 1802. Wife: Lucretia. Children: Mathew, James, William Rebecca, Hixy, Lucy, Gilly. Ex: wife, William Goodlow. Wit: Jonah Gentry, John Maupin, Thomas Parham.

MARTIN, JAMES. Aug. 5, 1796. March 1799. Wife: Sarah. Children: Christopher, David, William, Tyree, Robert, Hudson, Nathan. Son-in-law Pleasant Profith and wife Mary. Ex: wife and sons. "In case of dispute over settlement of property Thomas Clay, Green Clay and James French to have say as to decision."

MASON, WILLIAM. Oct. 22, 1793. Dec. 1793. Wife: Isabella. Children: Mary, Isabella, Jane, John, James and unborn child. Bro. James authorized to dispose of land in Virginia. Ex: wife, John Conchran, Matthew Scott. Wit: John Conchran, William Balch.

MAUPIN, DANIEL. Oct. 11, 1802. Feb. 1803. Mary Burnett, her dau. Lucy. Children: Sarah Stephenson, Mary Burnett, Elizabeth Rays, Margaret Goulding, Fanny Lynch. Ex: John Harris. Wit: Anna Harris, William Harris, James Oldham.

MAXWELL, THOMAS. Oct. 27, 1795. Jan. 5, 1796. Wife: Agnes. Children: Thomas, Robert, Bezaleal, Benjamin, Mary Terrell, Rebecca Schot, Ann Maxwell, Wit: Thomas Partin, William Morrison, James Dever. Ex: wife, Edmund Terrell.

MC KENNEY, JOSEPH. May 6, 1791. July 5, 1791. (Madison Co., Va.). "To my beloved Henry (bro.) all lands in Ky. and N. C. Sisters Hannah and Elizabeth. To my four sisters $50 N. C. currency and to my Honored Mother I lend my negroes. To John Maxwell my saddle and a good bridle and my hat." Ex:

friend James Crawford. Wit: George Adams, John Adams, James Barnett.

MILLER, ABRAHAM. July 3, 1798. Aug. 6, 1798. Nuncupative. "To bro. Benjamin and wife Mary." Wit: Oswald Townoon, Susannah Moore.

MOODY, ANDREW. SR. Feb. 2, 1800. --------. Wife: Katy. Children: Isaac, and four others not named. Ex: wife, James Anderson. Wit: John Moody, Joseph Moody.

MOORE, WILLIAM. Sept. 15, 1799. Oct. 1799. Wife: Margaret. Children: Joseph, William, James. To Martin, William, Hugh and Jean Glenn. Heirs of Albert Douglas, Gr. dau. Betsey Burnside. Ex: James Moore. Wit: David Elliott, Joseph Glenn, L. Allin.

MORRISON, HUGH. --------. Feb. 3, 1806. Wife: Mary. Property due from bro. in Tennessee, to wife. Wit: Isaac and John Anderson.

NOLAND, JOSHUA. Aug. 27, 1798. Dec. 1798. Wife and children mentioned but not named. Ex: Henry Noland, Joseph Shimor. Wit: William Toland, Samuel Hopper.

OREAR, JEREMIAH. March 4, 1798. Jan. 1, 1799. Wife: Nancy. Children: John, Benjamin, Daniel, also Ex: of will. Wit: David Rowland, Richard Rowland, Jesse Rowland.

OWSLEY, THOMAS. March 3, 1795. March 7, 1797. Wife: Mary. Children: William, Thomas, Henry, Anthony, Jonathan, Chloe Williams, Virlinda Huckwin, David, Mary Bryant, Patience Bledsoe, Elizabeth Goughe, Ann Williams, Daniel. Gr.son Thomas Chilton and Waler Williams. "To dau. Mary Bryant I bequeath 738 acres lying on the Old Buffaloe trace leading from Settlement of Beardstown to Bullets Lick". Ex: sons William and Daniel. Wit: Charles English, Absalom Brown.

PORTWOOD, LOYD. April 30, 1792. June 1792. Wife: Elizabeth. To son John when he becomes of age, and others not named. Wit: Thomas and Lude Portwood.

PORTWOOD, JOHN. April 28, 1795. -------, Wife: Elizabeth. Children: Solomon, Thomas and others. Ex: wife, John and Peter Wood. Wit: John Crook, Thomas Crews, Agnes Richards.

PROVINCE, JOHN. April 3, 1792. -------. Wife: Mary. Children: Sarah, William, Rebekah, Alexander, John, Ann. Mary. "To sons Alex. and John preemption on station camp in Cumberland". Bro. Andrew Province. Ex: wife, Alex., Denny and Samuel Woods. Wit: Joshua Nichols, Robert Henderson, Alex. Reed.

RABOURN, ROBERT. Dec. 27, 1805. July 6, 1806. Wife: Susanna. Children: John, William, Polly, Elizabeth, Susanna, Peggy, Rebecca, Joel, Mary, land in Augusta Co., Va. Ex: wife. Wit: Robert Tevis, William Blockined, John Bennett.

REYNOLDS, THOMAS. July 1792. Inventory.

ROBERTS, EDWARD. Feb. 22, 1802. April 5, 1802. Wife: Margaret. Children:

John and others not named. Wit: Nathan Robert, Robert Donoho, Rachel Barnes.

ROBERTSON, WILLIAM. July 23, 1804. ------. Wife: Sarah. Children: Payton, Anna Hawkins, Dorothy Pitman, William. Ex: wife, John Pitman. Wit: Peyton Robertson, William Robertson, John Bone, John Boyle, Echolas Hawkins.

ROBINSON, JAMES. Apprs: for James Mc Neely Dec'd. Aug. 12, 1788.

SAPP, NANCY. June 27, 1805. Aug. 1805. Bro. Fredrick Sapp, and dau. Nancy. Sister Margaret. Ex: Richard West. Wit: John Wheeler, Edmund Parrish, Hartley Sapp.

SCRIVNER, JAMES. Dec. 23, 1800. March 2, 1801. Children: Elizabeth Owens, Mary, Sarah, Benjamin, Thomas, Joseph, John, Reuben, James. Ex: sons Benjamin, Thomas, James. Wit: Alex. Garton, Jonathan Estill, Benjamin Estill.

SEARCY, BARTLETT. July 28, 1780. Nov. 1784. (of Granville Co., N.C.). Granville Co. Court, March 3, 1795. (Madison Co. Court). Wife: Lucy. Children: Samuel and others. Ex: wife, son Samuel, John, Williams. Wit: Elizabeth Searcy, Leonard Searcy, Thomas Searcy, Reuben Searcy.

SHACKLEFORD, JAMES. March 10, 1795. Aug. 4, 1795. Wife: Sarah. Children: Edward, James, Sarah Hinks, Betsy Sanderson, Ann Beasley. Wit: Thomas Chilton.

SHADMORE, THOMAS. Nov. 23, 1802. Oct. 1803. Wife: Not named. Children: John, Jean. Wit: John Kincaid, William Hook.

SMITH, REUBEN. Nov. 5, 1804. ------. Wife: Tobitha. Children: Malinda, Asa Cliford, Syntha, Mary Polly, William. Ex: Nicholas Hankins, Baird Maxwell, bro. Asa Smith. Wit: William Morison, Nicholas Hankins, Joseph Kennels.

STAPP, JAMES. Feb. 23, 1794. Nov. 4, 1794. Wife: Luce. Children mentioned but not named. Ex: John Stapp, Golston Stapp. Wit: Joseph Stapp, Elijah Stapp, Thomas Lowhorn.

STEPHENSON, EDWARD. Aug. 11, 1792. Oct. 2, 1792. Children: Betsy, William. Wife mentioned but not named. Ex: John Suddsy, James Stephenson, and son William. Wit: James Stephenson, Humphrey Best.

STEPHENSON, ELIZABETH. Feb. 8, 1791. April 3, 1792. Children: John, James, Elizabeth, others but not named. Estate to be divided among children except John and Elizabeth. Gr.dau. Jean Stephenson, Jean McKnigh. Wit: David Maxwell, Joseph Hunter.

STONE, BENJAMIN. Jan. 20, 1795. Aug. 4, 1795. Wife: Sarah. "I have exchanged my plantation that is in Guilford Co., North Carolina with Burges my son for a bond upon Ann Lewis". Children: Dudley, Samuel, Burges, Daniel, Elizabeth, Jane, Fanny, Susannah, Mary, Rebekah. Ex: wife, Ann Lewis. Wit: Aaron Lewis, Isaac, Thomas, John, and Sarah Lewis.

RICHARDSON, AARON. Dec. 19, 1803. April 2, 1804. Wife: Sarah. Children: Laviney, Thomas, William, Patty, Caley, Benjamin, John. Ex: wife, Daniel Richardson. Wit: Peter Bennett, Thomas Parsell.

TATUM, SAMUEL SR. Nov. 11, 1805. Feb. 1806. Wife: Sarah. Children: Nicholas, Laura, others not named. Ex: George Ateom. Wit: John Schooler, Nathan Schooler, William Vincent.

TIMBERLAKE, RICHARD. Feb. 16, 1795. May 5, 1795. Wife: Sarah. Children: Sarah Butler, John, Phillip. Ex: Martin Gentry, Thomas Butler. Wit: Will Irvine, John Bractten, Stephen Jett.

TIVES, NATHANIEL, SR. Aug. 29, 1798. Oct. 1798. Children: Nathaniel, Robert, Thomas, Jeremiah, Peggy, Susannah Wheeler. Wit: John Sappington, Robert Reburn, Edward Davis. Ex: Son-in-law John Wheeler.

WALDING, JAMES. Feb. 8, 1796. July 5, 1796. Wife: Ann. Children: Elizabeth Chizum, James, Jesse, William, Ann. Ex: William Walding, John Reed, Joel Short. Wit: Elijah Evins, Randal Yarber, Joel Short.

WATSON, JESSEY. June 1, 1790. Aug. 3, 1796. "Jessey Watson was seting at a Lick watching for a Deer, John Anderson going upon the same business had the misfortune to fire upon and wound him in mistake, upon the evening following getting very bad tho in his perfect sences and memory and expressing a great desire to see James Stephenson, at length took me by the hand and had some talk with me and then told me that his will was that his wife Milly Watson should have everything he had and that she should keep in possession and said gentleman bear witness given under my hand the day and year above mentioned. Wit: James Burnet, James Anderson, Evan Thomas Watson.

WATTS, JOHN. Feb. 4, 1796. July 5, 1796. Wife: Sarah. Children: Esther Sebree, Franky Quinn, Mildred Tomlinson, Betty Vawter, Amy Merry, Agatha Turner, Molly Watts. Ex: Jesse Vawter, Richard Sebree, wife Sarah. Wit: John Gess, Stephen Eastin, John Armstrong, Samuel Loyd.

WHITE, JAMES. Inventory. May 5, 1795. Apprs: John Reed, John Cloyd, Hugh Campbell.

WOOLSCALE, WILLIAM. Inventory. Nov. 1797. Inventory of William Woolscale produced by his widow Jane Woolscale. Children: Arp, Jiminey, Joseph.

MC CRACKEN COUNTY

BOOK A

1824 -- 1843

ADAMS, MATHEW. Inventory. Nov. 27, 1830.

BARLOW, WILLIAM. Feb. 14, 1838. April 9, 1838. Wife: Mahalia. Sons: John A., Joseph, Harding W.N. Daus: Sintha E., Polly H., Emmetha, Nin------(?), Mahalia C. Ex: wife: Wit: William T. Smith, E. Henson, William Titsworth.

BAYLES, JOHN. June 10, 1841. Feb. Court 1842. Wife: Susan. Dau: Sarah Margaret. Son: William. Son is to receive legacy from his grandfathers estate. Ex: wife.

CARSON, R. A. July 9, 1843. Feb. 13, 1844. Wife: Isabella. Son: A. L. Carson. Dau: Julia L. Carson. Land left to Noah Fuqua for benefit of his children. Ex: W. Phillips, Agustus L. Carson. Wit: Wm. Hall, J. S. Caldwell.

CLARK, WILLIAM. April 14, 1837. Sept. 13, 1838. Of St. Louis, Missouri. Sons: Merriwether, Lewis Clark, William Preston Clark, George Roger H. Clark, Jefferson Kenney Clark. Son Merriwether to have charge of education of son Jefferson. Ex: John O'Fallon, Merriether Clark, William Clark, George Clark (3 sons). Wit: S. W. Kearney, J. Fadford, A. C. Churchill, H. S. Coxe. (This will was probated in St. Louis, Missouri.). The testator was a son of John Clark of Louisvelle, Ky.

COOK, JOHN M. Sept. 27, 1838. Nov. 1838. Mentions A. M. Hicks, George Woolfolks (sons-in-law) but children not named.

COWLING, WILLIAM H. Sept. 26, 1844. ---------. Estate to wife (not named) and son Edwin. Wit: Edwin Ewell, J. Martin.

CULBERSON, ALEXANDER B. April 23, 1836. ---------. Nuncupative. Estate to brother Samuel Culberson. Proven by the oath of Elizabeth Thompson, Polly Hughs.

DUNCAN, LITHGO M. Dec. 1, 1843. Dec. 1843. Wife: Louisa. Legacy to James F. Willett for the benefit of L. M. Duncan's wife and children. Ex: James F. Willett, R. H. Stanton. Wit: J. B. Nicholson, H. J. Moss.

DICKINSON, JOSEPH. Dec. 15, 1836. ---------. Of Franklin County, State of Virginia. Estate is left to mother Martha Dickinson and brother Washington Dickinson. Ex: Brother Washington Dickinson.

DOYLE, JOHN. Inventory. Oct. 14, 1839.

DUFFY, JAMES. Nov. 10, 1841. Dec. 15, 1841. Estate to brother Thomas J. Duffy who is also named executor. Wit: Elijah Darnall, John Staton, Thomas Henderson.

ELROD, THOMAS. June 24, 1842. Oct. 10, 1842. Bros. Sidney G, George, Samson, Ranson, Jeremiah, James E. Sisters: Thessey Jane, Susan Elizabeth. Ex: Hiram Hall. Wit: John Potter, William Dent.

ELISON, WINIFER. Dec. 31, 1841. May 13, 1843. Estate to grand daughter, Winifer Ann Elison, Except $5.00 to son Andrew Elison, $5.00 to son Theophilus. Test: W. W. Lay, Alfred Gates.

ESSERY, JOSEPH. Feb. 18, 1836. Nov. 1836. Wife: Elizabeth. Son: John. Dau: Permelia Friend, Elizabeth Ward's children. Ex: wife. Wit: Andrew Newman, Robert Lovley.

FARANT, JOSEPH. Feb. 3, 1836. June 26, 1836. Nuncupative. Estate to Allen Richardson. Proven by oath of David Davis.

EWELL, CHARLES. March 18, 1830. May 11, 1830. Wife: Maria Dorcas. Legatees: John Ewell (son), Maria Virginia Ewell (dau.), Jesse Ewell, Joseph Fry, Edwin Henry, Sarah Ann, Lucy Ewell (last 4 gr.child.). Thomas Taylor and wife Martha (son-in-law and dau.). Mention is made of town lots in Dumfries, Va. and money due him from James Craik of Virginia. Ex: wife. Wit: A. W. Naylor, Lucy L. Taylor.

FORREST, EDMUND. April 12, 1832. June 1832. Wife: Sirena. Sons: Benjamin, William, Edmund, Joseph. Daus: Nancy Bennett, Mary Jarvis, Sary Careen Downs, Kizire May Squire. Wit: Elie Henson, J. Forrest.

GLISTEN, JOHN. Dec. 1835. Settlement. Admr: Abel Sullivan.

GRACE, SAMUEL. Feb. 29, 1844. Sept. 18, 1844. Wife: Nancy. Ruth Layman, Marthy Reaves (adopted daus.). Wit: John Smith, Alex. Ratcliffe, James McElya.

GRUNDY, GEORGE. Oct. 9, 1838. Nov. 3, 1839. Wife: Polly. Children mentioned but not named. Ex: William Grundy (son), Peter Stayton.

GRUNDY, WILLIAM. Inventory. --------1839.

HARRISON, ISAAC. Feb. 15, 1837. July 10, 1837. Wife: Deliah. Mentions Mary Elizabeth Collins, an infant in his care, to be educated. Property to be divided at wife's death between the following: William Arnet, Eliza Jane Alcock, Deliah Wood, Mary Elizabeth Collins. Ex: wife. Wit: William L. Smith, John Moore, B. L. (S?) Moore.

HAYNES, JOHN. Sept. 24, 1836. Nov. 12, 1838. Wife: Margaret. Children: David, Martha, and other children mentioned but not named. "To New Hope Church fifty acres". Ex: Andrew Haynes, David Haynes (sons). Wit: Robert Evans, Jacob Rudolph, Andrew Rudolph, Nathan Fentral.

HODGE, JAMES. Inventory. March 22, 1834.

HOUSE, GREEN. Inventory. April 21, 1828.

JOHNSON, WILLIAM. Settlement of estate. April 13, 1837.

KIMBLE, PHILIP. Dec. 29, 1829. March 8, 1830. Wife: Ann. Daus: Catharine Chrise, Jane Penrod, Mariah Penrod. Sons: Philip, David, Benjamin, Daniel,

Jorge (George). Ex: Benjamin Kimble (son), Israel Lynn. Wit: Elizabeth Carruthers, Peter Mahake (?).

LAY, WILLIAM. Feb. 5, 1844. July 15, 1844. Wife: Lucinda. Ex: wife. Wit: William Allen, G. A. Flournoy.

LOVELACE, ELIAS. March 23, 1832. Jan. 12, 1835. Wife: Nancy. "To Isaac Prather, son of Eli and Casander Prather, dec'd., to have 1 feather bed. Malinda Prather (sister of Isaac) to have one feather bed". Ex: wife, Andrew Newman, Andrew Lovelace. Wit: Archibald Lovelace, Andrew Lovelace.

MARTIN, JAMES. Inventory. Jan. 20, 1829.

MAYO, ABIGAIL. This will was probated in Richmond, Virginia, Oct. 9, 1843. Copy recorded in Paducah, Ky., Oct. 22, 1844. A will in eighteen sections, with eight codicils. Testator of Bellville, Henrico, Va. "To my son Edward Carrington Mayo land that was purchased in Richmond, Va., by my husband James Lysle, Sr." To grandson Edward (son of Edward) silver plate purchased since the death of late husband. "Among articles mentioned was a silver tankard having family arms engraved upon it, at that time it was in possession of testators daughter Sarah Mariah Scott, who was living in a place called Hampton Place, Elizabethtown, New Jersey. Legatees: Juliana Elizabeth Cabell (dau.), Louisa Patterson (sister), John Hart, Reuben Hart, William Hart ("three sons of my relative and friend, Robert D. Hart"). "To General Winfield Scott, Dr. Robert Henry Cabell, Edward Carrington Mayo, Samuel Marx, Joseph Mayo, to such as shall consent to act as trustees".

MC WORTHY, ELIAS. Jan. 4, 1837. Feb. 13, 1837. Wife: Margaret. Dau: Sarah Ann Rowe. Gr.son: Charles Washington Lewis Mc Worthy. Gr.dau: Elizabeth P. Adams, dau. of Mary Ann Adams (dau.). Wit: W. T. Best, Benjamin Wiles. Admr: Milton Mc Worthy.

MC WORTORS, SIBURN. Jan. 1, 1832. May 14, 1832. "Wife Nancy to have one black dress and bonnett taken from my trunk". "To sister Vany Mc Wortors one white dress to be taken from my trunk". Stepchildren, William Hill and Tabitha Hill to have land in Warren Co., Ky. Testators will was written in Tipton County, Tenn. Ex: Mathew Mc Wortors. Wit: A. H. Pope, Isaac Braden.

MORSE, SUPPLY C. April 5, 1833. ---------, Of Cincinatti, Hamilton Co., Ohio. The will was written in Parish West Feliciana, La. Estate in Ohio, Kentucky, Louisiana. Wife: Sarah. Wit: James E. Johnson, J. M. Perian, H. N. Anderson, J. P. Boswell, Henry Hiern.

MOSBY, JOSEPH. July 26, 1831. Aug. 8, 1831. Wife: Susannah. Six children mentioned but not named. Ex: wife. Wit: William Powers, Squire L. Stevall, Harmon Bone.

MUSGROVE, FIELDING CHARLES. August 9, 1843. Nov. 1844. Wife: Maretta. Ex: Hiram Smedley. Wit: George Smedley

NEWMAN, THOMAS. July 14, 1826. March 20, 1828. Wife: Elizabeth. Children mentioned: Andrew, Nancy Hill, Hiram, Thomas, Eli, Andrew. Ex: wife, Andrew Newman. Wit: Isaac Lovelace, Henry Garner.

NOBBS, BENEDICT. June 18, 1846. "Son James H. T. Nobbs to have one years schooling, dau. Nancy Mary to have five months in addition to what she had. Benedict N. Nobbs and Elizabeth Brown may be made equal in property to Joseph S. Nobbs. Hezekiah Anglin representative of deceased dau. Margaret Anglin children: Mary Elizabeth, Nancy Jane, Margaret."

OGLIVE, KIMBROUGH. Nov. 29, 1841. --------. Of Calloway Co., Ky. Wife: Nancy. Gr.son: James Benton Oglive. Ex: Vincent Wade. Wit: Joel Wear, Abner Johnson.

PHILLIPS, WILLIAM. April 12, 1844. May 25, 1844. Wife: Lucinda. Ex: Berry Hodge. Wit: R. Brownell, G. Magner.

PLUMMER, CHARLES. Inventory. July 17, 1826.

PRICE, WILLIAM. Inventory. Jan. 4, 1826. Apprs: Morgan B. Boren, James Talbot, L. Clanton.

RICHARDSON, JESSE. Oct. 15, 1839. ---------. Negro slaves to have their liberty for faithful services to himself and first wife. Mention heirs but does not name them. Test: John Duffy, Thomas Hugh.

SMEDLEY, JOHN. April 25, 1835. Nov. 9, 1835. Wife: Susan. Sons: John C., Amos. Daus: Agusta, Maria, Louisa. Ex: Christian Smedley (father), Hiram Smedley (bro.), Robert Fletcher. Wit: James O'Bannon, F. A. Harrison, F. H. Elrod.

SMITH, FRANCIS. Inventory. Nov. 20, 1835. Apprs: James Hawthorn, William Stokes, John C. Clannch.

SMITH, NICHOLAS. Jan. 2, 1838. Nuncupative. Wife Rachel to have land in Johnson County, Ill. Mentions the "four male children of brother William Smith". Proved by the oath of Lucinda Bullock, Martha Phillips, Martha McIntosh. Feb. 12, 1838.

STANLEY, ELIZABETH. April 13, 1844. Oct. 21, 1845. Children: Needham, Mason, Lucinda Allen. Ex: John Smith. Wit: R. G. Fletcher, John Smith.

STOVALL, SQUIRE. May 26, 1832. June 1832. Wife: Elizabeth. Ex: wife. Wit: Henry Buckler, John S. Stovall.

WATSON, ANNA. ------, ------Pro. 1835. "Land to bro. Benjamin Watson that I purchased from Col. James Thomas". Legatees: Eveline Watson (niece), Rosalie Gadsey (niece), Sally Francis (sister), Benjamin Watson (bro.), Samuel Watson (bro.). Ex: Benjamin Watson. Wit: William Smith, John Moore, Bryant Moore, Lewis Harvell.

WATSON, SAMUEL. Jan. 25, 1833. August 14, 1833. Mentions wife and children but does not name them. Ex: James Watson, John Stovall. Wit: James Watson, John Stovall.

WILCOX, JOHN. Dec. 18, 1836. Jan. 9, 1837. Nuncupative. Estate to Ralph Douglas. Proven by the oath of Thomas Best, Walter B. Padgett.

WOOLFOLK, GEORGE. Dec. 21, 1841. Dec. 11, 1843. Wife: Catharine. Sons: Robert Owen, George William. Daus: Ann, Frances Jane. Ex: ife, Robert Woolfolk (son), Dr. Robert Fletcher.

MERCER COUNTY

BOOK A

1786 -- 1795

ADAMS, WILLIAM SR. July 29, 1789. July 1795. Children: William, Samuel, David, Jennet, Anne, Margaret Curry, Mary Wilson. Ex: sons Samuel and David. Wit: Elizabeth Thomas, William Stewart, John Thomas.

ARMSTRONG, MARY. Dec. 13, 1792. May 1793. Legatees: Heirs of dau. Elizabeth and son William, sons Abel and Richard, Gr.son William son of Abel, Gr.son John, son of Richard, Gr.dau. Jean Steel, dau. of James, Gr.dau. Mary, dau. of James Armstrong. Ex: son Richard. Wit: Ninian Steel, John Bunton.

ARNOLD, STEPHEN. Dec. 26, 1793. March 1794. Wife: Jane. Children: Stephen, John, James, Elizabeth, Sarah, Jane. Son-in-laws Alexander Armstrong, Thomas Wilson. Gr.dau. Jenny Arnold, Dau. of Abegale. Ex: none. Wit: William Steel, Stanley Mc Clure.

BERRY, JOHN. Oct. 8, 1795. Oct. 1795. Wife: Anna. Children: Peggy, Rachel. Ex: Rachel Beery, Robert Mitchell. Wit: Thomas Gosh, Richard Berry, Elizabeth Ewing, Polly Berry.

BROWER, DANIEL. Jan. 15, 1791. Feb. 22, 1791. Children: John, Daniel, Abraham, Leah Stagg, Susannah Demaree, Rachel Cummings, Mary Demaree, Phebe Demaree. Ex: sons Abraham and John, Samuel Demaree, Sr. Wit: Peter Demaree, Francis Monfort, John Demaree.

BRUMFIELD, ROBERT. Feb. 7, 1790. Oct. 1794. Children: Job, William, James, Edah Prewit, Susan Richardson, Mary Prewit, Elizabeth Mitchel, Sarah, Rachel. Ex: son James, son-in-law John Richardson. Wit: Vincent Wren, Cloe Latimore, Agnes McLaughlin.

CANADY, RACHEL. Nov. 18, 1789. April 27, 1790. Children: Jeremiah Laws, Samuel Canady, Elizabeth Canady. Ex: Mariar Hansbrough, William Crow. Wit: John Underwood, George Hansbrough, Mariar Hanbrough.

COZINE, CORNELIUS. May 23, 1787. -----. Wife: Mary. Children: Daniel, Cornelius, Nancy, Sarah. Ex: John, Banta, Simon Vanarsdal, Albert Vorhis, Luke Vorhis.

DAVIS, JOSEPH. May 13, 1795. Nov. 1795. Wife: Jennet. Children: Samuel, John, William, Joseph, Robert, Jenny. Ex: wife, sons Robert and Joseph. Wit: William Gates, James Gates, John Davis.

DICKENS, DANIEL. Oct. 4, 1790. Feb. 28, 1792. Legatees: Three younger bros. and sisters: Charles, Winford, Lot Dickens. Ex: Chris. Dickens, Isaac Dickens. Wit: William Dickens, James Dickens, William Battou.

ESTES, ABRAHAM. May 23, 1788. Sept. 23, 1788. Wife: Kesiah. Children: Henry, Joel, Lucy, Rachel, Betty Ward, Jemimah, Franky. Ex: William Rice, wife, Robert Childers, Henry Estes. Wit: Joseph Robinson, James Lawrence,

Robert Lawrence.

FOSTER, ISAIAH. Nov. 29, 1794. Dec. 1794. Leg: Friends Absalom, Susanna and Jacob Froman, Michael Tothers, bro. Job and sister Rebecca. Ex: Jacob Froman. Wit: Peter Riley, John Everly, Emanuel Vantrees.

GILL, JOHN. Oct. 26, 1788. June 22, 1790. (Richland Co. South Carolina Oct. 9, 1789.) Wife: Margaret. Children mentioned but not named. Ex: (in Ky.) bro. William, John, and Thomas Pitman. Wit: William Mc Gowens, William Sanders.

GIVENS, SAMUEL, SR. Dec. 29, 1794. Aug. 1795. Wife: Martha. Nephew Robert Givens. Ex: Robert Caldwell, Sr., David Gillespie, Josiah Grover.

GRAHAM, BENJAMIN. Sept. 2, 1790. Oct. 1790. Wife: Faithful. Children: Alice, Mary, Jane, Elizabeth. Ex: Bro. Samuel, Elisha Thomas. Wit: Joshua Dodson, William McCachrow.

HALE, JOB. July 17, 1790. May 1793. Wife: Hannah. Children: John, Isaac, Betsy, Nancy, Sallie. Ex: John, Chiles, Capt. John Lillard. Wit: John Daly, John P. Steel, William Hoff.

HOLLOWAY, GEORGE. --------. March 1793. Wife: Mary. Children: Samuel, James, John, Mary Mc Gill, Charlotte Goodwin, 2 gr.children by Clayton Halloway (dec'd). Ex: wife, Thomas Allin. Wit: John Thomas, Peter Banta, Samuel Halloway.

HARRIS, WILLIAM. May 8, 1792. July 1793. Wife: Henrietta. Daus: Ann and Bradbourn. Ex: wife, George Thompson. Wit: James Taylor, Jr., William Clark Zachariah Field, George Thomason Jr., G. Thompson.

HARROD, JAMES. Nov. 28, 1791. Dec. 1794. Wife: Ann. Dau: Margaret. Ex: wife, William Moore, John Hardin of Nelson Co. Wit: John Winn, John Young, Israel Donaldson, Thomas Banfield, Samuel Naylor.

HARTLEY, THOMAS. May 15, 1789. June 23, 1789. Legatees: John Birney, Isaac Coffman, George Miles, Jean, Ann and William Birney Sr. Ex: William and John Birney. Wit: Vincent Wren, James Harlow, Daniel and Thomas Thornburg.

JAMES, ABRAHAM. March 30, 1791. May 24, 1791. Wife: Mary. Children: George, Sarah, Leah. Ex: wife, William Crow, Robert Mosby. Wit: William Rice, Philip Fulkerson, Francis Monfort.

JEFFERIES, MATHEW. Dec. 23, 1788. Aug. 1791. Wife: Isabella. Children: William, John, Agnes. Ex: son William, Capt. John Smith, Thomas Allin. Wit: Nathaniel Hart, Horatio Petty.

LITTLE, JOHN. July 7, 1794. Nov. 1794. Legatees: Polly (dau. of Col. John Smith), Peggy, Betsy, Patsy, Jennie, Sallie and John, and his bro. William Smith (sons of John Smith). Ex: Robert Mosby, Col. John Smith. Wit: James M. Graham, Andrew Shildrey, Samuel Graham.

LOWRY, PATRICK. July 25, 1781. ------. Wife: not named but mentioned. Children: John, James, Melvin, Margaret, Hannah, Betty, Mary, Jane Todd, unborn child. Ex: none. Wit: John Figgs, Elener Frake, Mary Conaway, Elisabeth Grundy.

MC AFEE, ROBERT. Feb. 28, 1795. Oct. 1795. Children: Samuel, Robert, John, Margaret, Janae, Sarah, Mary, Ann. Ex: John Braikenage, James McCoun.

MC COUN, JAMES. Aug. 31, 1790. Dec. 1790. Wife: Ann. Children: James, John, David, Elizabeth, Ann, Margaret, Mary. Ex: sons James, John. Wit: John Armstrong, Ann Mc Afee, James Legerwood, Robert Armstrong.

MC MURTY, JOHN. Sept. 6, 1790. Apr. 1791. Wife: Nancy. Children: James, Alexander, Samuel, William, John, Joseph, Mary. Ex: Mary Mc Murty. Wit: William Mc Kee, William Gordon, Henry Bishong.

MILLER, HANNAH. Aug. 16, 1786. March 1795. (wife of John Miller dec'd.). Children: Elizabeth, Jamime Thomas, Hannah, Mary. Ex: son-in-law William Fields, dau. Hannah Robinson. Wit: John Crow, William Crow, Elener Wright, Jean Owens.

NEELD, BENJAMIN. July 7, 1794. Oct. 1794. Bro. Nathan and bro. Robert. Niece Sarah Dau. of Nathan. Sister Jenny Steen. Ex: Augustin Passmore, Peter Casey, Nathan Neeld. Wit: John Steen, Robert Brown, John Daily.

NOELL, THOMAS. ------, June 23, 1789. Wife: Drucilla. Children: Elizabeth, Garnet, Muskow, John, Ann, Vancy, Lettie, Benjamin, Becky, Moses, Toby, Sally. Ex: wife, John Chiles Sr., Garnet Noell. Wit: David, Henry, and Elizabeth Chiles.

OVERTON, JAMES. Oct. 18, 1785. Jan. 25, 1791. Legatees: Bros. and sisters. Ex: Walter, Thomas and John Overton, Jr. Wit: William Pettus, Edmund Eggleston, Sarah Michir.

POFFE, GEORGE. Feb. 28, 1795. Oct. 1795. Legatees: John Willis. Ex: John Willis. Wit: Edward Willis, Samuel Devine, Mary Devine.

PRATHER, THOMAS. May 16, 1786. Aug. 1786. Wife: Mary. Children mentioned but not named. Theophilus Phillips. Ex: wife, James Coburn, Henry Prather.

ROBESON, JAMES. July 9, 1794. Dec. 1794. Wife: Sarah. Dau: Mary. Ex: none named. Wit: William Day.

SMITH, ADAM. Aug. 11, 1792. March 1793. Wife: Elizabeth. Children: Ezekiel, Benjamin, Solomon, Elizabeth. Ex: wife and son Ezekiel. Wit: Zacharias Smith, John Smith, John Samuel Mow.

STEPHENS, GEORGE WILLIAM. Dec. 27, 1784. April 28, 1789. Mother Mary Stephens, bros. Jacob, Isaac, Joseph, Lawerence, Bryan Martin Stephens. One half bro. John Stephens. Sisters Mary Earnest, Sariah Bowman. Ex: mother, bros. Joseph and Lawerence. Wit: Watson Henry, T. Hite, William Bowman, Robert Craige, James Bryan.

SUTTON, ROBERT. Dec. 28, 1794. Jan. 1795. Wife: Anna. Three daus. but only names Anne. Ex: wife, Benjamin Beall, Joseph Dickens. Wit: William Kennedy, Janette H. Beall, Mary Fields.

THOMPSON, JOHN. Aug. 20, 1792. Jan. 29, 1793. Wife: Priscilla. Children: John, Even. Ex: wife, son Even. Wit: John Wilcoxson, John Bennett.

THRELKELD, THOMAS. Jan. 3, 1790. March 23, 1790. Wife: Nellie. George and Daniel Threlkeld, sons of bro. John, Daniel Threlkeld Mc Konky, Armstead Long, Mary Buckey Threlkeld and Rachel Threlkeld (dau. of bro. Henry). Ex: wife, John Threlkeld, John Waggoner. Wit: Robert Pogue, Ezeliel Kennedy.

TILFORD, DAVID. July 23, 1794. Aug. 1794. Mother, Bro. Andrew, sisters Peggy Ewing, Polly Cull, Rachel Cloyd. Nephew Samuel Tilford (son of bro. Samuel). Remainder of estate to bros. and sisters not heretofore mentioned. Ex: Bro. Jeremiah and nephew James Mc Coun. Wit: Joseph Davis, Jeremiah Tilford, James Mc Coun.

VAN CLEVE, WILLIAM. Sept. 2, 1786. Feb. 1788. Wife: Abigail. Children: John, Ebenezer, William, Jonathan, Elizabeth, Jane, Mary, Phebe Harris. Ex: wife, William Crow. Wit: Thomas Gilmore, Rachel Van Cleve, Katherine Anderson.

WOODS, DAVID. (Of Virginia). Sept. 30, 1786. Dec. 1786. Mother, Ann Woods. Wife: Mary. Children: John, Billy, Nancy, Betsy. Ex: Samuel McAfee, John Gilmore. Wit: Bernard Noel, Capt. John Smith, Samuel Woods.

MUHLENBERG COUNTY

BOOK A

1799 -- 1814

ABOTT, JOHN. July 5, 1814. July 1814. Wife: Charity. Ex: wife, Silas Drake. Wit: William Weir, Josiah Underwood, Elizabeth Pitman.

ALLCOCK, RICHARD NELSON. March 9, 1805.)ct. 1807. Wife: Sarah. Sons: Counsel, Durand, James. Ex: Chas. Fox Wing, Chas. Lewis, Henry Davidge, Wit: Chris Thompkins, Sam'l Russell, David H. Stephens.

ALLISON, WILLIAM. April II, 1814. May, 1814. Children to receive estate on coming of age. Ex: William Imbler, Hugh Carter. Wit: Philip Murphy, John C. Groves.

ANDERSON, ROBERT. April 28, 1812. May 1821. Son: Thomas. Daus: Ann Dobyn, Martha Morris, Franky. Gr.son: Robert Littlepage. Ex: son Thomas, Amos Jenkins. Wit: Robt. Elder,Sr., Robt. Elder, Jon(John) Web (Webb).

BAILEY, THOMAS. Inventory. December, 1813.

BIGGERSTAFF, BENJAMIN. Inventory. November, 1799.

BIRD (BYRD), JOHN. June 22, 1808. ----- Wife: Rebecca. Sons: John, Mathias. Daus: Polly, Anne, Sally. Ex: wife, Leroy Jackson. Wit: R.D. McLean, Jacob Casebier.

BROWN, PETER. Inventory. Nov. 1811

BUTLER, GILBERT. Inventory. September, 1802.

CAMPBELL, PATRICK. August 28, 1799. Jan. 1800. Wife: Nancy. Son: William. Dau: Janitt (Janet?). Ex: wife, Patrick Campbell. Wit: C. Wing, A. McLean.

CAMPBELL, WILLIAM. Nov. 17, 1800. Feb. 1801. Wife: Tabitha. Son: Sam'l. Daus: Elizabeth, Tabitha, Ann, Polly, Jinny. Other legatees: Wm. Bradford. Ex: wife, William Russell, Robert Wilson, Wit:Jas. Blythe, B. Porter, Robert S. Russell.

CARTER, WILLIAM. Inventory. August, 1814.

COCKRUM, JAMES. Inventory. December, 1811.

COMBS (COOMBS), THOMAS. Inventory. February, 1807.

COOLEY, SUSANNA. Oct. 25, 1807. Dec. 1807. Son: Job Mathias. Dau: Susanna Reeves. Other legatees: Susanna Reeves (gr.dau), Justus Mathews (gr.son), Samuel Reeves (son-in-law). Ex: Jno. McFarland, Samuel Reeves. Wit: John McFarland, William McFarland, Samuel Reeves.

DAVIS, HENRY. -----April, 1805. Wife: Fanny. Sons: Randall, Henry. Dau: one mentioned but not named. Ex: Any David, Wm. Young. Wit: Lewis Kinchloe, Henry Davis, Warren Davis.(This Will was signed by Henry Young)

DOBYN, BATTEN. June 13, 1804. May, 1806. Wife: Frances. Sons: John, Lew, Washington. Daus: Elizabeth, Nancy, Susannah, Sally, Kitty, Polly. Ex: John Dobyn, Lew Dobyn. Wit: Thomas and Benjamin Littlepage.

DOBYN, JOHN. Inventory. May 13, 1813.

DURELLE, JOHN. May 13, 1800. August, 1808. Wife: Matha (Martha). Sons: David, Ephiram, Stephen, John. Daus: Rhoda, Matha, Rebecca. Wit: Jesse Reno, David Durall, Joseph Reynolds.

DURALL (DURELLE), SKINNER. Sept. 17, 1809. Oct. 1809. Wife: Elizabeth. Sons: Howard, Benjamin, Ark. Other legatees: Nancy Moore. Ex: wife, Elisha Durall, Wit: Micajah Wells, Spencer O'Neal, Robert Elder.

FISHER, JOHN. Inventory. Oct., 1814.

FORKER, THOMAS. Inventory. November, 1805.

GISH, CHRISTIAN. June 20, 1812. Oct. 1814. Wife: Barbary. Sons: David, Christian, John, Samuel, Joseph, George, Abraham. Daus: Elizabeth, Sally. Ex: John Hoffsinger, John Gish$\frac{3}{4}$ Wit: John Landis, James Walker, Fred. Haynes.

GOODMAN, SILVY. Inventory. July, 1809.

GROVES, JONATHAN. March 20, 1811. April, 1811. Wife: Edy. Sons: Isaac, Charles, William. Ex: wife, William Weir, David Groves. Wit: Joseph Groves, Susannah Gates.

HARRIS, JESSE. Inventory. April, 1806.

HELTSLEY, JACOB. Inventory. Jan., 1813.

LESLEY, VALENTINE. Inventory. December, 1802.

LEWIS, CHARLES. Nov. 1, 1806. Feb. 1808. Wife: Elizabeth. Sons: James, John, Charles. Daus: Suzean, Rebecca, Lizer, Elizabeth, Mary. Ex: wife, James Lewis, Isaac Pennington. Wit: Micajah Wells, Francis Wells.

McCARTNEY, JAMES. May 21, 1814. August, 1814. Legatees: nephews Thomas and James McCartney, Thomas, May Irwin. Ex: Thomas Irwin, Sr. Wit: Thomas Irwin, Jr., John Garvin.

McKINNEY, JOHN. Feb. 6, 1801. March, 1801. Wife: Mary. Sons: John, James, Gr. children: Mary McKinney, John McKinney (son of Sam'l.), John McKinney (son of James). Ex: wife, John McKinney, James McKinney. Wit: Charles Lewis, John McKinney.

McNARY, WILLIAM. Inventory. July, 1814.

McLEAN, JOHN. Inventory. December, 1800.

NAUGHT (VAUGHT), GEORGE. ----May, 1809. Sons: William, George, Isaac, Tamor. Daus: Mary McCaulis, Elizabeth McQuillion, Sally, Ruth. Ex: Jesse Reno. Wit: Armistead Morehead, Nancy Morehead.

NOFTZINGER, JACOB. Inventory. August, 1805.

PENROD, TOBIAS. Inventory. Oct., 1806.

MATHIS (MATHIAS), PERRIL. Dec. II, 1805. April 1806. Wife: Barbary. Ex: wife. Wit: John Stuart (son of D.S.), Eli Stuart.

OATES, W. Guardian's account. Oct., 1814.

PENROD, JANE. Dower. July 1813.

PROWSE, THOMAS. Inventory. Nov. 1810.

RENO, LEWIS. Aug. 28, 1799. Sept. 1799. Wife: Elizabeth. Son: Lewis. Dau: Milly Kincheloe. Wit: Isac (Isaac) Davis, Warren Davis, Moses Lucas.

RHOADS, DAVID. Oct. 6, 1811. Feb., 1813. Wife: Polly (second wife). Sons: Daniel, John, David, Henry, James, Lew, William, Ryla. Ex: wife, Solomon Rhoads. Wit: Henry Rhoads, Asa Hill, Bradford Rhoads.

RHOADS, HENRY. Aptil 15, 1812. August, 1813. Wife: Barbara: Sons: Daniel, Jacob, Henry, Solomon, David. Daus: Susannah Nighmyoir, Caty Jackson, Elizabeth Vanmeter, Hannah Jackson. Ex: bros. Daniel, Solomon, David. Wit: J.W. Connell, William Lunner.

RHOADS, JOSEPH. Sept. 17, 1799. Nov. 1799. Wife: Elizabeth. Sons: Jacob, Henry, John, Daniel. Daus: Hannah, Elizabeth, Catharine, Rachel, Mary (wife of Andrew Hunsaker). Ex: wife, bros. Solomon and Daniel. Henry Rhoads, Henry Right (Wright), Andrew Hunsaker, Solomon Rhoads.

ROSE, LENOX. August 28, 1806. Oct. 1806. Wife: Sarah. Children: six mentioned, but not named. Ex: wife. Wit: William Cross, Isaac Davis, Edward Williams.

SEVERS, FREDRICK. Feb. 28, 1804. April, 1804. Wife: Caterna. Sons: John, Solomon, Joseph, Michael, Gabriel, Jacob. Daus: Susannah, Elizabrth, Enlyanna. Ex: Solomon Rhoads, Jesse Jackson. Wit: Henry Rhoads, Abrm. Unsell.

SMITH, JOHN. March 26, 1803. May 1803. Wife: Mary. Sons: Elias, Jacob Keizer (stepson). Daus: Magdelena, Elizabeth. Other legatees: Rachel and Eva Tennet (nieces). Ex: son Elias, John Vaught. Wit: John Vaught, John Hopkins, John Zimmerman, Sam'l. Weir.

STOM, LEONARD. Inventory. May, 1814.

STUMP, FRANCIS. August 22, 1801. Oct., 1801. Wife: Rachel. Other legatees: David Washbough, George Hunsinger. Ex: John Vaught, John Stun, Rachel Stump. Wit: William Thompson, John Bowen, William Casebier.

TALBERT, JOHN R. Dec. 17, 1813. April, 1814. Wife: not named. Sons: Abner, Oliver. Ex: wife Nancy (?). Wit: Claibourne & Lucy Rice.

TYLER, RICHARD. Dec. 10, 1799. Jan. 1800. Wife: Sarah. Sons: John, Charles. Ex: wife, Isaac Davis. Wit: G. Tennille, Mary Davis.

VAUGHT, JOHN. June 11, 1813. July, 1813. Wife: Elizabeth. Daus: Margaret Smith, Eleanor, Polly. Sons: Abraham, John, Francis, Simeon, Martin, Samuel, Christopher. Ex: son John, Elias Smith. Wit: J. McConnell, Gilbert Vaught, Thos. Foster.

WARD, THOMAS. Inventory. October, 1808.

WARD, WILLIAM. Inventory. August, 1811.

WELLS, FRANCIS. April 7, 1812. May, 1812. Wife: mentioned but not named. Dau: Courtney Wells. Sons: Josiah, Wyatt, John, Micajah, Francis. Ex: Micajah and John Wells. Wit: A.B. Drake, Louis Solomon.

WILSON, ELIJAH. Feb. 22, 1812. -----Wife: Elizabeth. Son: Jeremiah. Daus: Esther, Elizabeth. Ex: Jeremiah Langley, Thomas Salsberry. Wit: Leron Jackson, Robert Robertson.

WOOTTON, ELIJAH. Inventory. Oct., 1814.

YOUNG, WILLIAM, SR. Inventory. July, 1814.

(Muhlenborg County wills were copied by Mr. Gayle R. Carver, Greenville, Ky.)

NELSON COUNTY

BOOK A

1784 -- 1807

ABELL, GEORGE. Sept. 2, 1803. ------. Wife: Elizabeth. Sons: Enoch Booth, Pollard, Francis. Daus: Ann, Judith, Catharine, Elizabeth. Ex: wife Elizabeth, William Abell. Wit: ------.

ADAMS, RICHARD. Inventory. July 1798.

ALLISON, WILLIAM. March 31, 1800. ------. Wife: Nancy. Children not mentioned. Sister: Mary Norris. Ex: Wife, bro-in-law James Stone. Wit: Thomas Bennett, Joseph Bennett, Henry Wilson.

ANDERSON, JOHN. Nov. 7, 1806. ----1807. John McGee to settle estate. Sons: John, Robert, James, Samuel, Archibald, David. Widow not named. Daus: Mary, Jean, Elizabeth.

ARMSTRONG, JOHN. June 27, 1800. Aug. 1800. To Mary Wilhite (hus. Tobias) and dau. Mary. Ex: Harmon Greathouse, Abraham Wilhite. Wit: Joshua Shearly, John Rush, Nancy Rush.

ASH, JOHN. Oct. 4, 1799. May 1800. Wife: Arabella. Sons: Reuben, Selvester, George, Joseph, Henry, Abraham. Daughters: Elizabeth. Ex: wife. Wit: John Mc Garvey, James Glass, William Pasley.

AYDELOTT, GEORGE H. Sept. 12, 1803. ------. Wife: Christiana Britingham Aydelott. Daus: Anna Reed, Elizabeth Bard, Mary Mc Dowell, Leah Holland. Sons: John, Benjamin, Zodack, Joshua. Ex: wife Christiana. Wit. ------.

BAIRD, THOMAS. Inventory. Jan. 16, 1792.

BAIRD, THOMAS. Dec. 13, 1790. Dec. 1791. To brother James, To brother John Shields. William Wilson. Ex: James Baird, Brien Neel. Wit: John Shields, James Shields.

BARNES, HANNAH. July 30, 1804. Sept. 1804. Children: Charity Fitzpatrick, Gr.dau. Ann Cole, heirs of Sally Welch, heirs of Andrew Hynes, heirs of Sarah Plummer. To daus. of Charity Fitzpatrick and Nancy Cole. Wit: Heli Kendall, John Lapley, Benjamin Kendall.

BARTON, ROGER. Inventory. March 9, 1792.

BELL, JAMES. Aug. 6, 1801. Nov. 1805. Wife: Ester. Children: Ester Evans, Dorcas Bell, Jenny, Elizabeth, Robert, Thomas, Samuel, James. Legatees: James and Sarah (dau. Samuel) Pendleton, Mary Moon, Nancy Scott (Isaac Scott). Ex: wife, John Bidford. Wit: John Young, Francis Davis.

BISSELL, THOMAS. Inventory. Feb. 25, 1803. By Rachel Bissett, Admr.

BLACK, JOHN. Feb. 5, 1795. March 5, 1795. To Jane Flemmon (sister), Abigail Black. Brother Jack Black. Mother Sarah Black.

BLAND, JOHN. Oct. 5, 1795. ------. Wife: Margaret. Children: Prudence Smith (hus. Timothy), Frances Hughes, Molly Randolph and sons, Samuel, John, Isaac, Elijah, Daniel, William. Nancy Bland, (dau. of Henry). Ex: wife, Daniel and John Bland. Wit. ------.

BLANDFORD, WILLIAM. Inventory. July 26, 1803.

BOARMAN, WILLIAM. Feb. 19, 1800. ------. To mother Dorthy Boarman. Legatees to be divided equally between four children of Ignatus Boarman: Elizabeth, John, Ignatus, Mary. Ex. Elizabeth Boarman. Wit: William Shaney, Mary Gristy, Dorothy Worthing.

BOGARTH, JOSEPH. (Of Nelson County, State of Virginia). May 5, 1790. Dec. 4, 1790. Wife:----. Sons: Joseph, John, Daus: and other small children not named. Ex: wife, brethern and friends, John Larue, Robert Hodges.

BRAKES, ROBERT. Appr. and Inventory. Aug. 8, 1799.

BRAY, HENRY. March 7, 1798. July 1799. Wife: Cathryn. Children: John Fredrick, Peter, William, Abraham, Peggy Ball, Jan Dewitt, Mary Davis, Cristner Robert. Ex: Aron Atherton. Wit: John Hill, Zacariah Masterson.

BRIGGS, WILLIAM. Dec. 9, 1800. March 9, 1801. Children: David, Thompson, Jane, Isabell, Ebenezer, Mary, Robert, George, Benjamin, Marian. Ex: wife Judith, Benjamin Edwards, John Robertson Esq., Thomas Hubbard, Thomas Duncan. Wit: James Brooks, David Gray, John Shields, William Wilson.

BRIGGS, WILLIAM. Inventory. April 10, 1792.

BROWN, PETER. Jan. 15, 1792. July 1793. Wife: Frances. Sons: Jereboam, Peter, Charles, Francis. Daus: Elinor, Rose, Mary, Ann. Ex: son Jereboam.

BURNS, MICHAEL. Dec. 4, 1795. Oct. 12, 1796. Wife: Priscilla. Children: Thomas, James, John, Ignatus, Michael, Robert, William, Joseph. Ex: wife, Joshua Grinwell. Wit: Atkinson Hill, John Finch.

CASEY, JAMES. August 11, 1795. Inventory.

CHINN, RAWLEIGH. Inventory. Nov. 4, 1801.

CLARK, JOSEPH. Aug. 6, 1796. May 1797. Wife: Mary. Children: Henry, James, Joseph, Elizabeth, Blanford, Ann Howard, Mary Thornburg. Legatees: Rebecca Thalls or Hall, Mary Hogan, Selah Clarch, Gr.children: Henry, James, Joseph, Elizabeth, Ann, Mary, Rebecca, Elinor, Selah. Ex: son Joseph Clarck. Wit: W. Charles Dorsey, Walter Stollard, Thomas Basye.

CLARKE, GEORGE. Nov. 1807. Dec. 1807. Wife: Sarah. Sons: James, Joseph, George. Other children not named.

CLEAVER, WILLIAM, SR. Aug. 28, -----. Dec. 1807. Wife: Hannah. Children: Benjamin William Stephens, David, James, Hannah. Ex: son Stephen.

CLEMENTS, JOHN. Nov. 16, 1803. Dec. 1803. Son: Leonard. Dau: Annie and her children: Polly, John, Creecy, D. Billy.

COMBS, DAVID. Inventory. June 6, 1801.

COMPTON, AUGUSTINE. Inventory. 1790.

COOMBS, JOHN. Aug. 12, 1800. Dec. 14, 1801. Wife: Elce. Children: Edward, Nelson, Asa, Samuel, John, Joseph, Sarah, Lettice, Elce. Ex: sons Edward and Nelson.

COPELAND, JAMES. July 16, 1796.

CRAVEN, JAMES. March 12, 1799. --------. Wife: Jemminah. Sons: James, Lefi. Dau: Hannah. Other children not named.

CRUME, WILLIAM. Inventory. Aug. 29, 1796.

CURTS, MARTIN. Jan. 26, 1795. Wife: Ann. Estate to be divided among heirs not named.

DAY, WILLIAM. May 12, 1800. July 1800. Wife: Nancy. Children: James, Susanna, Mary, William, Joseph, Heady, Peter, Yeartis, Nancy. Ex: sons James and William.

DEACON, MICHAEL ARCH. Inventory. Oct. 1792.

DOWNS, WILLIAM. Inventory. Dec. 4, 1798.

DRAKE, JONATHAN. June 11, 1791. Wife: Lucy. Son: Robert. Bro: John. Ex: wife and bro. John.

DUCKER, JOHN. April 1804. Wife: Elizabeth. John Ducker Spurrow, (son of Joseph) and Jerimiah Ducker, son of bro. Jeremiah.

EWING, SAMUEL. April 17, 1790. Jan. 10, 1792. Estate to Jacob Yoder, Jacob Ambrose, Stephen Ormsby.

FERGUSON. Inventory. Jan. 28, 1796.

FITCH, JOHN. June 20, 1798. July 1798. To friend William Rowan, "My beaver hat." To Dr. William Thornton of Washington D.C., Eliza Vail (dau. of Aaron), John Rowan. Ex: John Rowan, James J. Nourse.

FOGER, JOHN ADAMS. Dec. 8, 1804. Sons: Robert, Christian. Daus: Rebecca, Diana, Sarah, Annie. Ex: John and Benjamin Hammell.

FULKARTSON, FULKART. Feb. 10, 1797. --------. Sons: Jacob, Philip. Wife: Mary.

GREENWELL, JOHN. A. June 22, 1799. Sept. 14, 1801. Wife: Mary. Children: Henry, Ralf, Elizabeth, Robert, Ann, John. Ex: John Finch, Charles Smith, and wife Mary. Wit: Jesse and Elizabeth Ice.

GREEN, MARY. Sept. 1806. Feb. 1807. David Gill guardian of two sons, John and Caleb, until 21 years of age. John 12 years of age on 2nd of April next and Caleb 4 years of age on 28th of June.

GRIGSBY, NATHANIEL. May 13, 1797. Sept. 1801. Wife: Susannah. Sons: John, Nathaniel, Joseph, James, Samuel, Eskridge. Daus: Elizabeth, Mason, Susannah. Ex: wife, son Nathaniel.

HAMMOND, GEORGE. Jan. 9, 1801. Aug. 8, 1803. Wife: Mary. Children: Millie Stone, Job, Gervis, Nancy Edwards. Two slaves, old Letty and Patty, to have their liberty. Ex: wife, son Job. Wit: A. Hubbard, Joseph Morris, George and Rebecca Humphrey.

HAMMOND, JERVIS (GERVICE). Aug. 8, 1803. Nuncupative. Proved by the oath of Austin Hubbard, Isaac Ruble, Joseph Morris. Ex: Gervise Hammond, Jr. and Job Hammond.

HAND, JOSEPH. Jan. 8, 1793. May 1793. Wife: Nancy. Children: Joshua, William, Charles, Joseph, Elizabeth, Polly, Nancy. Ex: wife. Wit: Isaac Lansdale, John Davis, Peter Atherton.

HARDIN, MARK. March 1790.------. Sons: Henry, John, Mark, Benjamin. Wife: Ann. Daus: Lydia, Mary, Sarah, Catharine Hallet, Hannah Steelup. Ex: wife, sons Henry and John. Wit: Benjamin and John Hardin.

HARRISON, GEORGE. Division of property. Feb. 27, 1806. Wife: Elizabeth. Daus: Nancy Hynes, Fanny Harrison.

HART, MILES. Sept. 6, 1786.---1790. Wife: Elizabeth. Estate to wife and brother Silas Hart. Ex: Edward and Stephen Rawlings.

HART, SILAS. Inventory. June 12, 1790.

HEADY, THOMAS. August 12, 1799. July 9, 1804. Wife: Rebekah. Children: Stillwell, Thomas, Martha Goodwin, Elizabeth Collins, Rebecca Drake, Jane, Mary Silkwood, Charity Sturgeon. Wit: John Stone, Basel Nott, Daniel Bidwell.

HERRON, WILLIAM. July 1, 1793. Oct. 1793. Wife: Agnes. Children: James, John, Samuel, Elizabeth, Ann, Abigail, Isabel, Rachel, Mary, Margaret, Agnes, William. Ex: wife, son Samuel. Wit: Samuel Greer, James Allen, John Huston.

HOBB, ELIZABETH. ------Nov. 1796. Children: John, Walter, Stephen, Cyntha, Sarah, Elizabeth, Cassander, Margaret. Mentions husband Joshua Hobbs and daus. of Cassandrie, Elizabeth and Margaret. Ex:---- Wit: Elisha and Joseph Spurrier, Edwin H. Compton.

HOGLAND, RICHARD. Inventory. Oct. 1790.

HOWARD, JOHN. Dec. 9, 1802. Sept. 12, 1803. Wife: Elizabeth. Children: Henry, George, Charles, William, Joseph, Mary Corby, Sarah, Elinor Gray, Gr.sons: children of dau. Elizabeth. Ex: son-in-law Walter Seslee (hus. of dau. Sarah). Wit: Walter Burch, John P. Hill, Thomas Hill.

HUMPHREY, WILLIAM. Jan. 12, 1805. July 8, 1805. Wife: Mary. Children: George, Sarah Botsel, Susan, Elizabeth, Mary, John, William, Samuel, Simon, Nancy. Ex: wife, sons George and John. Wit: Joseph Ferguson, James Goodwin, Susannah Ferguson.

HYNES, ANDREW. July 21, 1800. July 1800. Wife: Elizabeth. Children: Abner, Thomas, Nancy, Alford Warford, Polly, Sarah Churchill, Elizabeth Harrison. Ex: --------. Wit: John Caldwell, Will R. Hynes, Alex. Mc Cown.

HYNES, THOMAS. March 4, 1796. July 12, 1796. Wife: Abigail. Children: William R., Andrew J., Thomas, Sally, Polly, Nancy. Ex: brother Andrew J. and son William R. Wit: Thomas, William, Isaac Crutcher.

JARBO, JOHN. March 10, 1792. June 1794. Wife: Ann. Son: John. Other children not mentioned. Ex: wife. Wit: Margaret Sands, George Hartt, William Newboutt.

JARBO, RANDOLPH. Aug. 9, 1796. Dec. 13, 1796. Wife: Elizabeth. Children: John, Walter, Elender, Bamel, Henry Bray, Joseph Brewer. Ex: wife and son John.

JONES, SAMUEL L. March 12, 1804. Dec. 1804. "Lots 3 and 4 to use of a grave yard. All property to be sold and money used to build a church on said lot. All preachers that preach Jesus Christ and Him crucified shall have free access to preach therein and every person that bares name of Christian there if it be their wish." Admr: Mr. Wilson, William Haynes.

JORDON, JOHN. Sept. 23, 1790. June 14, 1791. Wife: Ann. Children: Barbara, Jane, Andrew. Mentions bound children, James and Nelly O'Nail. Ex: wife, Henry Wood. Wit: W. Wright, John Harbison, William Jackson.

KAMPT, JOHN. Inventory. Dec. 18, 1800.

KENCHELOE, WILLIAM. Oct. 13, 1788. Aug. 1797. Wife: Molly. Children: Thomas, Peggy Davis, Stephen, Sally, Clary, Lewis, Eliss, Jesse, William. Ex: wife, son Lewis. Wit: Jesse and Travers Davis, Moses Milton, Bryan Young.

KING, VALENTINE. (Commonwealth of Virginia). Feb. 22, 1790. April 13, 1790. Sister Elizabeth Owens, bro. John Edwards King, Elizabeth Crisps, dau. of Nancy Brashear. Mentions mother and bros. William and Withers King. Ex: George and Cuthbert Harrison. Wit: Anthony Foster, Paul Kester, Cuthbert Harrison.

LANCASTER, RAPHAEL. March 1802. Peter Brown, J. Lewis. Inventory.

LAURENCE, SOLOMON. July 31, 1806. April 1807. Wife: Ann. Children: Elizabeth Pursley, James, William, Samuel, Robert, Fanny, Ann, Jenny. Ex: wife and Joseph Beathy. Wit: William Wells, Samuel Pursley.

LEE, SAMUEL. Inventory July 12, 1792. Apprs: John Davis, Charles Beeler, Jesey Rude.

LERUE, JOHN. Jan. 3, 1792. May 8, 1792. Wife: Mary. Children mentioned but not named. Ex: Robert Hodgen, Isaac Lerue Jr., Phillip Phillips. Wit: Sarah and Margaret Hodgen, Isaac Enslow.

LITCHING, ANTHONY. Inventory. Aug. 2, 1796.

LITSEN, ANTHONY. June 28, 1792. Sept. 1792. Children: Randolph, John,

Anthony, James, Henry, Matt, Sarah, Catharine, Mary, Nancy. Ex: Benjamin Ogden, William Hays. Wit: David Burcham, Samuel Robertson, John Stapleton.

MALIN, ISAAC. April 18, 1803. May 1803. Wife: Susanna. Children: Jacob, Gr.son Jonathan. Other children not mentioned. Six sons. Ex: Edmond Polk, Evan Williams, son Jacob. Wit: Moses Harrell, Elijah Wright, William May.

MARKS, WILLIAM. Sept. 4, 1804. -----. Wife: Mary. Children: John, James, Elizabeth, Jane, Margaret, Sarah, Mary. Ex: wife, sons John and James. Wit: Ebenezer Burkhead, Moses Crume, Mary Burns.

MARSHALL, JOHN. May 5, 1790. June 1791. Estate to friend George Hartt.

MARSHALL, WILLIAM. Nov. 1, 1803. May 14, 1804. Wife: Jane. Children: John, Jeremiah, James, William. Ex: wife, son William. Wit: John Risks, Isaac Taylor.

MCATER, LEONARD. Inventory, and sale. Nov. 1798.

MCCOLOMAN, JOSEPH. Sept. 3, 1800. Sept. 9, 1800. Wife: Elizabeth. Daus: Jean Kennedy. Other children not mentioned. Ex: wife. Wit: James Hady, Edwin Colton (or Cotton), William Woodman.

MCDANIEL, JOHN. ------. April 9, 1804. Wife: Mary. Children: Joseph, George, Solomon, James, Alex, William, Leah, Rebeccah. Ex: Eli Adams, George Medcalf. Wit: John Bullock, Richard Wright, James Cox.

MILLER, EBENEZER. Aug. 16, 1796. June 10, 1797. Wife: Mary. Children: James, Joseph, William, John, Stephen and son-in-law John King. Ex: wife, James Miller. Wit: James Deacon, J. Kennedy.

MILTON, RICHARD. Dec. 31, 1797. May 1801. Wife: Peggy. Children: William, John, Moses, Elijah, Nancy Davis, Sally Wilson, Francis Davis. Son-in-law Rawleigh Chinn, James Davis. Ex: sons Moses and Elijah, Gr.son James Moore.

MINOR, MARY. July 31, 1801. Dec. 1801. Children: William, Mary, Nicholas, John, Stephen, Spence. Ex: son William. Wit: Robert King, "Nick" Minor.

MORGAN, CHARLES C. Inventory. James Morgan, Admr. April 8, 1805.

MORRISON, JAMES. Dec. 5, 1798. May 1799. Children: James. Mentions James Nourse. Ex: James Nourse, Michael Kamp.

MURRY, JOHN. (MURRY). Wife: Darcus. Children: Jesse, Enoch, Margaret, Ann, John, Alfred, James, Elizabeth, Joseph.

NEELY, ISAAC. Inventory. July 12, 1792.

NEWITT, JOHN. Jan. 7, 1800. May 10, 1808. Wife: Ann. Children: John, Richard, James, Joseph, Ann Bowling, Ann Adams, Charles. Gr.chld: Joseph and Lucy Newitt. Ex: sons Richard and Joseph. Wit: Arthur Mc Lean, Samuel McLean, Walter Burch.

PATTON, JAMES. Aug. 9, 1796.

PAYTON, ELIAS. May 6, 1799. Aug. 13, 1799. Mentions cousin Polly Payton, dau. of bro. Elisha. Estate to be equally divided between brother and sister.

PENNEBAKER, PETER. (PANEBAKER). -----. Sept. 14, 1807. Wife: -----. Estate to children of daus. Margaret Couchman, Mary Mc Clelland. Ex: John Goodlett, Benjamin Grayson. Wit: Val Gray, Christian Binman, Thoman Langley.

POLK, THOMAS. Sept. 15, 1804. Nov. 9, 1807. Bros: Edwinond, Charles, Ralph Matson. Sister Sarah Polk. Wife: Lucy Polk. Step sons Samuel and Ignatus Abell. Ex: wife, and step son Samuel Abell. Wit: Edmond, Abell, Goodlove Kamp, William Kieth.

PRAYTHER, RICHARD. Inventory. May 11, 1801.

RANDOLPH, -----. Aug. 6, 1792. Inventory. John Karmady, James Colvin, W. T. Samuels, Apprs.

REED, CHARLES. (State of Virginia). Jan. 23, 1789. -----. Wife: Elizabeth, Children: John, Archibald, Charles, William. Ex: wife, Philip Phillips. Wit: James Anderson, John Phillips.

REEDE, JESSE. Jan. 30, 1791. April 1791. Wife: Maryann. Thomas and Ashley only children mentioned. Wit: William Mc Kime, James Brown, Asher Reede. Ex: wife, sons Thomas and Ashley.

RICKS, DINAH. March 14, 1796. July 1796. Children: John, Thomas, Ruth Crawford, Elizabeth, Mary. Ex: sons John and Thomas. Wit: William May, James Holtston, Rachel ------.

ROBERTSON, WILLIAM. March 14, 1796. July 12, 1796. Wife: Mary. Children: John, Elizabeth James, son-in-law Joseph James. Ex: son John and son-in-law Joseph James. Wit: William Wilkinson, John and Betsy Conway.

SCOTT, DANIEL. Inventory. January 24, 1807. Apprs: William Crutcher, Atkenson Hill, Leven Sprigg.

SCOTT, WILLIAM. Inventory. Jan. 15, 1807.

SHALLEY, ADAIR. Inventory. Aug. 20, 1803.

SHURELIFFE, THOMAS. (St. Marys Co., Maryland). June 15, 1786. July 1787. Wife: Elizabeth. Children not mentioned. Ex: wife. Wit: James Hamelton, Bennett Mattingly, Francis E. Shurliffe.

SHUMATE, JOHN. Sept. 16, 1792. ------. Wife: Margaret. Children: not named. Ex: wife Margaret, son Nimrod. Wit: William Smithers, William Young, Moses Milton.

SIMMONS, MARY. Dec. 5, 1788. Aug. 1792. Children: Edward, William, Jeminy, Vilandar, Griffin, Willett, Tabitha, Samuel, George, Rachel, Mary. Ex: James Willett (son). Wit: Edward Jones, Osborne Bland, Susannah Pottoneger.

SLAUGHTER, ROBERT. Feb. 22, 1803. May 1803. Wife: Peggy. Children not named. Ex: Brother Thomas and James. Wit: William Rogers, James Rogers, Thomas Bisress.

SMITH, MARY. Nov. 15, 1794. Oct. 1795. Children: Susannah Asher, Samuel Orr, Elizabeth Orr, Ann Dewett, William Smith, Gr.son Elijah Shockency, John Shockency, Hannah Devor. Ex: Bryan Stone, Thomas Morton. Wit: George Bruce, John Stoner, Hugh Crawford, Jr.

STIGLER, SAMUEL. Mar. 22, 1800. May 1800. Wife: Sarah. Children: Benjamin, Gilly, Mary Rawson, Sally Brown, Patty Snyder, Charlotte Eldridge, Nancy Dorsey. Ex: son James Brown, Charles Wortham, Beall Dorsey. Wit: Arthur Hall, Jeremiah Rees, John Brown.

TANNAHILL, SARAH. Aug. 30, 1792. Jan. 1793. Children: To dau. Rebecca Beall one half dozen table spoons and at her death to her dau. Sarah Beall and thirty pounds of Virginia money, to grandson Samuel Beall sixteen pounds of Virginia money and a half dozen silver table spoons. Son-in-law Walter Beall. To dau. Ann Harrison one half dozen silver teaspoons and forty pounds of Virginia money her gr.dau. Sally Harrison to inherit same at death of her mother. To friend Lydia Dorsey riding coat. Ex: Cuthbert Harrison (son-in-law), Charles Dorsey. Wit: Benjamin Frye, Jacob Yoder, James Latham.

TICHENOR, DANIEL. April 2, 1803. May 1804. Wife: Anna. Children: Peter, Jared, Silas, James, Joseph, Phebe Sutton, Jane Mash, Sarah Langsford, Anna, Daniel, Timothy, Elizabeth. Ex: wife Anna, sons Jacob and Peter. Wit: John Bruner, Jacob Fulkoyson, Thomas Bolden.

VAUGHAN, ANDREW. Inventory. Oct. 31, 1793. Jacob Decker, Admr.

VAUGHN, MARY. July 27, 1798. Nov. 1798. Children: All estate to dau. Mary May. Wit: Micajah Glascock, Jonathan Gore.

VEST, THOMAS. Inventory. Oct. 25, 1802. Admr: Samuel Niel.

WAKEFIELD, MATHEW. ------. Wife: Bridget. Children: Mathew, William, Mary (hus. Robert Samuels), John, Elizabeth (hus. Robert Kennady), Margaret (hus. John Bell), Jean (hus. James Russell).

WHITAKER, HENRY R. Inventory. Jan. 19, 1801.

WILCOCKS, WILLIAM. Inventory. June 1802.

WILLETT, SAMUEL. Oct. 1793. Apprs: Samuel Pettinger, Marak Carter, Richard Gardinier. Ex: son John. Dec. 13, 1797. Aug. 1799. Wit: John Huston, James Huston, James McClaskey.

WILSON, WILLIAM. Inventory. July 7, 1792.

WINSATT, IGNATUS. Dec. 2, 1806. May 1807. Wife: Eleanor. Ex: wife. Children: Ann, Ignatus, Puronella. Wit: William T. Shaneey, Richard Gardner.

WOODS, RICHARD. Inventory. Dec. 1805.

WORTHAM, SAMUEL. Inventory. Guardian appointed for heirs of Samuel Wortham, Charles and Lacy, 1786.

NELSON COUNTY

INDEX

BOOK B

Adams, Richard
Anderson, Benedict
Allen, Robert
Allen, James
Auberry, Thomas

Bean, John
Beall, Elisha
Beall, Walter
Bonehart, John
Brougher, Jacob
Brown, James
Brown, Sally
Brown, Thomas
Burke, A.
Burton, ------.

Calvert, Thomas
Clark, James
Clark, John
Clark, George
Colton, John
Clement, John
Couchman, Michael
Cox, Gabriel
Crutcher, Isaac

Edwards, William

Farmer, John
Folks, Mary
Fuller, John

Glaze, Earhart
Grable, Joseph
Greenwell, John A.

Hagan, Mary
Harding, James
Head, Catherine
Heady, Thomas
Hobbs, Joseph
Howard, Thomas
Howard, Charles
Huston, William
Humphreys, William

Humphreys, Mary
Hynes, Andrew

Johnston, Samuel
Johnston, William
Jones, Samuel

King, William

Leasher, John
Lightfoot, John
Long, James

Marks, George
Marks, Sarah
Martin, Edward
Mc Cabe, ----
Mc Clary, John
Mc Atee, Leonard
Mc Garvy, John
Mc Gee, John
Merryman, Zacariah
Miles, William

Polk, Thomas
Prather, Richard

Remey, Thomas
Ricks, Thomas
Roberts, Thomas

Smiley, William
Stewart, Charles
Stone, Elijah

Taylor, William

Vorols, John

Walker, Gideon
Weller, Daniel
Wells, Frances
Willett, George
Woodsmall, James

NICHOLAS COUNTY

BOOK A

1800 -- 1816

BAKER, MARTIN, SR. July 7, 1812. Oct. 1812. Sons: John, James, William, Thomas, Benjamin, Martin. Gr.son: Martin Mc Clure. Dau: Sarah Kimbrough. Ex: children, William Cook, James Mc Clure. Wit: James Cole, E. P. Rall.

BARLOW, THOMAS. Sept. 10, 1808. Nov. 1808. Wife: Eleflet. Sons: William, Jesse. Daus: Elizabeth, Jane, Mary Epison, Edith King (Fing), Liency Saddler, Milly. Ex: William Barlow, Jesse Baskett.

BEARD, WILLIAM, (BAIRD). May 4, 1801. April 1802. Sons: George, William, John. Daus: Martha, Nancy. Sons-in-law: Walter McFarland, George Workman. Ex: George Beard, Cornelius Hall. Wit: John Baird, George Workman, George Baird, Martha Baird, Nancy Baird.

BELL, ROBERT. Feb. 15, 1803. May C. C. 1803. Wife: Jane. Children: Jane, Sally, Polly, Robert. Mentions brother Samuel Brown. "I do allow to David Brown my ankeen Jackett and Breeches and all rest of my wearing apparel." Ex: David Brown and James Ardrey. Wit: James Graham, Alex Clark.

BOYD, WILLIAM. Inventory. Aug. 24, 1805. Admr: Ally Boyd.

BRADENBURY, MATHIAS. Inventory. April 11, 1807. Admr: Esther and David Bradenbury.

BRITTON, JOSHUA. Inventory. Dec. 20, 1806.

BUCHANAN, JAMES. Inventory. June 10, 1806. Apprs: William Williams, John Allison, Thomas West.

BUCKNER, ROBERT. Nov. 4, 1805. Wife mentioned but not named. Children: Samuel, Henry, Sharlotte, Harre? Martin? and Liddy? Ex: Cordin Hall. Wit: C. Hall, Elizabeth Ammon.

BURDIN, JAMES. April 5, 1806. Dec. 1806. Wife: Mary. Children: Charles, Elijah, several daus. but does not name them, (children of former wife). Ex: William Baker. Wit: Charles Dotson, James Adams, Robert Barrings.

CASADY, DANIEL. April 25, 1812. April 1814. Children: Thomas, Jeremiah, William, Nelly, Mary. Gr.dau. Nancy. Ex: sons James and Jeremiah. Wit: Thomas Davidson, H. Roberts.

CASADAY, THOMAS. July 1815. Oct. 1815. Bro. Jeremiah and his dau. Polly. Ex: bro. Jeremiah. Wit: Thomas Davidson.

CORBIN, ABRAHAM. April 14, 1813. -------. Wife: Eleanor. Children: not named. Wit: William Mc Dowell, Phebe Galbreath, Rachel Corbin.

CRAWFORD, SAMUEL. Sept. 30, 1804. July 1806. Wife: Mary. Children: Mary, John, Isabel. Ex: wife.

DAILEY, BRYAN. Dec. 2, 1803. Feb. 1804. Children: John and others not named. Ex: wife but not named. Wit: Robert Davis, William Asberry Jr., Elihu Harding.

DAVIDSON, JOHN. Sept. 12, 1815. Oct. 1815. Wife: Nancy. Children: Jane Riddle and her heirs, Isabella Barnes, Christiana Nukam, John, James, Martha Dampeer? Ex: David Rogers. Wit: David Byers, John Forsyth.

DEAL, MATTHEW. Jan. 15, 1813. -----. Wife: Keaty. Children: Isaac, James, Mathew, William, John. Ex: son Isaac. Wit: David Byers, John Bannester.

DOWNEY, ARCHIBALD. March 21, 1814. May 1815. Wife: Sarah. Children: Jenny and others not named. Ex: James Thompson Jr. Wit: Robert Caldwell, Edward Pendergart.

DRUMMONDS, JAMES. March 11, 1812. Jan. 1814. Wife: Rebecca. Children: Eleanor, Polly Wilson, Elizabeth Godman, Rachel Batson. Ex: wife, Samuel Griffith. Wit: Samuel Irwin, Joseph Steel.

DUNSMORE, SAMUEL. Nov. 7, 1807. Jan. 1808. "I give white straight coat and gray coat that is at the Taylors to my sister Margaret Mullenberginz. Sister Elizabeth Wammeter, bros. John D., Henry. Ex: bro. John.

FORSYTHE, WILLIAM. Inventory. Aug. 13, 1800. Apprs: John Mitchell, William Thompson, Alex. Thompson.

FOSTER, THOMAS. Oct. 30, 1808. Nov. 1808. Wife: Rhoda (alias Howard). Children: Susana Yates, Mary Mouide?. "To wife Rhoda is best entitled to it from her care, conduct, circumspection, and attention to me in all my infirmities. In short under God what property I have she has been the means of acquiring and keeping together under present disorders I labor under she has been my nurse, my consolation and my friend as she is best deserving of enjoying what she has so faithfully and justly assissted in acquiring." Ex: George and Christian Summit. Wit: James Musset, John Frye, Edward Stoker.

GRAY, JAMES. Dec. 23, 1812. April 1813. Wife: Hannah. Children mentioned but not named. Ex: wife and Alex. Blare. Wit: Richard Tilton, Joseph Williams, David Heth (Heath).

HALL, CORNELIUS. Feb. 1, 1814. Feb. 1814. Noncupative will. Wife: Keturah. Daus: Pamelia and Jane. "If estate received from mother in Virginia same to go to Pamelia." Proved by oath of Hamblin Stokes.

HARNEY, MILLS. March 23, 1814. -----. Wife: Nancy. Legatees: Rowland, Hiram, Rhoda, Thomas, Hannah, Ricely, Samuel, Shelby, Mills and Caty Harney. (Undoubtedly his children). Ex: wife, William Powell. Wit: John Grohigan, Nancy Rickey, William Powell.

HARRIS, SAMUEL. June 10, 1814. July 1814. Wife: Molly. Children: Betsy Dallas, Samuel, Sarah Barton. Ex: son-in-laws Elijah Barton, William Dallas.

HELTMAN, JOHN. Dec. 12, 1812. Feb. 1813. Step dau. Elizabeth Grosvenor. Equal parts of estate to John Grosvenor and Elizabeth Davis. Ex: Richard Grosvenor. Wit: William Baker, Polly Hainey.

JONES, JOHN. March 11, 1802. Sept. 1802. Wife: Sarah. Children: John, Dumas, Elizabeth Mann, David, Moses, Nancy Willas. Ex: Moses Jones, Hubbard Williams. Wit: John Kimbraugh, Richard Kimbraugh, Jesse Baskett, William Barlow.

KIMBROUGH, NATHANIEL. Sept. 23, 1807. Feb. 1808. Wife: Elizabeth. Children: Sarah, Major, George, Mary, John. Wife to keep possession of estate until youngest son John reaches age of 21 years. Charlotte Williams. Ex: wife and Jesse Baskett. Wit: A. Lilly.

KINHART (KINCART), SAMUEL. Sept. 7, 1813. -------. Wife: Isabel. Children: James, Samuel, John, Susannah, Isabela, Mary Archer. Ex: son John. Wit: David Byers, Thomas Nesbit, Moses Hall.

LINNELLE, WILLIAM. Inventory. Sept. 13, 1799. Apprs: James Crocket, John Mc Donald, John Bigger.

MC ANULTEY, JOHN. May 5, 1815. July 1815. Estate to bros. James and Joseph, sisters Sally, Jane and Elizabeth. Ex: Alex. Blair, (guardian for bro. Joseph) and Hugh Cowan. Wit: Hugh Wiley, Samuel Thompson, James Hill.

MC CORMICK, JOHN. May 1805. Inventory. Apprs: Robert Mc Intire, Jonathan Johnson, William Barlow.

MITCHELL, WILLIAM. Oct. 3, 1801. Dec. 1801. Wife: Mary. Children: James, William, Thomas, Jenny Graham. Ex: James Mitchell (son) and son-in-law James Graham. Wit: James Parks, John Mitchell, Thomas Nesbit.

MITCHELLTREE, JOSIAS. Jan. 2, 1807. Jan. 1810. Wife: Nancy. Children: Mary Mc Gunnis, George. Ex: William Mc Gunnis. Wit: Edward Hillock, Edward Thomas, James Hillock.

MORGAN, JOHN. Dec. 20, 1807. Feb. 1808. Wife: Agnes. Children: Mariah, Jefferson. Ex: wife, Rice Morgan. Wit: James Avery, Francis Bay.

MUMFORE (MANFORD), WILLIAM. April 29, 1804. May 1804. Wife: Sarah. Children: Polly, John, James, Margaret. Ex: William Boid, William Gray. Wit: John Boyd, Andrew Yates, Walter Caldwell.

MONCRIEFF, MAXA. Inventory. June 10, 1801. Feb. 1802. Apprs: Jacob Jones, John Anderson, Jacob Ashcraft, Joseph Duncan.

NANHOOK, THOMAS. Inventory. ---------1814?

OLIVER, JOHN. April 21, 1802. July 1802. Wife: Elizabeth. Children: Archibald, Margaret, James, Elizabeth, Nancy Henderson. To Samuel Fulton, mentions money owing him in Redstone Settlement, Pa. Ex: Alex. Blair, Thomas Nesbit. Wit: James Parks, John Mitchell, Mordecai Mc Donald.

PHILLIPS, MICHAEL. April 16, 1802. July 1802. Wife: Isabel. Children: Jena, John, David and others not named. Wit: Thomas Cotrill, William Frazier, Hiram Harney.

PRATER, JEREMIAH. Oct. 5, 1812. Jan. 1813. Wife: not named. Zephuriah Prater, Thomas Rucker Prater, Reason Prater. Prop. to be divided among

Jeremiah, Zephemiah and Ashford Prater and Patsy Collins. Ex: Jeremiah and Zephemiah Prater. Wit: Eli Metcalf, Zephemiah Prater, John Hunter.

RIMBROUGH, SAMUEL. Feb. 12, 1810. Feb. 1810. Wife: Cary. Children: John, Robert, William, Betsy Baker, Sally Barlow. Ex: William Barlow, William Rimbrough. Wit: John Collier, John West.

ROBINSON, ALEXANDER. July 21, 1809. Nov. 1813. Wife: Jane. Sisters Agnes Davidson, Anney Trusdale. Bro. James. Ex: wife. Wit: David Byers, Moses Hall.

SADLER, JOHN. Nov. 16, 1813. May 1815. Wife: Lucy. Children mentioned but not named. Ex: wife. Wit: Thomas Dupree, Holladay Stearn.

SNAP, GEORGE. Sept. 4, 1807. April 1808. Wife: Magdalene. Children: Catharine Fryman, George, Betty Richard, Magdalene Richey, Peter, Adam, Margaret Rannels, heirs of son John. Ex: wife. Wit: Robert Mc Intire, John Sharp, Jesse Baskett.

STEVENSON, JAMES. July 29, 1810. Oct. 1810. Wife: Elizabeth. Children: Mary (wife of Edward P. Criswell), Sally (wife of William Reding). Ex: bro. William, bro-in-law Robert Criswell, Jr. Wit: Archibald Ramsay, John Riley, Jeremiah Casady.

STEPHENSON, WILLIAM. July 12, 1814. -------. Wife: Rebecca. Children: William, John, Margaret, Jane, Nephew William Stephenson. Robert and James Wiley sons of Hugh Wiley and dau. Betsy. Ex: son Robert, son-in-law Hugh Wiley. Wit: Archibald Ramsay, John Williams.

STEWART, JOHN. Dec. 31, 1804. Feb. 1805. Wife: Mary. Children: Mary, Lucy, Jesse, Joseph, William, John, James, Elizabeth, Liddy. Gr.dau. Elizabeth Stewart (dau. of Robert Stewart). Ex: Jesse Baskett, William Baker. Wit: John Hudleson, Robert Mintur, Samuel Eslick.

THOMSON, ALEX. Jan. 5, 1811. Aug. 1811. Wife: Susy Anna. Children: James, Polly, John. Ex: wife. Wit: Samuel M. Waugh, Samuel Hall.

TROUSDALE, WILLIAM. March 21, 1803. Sept. 1803. "About to leave the land of my nativity for sometime." William Wait, son of sister Mary Endicott, sisters Ann, Hannah. Ex: William Endicott, Thomas Corruthers. Wit: John, Wait, Nathan Lowe, William Lowe.

TRUSDALE, JOHN. Oct. 24, 1799. Jan. 1802. Children: William, Hannah, Ann, Mary. Wit: Hugh Wilson, John Wait, Matt Scott.

WELCH, MICHAEL. March 12, 1796. April 1800. Wife: Mary. Children: John, Abraham, Abigail, Margaret, Catharine, Mary. Ex: wife and son Abraham. Wit: John Steele, William Miller, John Smith.

WELLS, AARON. Sept. 2, 1811. Feb. 1813. Wife: Ruth. Children mentioned but not named. Ex: wife. Wit: Thomas Throckmorton, John Throckmorton, William Wiggins.

OHIO COUNTY

BOOK A

1798-1824

ADAMS, JAMES. Inventory. July 25, 1812. Apprs: Jas. Bates, Jas. Smeathers, Thos. Milley. Admr: Benj. Duncan.

ANDERSON, ATHEL. Inventory. Oct.--1815. Apprs: Jno. Hoover, Jno. Lucas.

ANDERSON, JOHN. July 3, 1817. Nov. 9, 1818. Wife: Frances. Children: Polly White (hus. Joseph), Sarah Stevenson (hus. Jno.). Ex: wife. Wit: Richard Barrett, Joseph Johnston.

ASHBY, GEORGE. Inventory. August 27, 1811. Apprs: Joshua Griffith, William Tanner, Sr., James Smith.

ATHERTON, CHARLES. Inventory. May -1818. Apprs: John Austin, Matt. Sheeths, Henry Coleman. Admr: Thomas Pender.

AUTRY, ALEX. Inventory. March 25, 1826. Apprs: Samuel Wilson, Samuel Lee, Jno. Drake. Admr: I. F. Harris.

BARNARD, JOSHUA. Inventory. Nov.- 1808. Apprs: Wm. Barnard, Nicholas Hocker.

BARNETT, ROBERT. Inventory. April 7, 1801. Admr: Alex. Barnett. Apprs: J. Crow, Capt. Samuel McGrady, H. Davidge.

BARNES, JOSEPH. May 18, 1821.------Wife: Mary. Children: Joshua, John, Ellenor, Weaver, Charletey Rendon (hus. Robt.), Nancy Perk. Gr.son: Joseph, son of Joshua. Ex: sons Joshua, John and son-in-law Robt. Rendon. Wit: James Kidson, D. Lemorrison, Stephen Stateler.

BARRETT, THOMAS. Jan. 16, 1819. May 10, 1819. Wife: Eliz. Children: Sally Pate, Richard, Joshua, Matilda, Thos., Jas. Test: Jno. Ridgeway, Thos. Smith.

BARRETT, Thomas. Inventory. Apprs: Jacob Iglehart, Jno. Iglehart, David Bell.

BEALL, ELI. Feb. 15, 1814.----- Wife: Nancy. Children: William, other mentioned but not named. Ex: wife, son William. Wit: Joseph Thompson, Thos. Jones, John Dairy.

BEALL, NATHL. Inventory. April 28, 1814. Apprs: Joseph Thompson, Thos. Jones, John Jones. Admrs: William Beall, Nancy Beall.

BELT, WILLIAM. Sept. 13, 1822.---Legatees: Henry J. Belt (bro.), Carlton Belt (father), Charity Belt (cousin), Higginson Belt.

BIGGAR, SAMUEL. Inventory. August, 1804. Apprs: Robt. Cooper, Benj. Thompson, William Meek.

COLEMAN, MARTIN. Inventory. Sept. 1804. Apprs: Harrison Taylor, Matthew Shults, John Eathernton.

CONDICT, BRYAN. July 7, 1815. Oct. 1816. Wife: Polly. Children: Ann Elliott, John, Peter, Jacob, Philip, Edward, Emeline, nephew Daniel Lindley. Ex: wife, sons Peter, John. Wit: David Condict, Benjamin Humphrey.

CRAWFORD, SAMUEL. Feb. 11, 1818. Nov. 12, 1821. Wife: Mary. Children: William, Samuel, Peggy Allen, wife of Joseph Allen. Ex: Joseph Allen, Edward Blacklock and wife. Wit: Francis W. New, Wm. Erwin, Benj. Burch.

CUNDIFF, JOHN. Inventory. June 14, 1815. Apprs: Elijah Hogg, Moses Milton.

DUNN, VINCENT. Inventory. Jan. 1812. Admr: Polly Dunn. Apprs: Joseph Thompson, Thomas Jones, John Keith.

DOUGLAS, GORDON. Inventory. Apprs: Alex. Barnett, Jno. Bennett, Chas. Calloway.

ERVIN, EDWARD. Inventory. August 10, 1819. Apprs: Thomas Stevens, H. Belt.

FELIX, JOHN. Inventory. Oct. 5, 1824. Apprs: William Carter, Joseph Gentry, David Kelly.

FIELD, JOHN. August 30, 1801. June 1802. Wife: Sally. Children: William, Elizabeth, Hannah, Nancy, Zachariah, James, Aquilla. Mentions George Ashby. Ex: Benj. Field. Wit: Thomson M. Jones, Moses Jones,---Ferguson.

FULKERSON, PHILIP. Sr. June 21, 1813. August 1813. Wife: Elizabeth. Children: Jacole, Adam, Philip, Fulkard, John, Rachel, Betsy, Pamelia. Other legatees: Reed McGrew, bro. John Fulkerson. Ex: son Fulkard. Wit: Sam Hedd, Geo. Coleman

GARNER, EPHIRAM. Inventory. Oct. 3, 1808. Apprs: Moses Thomas, J. Lewellyn.

GIBSON, JOHN. Inventory. Nov. 1807. Apprs: Wm. Tanner, Jno. McFarland, Walter McFarland.

GIBSON, WILLIAM. Inventory. Nov. 1807. Admr: John Gibson. Apprs: Andrew Kelly, William Tanner, James Smith.

GRANT, WILLIAM. (Of Bullitt Co.) Jan. 7, 1819. August 13, 1821. Children: John, William, Tibelow, Whitledge, Elsy, Harriett, Daniel. Gr.children: Eliza and Daniel (child. of son Daniel), William (son of Wm.), William and Posy Grant. Ex: sons. Wit: George Marshall, William Barnes.

GRIGSBY, AARON. August 31, 1818. Nuncupative. Leaves estate to Willis Chapman with request that he care for the Grigsby family. Wit: Stephen Williams, Sally Williams, F. Fulkerson.

GUARDIAN, HENRY. Nov. 8, 1812. Nov. 1813. Legatee. adopted son John Joseph Smith, walso named executor. Wit: James Baird, Jno. Woodward, Benj. Woodward.

GUINN, MOSES. Inventory. July 8, 1813. Apprs: Jno. Galloway, Obidiah Brumfield.

HEDGES, PETER. Inventory. July 1, 1811. Apprs: Baxter Davis, W. Condict.

HELT, JANE. Inventory. Feb. 25, 1818. Apprs: Joseph Barnett, Thomas Barnett, John Pate.

HOLT, DANIEL. Nov. 24, 1803. Estate to be sold and proceeds to go to slave Mary and two mulatto boys. Ex: Jno. Vannada. Wit: Peter Davis, Abrm. Harriman.

HOCKER, PHILIP. June 25, 1820. August 30, 1821. Children: Nicholas, Richard, Weaver, Philip, Deliah, Dorcas, Polly, Sarah Davis, heirs of dau. Betsy. Ex: Robt. Render (Rendon). Wit: Elijah Williams, Jno. Austin, Samuel Heel.

HORSEMAN, ----. Inventory. Feb. 20, 1826.

LANHAM, RICHARD. Sept. 6, 1806. May 1807. Wife: Rachel. Sons: Elias, Elijah. Sons to be taught to read and cypher, daughters to be given education that meets with approval of wife. Wit: George Hart, Moses Thomas, John Peak.

LEACH, WILLIAM. August 5, 1808. Wife: Aleys(?). Children: Leonard, Susan, Patsy Miller, Lisbeth Cox, William. Ex: son Leonard. Wit: Wm. Cooper, Benjamin Cox.

MARTIN, OBIDIAH. Inventory. Oct. 11, 1824. Apprs: Geo. Render, Robt. Render.

MCGRADY, SAMUEL. Inventory. Nov. 1814. Apprs: Thos. Myers, Chris. Jackson

MCLURE, ALEX. Inventory. Sept. 17, 1823. Apprs: J.G. Stevens, Abraham Foreman, Julius C. Jackson.

MILLER, JOHN. Oct. 29, 1816. ------Wife: Ruth. Children mentioned but not named. Wit: Benjamin Kelly, George Bone.

PARKER, THOMAS. Inventory. Jan. 1805. Apprs: Richard Taylor, William Taylor, Robert Howard.

PATE, JOHN. Feb. 22, 1820. Wife: Jennet. Children not named. Wit: Benjamin Kelly, John Ridgway, Joseph Gentry.

POWERS, JOHN. Inventory. Oct. 2, 1824. Apprs: John Crow, Leonard Bruce.

PRUDEN, DANIEL. Inventory. March 1820. Apprs: Jno. Lucas, Robert Barnett, Thomas Barnett.

WALLACE, ARTHUR. Inventory. Feb. 1823. Admr: Mary Wallace, James Johnson.

WHITAKER, JAMES. Sept. 3, 1816. -----All debts to be paid by bro. Alex. Whitaker, Sary Parker. Ex: Alex. Whitaker. Wit: Rice Whitaker, Nathan Grigsby.

WHITE, LEMUEL. Inventory. March 14, 1815. Apprs: Jno. Davis, Anthony Thomson.

WOOD, THOMAS. Inventory. Second Monday in Sept. 1824. Apprs: William Taylor, Richard Taylor, William Leach.

WOODWARD, JOHN. Inventory. No date. Apprs: Jeffries Bennett, Benjamin Benton, James Baird, Jr.

OHIO COUNTY

INDEX

BOOK B

Allen, Theophilus
Austin, Zachariah
Autry, Burwell

Barnett, Andrew
Barnett, Eliz.
Barnett, Felix
Barnett, Jane
Barnett, Joseph
Barnett, Thos.
Baird, James
Ballzel, Elinor
Barnard, Joshua
Bean, Leonard
Bell, Eli
Bennett, John
Bennett, Lewis
Bennett, Reuben
Bennett, Samuel

Carlin, John
Chapman, Joshua
Coleman, Martin
Cooper, William
Cooper, Jacob
Cooksey, James
Condell, Lewis
Cox, Joseph
Crow, Avery
Crow, Elijah
Curtis, John
Cundiff, John

Davenport, Robert
Dodson, Eli
Duke, John
Duncan, Roley
Dunn, Vincent

Elliott, Richard
Erwin, William

Field, Aquilla
Ford, John
Ford, John B.
French, David
Fulkerson, Phil

Gentry, Moses
Gibson, John
Goldsmith, John
Greer, George
Guinn, Moses

Hatcher, James
Hayden, Samuel
Haynes, Chrles
Haynes, E.
Hedees, Peter
Hocker, Phil
Hocker, Nicholas
Howell, John
Huff, Chas.

Iglehart, James
Iglehart, William
Iter, Perry

Jackson, Chris.
Johnson, Grant

Kelly, Benj.
Kelly, Dave
Kelly, John
Kelly, Levina
Kikins, Mark

Martin, John
Martin, Richard
McCreery, Chas.
McGea, Edward
McLaughlin, Wm.
Miller, Jno. H.
Milligan, Jas.
Morgan, David
Monroe, Eliz.
Monroe, John
Morris, Pressley
Moseley, Robt.

Nall, Richard
Newcumb, Samuel

Owens, Henry

Peake, John

Pearl, A.R.
Pender, Thos.
Powers, John

Raley, Jona.
Raw, Thos.
Render, Judith
Render, Thos.
Robinson, Roger
Robinson, Sarah
Roger, John C.
Ross, Joseph

Shreoder, George
Shultz, Mathew
Skinner, Leonard
Smith, James
Smith, Jesse
Smith, Thomas
Stevens, James
Stevens, John P.
Stevens, Richard
Stewart, Archibald
Stull, Philip

Taylor, John
Tabler, Pardon
Tapley, Hosea
Taylor, Thomas
Thomas, Moses
Thompson, Anthony
Thrasher, Mary E.
Tichenor, John F.

Underwood, Mathew

Webber, Peggy H.
Whelter, Tarlow
Williams, Evan
Williams, Elijah
Williams, Rezen
Wilson, Edward
Wilson, Samuel
Wilson, William
Woodward, Benjamin

SCOTT COUNTY

BOOK A

1797 -- 1809

ADAMS, NATHAN. Dec. 18, 1803. Aug. 1804. Daus: Sarah, Mary, Betsy Tull, Ellgood. Son: Nathan. Wit: John Garth, Robert Griffith, Minor Ratcliff.

APPLEGATE, RICHARD. July 31, 1798. Dec. 1800. Wife: Rebecca. Daus: Mary, Rebecca, Alletta Lantaman, Cather Leman, Elizabeth Mc Can, Alsa Walls. Sons: Benjamin, Daniel, William. Ex: Joseph Wilson. Wit: William Ward, William Fisher.

BEATTY, WILLIAM. August 1800. Dec. 1803. Wife: Sarah. Sons: George, Joseph, Howard, Steward. Son-in-law: George Beaty. Daus: Sally, Nancy. Children by a former wife: John, William, Molly (wife of James Beaty), Betsy Craigmiles, Joney Beaty. Ex: Saray Beaty (wife), George Beaty (son). Wit: ------. Robert Smith is made guardian for Winifred Beaty, Feb. 24, 1804.

BERRYMAN, JOHN. Of Spottsylvania Co.; Va. Feb. 18, 1799. Sept. 25, 1799. Bros: Newton, Francis, Josias. Nephews: William Monroe, Josias Berryman, Jr. (son of Newton Berryman), Francis Berryman. Nieces: Elizabeth Berryman, dau. of Gerrard Berryman), Winfred Berryman. Sisters: Winifred Monroe, Eliza Berryman (dec'd). Ex: Newton Berryman, Josias Berryman, Francis Berryman (bros.). Wit: Sherod Horn, Martin Brent, Peter Hicks.

BROOKS, THOMAS. Inventory. Nov. 26, 1802. Apprs: Samuel Sheppard, Adam Johnson.

BURBRIDGE (BEURBRIDGE), THOMAS. Sept. 27, 1794. Jan. 1795. Bros: Lunsfield, George. Sis: Mildred Robinson, Sarah Elley, Frances Smith, Elizabeth Branham, Mary Bullitt. Ex: Lunsfield Burbridge, George Burbridge (bros.), Henry Elley, Robert Smith, Benjamin Robinson, Taviner Branham (bros.-in-law). Wit: Edward Elley, Matthew Gale, Sr., William Wood.

BURDET, FREDRICK. Inventory. Nov. 25, 1795.

CLARVO, HENRY. April 28, 1808. May 1808. Wife: Not named. Dau: Mary, alias Polly. Son: John. Ex: William Jenkins (bro.-in-law). Wit: John Howard, James Twyman.

COPPAGE, ISAAC. Feb. 10, 1807. March 1807. Sons: Charles, Rodden. Daus: Lucy Kearn, Nancy Coppage, Gracy Philes. Ex: Rodden Coppage (son), Fielding Bradferd. Wit: William Stut, Jesse Threlkeld, Thomas Foster.

CRAIG, ELIJAH. May 13, 1808. June 1808. Sons: Simon, John, Joel. Daus: Lucy, Mary. Ex: John Craig (son), Thomas Hawkins, Josiah Pitts. Wit: Alex. Smith, Archibald Ruland, Alex. Henderson, Philip Rodes, Val Sanders.

CRAIG, WILLIAM. ----1804. Admr: E. Craig, Jr.

CULBERTSON, MARTHA. Jan. 23, 1807. Feb. 1807. Sis: Nancy Adams, Prudence, Jane Adams, Polly Culbertson. Bro: Robert Culbertson. Ex: John Adams,

James Lindsay. Wit: James Stephens, William Stephens.

CULBERTSON, SAMUEL. July 8, 1806. Nov. 1806. Wife: Martha. Sons: Joseph, Alexander, Robert. Daus: Hetty, Eliza, Patsy. Ex: wife, Joseph Culbertson (son).

DUVALL, HENRY. Oct. 22, 1806. Dec. 1806. Legatees: Keriah Duvall (mother), John Duvall (bro.), John Duvall (nephew). Ex: Cornelius Duvall (father). Wit: Rodes Smith, Samuel Lowery.

ERVING, SAMUEL. July 24, 1808. Aug. 1808. Wife: Ellena. Dau: Martha Murray. Sons: John, Joseph, William, Robert, James, Samuel. Ex: wife, Joseph Erving (son). Wit: Robert Erwing, James Erwing.

FAUQUIER, RACHEL. Feb. 23, 1802. Sept. 1802. Daus: Elizabeth Clinton, Jane Mc Cumsay (Mc Cumprey), Mary Nickson. Gr.sons: John and Robert Cumprey, James Barclay, Matthew Barclay. Gr.dau: Mary Mc Dougal, Sarah Mc Dougal, Ann Mc Dougal. Son: James. Ex: Hugh Emison, John Watkin, Lewis Heath. Wit: Thomas Mc Picking (?), John Comason (?), William Duly.

FIELDS, WILLIAM. Dec. 1808. Admr: James Field. Apprs: James Fields, John Mulberry.

FREELAND, FRISBY, JR. Of Calvert County, Maryland. Nov. 16, 1803. --------. Wife: Sarah. Ex: wife. Wit: Thomas Bowie, Thomas Chew, Evansfield Bowie.

GATTIWAY, GEORGE. Inventory. Dec. 23, 1796.

GRAHAM, JOHN. Inventory. June 19, 1802. Apprs: William Steel, Alex. Tilford, James Withers.

GRANT, ISAREL. Oct. 7, 1796. Oct. C. C. 1796. Wife: Susannah. Sons: James, William, Jesse. Daus: Sally, Rebecca. Ex: George G. Boswell, David Bryant, Jonathan Bryant, John Mosly, John Hawkins. Wit: James Bryant, James Lemon.

GRAY, WILLIAM. May 27, 1803. Apprs: Samuel Shepherd, Benjamin Quinn.

GREEN, SPENCER. June 29, 1798. Dec. 1798. Wife: Ruth. Dau: Nancy. Sons: James, John, Joshua, other children not named. Ex: wife. Wit: John Mc Kinney, Martha Mc Kinney (Mc Kinny).

HALL, JOHN. Inventory. August 11, 1803.

HAWKINS, JOHN. Oct. 30, 1804. Sept. 1806. Wife: Sarah. Daus: Betty Thames, Peggy, Sally Smith, Nancy Carson, Fanny Thomas, Betsy Faulkner, Caty, Lucinda. Sons: Jameson, Philamon, William. Ex: wife, Philemon Hawkins, Thomas Hawkins, John Hawkins, John Payne. Wit: Toliver Craig, Andrew Johnson, Lew Hawkins.

HEARNDON, LEWIS. Sept. 17, 1789. July 1796. Wife: Frances. Dau: Isabell Brown, other children but not named. Ex: James Hearndon (son), Henry Elly. Wit: Thomas Ficklin, Thomas Dinwiddie, Colby Shipp.

HENDERSON, JOHN. August 4, 1799. --------. Children mentioned but not named.

Sons-in-law: Alex. Smith, John Miller. Wit: Peter Kerns, A. Hambleton, (Agnes Smith)?.

HEAD, JOHN ALFRED. -----. -----. Wife: Elizabeth. Sons: William, Benjamin, Alfred. Daus: Anna Ransdale, Sarah, Fanny. Ex: wife, William Head, Martin Hall(?), Jr.

HUTCHINSON, JAMES. Sept. 22, 1806. Inventory. Apprs: Archibald Collins, Bartlett Collins.

INGRAM, JACOB. Jan. 25, 1802. Sons: Samuel, Joseph, Josiah, -----, Seth. William Wilson appointed guardian of above named children.

JONES, JOHN. Jan. 22, 1796. Joseph Jones, Ex.

JOHNSON, HENRY. Jan. 9, 1806. March 1806. Wife: Mary. Children: not named. Ex: wife, William G. Johnson. Wit: Matthew Mickie, John Watkins, George Wood, Samuel Thompson.

KEENE, THOMAS. Oct. 9, 1802. March 1804. Wife: Mary Keene, Sons: Vatchel, Richard. Ex: John Ccur----(?). Wit: Robert Hunter, Charles Keene.

KEENE, WILLIAM. Nov. 12, 1801. May 1802. Legatees: Richard Keene (son), Capt. John Hunter and Mary, his wife. Ex: Dr. Samuel Keene, Capt. John Hunter. Wit: J. Hopewell Keene, James Price, W. Warren, Jr.

LAMBERT, DANIEL. June 18, 1804. -----. Wife: Ruth. Sons: Benjamin, John, Baldwin. Daus: Mary, Phebe Thomson. Ex: sons John, Benjamin. Wit: Rodes Smith, John Brock, Hugh Dickey.

LINDSAY, JOHN. Sept. 29, 1805. Jan. 1806. Wife: Ann. Sons: John, Robert, other children but not named. Ex: William Henry, William Cave. Wit: J. Burnett, Betty Glass.

LOWERY, ALEX. Settlement Nov. 1808. Cary L. Clark, C. C.

MARTIN, THOMAS. Feb. 2, 1800. Sept. 1800. Wife: Margaret. Sons: Robert, Thomas, John, James, Samuel, Benjamin, Alexander. Daus: Margaret, Mary. Ex: sons James, Thomas. Wit: Daniel Sinclair, Early Scott, John Van Zandt.

MC CLURE, MARY. ----3, 1804. Sept. 1807. Sons: Holbart, Nathan, Moses. Daus: Rebecca Anderson. Wit: Lewis Nickolls, John Kennedy, John Mc Clure.

MC CORMICK, HUGH. June 17, 1797. Oct. 1797. Wife: Katherine. Sons: George, William. Daus: Elizabeth, Mary. Ex: sons, George, William. Wit: James Ruggless, Jane Stephenson.

MILAM, ARCHIBALD. April 12, 1806. June, 1806. Wife and children mentioned but not named. Ex: David Thomson, James Liggett, John Scott. Wit: John Stile, Jan Milam, Richard Stutts.

MONTEITH, DAVID. August 4, 1797. -----. Wife not named. Children: William, David, Esther. Ex: John Carnagy.

MORRIS, ELIZABETH. Aug. 9, 1796. Jan. 1797 (?). Dau: Sukey Oldham. Ex:

George Oldham (son-in-law).

NASH, SOLOMON. Sept. 26, 1803. Apprs: Robert Saunders, John Snell, John Thompson.

NEALE, DANIEL. May 10, 1802. Sept. 1804. Wife: Jemina. Sons: Daniel, William, Pressley, John, Teadius, Rhodham. Daus: Nancy Kelley, Jemina Leach, Penelope, Susanna. Ex: James Kelley, Rhodham Neale, Daniel Neale. Wit: Chris. Neale, Joseph Wilson, John Hawkins.

NEWINGHAM, NATHANIEL. Sept. 25, 1797. Sale. Apprs: Joshua Newingham, John Hawkins.

OSBURNE, THOMAS. Inventory, June 20, 1803. Apprs: Samuel Daharen, Rhodin Coppage, Fielding Bradford.

PATTIN, PHILLIP. May 22, 1808. Sept. 1808. All his estate to his negroes, viz: Grace, James, Jeremiah, Samuel. Wit: John Carckwell, Rhoda Thomason, Susanna Carckman.

PLUNKETT, PHEBE. Feb. 10, 1804. Children: William, Hampton, Harry, Richard, Anthony, Nelly. Wit: David Herndon, George Burbridge, Rodes Smith.

REED, JOHN. Sale. Jan. 23, 1802. Admr: Bartlett Collins.

RISK, JOHN. Sept. 4, 1805. March 1808. Wife: Jane. Sons: John, Robert, James, William, Moses. Daus: Margaret, Elizabeth, Mary Ann, Jane, Martha, Susanna, Rebecca, Nancy. Ex: Robert Morris, David Morris. Wit: Isaac Beauchamp, Sally Brown, Daniel Brown.

ROSELL, MATILDA. June 25, 1804. Orphan of N. Rosell. Apprs: Clifton Hornsby, George Marshall, Ephiram Holland.

ROSS, WILLIAM. Late of Sussex Co., Delaware. March 9, 1802. May 1802. Wife: Anna. Sons: Clement, Hewitt, William. Daus: Peggy Latan, Rebecca. Ex: wife, son William. Wit: Robert Griffith, John Nulton, David Layton.

SAUNDERS, ROBERT. May 11, 1805. ----. Wife: -----. Dau: Nancy. Sons: Toliver, Benjamin, Thomas, Walker, Valentine. Ex: John Thomson, Peter Gatewood, son Valentine to be executor when he comes of age. Wit: James Barton, Benjamin Wharton, Henry Henderson.

SHIRLEY, WILLIAMS. Sept. 30, 1799. March 1805. Wife: Margaret. Sons: Robert, William, Richard, John. Daus: Rebecca, Sarah Johnson. Ex: wife. Wit: John Rodes, Walker Rodes.

SMITH, THOMAS. Sept. 11, 1799. ----1800. Wife: Tilly (Davis). Sons: James, Thomas, William, John. Daus: Peggy Bryant, Fanny Davis, Mary Davis. Ex: son John. Wit: William Ward, William Mc Garrick.

STERRETT, JAMES. Settlement. Nov. 1794. John Sterrett, Admr.

THOMASON, SAMUEL. Oct. 23, 1793. Apprs: Achille Stapp, Thomas Branham, Henry Elly, Benjamin Quinn.

THARP (Indexed as Allantharp), BENJAMIN. Jan. 5, 1806. March 1806. Bros: William, George. Sis: Martha. Ex: John Allentharp (father). Wit: John Talbott, Samuel Young, Daniel Mitchell.

THOMASON, NELSON. ----1803. Nov. 1803. Legatees: Winny Gough (niece), Frances Thomason (dau. of Richard Thomason), Elizabeth Herndon. Ex: Nathaniel Craig. Wit: Cornelius Gough, Thomas Herndon.

THOMASON, RICHARD. June 12, 1802. Sept. 27, 1802. Wife: Sarah. Children: Frances, others not named. Ex: Harry Jenkins, Nelson Thomason, David Shelton. Wit: Henry Dehoney, Nancy Thomason.

THOMPSON, ANN. June 17, 1798. Son: David. Daus: Ann Walton, Mary Wigglesworth, Unity Smith, Elizabeth Rodes, Lydia Ferguson. Ex: Rodes Smith (son-in-law), David Thompson (son).

TROTTER, WILLIAM. June 26, 1797. Oct. 1797. Wife: Margaret. Sons: Joseph, William, David, Stephenson (?). Ex: wife, bro. John Trotter, William McClure. Wit: George Trotter, Robert Kay, James Lindsay.

UTTER, WILLIAM. Aug. 1, 1797. Sept. 1797. Wife: Margaret. Dau: Margaret. Wit: William Hicklin, Ash Emison.

VAUGHN, EDMUND. August 1796. Inventory. Apprs: John Suggett, Daniel Neal.

WALKER, JOSEPH. Jan. 22, 1806. Aug. 25, 1806. Wife: Grisel. Daus: Nancy Womack (wife of Michael Womack), Mary Hays, Jane Walker, Gr.dau: Jenny Walker (dau. of Samuel). Gr.sons: Joseph Walker (son of James Walker), Joseph Henderson (son of Alex. Henderson). $20. to support of the Gospel, Cherry Springs Congregation. Ex: son Samuel, Samuel Finley. Wit: John Hutchinson, Michael Wamick, Josep Wamick.

WARD, SAMUEL. Sept. 1803. Nov. 1803. Wife: Sarah. Children: William, other children not named. Mentions father William Ward. Ex: wife, son William. Wit: John Adkins, Ira Cook.

WHARTON, VALENTINE. July 20, 1799. July 22, 1799. Son: Benjamin. Daus: Nancy Landes, Fanny Wharton. Wit: Thomas Cavendar.

WILSON, JAMES. Feb. 1805. -----. Mentions his parents. Bequeaths his stills to bro. Richard. Ex: bro. John. Wit: Nathaniel Wilson, Hans Murdagh.

SCOTT COUNTY

INDEX

BOOK B

1809 -- 1817

Abbott, Robert
Abbott, Henry
Abbott, William
Allen, Polly
Allen, Tharpe William
Allen, Robert
Acuff, Chris.

Barten, William
Beatty, John
Bettis, Harry
Benson, ---
Bird, Lee
Boswell, George
Browning, James
Brooks, James
Browning, Jane
Bradley, Robert
Brent, Hannah
Branham,
Brown, Joel
Burdett, Polly

Campbell, Porter
Carroll, E.
Cave, Henry
Cobb, Samuel
Conder, Samuel
Coppage, John
Cowden, Samuel
Coppage, Isaac
Craig, Martin
Conner, Newlin
Craig, William

Davis, Joseph
Deane, Joseph
Denning, Fielding
Drake, Thomas
Doyle, Alex.
Duncan, James
Dunn, Sally

Estill, Thomas

Fields, Reason
Fox, John

Grant, William

Green, James
Gattenway, Samuel
Griffith, Paris

Hannah, Andrew
Hayden, Turner
Henderson, Fanny
Holland, Ephiram

Johnson, Henry
Johnson, Jacob
Johnson, Adams
Jones, Benjamin

Keene, Samuel

Lowery, Abraham

Martin, Thomas
Mc Cullough, Joseph
Mc Fall, John
Mc Coy, Abraham
Mc Kinkey, David

Neale, Daniel

Pugh, Joseph
Pierce, Adams
Polk, John

Redding, Joseph
Risk, -----

Scott, John
Shortridge, William
Short, Eli
Smith, Joseph

Tharp -----
Tilford, David
Tyre, William

Vandebark, Jordan
Viley, ------

Ward, William
Wilson, Thomas

Yates, -----

SHELBY COUNTY

BOOK A

1795--1804

ANDERSON, JOHN. Inventory. March, 1799. Admr: Margaret Anderson.

BOYLES, DAVID. Inventory. June 30, 1798. Admr: Rebecca Boyles.

BOYD, WILL. Inventory. Nov. 16, 1798. Admr: John Winlock, Robert Allen, James Ballard. Mary Boyd, widow, receives dower Feb.,1799. Children: John, Hannah, Jane, William, Mehitable.

BOWLING, WILLIAM. May 3, 1794. March, 1795. Wife: Margaret. Son: John. Ex: Daniel Ketcham, Sim Bowling. Wit: William Morris, Alex. Montgomery, M. Warford.

BREEDING, RICHARD. May 20, 1798. -----Wife: Frances. Sons: William, Paul. Dau: Elizabeth. Ex: wife. Wit: William McCroy, Isaac Whitaker. Apprs: William Brodie, Peter Bailey, Elijah Whitaker.

BRISCOE, JAMES. Feb. 23, 1804. Dec. 1804. Wife: Catharine. Daus: Mary Massey, Caty, Sarah. Ex: John Briscoe, Edward Briscoe (bros.). Wit: Jona. Tinsley.

BROWN, JAMES. August 28, 1799. Nov. 1799. Wife: Liddy. Ex: Daniel Colgan, Jonathan Cox. Wit: W. Bullock, Thomas Allen, James Moore.

BUCKHANNON, WILLIAM. Jan. 26, 1797. July, 1798. Wife: Agnes. Children not named. Ex: wife, Victor Buckhannon. Wit: Thomas Robertson, Thomas Allison.

BUTLER, ELIZABETH. Sale. Oct. 10, 1803. Admr: Arthur McGaughey.

BUZAN, JESSE. Inventory. Sept. 13, 1794. Apprs: Sam'l McKinley, Nicholas Smith, James Pritchard.

CLARK, JOHN. (Of the County and Parish of Henrico, Va.). Sept. 2, 1783. Sept. 3, 1798. Wife: Elizabeth. Ex: wife, sons Abidiah, Benjamin. Wit: Roger Gregory, James Grinstead, Lear Hensley.

CONNELLY, JOHN. July 8, 1798. Oct. 1798. Wife: Sarah. Sons: William, Thompson, Jesse, James, Stephen. Daus: Mary, Sarah, Elizabeth, Nancy. Ex: wife, Anderson Allen. Wit: Benjamin Kersie, James Brooks.

DANIEL, ROBERT. August 8, 1792. August 1797. Legatees: Thomas, Coleman, and Martin Daniel (bros.), John Daniel (father), Sukey Morris, Betsy Merriwether, Martin, Reuben (last 3 children of sis. Clark). Ex: Martin Daniel, Nicholas Merriwether. Wit: Daniel Farley, Sam'l. Pryor.

DORNAN, OLIVER. Inventory. Dec. 1801. Apprs: Ebenezer Patton, John Martin, John Bushirk.

ELAM, RICHARD. No dates. Apprs: John Shannon, Thomas King, Moses Hall.

FORD,JOHN. April 13,1803. Oct. 1803. Wife: Catharine. Sons: Elisha,Spencer, Samuel,Edward,William. Daus: Ann, Jenney. Ex: sons Samuel,William,Elisha. Wit: David Denny,Oswald Thomas,David Thomas.

FELTY,JOHN. July 22,1795. Apprs: William Butler,David Farley.

GARRETT,JOHN. August 30,1794. May 1799. Children: Isaac,Nancy,Esther,Margaret. Ex: Margaret Garrett,Isaac Garrett. Wit: Isaac Edwards,Jas. Mc Quaid.

GASSAWAY,RICHARD. June 17,1801. Nov.9,1801. Wife: Nancy. Sons: Samuel,Henry, Nicholas,James. Daus: Nancy,Elizabeth. Ex: wife,son Nicholas.

GREEN,JONATHAN. Oct. 12,1794. May 1798. Wife: Caty. Sons: George,William. Dau: Polly. Ex: wife. Wit: Nicholas Smith, Nicholas Smith,Jr.,Simon Smith.

HARTMAN,ANOTHY. August 22,1799. April 11,1803. Wife: Margaret. Sons: Abraham, Daniel, Anothy, David, Solomon,Joseph, Jonathan. Daus: Ester Hostetler, Catharine Miller,Agnes Hosteler. Ex: sons David and Solomon. Wit: Isaac Murphy,Catharine Murphy.

HANIEL,PHILIP. August 1796. Inventory. Apprs: Joseph Irwin, Robert Irwin, Samuel Mc Kinley.

HANSBROUGH,MORIAS. July 22,1799. August 1800. Wife: Mary. Sons: George,John, Joel. Dau: Susannah. Ex: wife, son George, John Underwood. Wit: Peter Hansbrough,Daniel Colgan,Isaac Ellis.

HILL,HARDY. Dec. 17,1798. March 1799. Wife: Margaret. Son: Isaac,other children not named. Ex: wife, George Cavinston. Wit: Archibald Cameron,Isaac Miller

JACOB,THOMAS. May 19, 1797. Apprs: Anthony Jenkins, Nimrod Duncan,Robert Tyler,John Cline,admr.

JOHNSTON,PHILIP. May 17, 1798. July 1798. Wife: Elizabeth. Daus: Elizabeth Payne, Catharine Thomas,Fanny Payne. Sons: Thomas,Philip. Gr.son: George Payne(son of Joseph Payne). Ex: wife, Joseph Johnston(son). Wit: Isaac Payne,Rowland Thomas.

LANE,LAMBERT. Sept. 27,1804. Apprs: Caleb Reed,Isaac Nieman,Henry Johns. Admr: Anne Lane,widow.

LAWERENCE,DAVID. Nov. 10,1804. Dec. 1804. Children: Hannah,Charlotte,Mary, Betsy, Thomas,James,David,Thomas Arbuckle and wife to have charge of the children. Wit: Solomon Lawerence, Thomas Prather.

LEATHERMAN,JOHN. Jan. 15,1796. Wife: Hannah. Legatees: Christian,son of bro. Bazell Fugarden,mentions other children of his brother but does not name them. Ex: David Miller,George Humphrey. Wit: Thomas Craig,Henry Newman, John Harrison.

LEWIS,JOHN. Jan.30,1804. Wife: Margaret. Children: Bluford,Patsy,Henry, Polly, Keziah,Catharine,John,William, Fanny. Apprs: William Bridgewater, James McDavitt,John Shackleford.

MC CLAIN, JOHN. Dec. 1801. Admr: Catharine Mc Clain. Apprs: Joseph Robinson, Albert Bright, A. Mc Gaughey.

Mc CLAIN. Nov. 1801. Inventory. Apprs: A. Bright, Burton James, James Hoagland.

MC CAMPBELL, SAMUEL. Dec.12, 1803. August 1804. Wife: Martha. Sons: James, John, Andrew. Daus: Margaret, Nancy Elliott, Molly Lawson. Ex: sons James and John. Wit: Isaac Collett, Daniel Colgan. Andrew Mc Campbell.

MEEK, JESSE. ---May, 1802. ---- Wife: Sarah. Son: Silas, other children not named. Wit: A. Holmes, J. Stout, A. Shelburne.

METCALF, JAMES. Nov.7, 1798. Apprs: Daniel Kitcham, Gikes Smith, Margaret Metcalf (widow).

NEWLAND, JACOB. August 12, 1800. Nov. 1800. Nuncupative. Wife: Lucy. Sons: John, Isaac, Benoi, Robert, Abraham, Jacob, William. Daus: Isabella, Elizabeth, Polly, Amy. Ex: wife, son John.

OWEN, BRACKETT. Dec.5, 1801. May 1802. Children: William, Jesse, Samuel, Sally Glass, Jacob, Nancy Gwin, John, Abraham, David, Joseph. Ex: Thomas Gwin(son-in-law], Abrm. Owen(son). Wit: William Lively, Daniel Lively, John Lively, Ann Bainbridge.

OWEN, GEORGE. May 1794. Inventory. Apprs: Jacob Fullinwider, Samuel Ryker, William Cooper.

PENNINGSTON, ISAAC. Nov.14, 1801. Appr: John Beadle. (Isaac Pennington married Polly Lockhart, Feb. 18, 1799.)

PERKINS, WILLIAM. Dec. 1795. Inventory. Apprs: Thomas Gwin, Arthur Mc Gaughey, Aquilla Whitaker. Jane Perkins, widow.

POWELL, WILLIAM. Sept. 1802. Inventory. Apprs: William Taylor, Fielding Ashby. Polly Powell, widow.

PRUITT, MICHAEL. Feb. 18, 1798. May 1798. Sons: James, Elisha, Michael, Byrd, Joseph, Robert, Joshua. Daus: Betsy Adams, Judith Mitchell. Ex: Elisha Pruitt, Daniel Mitchell. Wit: Jeremiah Crabbe, William Grigsby, Richard M. Booker.

REED, JAMES. July 7, 1804. Inventory. Apprs: David Colgan, Bland Ballard, Chris. Bryant. Susan Reed, admr.

REDDING, WILLIS. August 25, 1804. Inventory. Apprs: Elisha Ford, Masterson Ogden, Thos. Mitchell.

ROBINS, WILLIAM. Oct. 1795. Inventory. Apprs: G. Ryker, Mason Watts.

SHANNON, WILLIAM. Sept. 22, 1793. May 1794. Legatees: Sarah. Shannon(mother), Margaret Byers, William Shannon(son of bro. Thomas), John Shannon(son of bro. Samuel), David Staniford. Ex: David Staniford, Samuel Shannon. Wit: Joseph Winlock, William Adams.

SHANNON, THOMAS. April 12, 1797. Nov. 1800. Wife: Mary. Sons: Sam'l., James. Daus: Jane Reed, Agnes Wallace, Mary Shannon. Ex: wife. Wit: Mathais Ham, Jacob Caney.

SHIELDS, PATRICK. August 3, 1797. Inventory. Apprs: Richard Rees, James Dodd, Robert Lowden. Mary Ann Shields, widow.

SHUCK, ANDREW. March 20, 1803. May, 1803. Wife: Margaret. Sons: John, William, Mathew, Andrew, Cornelius. Daus: Hannah Batise, Helena Banta, Margaret Sharp, Sarah Banta, Mary Pollard. Ex: Albert Verhees, Peter Banta, Wit: John Verhees, David Demaree.

SQUIRE, JOHN. May 14, 1804. Inventory. Apprs: A. McGaughey, Wilson Maddox, Dyansius Shelburne.

STOUT, JAMES. Inventory. August, 1799. Apprs: Richard Steel, Philip Ficklin.

THOMPSON, THOMAS. Inventory. Dec. 18, 1797. Apprs: Bland Ballard, John Wilcox, William Beene, Elizabeth Thompson, widow.

Van CLEAVE, RALPH. Sept. 5, 1798. Apprs: John Ryker, Sam'l. Ryker, John Teague, Lydia Van Cleave, widow.

WALKER, JOSEPH. August 18, 1800. Sept. 1800. Wife: Polly. Children: Polly, Nancy, James. Ex: wife, James McCroskey, James Parks. Wit: Sam'l. Walker, Michael Warnock, Joseph Walker, Jr., James Logan.

WILSON, SAMUEL. August 30, 1794. Wife: Margaret. Ex: wife, Hugh Wilson (bro.), Wit: William Smiley, Rememberance Wilson.

WHITAKER, JOHN. Feb. 13, 1797. March, 1798. "To wife, Mary plantation whereon I now live, together with all my horses, cattle, sheep, hogs, together with all household furniture. To heirs of son John, dec'd., five pounds each at the decease of my wife. To sons Charles, Abraham, Elijah, Aquilla, Isaac, Jesse, the land and plantation that I give and bequeath unto my wife Mary during her natural life or widowhood, I give and bequeath unto whole of my sons, to be equally divided between them at decease of my wife. Also a certain tract of land lying on the north side of Buffalo road, the place whereon I once live in Nelson County, to be equally divided among my children at decease of myself. I give and bequeath unto dau. Hannah a second rate cow and calf, no more at decease of my wife." Ex: sons Isaac and Jesse. Wit: Josiah Herbert, David Reed, John Stilwell, Jonah Glavock. (Rev. John Whitaker, of Maryland, was one of the early Baptist ministers of Kentucky.)

WHITAKER, JOHN. Sale. Account of sale returned May County Court, 1799.
Aquilla Whitaker,........1 book
Isaac Whitaker..........1 dictionary & hymn book
Jesse Whitaker..........2 big books
Charles Whitaker........1 Rifle gun
Abraham Whitaker........1 handsaw & pot
Daniel Applegate ....1 cresent saw
Martha Whitaker.........1 big pot
William Collins.........Sundry of old iron
John Elliott............1 drawing knife

Daniel Applegate ....1 hewel and plane
John Engle...................1 mattock
Mordicai Nerus ....5 pounds of iron
Daniel Applegate ....1 pair of scales and weights
Abraham Whitaker ....1 hone razor & cock
Mordicai Nerus ....1 mowing knife & crank
Daniel Applegate ....2 sheep
David Shaver ....4 sheep
Abrm. Hoff ....2 sheep
John Whitaker ....2 sheep

WHITAKER, ABRAHAM. Nov.4,1815.-----1815. Wife: Susannah (Humble). Children: John, Seth, Nimrod, Elijah, Charity, Eliza, Levisa, Dorcas, Ballard, Levi, Malida, Polly. Ex: son Seth. (Will Book C)

WHITAKER, ELIJAH. Inventory. April Court, 1826. Admr: James S. Whitaker(nephew). Apprs: William Owen, Henry Radford, William Smith, James Owen.(Will Book D)

WHITAKER, JESSE. Nuncupative. Sept. 6, 1800. Wife: Lydia. Children: Rachel, Squire, Lee, Mary. Proved by the oath of Elijah and Isaac Whitakerv(bros.).

YOUNG, ADAM. Jan. 16, 1798. Logatee and executrix:Mary Crawford (niece). Wit: John McCARTY, John Howard, William Smiley.

SHELBY COUNTY

BOOK B

1804 -- 1811

ADAMS, SIMON. Inventory. August C. C. 1811. Apprs: James Mitchell, George Bearcy, Jr., Thomas Davie.

ASHBY, SILLS. Inventory. August C. C. 1810. Apprs: William Harris, William Pollard, Thomas Davis.

BANTA, HENDRICK. Dec. 13, 1799. ------. Wife: Anna. Ex: Albert Voris, Cornelia Banta, John Voris. Wit: Christopher Bergin, Simon Vausdal, Rachel Vausdele.

BEADLE, JONATHAN. Settlement. March 2, 1807. Admr: Isaac Whitaker, Ellis (Elijah) Whitaker.

BLACK, CHARLES. May 30, 1806. ------. Wife: Elizabeth. Stepson: Bazell Teagarden. Ex: wife. Wit: James Johnson, Laney Johnson.

BOOKER, RICHARD. Feb. 7, 1805. March, 1805. Sons: Richard, John, William, Parham, Samuel. Sons-in-law: John Calloway, Joseph Young. Dau: Elizabeth Baker. Mentions son Edwards wife but does not name her. Ex: David Sandifor, Matthew Flournoy, William Ford of Henry County. Wit: James Mc Achran, Robert Mitchell.

BOONE, GEORGE. Of Madison Co., Ky. Legatees: Father, mother, sister Maris Steel. Wit: Sally Simpson. Oct. 2, 1810. Nov. 1811.

BOZELI, GEORGE. Inventory. Dec. 29, 1808. Admr: Nancy Bozell. Apprs: William Polk, Philip Taylor.

BRADSHAW, WILLIAM. Inventory. Jan. 21, 1811. Apprs: Gwin, Plummer Thurston, Singleton Wilson.

BRITE, LEWIS. Inventory Nov. 5, 1807. Apprs: Wilson Maddox, Davis Shepherd, William Hinton.

BULL, EDWARD. Inventory. Jan. C. C. 1808. Apprs: David Standeford, Joseph Metcalf, Abraham Rutledge.

CANNON, TUBMAN. Inventory. Aug. 1806. Apprs: Joseph Winlock, John Knight, Joseph Simpson. Admr: Betsy Cannon.

CHILDRESS, SUSANNAH. Sale of land. Susannah Childress was formerly Susannah Coburn, the widow of James Coburn.

CAN, MOSES. Inventory. Apprs: Thomas Foreman, Joseph Mc Grew, Jonathan Osburne. May, 1810.

CHILES, WALTER. May 17, 1805. ------. Wife: Phebe. Daus: Susannah Day, Nancy Thomas, Agnes Wallace, Betsy, Huldah, Phoebe. Sons: William, Thomas,

Lear, Lolly, Walter, Wallace. Ex: sons William, Walace, Walter. Wit: Froeborn G. Crenshaw, William T. Webber, Tarlton Lee. No date of probation.

CHURCHILL, RICHARD. Inventory. No Date. Apprs: William Collier, Admr: Mary Churchill.

CLARK, JAMES. Inventory. May C. C. 1811. Apprs: Simon Phyle, James Martin, Zachariah Clark.

COOPER, ELIAB. April 27, 1808. August 1810. Wife: Jeminah. Sons: Jesse, Eliab, Sarahan, Joseph. Dau: Gateen Collins. Ex: Walter Stallard. Wit: William Keston, William Hansbrough, John Able, George Wells.

CRERENSTAN, RICHARD. March 16, 1811 ------. Mentions six daus. but does not name them. Wit: Stephen Beard, William Mc Kinley, Margaret Hill.

DEMAREE, SAMUEL. Dec. 20, 1810. March C. C. 1811. Sons: David, Samuel, Cornelius, Daniel. Daus. Mary (wife of Cornelius Bice), Caty (wife of Tunis Van Nuys). Ex: sons David, Samuel, Cornelius. Wit: Christopher Bergen, George Bergen, George Lest.

DUGAN, HUGH. Inventory. Dec. C. C. 1809. Apprs: Andrew Holmes, John Todd.

EAKIN, ROBERT. No dates. Inventory. Apprs: Ellis Oglesby.

ELLIOTT, ROBERT. Inventory. April, 1806. Admr: Elijah Booker.

ELLIOTT, JESSE. Inventory. Dec. 14, 1811. Apprs: JOhn Williams.

FINLEY, WILLIAM. May 29, 1806. July 14, 1806. Wife: Sarah. Sons: William, Andrew, John, James, Lycurgus. Daus: Elinor, Jenny, Ann, Nancy. Ex: wife, sons John, James. Wit: James Shannon, James Alexader, Robert Weir.

FULTON, JOHN. Inventory. July 22, 1809.

GASH, JAMES. Inventory. March 1810. Apprs: Elisha Prewitt, Sr., William Jewell, Jr., Joseph Prewitt.

GILLESPY, JAMES. Inventory. 1806. Apprs: Samuel Van Cleave, William Allen, Robert Carson.

GRAVES, DAVID. Jan. 9, 1808. Feb. 1808. Wife: Agnes. Agnes Connelly (Gr. dau.), children mentioned but not named. Admr: Richard Graves, Andrew Holmes. Wit: Andrew Holmes, John Caldwell.

HERMAN, STEPHEN. Inventory. A. Holmes, M. Daniel, Aaron Tully. Apprs.

HORNSBY, JOSEPH. Of Virginia. March 6, 1799. Dec. 1807. Sons: Joseph, Thomas, Francis (dec'd). Daus: Hannah, Margaret. Son-in-law: William Nicholas, Merriwether Lewis. Ex: Joseph Hornsby, Thomas Hornsby, William Nicholas, Merriwether Lewis. Wit: John Knight, Joseph Winlock, William Mc Coy, John Mc Coy.

JEWELL, WILLIAM. Inventory. July C. C. 1811.

JONES, RICHARD. Dec. 28, 1807. April. 1808. Wife: Elizabeth. Sons: John, Silas. Daus: Polly Johnson (dec'd). Children: Nancy, Elizabeth Metcalf, Fanny Metcalf, Jane Crook, Annie Metcalf. Ex: wife, son John. Wit: ------.

LAWRENCE, DAVID. Inventory. Dec. 1804. Apprs: William Crow, John Lawerence.

LEE, DANIEL.. Inventory. March 24, 1810. Apprs: Samuel Miles, Jesse Lewis, John Lewis.

LEWIS, JOHN. Feb. 12, 1808. Settlement of estate. Admr: Margaret Hall who was Margaret Lewis, widow of John Lewis.

LEWIS, JOHN. Austin Hall is named guardian of John Lewis' children, viz: Henry, Polly, Keziah, Caty, John, William, Phaney. August, 1807.

MATTHEW, JOHN. Inventory. Dec. 19, 1807. Apprs: Robert Allen, James McDavitt, William Polk.

MC CAMPBELL, SAMUEL. Inventory. Nov. 1, 1804. Apprs: George Wilcox, Jacob Follinwade, Alex. Mc Dowell.

MC CLAIN, JOHN. Inventory. July 19, 1804. Apprs: A. Mc Gaughey, Moses Boone, Joseph Robinson.

MC CLAIN, DAVID. July 25, 1803. ------. Sons: John, Thomas, James, Alexander. Daus: Agnes, Mary. Ex: William Collins, John Caldwell (friends).

MC CRACKLIN, DAVID. Inventory. August 9, 1809. Apprs: Uriah Gloren, Nicholas Ware, Drury Malone.

MC FALL, DAVID. Settlement of estate. May 24, 1807.

MC FALL, LETTY. August 31, 1807. Feb. 1808. Estate to Samuel Methanton (son of James & Nancy). Ex: Tinson Ashby, Stephen Ashby, Polly Ashby.

MC KINNEY, JOHN. Inventory. April 6, 1805. Admr: James Hall.

MC QUADE, HENRY. Inventory. Sept. 1805. Admr: Ellis James, James Ballard.

MC WARD, MARGARET. Sept. 1805. Oct. 1807. Admr: Thomas Dickinson, Francis Jackson.

MC WADE, HENRY. May 13, 1805. Apprs. of estate of Margaret his wife. Oct. 15, 1808. Admr: James Anderson, James Ballard, James Simrall.

MILES, SAMUEL. March 11, 1811. ------. Wife: Sarah. Son: Benjamin. Ex: Eveen Miles, Samuel Miles (sons). Wit: James Cristy, Sr., Israel Christy.

MOORE, B. M. Inventory. Dec. 21, 1805. Apprs: A. Holmes, W. Daniel, Aaron Tilley.

PAYTON (PEYTON), CHARLES. Inventory. May 5, 1807. Apprs: John Gee, Dennis Onan, Thomas Mitchell.

PEARCY, GEORGE. Inventory. Nov. 11, 1811. Apprs: Jesse Duncan, Matterson Ogden, Nathanial Terrill.

PERRY, RODERICK. August 8, 1808. -----. Wife: Jane. Dau: Elizabeth, other children but not named. Ex: sons (?) Randolph, Robert, Roderick, Franklin. Wit: Thomas Baskett, Archibald Bailey, John Shepherd, Elijah Shelburne.

POLLARD, HARRY. Inventory. Oct. 23, 1811. Apprs: Thomas Mitchell, Elijah Pollard, Nathaniel Mc Grew.

POLLARD, HARRY. Aug. 8, 1811. Wife: Rachel. Children: Elijah, Rachel, Finley, other children not named. Ex: Rachel Pollard (wife,) Elijah (son).

PREWITT, JAMES. Inventory. Sept. 1811. Admr: William Mc Lane.

PREWITT, NATHANIEL. Inventory. Nov. 15, 1810. Admr: William Lane.

REED, SUSANNAH. Inventory. June 11, 1811. Apprs: Robert Tevis, Christopher Brant, George Robinson.

REDDING, WILLIAM. Inventory. July 13, 1805. Admr: Reuben Redding, Timothy Redding.

REID, JAMES. Sale. May 10, 1805. Admr: Isaac Collett.

RIDWAY, RICHARD. Inventory. March 26, 1806.

ROBINSON, JAMES. May 23, 1805. August 1805. Wife: Elizabeth. Sons: George, John. Daus: Sarah Sawyer, Mary Gillespy, Jean Carson, Elizabeth Metcalf, Rebecca Carson. Gr.dau: Elizabeth Fulton Metcalf. Ex: wife, John Sawyer, Stephen Allen.

RUTLEDGE, JOHN. Inventory. June 14, 1802.

SIMPSON, JOSEPH. March 17, 1807. -----. Wife: Betsy. Sons: William, Benjamin, John. Dau: Polly. Ex: wife. Wit: George Armstrong, John Simpson, James Moore.

SNYDER, PETER. Feb. 25, 1805. April 1, 1805. Wife: Susannah. Sons: Peter, John, Jacob, Daniel. Dau: Katherine. Ex: Christian Hostettler & Adam, his son. Wit: Henry Cochrane, James Gray.

STONE, GEORGE. Oct. 9, 1810. Wife: Anna. Children not named. Ex: Jacob Stone (father), Robert Cochrane.

TALBOT, EZEKIEL. Inventory. July 1805. Katharine Owen, formerly Katharine Talbot, widow of Ezekiel Talbot, given her dower in his estate by following commissioners: Francis Jackson, Blan Ballard, Aquilla Whitaker.

THREKELD, THOMAS. Of County of Mercer, Va. Jan. 30, 1790. ------. Wife: Nelly. Legatees: George, Daniel, Thomas (sons of bro. John Threkeld), William (son of Moses Threkeld), Daniel Threkeld Mc Conkey, Armistead Long, Buckley & Rachel (daus. of bro. Henry). Ex: wife, John Threkeld (bro.). Wit: Robert Pogue, Zeke Kennedy.

UTTERBACK, HENRY. Inventory. Dec. 1805. Apprs: Aaron Watts, Aaron Martin, John Martin. Dower given the widow, Patsy Utterback, April 23, 1810.

VARDMAN, PETER. July 23, 1808. ------. Wife: Prudence. Daus: Naomi Marshall, Prudence Marshall, Dorcas Overell, Naomi Nash, Sally Lancaster, Molly Menefee and her dau. Patty. Son: Thomas. Ex: Thomas Lewis, George Marshall (sons-in-law). Wit: John Ford, Jesse Rice.

WEAVER, MYRTLE. Inventory. No dates. Admr: Littleberry Weaver.

WHITE, MATTHEW. Inventory. Nov. 15, 1808. Apprs: Gaither, Matthew Bucey, Robert Tyler.

WOOD, JOHN. March 26, 1810. Nov. 1810. Sons: James, William. Daus: Elizabeth Lutteral, Sarah Wood, Synthia Coleman, Nancy Herndon, Lidia Herndon. Ex: James Lutteral, James Herndon. Wit: George Wilcox, Jacob Hansbrough, John Jones. Synthia Coleman (wife of Richard Coleman).

SPENCER COUNTY

BOOK A

1824 -- 1833

"At the first County Court began and held at the house of Leander Murphy in town of Taylorsville on Monday, 19th of January, 1824. Present: Stephen Baird, Joptha Barkley, Mastin Shelburne, Jonathan Cox, Thomas Newman, Gideon Walker, John Huston, John Lilly. All were duly qualified by taking oath prescribed by the constitution and laws of the State. David L. Wilson produced his commission as sheriff of this county, therefore took oath of office."

ASHBY, BEADYS. Inventory. March 1825.

ASHBY, ROBERT. August 20, 1831. Inventory.

BENNETT, BAZIL. March 5, 1830. --------. Wife: Matilda. Children not named. Ex: wife. Wit: Josiah Reason, Joseph Readman.

BIRDWILL (BRIDWELL), PRESLEY. June 12, 1832. ------. Sons: Ronal, Stephen, Presley. Dau: Peggy. Mentions father and mother. Ex: Stephen Birdwill, Stephen Beard.

BOSTON, JESSE. August 21, 1830. Wife and Ex: Mary. Sons: Rdward, Jesse, James. Dau: Harriet Stone.

BOTS, SETH. Sept. 1827. Daus: Esther, Sary Elkins, Alyee Elkins, Nancy Taylor. Gr.children: Benjamin and Polly Elkins. Wit: William Sterling, Charles --------.

BOYD, JOHN. Oct. 1833. Wife and Ex: Fabith. Sons: Robert, John, James, George. Daus: Betsy Veech, Polly Stone, Ruth Carling. Wit: ------.

BOYD, WILLIAM. April 27, 1830. Wife: Ruth. Children mentioned but not named. Ex: wife. Wit: William Lowe, Edward Stone.

BRISCOE, JOHN. June 1830. Allotted slaves from estate of late father, John M. Briscoe.

BUCKNOR, THOMAS. Dec. 26, 1831. Dau: Sally Ann. Son: William Presley. Ex: son Presley.

BURDETTE, JOHN. Sept. 1831. Estate to wife Easter. Mentions nephew Dr. Morrison Burdette.

BURNETT, JOHN C. May 16, 1833. Wife: Ann Morian. Ex: John Mc Gee, Thomas Burnett (bro.).

CARICO, ELIZABETH. June 18, 1824. Estate to be divided among children, not named. Ex: Vincent Carico (son). Wit: Fanny Spalding.

COCHRAN, ROBERT. --- 22, 1824. Daus: Polly Thomas, Anna Kinchloe, Patsy

Yantes. Ex: John Cochran (son), Peter Strong.

COLLINGS, BENJAMIN. Inventory. July 28, 1830. Wife: Sarah

CUNNINGHAM, FRANCES (FRANCIS). July 24, 1821. Son: Robert. Gr.dau: Meriah Hill, Jenit Cratherz, Peggy Hill. Ex: William Neil, John Boyd.

DAVIS, ELIZABETH. Jan. 28, 1832. Allotment of dower.

DAVIS, WILLIAM. Dec. 5, 1833. ---------. Estate to bros. Vincent and David, Nephews and neices.

DARNE, CATHARINE. Aug. 5, 1834. Dau: Mary Ann Brown.

DORNE, (DARNE), CHARLES. Inventory. Nov. 25, 1830.

DULIN, EDWARD. Inventory. Nov. 23, 1827. Wife: Mary.

STEWART, JAMES. Inventory. June 1825. Joseph Russell named guardian of James Stewart's children: James, John, Rebecca, Lucinda. Elizabeth Stewart wife. Admr: Peter Stout. Apprs: Reuben Dale, Daniel Bennett, H. Day.

SPENCER COUNTY

INDEX

BOOK A

1825 -- 1834

Ashby, Beady
Ashby, Robert

Barker, Milley
Beauchamp, Isaac
Bennett, Bazil
Bellwood, ------
Birdwill, Presley
Boyd, John
Boyd, William
* Boston, Jesse
Briscoe, George
Briscoe, John
Brown, Joseph
Burnett, John
Burdette, Benjamin
Burdette, John
Buchanan, Archibald
Buskirk, Thomas

* Bots, Seth

Carico, Elizabeth
Cochran, Robert
Collings, Benj.
Cook, William
Cunningham, Frances

Davis, Elizabeth
Davis, William
Darne, Catharine
Darne (Dorne), Charles
Dulin, Edward

Forman, Thomas
Froman, John

Goodwin, John
Gray, John S.
Gray, Joseph
Grigsby, Redman

Hatfield, William
Hatfield, Eliza
Hidden, Jacob
Hopewell, John

Irwine, Richard

Jackson, Francis
Jarboe, Joseph
Jones, Mildred

Luckett, James
Lunderman, John

Mc Cullom, Joseph
Mc Gee, Ahijah
Mc Grew, Joseph
Mc Lauhten, Jesse
Meartin, John
Milton, William
Miller, John H.
Moxley, Daniel

Norman, Isaac

Onan, (heirs)
Ozburn, Abner

Phillips, John
Prewitt, Martha

Redman, -----
Roberts, Abner
Rodgers, Andrew
Russell, Rachel

Scott, John
Shields, Frances
Smallwood, George
Snider, Adams
Stewart, James
Stone, Guilford

Terrill, Micajah
Turnham

Veach, Elliott

Weeks, James
Woods, Nathaniel

TODD COUNTY

BOOK A

1820 -- 1826

ALLISON, ABRAHAM. Sept. 12, 1825. Joseph Wilson is guardian for Abraham Allison, son of Robert Allison (Ellison).

ALLISON, ROBERT. March 23, 1816. Sept. 1823. Sons: William, Robert, Samuel, Joseph, James. Daus: Mary Beaty, Elizabeth Heyton. Ex: James Allison, Joseph Allison (sons). Wit: M. Wilson, F. T. Pennington, John Mc Kinney.

ANDERSON, RACHEL. Jan. 1, 1825. Receives her dower from estate of husband, Reuben Anderson, dec'd.

ANDERSON, REUBEN. March 14, 1825. Settlement with the heirs of Reuben Anderson. Heirs: Martha Anderson, Jasper Anderson, Sarah Anderson. Guardian: John S. Anderson.

ANDERSON, REUBEN. Inventory. August 9, 1824. Admr: Will Earham.

ARMSTRONG, ROBERT. Inventory. Dec. 1823.

BOURNE, AMBROSE. Oct. 9, 1823. Nov. 11, 1823. Wife: Charity. Sons: Alexander, John M, Josiah Fort. Daus: Fanny Watkins, Jane Greenfield, Piety Horn Bourne. Mentions brother Foster's daughter and Elisha Bourne's two little daughters Sally and Agatha. Ex: Whitneel Fort, John M. Bourne (brother). Wit: Thomas Dill, John Cockrill, Samuel Johnson.

BRONAUGH, THOMAS. Oct. 30, 1820. Dec. 15, 1820. Daus: Betsy Peters, Polly Baker. Mentions Margaret Elizabeth Gaines, Thomas Francis Gaines, Edward Gaines, Francis Pendleton Gaines, (possibly grandchildren). Ex: Taliferrio Bronaugh (brother), William C. Davis. Wit: Joseph Mason, William Daniel, Alexander Gilmore.

BROOKS, THOMAS. Inventory of Thomas Ross (infant). Charles Mills Guardian, 1823.

BROWN, FRANCES. May 1, 1824. March, 1825. Sons: Elijah Gartin Brown, John Brown, Nathaniel Griffith Brown, William Gartin Brown. Daus: Fanny Shanklin, Elizabeth Douglas. Mentions heirs of Uriah Gartin and Richard Gartin. Ex: John Brown (son). Wit: W. Mc Kee, William Simpson.

CARPENTER, CHRISTIAN. May 8, 1822. June 1822. Wife: Katy. Mentions five youngest daus: Fanny, Polly, Nancy, Katy, Minerva. Sons: Peter, John, Robert, Christian. Daus: Sarah, Elizabeth. Ex: wife, Robert Carpenter (son). Wit: John Brown, William Mc Kee.

CARNALL, GEORGE. Oct. 17, 1825. Dec. 14, 1825. Wife: Mildred. Sons: David, James, Perry, Patrick, Fleming, Elijah H. Daus: Rhoda, Roxanna, Keziah, Esther, Ann, Mary. Ex: wife, Patrick Carnall, Fleming. Carnall (sons).

Wit: Chris. Collins, Benjamin Dyar Carnaugh.

DAVIS, THOMAS. March 15, 1826. May 8, 1826. Wife: Mary. Daus: Sarah Ann, Mary Elizabeth. Ex: John Pendleton. Wit: Benjamin Downs, George Fristoes, William Burgess.

DILLS, THOMAS. April 1825. August 1825. Wife: Mary. Children not named. Ex: Anthony North, John Graham.

DONNER, BENJAMIN. Inventory. May Court, 1826. Admr: Elizabeth Donner. Apprs: Henry Tandy, Jackson Tandy, George Fristoe.

DUVAL, SAMUEL. ----1825. May 1825. Estate to Daniel Dunscomb and Samuel S. Duval, they are also named as executors. Mentions daus. Lucy Clayburn Dennings, Nancy Dunscomb. Wit: James Black, Joseph Black, John Black.

EDWARDS, ELISHA. Oct. 1823. Nov. 1823. Wife: Martha. Children: Mary Beall, Martha Maria, Margaret Louisa, Benjamin Tazewell, unborn child. Ex: wife, Presly Edwards (brother), Cyrus Edwards (brother). Wit: William R. Stewart, Thomas Kirkman, B. F. Edwards.

FRISTOE, DANIEL. Inventory. 1826. Wife: Margaret. Daus: Nancy, Mary.

GIBSON, JOHN. July 1821. Dec. 1821. Wife: Mary. Daus: Gressy, Betsy, Sally, Mary. Granddau: Sally Gibson, dau. of son John. Gr.daus: Jane and Catharine daus. of son Hugh. Wit: P. Hazelwood, Cornelius Riddle.

GREENFIELD, SAMUEL. Sept. 26, 1823. Nov. 1823. Wife: Polly. Dau: Mary Jane. Sons: James Thompson Greenfield, Gideon Thompson Greenfield. Ex: Gideon Thompson, Thomas Greenfield, Sr., William Greenfield. Wit: James Kendall, J. Thompson, Warren Greenfield.

HENDERSON, JOHN. August 30, 1819. Dec., 1824. Wife: Susa. Children mentioned but not named. Ex: John Sperlin. Wit: Judith Henderson, William Blalock.

HILL, BENJAMIN. April 8, 1818. Nov. 1820. Wife and children mentioned but not named. Wit: Willis Read, C. H. Babbitt.

JAMESON, ROBERT. Dec. 12, 1825. Feb. 1826. Wife: Nancy. Sons: Enos, Sidney, Ephiram, Andrew Jackson, Thomas, Robert, Isaac. Dau: Permelia Presley, Rose Alinda Ring, Sarah. Ex: wife, son Enos. Wit: Spottswood Smith, S. W. Carney, Richard Bowlding.

LOWRY, SAMUEL. Feb. 15, 1821. Nov. 8, 1824. Wife: Susannah. Ex: wife. Wit: Matthew Cunningham, Robert Miller, Nancy Gallaher.

LUNNSDEN, WILLIAM. Feb. 25, 1823. Dec. 1825. Wife: Nancy. Children mentioned but not named. Ex: wife, James Graham, John Graham. Wit: Roger Burrus, James Atlin.

MC VEY, JOHN. Sept. 3, 1820. Nov. 1822. Wife: Rachel. "To six youngest children who have received no part in my estate, viz: Charles, Nathaniel, Samuel W., Edly P., Jane". Ex: wife, Thomas Mc Vey (son), Samuel Shamwell. Wit: Patrick Carnall, Elijah Latham, Bazel Latham.

MILLS, ADAM. Feb. 20, 1823. Feb. 14, 1825. Wife: Nancy. Sons: Andrew, Robert, David. Dau: Jincy, Polly. Ex: Robert Graham, Matthew Graham, William Harlan. Wit: William McKee, Barnes Jeter.

MOORE, JAMES. Sept. 2, 1820. Dec. 14, 1820. Wife: Sarah. Sons: David, Alexander, William, James, Samuel. Dau: Margaret Saunders, Elizabeth. Ex: wife. Wit: Robert Allison, Joseph Allison, Asher Shelton.

PAYNE, CHARLES. April 13, 1822. June 1822. Wife: Polly. Sons: William, Joseph, Robert. Daus: Elizabeth, Susanna Jeters, Harriet Haygood. "To infant children of Thomas Payne, Augustus and William." Ex: not named. Wit: Samuel Hargroves, William H. Terry.

PAYNE, JOSIAH. Nov. 15, 1820. Aug. 1821. Wife: Mary. Sons: William, Robert, Josiah. Dau: Mary, Rachel, Lettice (?), Camalito (?). Ex: wife, Robert Starks. Wit: A. Shelton, Thomas Hunt, Robert Haymes.

ROSS, SAMUEL. Feb. 18, 1826. March 1826. Wife and children mentioned but not named. Ex: Thomas Acock. Wit: John Christian, John Driskill.

SINGLETON, FRANCES. Oct. 27, 1825. Jan. 9, 1826. Sisters: Agnes Singleton, Elon Miller. Nieces: Nancy Miller, Agnes Young. Bro: Vincent. Mentions mother but does not name her. Ex: James Gray (friend). Wit: Susan Mitchell, William Young.

STUBBLEFIELD, BEVERLY. July 1, 1820. Feb. 1824. Estate to wife, Mary, and five youngest children, viz: John, Elizabeth, Maria, Virginia, Mary. There were three older children but only dau. Susan, wife of James Clark, was named. Ex: wife. Wit: William F. Gray, C. P. McReynolds.

TALIAFERRO, FRANCIS. April 29, 1821. ----1826. Wife: Lettisia. Sons: Samuel Walker, Le Roy. Daus: Nancy French Edrington, Sally Hughes. Ex: wife. Wit: Alfred Lomax, Washington Lively.

TERRY, JAMES L. AND NAPOLEON. Inventory. August 14, 1826. Appraiser and guardian: Henry Gorin (Lorin?).

TERRY, STEPHEN. Inventory. Oct. 1822. Admr: William M. Terry. In 1824 there was a settlement of accounts of William M. Terry with Elizabeth Terry, Amanda Terry, Mildred Terry.

THOMPSON, JOHN. Oct. 26, 1816. Dec. 1816. Wife: Sophia. Daus: Jane Snowden, Sophia, Nancy, Isabella. Sons: John, Alexander, Robert, James. Dau: Polly McFarin. Ex: not named. Wit: Finis Ewing, Thomas Bryan, George Snoden.

THOMPSON, SAMUEL. Inventory. Sept. 5, 1822. Apprs: Henry Floyd, Leven King, Jonathan Cox.

VARMAY, BRAZILLA. Inventory. Sept. 1822. Apprs: Granville Wadill, Pouncy Anderson, John Stephenson. Admr: William Harlan.

WALLACE, SIMON. Sept. 5, 1822. Dec. 1822. Wife: Rachel. Children not named. Ex: wife, John Graham. Wit: William Randle, Bernard Anderson.

WILKINS, JAMES. Sept. 6, 1822. March 1823. Wife: Elizabeth. Sons: William, Thomas, John, James, Alexander. Dau: Isabella. Children of son James viz: Shaw, Hugh, Chesterfield, George Hunseker. Ex: wife, son James. Wit: Edward Shanklin, Robert Shanklin, William Hopper.

YANCY, JOHN. Jan. 4, 1824. Dec. 4, 1825. Wife: Susannah. Son: Gabriel. Gr.children: Maria Louise, Preston I. Yancy, Robert Yancy. Ex: Gabriel Yancy (son), Joseph P. Graves. Wit: William Smith, Edmund Fulcher, Benjamin Allen, Joseph Graves.

TODD COUNTY

BOOK A

Fry, Thomas	Kennedy, Senneca
Graham, Rachel	Mahen, Jane
Humphrey, James	New, Emily
Hadley, Martin	Rice, Jesse
Hodges, Robert	Sanders, William
Jameson, Mahala and Susanna	Terry, James
Johnson, Mary	Waggoner, James, Sr.
Kennedy, James	Willis, Reuben

Inventories and guardian accounts.

WARREN COUNTY

BOOK A

1796---1814

ALEXANDER, ANDREW. August 1798. Inventory. Admr: W. Chapline.

AYERS, DAVID. Nov. 29, 1800. May 1801. Wife: Polly. Children: Zury, John, Thomas. Ex: wife. Wit: Thomas Slayton, John Willoughby, Isaac Scaterfield.

BARTEN, BARBESTER. May 16, 1813. Oct., 1813. Wife: Elizabeth. Sons: John, Barry, Ward, Obed, Leroy, Bently. Ex: wife, son Barry. Wit: Benjamin Letchworth, Green Graham.

BEARD, BRIZELIA. Dec. 1802. Inventory. William Chapline, C.C.

BLACKFORD, REUBEN. Jan. 25, 1804. May, 1804. Wife: Elizabeth. Children: Elizabeth, Anna, Easter, Reuben, Ex: Durham Turner. Wit: Phebe Turner, Elizabeth Blackford, Thomas Blackford.

BUNCH, CALLOWAY. Nov. 11, 1807. Jan. 4, 1808. Wife: Nancy. Children: William, Patsy, Simion, Elizabeth, Pemelia, Polly, Joseph Hendersob (stepson). Ex: wife, bro. George. Wit: David Hudspeth, William McWilliams, Karak Wilkinson.

CARVER, HENRY. Sept., 1802. Inventory. Apprs: William Hays, John Nestor.

CHAPLIN, WILLIAM. May 30, 1811. Inventory. Apprs: A. Graham, Samuel Barclay, H. Crump. Admr: Eliza Chaplin.

CHAPMAN, ABNER. Nov. 7, 1812. Inventory. Apprs: Jonathan Holloway, James Hay, Jacob Holloway.

CHASON, JAMES. April, 1808. Inventory. Apprs: Jonathan Holcomb, Collin Lanter, Jesse Berryman.

CHASON, PEGGY. July 15, 1809. Dower. (Now Peggy Miller) Apprs: John Hudson, John Aden, Jonathan Holcomb.

CHASTIAN, JAMES. Nov. 1813. Division of land. Children: John, David, Thomas, Nancy, Edward, Polly, Sally.

COLE, ZACHARIAH. May 15, 1813. Oct. 1813. Wife: Mary. Children: Abraham, Samson, Zachariah, George, Mary, Abenezer, Elizabeth Nealy, Hue, Freelove Henderson, Joseph, Phoebe, Alexander, John. Ex: wife. Wit: Richard Pope, Joseph Sherman, William Sherman.

COMPTON, DARNAL. July 1799. Inventory. Apprs: James Campbell, John Barley.

COWLES, EDWARD. Aug. 10, 1813. Feb. 1814. Admr: Henry Cowles (uncle). Wit: Vincent Cowles, James H. Cowles.

CRAWFORD, ISAAC. March, 1799. Inventory. Apprs: Alex. Davidson, Daniel Gage, Robert Wallace.

CURD, WILLIAM. Of Jessamine County. Inventory. Nov. 30, 1799. Apprs: Abraham Fulkarson, Benjamin Bradshaw, Will Lewis.

DOBSON, ELIAS. Sept. 1802. Inventory. Admr: Sarah Dobson, Bartholomew Stoval.

DOYLE, THOMAS. Sept. 14, 1806. Oct. 1809. Wife: Mahaly. Children: Elizabeth, John, Hannah. Ex: Gregory Doyle. Wit: John Rountree, John Davis, Peggy Smith, Peggy Doyle, Samuel Doyle.

Dye, Benjamin. July 1, 1805. Dec. 1805. Wife: Fanny. Children mentioned, but not named.

DYER, ABNER. Oct. 10, 1812. Inventory. Admr: Nancy Dyer. Apprs: William R. Paine, John Whitsitt, William Derby.

EUBANKS, WILLIAM. Dec. 4, 1812. April 13, 1813. Sons: John, William, Nimrod, Benjamin Rawlins (son-in-law). Gr.dau: Fanny Rawlins. Ex: son John, Thomas Hay. Wit: John Hay, Philip Bush, Edward Harris.

FICKLIN, JAMES. Feb. 7, 1811. May 1811. Wife: Esther. Sons: Robert, Joseph Pulliam (son-in-law). Mentions a law suit pending in Virginia. Ex: son Robert. Wit: John Ray, Henry Miller, Asa Pepa.

FICKLIN, ROBERT P. March 26, 1813. Legatees: Katharine Ficklin (wife), Esther Ficklin (mother), Robert Pullian (nephew), heirs of Joseph Pullian. Wit: John Ray, L. Garrison.

FOSTER, JAMES. May 20, 1813. Inventory. Apprs: Drury Foster, James Sherman, James Wilson, Peter Wagoner.

GOODMAN, SAMUEL. JAN. 16, 1814. Inventory. Apprs: Peter Jones, Eriel Floyd, James Young.

GRAINGER, JOHN. March 1808. May 1808. Son: John. Dau: Sally, other children not named. Ex: bro. Jacob. Wit: J.W. Covington, James Mitchell, George Carson.

GREER, ISAAC. Feb. 16, 1812. July 1812. Wife: Mary. Children: Sary, Levi, Hannah, Lorry, Permely. Ex: wife. Wit: Edward Chaston, Thos. Crabtree, David Owen.

GRIDER, HENRY. Appointed guardian for Daniel Gillespie, Nov. 1801.

HALL, MATTHEW. Oct. 1813. Inventory. Apprs: Robt. Herrale, George Frazier.

HAMMOND, ELIJAH. Admr. for estate of John Merry . May 8, 1805.

HAYS, SAMUEL. ----April, 1805. Wife: Elizabeth. Ex: son James. Wit: William McFARin, Samuel Hays, Reuben Fox.

HENDRICK, JAMES. May 29, 1812. August 1812. Wife: Mary. Children,but only son William named. Ex: John Hendrick. Wit: Jas. Howland, Jas. Hendrick, Joseph Shutts.

HENDRICK, JOHN. March 25, 1814. Nuncupative. Wife: Fanny. Children not named. Proved by the oath of John and James Hendrick.

HILL, MOSES. Inventory. Nov.,1809. Apprs: Joseph Duncan, Thomas Eubanks.

HICKERSON, THOMAS. Inventory. August 11, 1812. Appr: Daniel Doughty.

HODGE, WILLIAM. Inventory. Nov. 1, 1811. Apprs: Denton S. Porter, Jeremiah Henton.

HOWARD, CHARLES. Jan. 4, 1815. Apprs: James Hay, James Gray.

HUDSPETH, JOSEPH. March 5, 1809. April, 1809. Wife: Anna. Sons: James, John, Dunham, George, Solomon, Thomas. Dau: Dolly. Ex: sons Thomas, John, and bro. George. Wit: Aaron William, John Whitsitt, William & George Harris.

JENNY, ABEL. Inventory. April 19, 1807. Apprs: William Hodges, Mark Garrison, Robert McReynolds.

JOHNSON, JOHN. Inventory. Nov.,1807. Admrs: Peggy Johnson, John Johnson. Apprs: William Thomas, Robert Lee, Mark Reeves.

KEY, SIMON. Dec.11, 1800. June 1801. Wife: Elizabeth. Children: Bennett, Simon, Lucocy, Obidiah. Ex: wife, son Obidiah. Wit: John Ray, B. Freeman.

KING, ROBERT. Inventory. Dec.13,1800. Apprs: John Moore, Thomas Chapman, Thompson Buggs.

KIRBY, DAVID. April 26, 1811. July 1811. Wife: Elizabeth. Children: Jesse, Leonard, Samuel, Asa, Isabel, Solomon, Agnes Tully, Sally Scroggin, Jeporath Pace, Elizabeth Piles. Ex: Children to select executor. Wit: John Loving, John Hightower, Jacob Skiles.

LEWALLEN, WILLIAM. Aug. 29, 1811.----Wife: Miram. Children not named. Wit: Isiah Lewis, William Milton.

LIGHTFOOT, CLEYBOURN. Inventory. Nov.,1810. Apprs: Micajah Hermans, Mathew Caldwell, Roley Williams.

LITTEN, THOMAS. Inventory. August, 1810. Appr: John Porter.

LONG, MARY. Inventory. July 12, 1809. Apprs: Joseph Ficklin, Samuel Barclay, Willis Mitchell,Sr.

LOVING, James. Sale. Jan.16, 1801. Admrs: Joseph Snodgrass, Jean Loving.

LOWERY, WYATT. April,1814. Legatee: bro. Stephen. Ex: Benjamin Temple, bro. Stephen. Wit: Benjamin Temple, Byrd Hendrick, Thomas & John Smith.

LOWERY, JAMES. Inventory. Jan. 16, 1801. Apprs: George Higgeson, Thomas Fletcher, Thomas Ford, Samuel Cox.

LLOYD, CHARLES. Jan. 1,1811. Nov.,1812. Wife: Catharine. Children: John, Elizabeth, Catharine, Polly. Ex: John Hendrick, Catharine Lloyd. Wit: Jane Hendrick, John Davenport, Catharine Renner (?).

LOYD, JAMES. Settlement. Feb., 1804. Apprs: Jonathan Rosell, Robert Wallace.

LUCAS, NATHANIEL. May 4, 1807. Sept. 1807. Wife: Sarah. Children: John, Robert ("land I possess in Montgomery Co., Va.), Nancy, Elizabeth, Tabitha, Sarah, Rebecca. Ex: Henry Fox, Tarlton Drake, John Dixon, Sr. Wit: J. Dixon, Joseph Carter, Kensley Dixon.

LYLES, MANCE. Inventory. Apprs: John Blackwell, John Gibson, Peter Waggoner. May 8, 1810.

MADISON, ROWLAND. Inventory. Oct. 19, 1802.

MAGNIS, PEREGREN. May 8, 1800. July 1800. Wife: Mary. Ex: George & Joseph Magnis. Wit: William and John Black.

MARMEN, WILLIAM. Sept. 4, 1811. Jan. 1812. Children: Hardy, Acy, Stephen, Charlotte, Milly. Wit: Eless McFaddin, William Hays, Shadrack Hays.

McCALIEY, DANIEL. Feb. 8, 1806. March 1806. Son: James. Admr: Sam'l Doyal.

McCURRY, JOHN. Inventory. Aug. 20, 1808. Apprs: James Renfro, David Sample Martin Elmon.

McFADDIN, JOHN. Inventory. Apprs: Isaac Lewis, Aaron Lewis, Robert Bryan.

McGINNIS, THOMAS. Inventory. Admr: John Curd.

MOORE, ROBERT. Feb. 18, 1802. April, 1810. Wife: Mary. Sons: Lewis, William, Nathan, Warren, Cleric. Sons-in-law: Fredrick Fort, William Shackleford, James H. Cole. Ex: William Moore. Wit: James Renfro, William Collins.

MORRIS, VALENTINE. Sept. 1807. July 1808. Wife: Ruth. Children: Elijah, Edward, Moses, Jacob, Rhoda, Milly, Patsy, Kelly, Rachel, Betsy, Becky, Esther, Ann. Wit: Charles Eades, Samuel White.

MORRISON, JOHN. Inventory. March 24, 1814. Apprs: D. Conwell, J. Birmatt.

MOTLEY, JOHN. June 13, 1811. Dec. 1811. Wife: Elizabeth. Sons: Mathew, Henry, James, Edwin. Daus: Sally Smith, Caty Johnson, Polly Johnson, Denny Lynn, Nancy Woatherspoon. Ex: sons Mathew and Henry. Wit: John Ray, John Landis.

MARSHALL, JOHN. Inventory. Feb. 16, 1811. Those mentioned: Merry, William, and Gilbert Marshall, John Stephens.

MILLER, GEORGE. March 17, 1812. May 1812. Wife: Mary. Daus: Ann, Susanna. Ex: Micaja Miller, Berryman Roe. Wit: William Newton, Mathew Boren, Francis Boren

MILLER, ISAAC. Nov. 16, 1809. Jan., 1810. Wife: Margaret. Isaac Hammette (nephew Ex: Benjamin Cullen. Wit: Josiah Wright, William Stephen, George Davidson.

MOBERLY, CHARLES. Inventory. Aug. 23, 1811. Admr: Elijah Hammette. Apprs: David Shaggs, William Hill, Nathaniel Ewing.

NESTER, JOSEPH. Jan. 5, 1810. Feb. 1810. Wife: Jenny. Son: Samuel. Ex: wife. Wit: Henry Caldwell, Hugh Brown, Elizabeth Cowles.

PHELPS, MARTHA. Inventory. Oct. 26, 1811. Apprs: Joseph Gray, William Hays.

RAWLIN, CHARLES. Inventory. May 1808. Apprs: Thomas Crawford, George Reed.

ROBINSON, JEREMIAH. Sept. 13, 1810. Oct. 1811. Wife: Isabell. Sons: Jeremiah, Alexander. Ex: wife, son Alex. Wit: Hugh Shannon, Elijah Simons.

ROBINSON, JOHN. Inventory. August 11, 1808.

ROSS, WILLIAM. Inventory. Nov. 4, 1806.

ROWLAND, DANIEL. Inventory. Dec. 1805. Apprs: James Dell, Jona. Helemon(?)

SMITH, GEORGE. Dec. 1811. March 10, 1811. Wife: Elizabeth. Children: Peggy Elizabeth, Mary, Caty, George, Henry, John, Christian, Paps, Clary Walker Barberry, Henrietta. Wit: Howard Smith, Henry Duberg.

STEWART, CHARLES. Aug. 7, 1799. Oct. 1799. Wife: Elinor. Son: Stephenson, other children not named. Ex: Burwell Jackson, Robert Herrill.

STEWART, JAMES. Aug. 24, 1810. ---1812. Children: Alexander, Charles, James Nancy, Polly, Simon Hubbard (son-in-law). Wit: Leander Sharp, A. Hubbard.

STEWART, WILLIAM. Inventory. ----- Apprs: Benj. Pullian, Sam'l. Kirkland, John McIntosh.

STOVAL, BARTHOLMEW. March 25, 1807. April 1807. Wife: Susanna. Children: George, Jesse, Thomas, Nancy, Edy. Sons-in-law: William Oliver, Thomas Dobson, Gr.children: John, James, Betsy, Suky, Sally, all heirs of dau. Delicia Dobson, dec'd. Ex: John Ray. Wit: William Merino, William Gibson.

STROTHER, ROBERT. Oct. 14, 1800. March 1801. Sons: John Dabney Strother, Benjamin. Daus: Nelly, Elizabeth, Nancy. Ex: Samuel Strother, Nelly Strother. Wit: F. Walker, John D. Strother, A. Hubbard.

TIGERT, JAMES. March 17, 1809. Wife: Joan. Children: John, William, Hannah. Ex: wife, brother John Tigert.

TURNER, HARDIN. Nov. 30, 1812. Jan. 1813. Wife: Rachel. Children: Sally, William, Nathan, Elizabeth. Ex: Alex. Graham, Thompson Briggs.

WHITTEN, ELIJAH. Inventory. July 16, 1812. Apprs: Joseph Gray, Charity Whitten.

WILLIAMS, JOHN. (Of Breckenridge Co., Ky.) Feb. 23, 1807. July 1807. Wife: Silvey. Children not named. Wit: Mathew Caldwell, John Letherman.

WRENN, NICHOLAS. August 6, 1808. ----- Wife: Elizabeth. Ex: sons John, Isaac.

WASHINGTON COUNTY

BOOK A

1792 -- 1808

ABELL (ABETT), SAMUEL. Feb. 1, 1795. June Court 1795. Sons: Edmund, Barton, Peter, Ignatus. Daus: Elizabeth Fenwick, Henrietta Thompson, Susannah, Mary Ann. Grandsons: John Thomas, Bennett Thomas (Thompson), Joseph Abett, Joshua Abell. Ex: Joshua Abell (son). Wit: Benid Spalding, Robert Abell.

ALVEY, JOSEPH. August 23, 1803. Jan. 2, 1804. Wife: Ann. Sons: Basil, Thomas, Clement, James, William. Daus: Eleanor, Ann. Ex: Robert Alvey, Zacariah Riney. Wit: John Watham, John Warren, Thomas ----(illegible).

ASKIN (ASKEN), JOHN. Jan. Court 1801. Inventory. Apprs: Edelin, Thomas Stayton, Obidiah Staton.

ASKREW, WILLIAM. Sept. 29, 1798. Dec. 1798. Wife: Hannah. Children mentioned but, not named. Ex: wife, John Asken, Thomas Robb. Wit: Nathan Springer, Ezekiel Montgomery, John Waller. (Name is indexed Askrean, signed Askrew).

BARNES, GEORGE. Inventory. Jan. 16, 1802.

BEALLE, ANDREW. August 27, 1803. Sept. 1803. Legatees: Nancy Oxbury, Richard Bealle, Peter Brown, Benjamin Brown. Ex: Richard Bealle, Peter Brown, John Beasland. Wit: Philemon Waters, E. B. Gaithers, Sarah Brashoars.

BEALL, MARGARET. Inventory. Sept. 5, 1797. Apprs: James Molyhon, Edward Clarkson, John Cunningham.

BEALLE, NATHAN. July 29, 1802. Sept. 6, 1802. Wife: Sarah. Sons: Jesse, William, Washington. Daus: Tabitha Hudspeth, Polly Bealle, Nancy Bealle, Elizabeth Noland (husband Bernard Noland). Ex: wife. Wit: Henry Miles, William Bucket, William Puckrill. Mentions estate in Maryland.

BERRY, RICHARD. Aug. 19, 1797. Dec. 1798. Wife: Rachel. Sons: Richard, Francis, Edward. Daus: Jane, Joanna, Sarah, Rachel. Ex: Richard Berry, Francis Berry (sons). Wit: James Ryan, Richard B. Brownfield, William Brownfield.

BLANDSFORD, IGNATUS. Inventory. Jan. 16, 1808. Apprs: Coleman Brown, Francis Spark, George Summers.

WILL OF RICHARD BERRY: IN THE NAME OF GOD AMEN, the Nineteenth day of August, in the year of our Lord, one thousand, seven hundred and Ninety Seven. I, Richard Berry, of the State of Kentucky and County of Washington, now in my proper senses and memory do make this my last Will and Testament, viz:

I give to my sons Richard and Francis Berry, each a tract of land as it was laid off by Archibald Bilbo, which they have improved.

Also I give to my son Francis Berry a good feather bed and furniture and ten pounds.

Also I give to my son Edward his mare and saddle and cow and a rifle gun and my negro boy called Fill and a good feather bed and furniture and a big plow and tacklin.

1 also give to my beloved wife Rachel Berry the mare colt, Plesure, a good saddle and a bead (bed) and furniture to dispose of as she sees cause. I lend to her my plantation I now live on and all the rest of my estate during her life and after her death I give said Plantation to my son Eward Berry, then an equal division between my seven children: Joanna, Sarah, Rachel, Richard, Francis, Jane, Edward, of the rest of my property.

Also I authorize my son Edward to make a sale of a tract of land on Doctors fork in Mercer County for use and benefit of John Berry's two children.

I appoint Richard and Francis Berry to be executors of this my last Will and Testament.

In Witness whereof I have hereunto set my hand and affixed my Seal this Nineteenth day of August, One Thousand Seven Hundred and Ninety Seven. (1797).

Acknowledged in the Presents of James Ryan, Richard B. Brownfield, William Brownfield.

Signed: Richard Berry.

County Court, 4 December, 1798, this will was proven by the oath of James Ryan, William Brownfield.

(Richard Berry was an uncle of Thomas Lincoln, and it was at his home that Thomas Lincoln and Nancy Hanks (parents of Abraham Lincoln) were married.)

BOOTH, BASIL. Oct. 20, 1794. Nov. 5, 1795. Wife: Elizabeth. Daus: Ann, Jane. Ex: wife. Wit: William De Rohan, John Brothers, Honay Lucas.

BOOTH, JANE. Inventory. Dec. 1799. An infant orphan of Basil Booth.

BOYD, ELIJAH. Inventory. May 4, 1803. Apprs: Josiah Wilson, James Mc Ilroy, John Sandusky.

BREWER, WILLIAM. March 17, 1799. April 1799. Wife: Susannah. Daus: Mary Shanks, Sary Mattingly. Sons: John, William, James. Ex: wife. Wit: John Brothers, George Brothers.

BROTHERS, CORNELIUS. No date. 1803. Wife: Elizabeth. Sons: James, Jeremiah, George. Dau: Mary. Gr.sons: John Brothers (son of Cornelius Brothers), Cornelius Brothers (son of John Brothers). Daus: Dority Brothers, Elizabeth Brothers. Ex: wife, James Brothers. Wit: Henry Smock, Garrett Smock, Henry Peterson.

BROTHERS, CORNELIUS. Inventory. April 16, 1793. Appr: Wilford Hayden.

BROWN, ANN. Dec. 24, 1804. April, 1808. "My estate to my son Wilford, his wife and heirs but, should he die without heirs then estate to go to Charles Mills and wife, after their decease to their son Stephen " Wit: Henry Smock, Anthony Brown, Samuel Brown.

BROWN, BASIL. August 22, 1798. Nov. 3, 1801. All estate to wife Mary. Wit: John Helm, Sally Helm -----Allen.

BROWNFIELD, JAMES. July 23, 1795. Jan. 7, 1796. Wife: Joannah. Sons: Robert, Richard, William, James, Obadiah, Samuel. Dau: Rachel. Ex: Richard Berry, Richard Brownfield (son), John Caldwell. Wit: Stith Thompson, Francis Berry, John Mc Glathon.

BUCKMAN, IGNATUS. Sept. 2, 1794. Inventory. Apprs: Benjamin Spalding, Leon Hamilton, Sam Abell, John Dyer.

CARSON, THOMAS. No date. Dec. 12, 1808. "Estate to wife and children". Fails to name them. Ex: James Carson, Josiah Neilson. Wit: James Graham, William Patton, Joseph Feland.

CLELAND, PHILIP. Inventory. July 1, 1800. Apprs: Edward Hughes, Benjamin Lawless, Charles Wickliff.

CLELAND. Horatio Cleland, Harriett Cleland infant orphans of Philip Cleland.

CLIFTON, BURDETTE. Jan. 1, 1799. Inventory. Apprs: John Mc Cawlin, John Davis, Henry Purtle.

CLIFTON, HANSON. May 2, 1794. June Court, 1794. Wife: Nancy. Children: William, others not named. "Money to be paid brother Baldwin Clifton before Estate is divided. " Ex: wife, Baldwin Clifton (brother), Col. John Caldwell. Wit: Sarah and Baldwin Clifton.

CONDER, GEORGE. July 5, 1790. Sept. 1799. Wife: Barbara. "Estate to be equally divided among my children, except George Conder and Margaret Young." Other children not named. Ex: wife, Peter Conder, John Conder (sons). Wit: Benjamin Patton, Philip Weser, Isaac Konkright.

COPEL, PETER. August 25, 1803. Nov. 1803. Wife: Elinor. All estate to wife. Wit: Edwin Beaver, Delijah Vessels (Elijah).

CORN, EDWARD. Inventory. Dec. 4, 1798. Apprs: Joseph Callico, William Worland, Peter Powel.

CUNNINGHAM, THOMAS. Inventory. Jan. 3, 1801. Apprs: William Allen, William Yates, William Jackson.

CURTSINGER, CONROD. Inventory. Jan. 7, 1805.

DANT, JOHN. June 14, 1807. Feb. Court 1808. Wife: Elizabeth. Sons: James, Joseph. Dau: Mary Elliott (hus. Stephen Elliott). Gr.daus: Elizabeth Elliott, Teresa Dant. Testator leaves to son Joseph "his great coat", to son James "balance of my clothes". To Stephen Elliott "a grey mare". Ex: James Dant (son). Wit: John Lancaster, Thomas Shearcliffe, Wilford Newton, John Riggs.

DAWSON, WILLIAM. Inventory. August 9, 1806. Apprs: John Thomas, Richard Gregory.

DOOM, JACOB. June 4, 1798. Sept. 4, 1798. Wife: Abigail. Children mentioned but not named. Estate to be sold when youngest child comes of age. Ex: wife, Jacob Yoder. Wit: Phillips, Thomas Phillips, Thomas Brown, Henry Faith.

DORAN, THOMAS. Inventory. Nov. 23, 1807. Apprs: John Muldrough, Abram Irvine, Richard Spalding.

DOWDALL, JOHN. Nov. 18, 1801. April 2, 1804. Wife: Stacy. Daus: Polly Lewis, Milley Meredith. Gr.children: Betsy Lewis, Thomas Dowall Lewis, John D. Lewis, Sally Lewis, Davis Meredith. Ex: Mathew Walton, William Bryant. Mentions John Pain, uncle of his wife, also mother-in-law Elizabeth Ball to be cared for from estate. Negroes to be given their liberty upon reaching the age of thirty one years.

EDMONSON, JOSEPH. Inventory. Nov. 28, 1806. Apprs: Edward Hughes, John Hammett, Francis Graham.

EDMONSON (EDMINSON), POLLY. Jan. 11, 1802. Feb. 1803. Sons: John, James, Joseph, Robert. Dau: Chandler, Polly Scanland, Sally Evanson, Nancy Bland, Betty Embree. Ex: Robert Edmonson (son). Wit: Owen Owens, John Brown.

ELDER, IGNATUS. Sept. 5, 1801. Inventory. Apprs: Samuel Lowe, William Piles, Francis Berry.

EWING, CHARLES. Inventory. Nov. 26, 1795. (Appraisers names missing, part of Book A has been destroyed by mice.)

FLANAGAN, PATRICK. Nov. 9, 1807. Jan., 1808. Legatees: Patrick Flanagan, son of Terrence Flanagan (cousin), John Rony, John Flanagan. "Whats left to the Church for saying Mass." Wit: Henry Hagan, Terrence Flanagan, Patrich Flanagan.

FORD, IGNATUS. Nov. 10, 1806. Feb. 20, 1807. Legatees: Mother, Benny Ford (brother), uncle Benedict Spalding. Wit: C. Hamilton, Moses Jeffries, Ann Hamilton.

FOURNIER, MICHAEL. Feb. 11, 1803. "Estate to Michael Fagan, after his decease to Vincent Gates and his sister Eleanor Ryan." Mention is also made of Rev. Stephen Theodore Baddin (priest", Elizabeth Wells, Mrs. Garet Hayden. Ex: Joshua Abell. Wit: Benjamin Spalding, Ignatus Ford, Benedict Spalding, Jr.

FROMAN, ISAAC. Oct. 10, 1808. Apprs: Benjamin Hardin, Joseph Rickman.

GATES, JAMES. Inventory. Sept. 15, 1803. Apprs: William Wright, Zachariah Laham, Jeremiah Harcort.

GIBBONS, GEORGE. Inventory. April 7, 1801.

GOLDMAN, HENRY. Inventory. Sept. 1, 1796.

GOODMAN, HENRY. Inventory. Sept. 1, 1796. Apprs: Samuel Reed, John Galloway, Philip Walker.

GRAHAM, JOHN. Inventory. Oct. 19, 1798. Apprs: John Hammett, Akin Irwin, Thomas Stayton.

GRAHAM, MARY. Inventory. Sept. 23, 1806. Apprs: Thomas Stayton, Joe Dean, Abraham Brown.

GRAVES, CHARLES. March 20, 1796. "Estate to wife Ellender, after her death to be divided among the surviving heirs". Children names not given. Ex: Joseph Allevey, James Austin. Wit: David Winfield, Thomas Riney, John Mc Carter.

GRUNDY, CHARLES. Oct. 6, 1793. April 1794. Mother: Elizabeth Grundy. "Clothes to brother Felix Grundy, provided he pays Garner(?) Grundy for a saddle and a gun I now have to take on the campaign". Ex: mother, Thomas Turnam. Wit: Edward Jenkins, Overton Cosby, Samuel Allen, Polly Grundy.

HAND, JOHN. May 2, 1802. Sept. 1802. Estate to wife Monica (?). Wit: John Riggs, Mary Riggs, William Dervan.

HARDIN, JOHN. July 2, 1788. April 4, 1793. Wife: Jane. Sons: Martin, Mark, Davis. Daus: Sarah, Mary. Ex: wife, Martin Hardin (brother). Wit: Samuel Robinson, John Hardin, Mary Robertson.

HAYDEN, BASIL. June 15, 1804. June 21, 1804. Wife: Henrietta. Sons: Stanislaw (eldest), Edward, Lewis, Daus: Ann, Teresa. Mentions wife's son William Hayden. Ex: John Lancaster (?). Wit: Charles Hayden, George Hayden.

HAYDEN, BENNETT. April 1794. July, 1794. Wife: Elenor. Children: John, Elizabeth, unborn child." Forty shillings in cash to be paid Rev. William Rohan and Mr. Barries to say Masses for my soul to God to forgive my sins." Ex: wife, Philip Lee, Basil Hayden (uncle). Wit: William Rapier, Charles Hayden, James Elliott.

HAYDEN, HENRIETTA. "To worshipful Court of Washington County, I, Heniretta Hayden of said county do hereby declare that I will not take or accept the provision made for me by Will of my late husband, Basil Hayden, dec'd., or any part thereof and I do hereby renounce all Benefit which I might claim by said Will, because I have lately discovered unexpected Danger in said Will, and I hereby claim Dower as the law directs. As witness my hand and seal this 9 day of February, 1805. Wit: William Hayden, Lewis Hayden." Recorded April Court, 1805.

HAYDEN, ROBERT AND WILLIAM. Inventory. Sept. 1802.

HAYDEN, ROBERT. Aug. 20, 1806. Nov. 1806. Brother Stanislaw to manage estate and be guardian to testators three children: Sarah, Amalem(?), Mary. Wit: John Lancaster, Charles Cough, Robert Constable. Ex: Brother Stanislaw.

HAYDEN, WILLIAM. March 24, 1794. June 1794. Wife: Milleta Hayden. Sons:

William, Robert. Daus: Molly, Elizabeth. Mentions dau. Anney's (dec'd) children. Ex: wife, Halton Hilton. Wit: Luke Mudd, Basil Hayden, Jr., Bob Hayden.

HEAD, EDWARD. Nov. 8, 1796. Dec. 6, 1796. Wife: Priscilla. Daus: Martha, Lucy, Mary. Sons: Henry, Bigger John. Sons-in-law: James Paxton, Zadock Richards. Gr.son: Edward Edler. Ex: Bigger Head (bro.), Henry Head (son), John Head (cousin). Wit: John Mc Cloughlin (?), Peter Adams, Richard Brownfield.

HILTON, HENRY. Dec. 29, 1801. "Estate to father William Hilton and Mildred, his wife." Ex: Mathew Walton. Wit: John Bullock, Fred Nances, Leroy Gregory. Probated May 2, 1803.

HOWARD, JAMES. Feb. 15, 1802. July, 1803. Wife: Mary. Sons: Charles, James Richard. Daus: Molly, Susannah Tricey, Kattey. Ex: wife. Wit: Henry Smock, William Vessels, James Vessels.

JARBOE, BARTON. June 29, 1802. -----. "To brother Joshua estate in St. Maries County, Maryland, now in possession of my mother." Wit: Lean Hamilton, B. Spalding, Ignatus Mills.

JENKINS, EDWARD. Oct. 6, 1793. April 3, 1794. "About to set out on an expedition against the Indians. My estate to my brothers, James F. Jenkins, Richard Jenkins." Mentions the following: Sam Overton (half brother), William Jenkins (brother), Mary Overton, Amelia Overton (nieces), Samuel Seay (nephew), Jacob Seay (bro.-in-law). Wit: Nathan Walton, John Bullock, John Overton.

MARKS, ISAAC. Inventory. Sept. 4, 1801.

MC ELROY, HUGH. Jan. 30, 1794. June 5, 1794. Wife: Easter. Sons: James, John, Samuel, Hugh, Abraham. Daus: Peggy, Sally Sandusky, Mary Simpson, Elizabeth Mc Elroy. "Stills to be disposed of as wife may think proper." Ex: wife, James Mc Elroy, John Mc Elroy (sons). Wit: John Irvine, Philip King, Thomas King.

MILES, ELEANOR. January 23, 1806. July 7, 1806. Daus: Audrey Vain, Priscilla Osborne, Sarah Montgomery. Sons: William, Barton E., Joseph. Gr.sons: Rhodias E. Mudd, Thomas Mudd (children of dau. Henrietta Mudd). "To dau. Priscilla my fire tongs, to dau. Audrey Vain, my shovel, to gr.son Rhodias Mudd my looking glass." Ex: William Miles (son), Priscilla Osborne (dau.), Thomas Osborne (son-in-law). Wit: John Lancaster, Matthew Cipele, Ignatus Mattingly.

MOLOHAN, JAMES. March 22, 1801. July 7, 1801. Children: Charles, Alleweze Higden, Jane Drury, Lusansia Horskin, Margaret Thompson, James. To the last three named children the testator leaves three shillings each. Wit: Jonathan Goldsbury, John B. Cough.

MOORE, WILLIAM. Inventory. May 7, 1801. Apprs: Nicholas Moore, Absalom Moore, John Beavins.

MUDD, WILLIAM. Oct. 16, 1801. Feb. 6, 1806. Wife: Elizabeth. Sons: Richard, William, Walter. Daus: Henrietta Sansberry (wife of Nicholas), Mary

Boone (wife of Henry). Ex: wife, Richard Mudd (son). Wit: Edward Clarkson, William Montgomery, Joseph Hoskins.

NOTTINGHAM, BENNET. --------. July 7, 1801. "To Henry Baily twenty five pounds of Maryland currency, to heirs of Philip Nottingham, dec'd., to wit: Ignatus, Joseph, Elizabeth, Benedict, Stephen. To Rev. Furmay five pounds, sixteen pounds to be paid Jeremiah Gough." Other Legatees: Catharine Greenwell, Elinor W-----(?), Barbary Bailey, Elizabeth Medley, Rebeckah Nottingham. Ex: Thomas Caddin of St. Marys Co., Maryland. Wit: Henry Smock, Richard Sedwick Spalding, John Taylor.

NOTTINGHAM, IGNATUS. Dec. 8, ------. April 4, 1808. "To Ignatus Lucas full share of Bennet Nottingham's estate left me". "I bequeath to my wife Mary, my roan mare, corn, household furniture." Wit: Henry Smock, Stephen Wingate, Joseph Wingate.

OVERTON, JOHN. Nov. 1, 1800. Feb. 3, 1801. Wife: Mary. Son: John. Dau: Mary Kindle. Ex: wife, John Overton (son). Wit: John Nall (Nalle), Coleman Brown.

PARKER, GRIZZLE. Dower. Dec. 11, 1799. Widow of Richard Parker.

PARKER, RICHARD. Inventory. April 8, 1799. Apprs: John Cosby, John Slack, Peter Peters.

PARKER, ROBERT. Inventory. Sept. 29, 1795.

PEARCE, THOMAS. April 10, 1793. June 6, 1793. Wife: Lydia. Sons: John, Isaac, Adams, Jacob, William, Thomas. Daus: Mary, Betsy, Tena. Ex: Jeremiah Briscoe. Wit: John Sandusky, John Barnet, John Springer. (The name is also spelled Pierce, Perce.).

PETER, SAMUEL. May 20, 1807 (?). Nuncupative. Wife: Mentions but does not name. Sons: William, Zachariah, Simon. Legatees: Milburn Hogg. Proved by oath of William Peters, William Shoemaker.

RICHARDS, GEORGE. May 25, 1803. Nov. 6, 1804. Wife: Nancy. Sons: Reason, Zadock, William, Samuel. Daus: Sarah, Cathie, Jemina Wallace, Polly Elder. Wit: Thomas Cleland, John Mills, John Gray.

RIDGE, WILLIAM. Inventory. Dec. 3, 1795. Apprs: John Springer, Anthony Sandusky, John Sandusky.

RIGGS, BENJAMIN. Jan. 14, 1804. May 7, 1804. Wife: Dolly. Sons: Benson, Dowel, Charles. Daus: Sarah, Charity. Ex: wife, Samuel Grundy. Wit: Jordan Grundy, William Fetheringgille, Thomas Russell.

RINEY, THOMAS. Inventory. Dec. 3, 1795.

ROBBINS, MARY. Nov. 23, 1799. Jan. 7, 1800. Nuncupative. Legatees: Daniel Robbins, Mary Smith (dau.), Clarecy Smith (gr.dau.). Proven by the oath of Catharine Bosworth, Delilah Stillwell.

ROBERTS, WILLIAM. Feb. 6, 1803. May Court, 1803. Wife: Mary. Mentions children but does not name them. Ex: wife. Wit: Phil Wasburn, Joseph Medley.

SANSBERRY, NICHOLAS. Jan. 1, 1807. May 1807. Wife: Henrietta. Son: Hillary, other children not named. Mentions Elizabeth Mudd, mother-in-law. Ex: wife, Reuben Mudd (bro.-in-law). Wit: Elisha Mater, James Murry, Charles B. Moreland.

SIMPSON, THOMAS. Nov. 23, 1799. Jan. Court 1800. Wife: Sary. Dau: Jean. Son: James. "If James (son) thinks proper to keep the Still, he must pay his sister twenty pounds". "To brother John Simpson part of pre-emption." Ex: wife, James Simpson (son). Wit: John Simpson, John Ewing, Jr.

SIMMONS, NANCY. Inventory. Feb. 5, 1804.

SISSEL, JOHN B. Inventory. April 2, 1799. Apprs: Leonard Mattingly, Sr., James Parson, Ignatus Mattingly. Admr: Ann Sisel.

SLACK, RANDAL. Feb. 20, 1795. April 1795. Wife: Sarah. Son: Richard, other children not named. Ex: Joseph Caldwell, John Slack. Wit: John Pertle, Henry Barlor, William Mc Antire (Mc Intire).

SMITH, JAMES. May 7, 1807. Jan. 4, 1808. Wife: Mary. Dau: Anne Matilda Coombs, other not named. Ex: wife. Wit: John Lancaster, Robert Yates, James Molohan.

SNODGRASS, SAMUEL. Inventory. Feb. 4, 1800.

SPALDING, HENRY. June 25, 1801. July 7, 1801. Wife: Nancy. "To brother Ignatus Spalding, my clothes, wife to have one-third of estate, two thirds to bro. Peter Richard Spalding, sisters Mary and Anne Spalding. If there should be a child then estate to go to heir." Ex: Isaac Williams, John Simms. Wit: George Humphreys, William Moore.

SPALDING, JOHN BAPTIST. August 20, 1802. Dec. 20, 1805. Wife: Anne. Daus: Anne Billinder Dailey, Susanna Howard, Stephen, Barbary, Teresa. Ex: wife. Wit: Edward Mattingly, William Haden. Testator from the County of St. Mary, Md.

SPRINGER, PETER. Dec. 13, 1798. April, 1799. Wife: Jeane. Children mentioned but not named. Ex: wife, Ezekiel T. Hickman. Wit: John Walter Fower, John Silver, Samuel Silver.

STALCUP, -----. Inventory. Dec. 29, 1792.

TAYLOR, ELIZABETH. April 22, 1794. July, 1794. Daus: Mary, Nancy. Money to Coonrod Curtsinger in payment of a debt. Wit: Edward Bird, Jacob Barlow, Cornelius Barlow.

TAYLOR, ZACHARIA. May 3, 1794. Nov. 1794. Wife: Prudence. Sons: Zachriah, John, George, Mormon, Uriah. Daus: Ann, Mary, Elizabeth. Ex: John Taylor, George Taylor, Samuel Peters. Wit: Richard Peters, Thomas Turpin, Cleton Taylor.

THOMPSON, JOSEPH. Dec. 3, 1803. April 1804. Wife: Nancy. Sons: James, Thomas. Ex: wife. Wit: Joseph Maxwell, William Phillips, Charles Thompson.

THOMPSON, STITH. Nov. 5, 1795. June 1796. Wife: Elizabeth. Sons: Reves,

Stith, William, Charles, James, Starling, Stephen. Ex: John Davis, John Caldwell, John Thompson, Richard Thompson. Wit: John Pertle, John Shackleford, John Mc Claughton, Adam Row.

TOY, JAMES. Sept. 13, 1807. Nov. Court, 1807. Bro. John Toy. Sister: Margaret Toy. Ex: Thomas Cosgrove, Thomas Fitzpatrick.

WATHAN, HENRY. Inventory. Dec. 11, 1806.

WATHAN (WATHEN,) SILVESTER. Sept. 16, 1803. Nov. 1803. Wife: Sarah. "School my children and advance them through the rule of three." Children not named. Ex: John Wathan (father), Rudolphus Syms. Wit: John Warren, George Thompson, Zach Riney.

WATTS, AARON. Sept. 24, 1802. Nov. 1802. Estate to mother. Ex: John Hungate. Wit: Thomas Calvert, Charles Doyal.

WAY, WILLIAM. June 29, 1798. Jan. 1803. Wife: Sarah. Children mentioned but not named. Ex: wife, Jesse Head. Wit: Felix Grundy, Daniel Easterday, Cornelius Buckler.

WILSON, JOSIAH. Sept. 21, 1803. Feb. 6, 1804. Wife: Hannah. Sons: Jonathan, Josiah, Samuel, John, William E., Anthony, Humphrey, George. Daus: Mariah, Harriet. Wit: Joseph Head, Jacob Sodusky, Samuel Robertson.

WOOLEY, MICHAEL. Oct. 30, 1796. Jan. 1797. Sons: William, David, John. Daus: Rebeckah, Barbary. Wit: Thomas Hopp, Christopher Wooley, David Hogin.

VAUGHN, SAMUEL. Oct. 9, 1797. Jan. 1798. Wife: Prudence. Sons: Claiburn, Luke, John, Joel, Samuel, Chesly, Peter, William. Daus: Dise, Sally, Betsy, Patty. Ex: wife, sons William, Luke. Wit: John Hurst, Henry Hurst, Starkey Hayes.

AN INVENTORY of the Estate of Elisha Sherrill Dec'd. taken the 9th ruary, 1818.

1 half bushel
1 cupboard
1 shovel plow
1 "   "
5 sheep
1 Brashear plow
1 pair of Iron gears
1 pair of hames and bridle
1 cutting knife
1 kittle
1 pale (pail)
1 full tub of pickles
1 slay
1 saddle
2 wooden dishes
1 Mattick
1 hoe
1 bolt of yarn
1 hoe
1 Iron Wedge
1 pair of weaving geers
1 set of spools
1 churn
1 small pail
1 pair of double trees
1 frying pan
1 teapot and mug
1 pair of Iron geer
1 Bay mare
Cupboard ware
1 halter chain
1 flax hackle
1 small pail
1 churn
1 pickling tub
1 mortar and gum
2 barrels
1 slay
1 flax hackle
1 sithe and cradle
1 log chain
Sundry tools
1 pott
1 tea kettle
1 Bible and sickle
1 Loom
1 black horse
1 sorrel horse
1 waggon
1 steer
1 bull
1 cow
1 cow and calf

1 cow & calf
1 cow
1 heifer
12 "
"   "
1 steer
1 heifer
1 heifer
1 calf
5 hoggs
3 sows - 14 piggs
5 hoggs
1 bed and furniture
1 bedstead and furniture
5 sheep
5 "
5 "
1 dozen Geese
1 "   "
1 "   "
1 "   "
1 "   "
8 "   "
1 Oven and hooks
1 Hogsheads
1 Oven
Sundry pails
1 flax wheel
1 flesh fork and ladle
1 slay
1 lot of spools
3 small pails
1 hoe
1 gray mare
1 cow
1 cow and calf
1 cow and calf
5 Barrows
Bed and furniture
1 bed and furniture
1 counterpin
7 sheep
1 dozen Geese
1 pott
1 oven and hooks
1 pott and hooks
1 baker
1 small pail
1 churn
1 pickling tub and pail
1 reel
1 flax wheel

1 flax wheel
1 "   "
1 coffee mill
Sundry cupboard ware
Spoons, knives, forks
crocks and bottles
Ball and lifters
1 small table
1 Testament
Sundry Pewter
Sundry cupboard ware
1 pair of mill stones
Sundry cupboard ware
25 barrels of corn
1 Looking glass
1 shovel
1 grindstone
1 cotton wheel
25 Barrels of corn
25 "   "   "
1 stay
1 stay
1 flax wheel
1 peweter dish
1 try and sifter
1 coffee Mill
Cupboard ware
1 peweter dish
1 bottle
1 pewter basin
1 "   "
1 Shugar desk
1000 bundles of Hay
1000 "   "   "
1000 "   "   "
1000 "   "   "
1000 "   "   "
Parcel of flax

25 bundles of oats
25 barrels of corn
25 "   "   "
25 "   "   "
25 "   "   "
1 stack of rye
25 bushels of wheat
1 bed and furniture
1 lott of spun yarn
1 lott of cotton and basket
2 pair of cards
1 chest
1 faln table
1 candle stick
2 bells
3 churns
4 "
4 "
4 "
3 "
1 chest
1 candle stand
1 smoothing Iron
3 meal baggs
1 Branding Iron
2 Riddles
1 cotton wheel
1 small bell
1 Lott of spun yarn
7 bushel & 14 pounds of Fatt
2 pair of Horse Shoes
1 claw hammer
1 bundle of hay
25 bushels of wheat
4 bushels of corn
25 dozen of oats
25 "   "   "
25 bushels of wheat
25 dozen of oats.

Aaron Sherrill, Administrator.
C. W. Mc Clain, County Clerk.

WASHINGTON COUNTY

BOOK B

INDEX

1808 -- 1816

Alvey, Joseph
Ayrs, May
Ayers, Thomas
Able, Joshua

Barlow, Henry
Baxter, William
Boone, John
Brown, Susannah
Brown, Charles
Brown, James
Brownfield, Robert
Brothers, Jeremiah
Buckman, Francis
Bullock, Thomas
Burnett, William

Cash, Caleb
Canon, Thomas
Canary, Christopher
Caulk, Benjamin
Cambron, John B.
Champion, John B.
Compton, Benedict
Clark, Thomas
Curtsinger, ----

Dawson, William
Davenport, Sarah
Decker, William
Dorothy, Archibald
Duffield, William

Edwards, Charles
Edwards, Thomas
Edlin, George

Flanagan, John
Fowler, John W.
Fogle, Adam
Foler Orphans
Frowman, Isaac

Gardner, Thomas
Gilbert, John
Goundy, John , (Grundy)

Green, Thomas E.
Greenwell, Charles

Humphrey, George
Head, Edward
Haden, Charles
Hager, James
Hardestry, ----
Hamilton, Richard
Hammett, John
Handley, Anthony
Hovey, Aaron
Harron, Allen
Handly, John

Jarboe, John R.

Leaton, Joseph
Lewis, Thomas

Mattingly, Joseph
Mattingly, John
Marks, Joanna
Montgomery, Charles
Montgomery, Bernard
Myers, Jacob
Montgomery, William
Medley, John
Michael, James
Mills, Nicholas
Moore, Harbin

Newton, Ignatus
Newman, ----

Obannon, James
Obbouren, Thomas

Parker, Martin
Parker, Nathan and Sar
Parris, William
Perry, John
Pike, Samuel
Prewitt, John
Purdy, John

Robertson, Mary
Rodman, Esther
Robertson, George
Robey, Hezekiah
Robins, John
Russell, Charles
Ryan, James

Sandusky, Anthony
Sandusky, Rebecka
Sally, George
Silver, John
Simpson, John
Simens, John
Smock, Barrett

Smock, Henry
Smith, Basil
Smith, Clement
Spalding, Benedict

Taylor, Samuel
Thurman, Livingston
Tilford, Samuel
Thompson, John B.
Thompson, George
Tubman, John

Vancleave, Aaron
Vowles, John

Walker, William

WASHINGTON COUNTY

BOOK C

INDEX

1816 -- 1823

Abell, Mary
Abell, John

Cock, Stephen
Cock, Amey

Dickens, William
Davis, Jodwick
Davis, Thomas
Daily, John
Dowdell, Stacy
Durr, Reuben
Dyer, John

Edelin Heirs
Edmonson, James
Enose, William
Elliott, Thomas
Elliott, Richard
Everhart, Martin

Fagan, Michael
Farris, Zephariah
Fenwick, Henry
Fetty, Rachel
Fogle, Adam
Fitzgerald, Thomas
Flannagan, Terrence

Gaston, Mariah
Grundy, George
Gilbert, John
Gillis, William
Graham, Francis
Gregory, Richard
Graham, James
Graham, David
Green, Leonard
Grigsby, James

Hayden, Benjamin
Hayden, William
Haygan, Isaac
Hardin, John
Hatten, John
Hamilton, Leonard
Hamilton, Samuel
Hamilton, Isam
Hays, William
Hardin, Benjamin
Hargroves, William
Head, Biggers
Herregan, Patrick
Hewett, Terry
Hundley, William
Hundley, James

Jones, John
Joseph, Jesse
Jackson, William
Joseph, Henrietta
Jarboe, Charles
Jones, Richard

Knott, Jeremiah

Lee, Philip
Lanham, Stephen

Mattingly, William
Mattingly, Joseph
Magee, Matthew
Medley, John
Mahan, William
Mills, Absalom
Montgomery, Samuel B.
Moore, William
Mullican, Terrence
Mullican, Basil

Northcraft, William

Paddock, William
Patterson, Beverly
Peak, William
Polin, David
Purdy, John

Purdy, William
Prewitt, William

Ray, Nichola
Ray, Joseph
Ramder, James
Rinehart, Daniel
Rollins, Henry
Rounder, Joseph
Rudd, Susannah
Robertson, Hannah

Sandusky, John
  Scantland, James
Sherrill, Elisha
Silvers, John
Smith, Edward
Springer, Levi
Springer, Eliza
Springer, John

Vandike, Richard
Vandike, Mary

Whalen, Michael
Walton, Mathew
Waters, Theodore
Worland, Charles
Woods, Henry
Wickliffe, ------

WOODFORD, COUNTY

BOOK A

1788 -- 1811

ALLISON, CHARLES. Inventory. June 1792. Apprs: Thomas Howard, Robert Quinn, Thomas Johnson.

ALLISON, JOHN. ------. Nov. 3, 1791. Wife: Isabella. Children: Halber A., Sarah, Isabella. Ex: wife, David Steele. Wit: James Stevenson, William Ellis, James Risk.

BAILEY, SAMUEL. Inventory. June 7, 1795. Appr: Thomas Mosely, John Arnold, Edward Mitchell.

BEASELY, BENJAMIN. Jan. 16, 1796. ------. Wife: Caty. Children: Sarah, Tabitha, Thomas, Phoebe, Elizabeth, Charles. Ex: Edmund Beasely. Wit: James Bowdry, William Dale.

BELL, THOMAS. Sept. 1791. April 1792. Woodford Co., State of Va. Wife: Elizabeth. Children: Robert, William, Thomas. Gr.son: Thomas Montgomery, Mrs. Elizabeth Bell (widow of John Bell), and other children not named. Ex: wife, son Thomas. Wit: Samuel Shannon, Lewis Snead, Chapman Taylor.

COOK, HOSEA. Inventory. Dec. 1792. Apprs: William Ware, Edmund Ware, Carter Blanton.

COX, AGNES. Dower, estate of Samuel Cox. Jan. 1794.

COX, SAM. Inventory. Dec. 1793. Appr: Harry Bartlett, Richard Apperson, Nathaniel Sanders.

CRINES, PETER. Inventory. Oct. 1790. Apprs: Jacob Martin, James Fisher, John Hutchinson.

CURRY, JOHN. Inventory. Jan. 1795. Wit: Cave Johnson.

DAVIDSON, ROBERT. Inventory. Dec. 1790. Apprs: Dudley Mitchum, Henry Anderson, Richard Young.

DRISKILL, TIMOTHY. Aug. 8, 1795. March 1796. Wife: Priscilla. Children: Amy, Anne, Elijah, Jonas, Dennis, Druscilla, Sarah Plough, Elizabeth, Polly, Rebecca. Ex: wife, Samuel Brooking, Isaac Ruddle. Wit: James and William Garnett.

EDWARDS, URIAH. Inventory. April 1792. Appr: John Hatton, Archibald Curry, Stephens Archer.

ELAM, JOHN. Oct. 2, 1794. Jan. 1795. Sister Ann Brown and her heirs. John Brown. Ex: John Brown, William Brown. Wit: Bennett Pemberton, William Hickman, Thomas Settle.

FULTON, WILLIAM. Inventory. May 1795. Appr: John Ewing, James Stephenson, William Lindsey.

GRANT, SAMUEL. Aug. 10, 1789. Sept. 1789. Wife: Elizabeth. Children: Elijah, Elizabeth. Ex: wife, Elijah Craig, William Grant, Jr., Isarel Grant. Wit: John Cave, Henry Herndon, Frances Stewart.

GRESHAM, WILLIAM. Inventory. Dec. 1791.

HADDEN, WILLIAM. Inventory. Oct. 1794. Apprs: Andrew Hamilton, Julius Blackburn, Samuel Kyle.

HARRIS, HARRISON. --------. Sept. 1799. Wife: Martha. Children: Randolph, Susanna, David. Ex: sons Randolph and David. Wit: T. Marshall, Samuel Deweese, Caleb Wallace.

HASTINGS, WILLIAM. Inventory. Sept. 19, 1789. Apprs: J. Finney, James Furney, John Burton.

HATTON, ROBERT. Inventory. April 1792. Apprs: George Shannon, John M. Hatton, Stephens Archer.

HAYNES, ELIZABETH. April 20, 1795. July 1795. Elizabeth and Sarah Raglin, (aunts). George and David Rowland, (uncles). Wit: Joshua Mc Clean, John Goudy, William Mc Adams.

HOLMAN, HENRY. Mar. 6, 1789. Sept. 1, 1789. Fayette Co., Va. Wife: Jane. Children: Nicholas, William, Isaac, Jesse, Edward, Rozetta, Elizabeth, Mary. Ex: son Edward, David Daret. Wit: James Fisher, Edward and George Holman, Sarah Williams.

JACK, FRANCIS. (woman). May 30, 1789. Oct. 1789. Children: Samuel, Patrick, Nancy, Fanny, Elizabeth. Ex; John Watkins, Cave Johnson.

JANUARY, PETER. Feb. 26, 1787. July 1789. Fayette Co., Va. Wife: Deborah. Children: John, Samuel, James, Ephiram, Sarah, Nancy. Ex: sons James and Ephiram. Wit: Caleb Wallace, James Fraser, Samuel Walker.

JARVESON, JAMES. Feb. 2, 1791. Nov. 1795. Wife: Martha. Children not named. Friends: James Waugh, James Bain (school master in Cane Run). Ex: James Waugh, James Bain. Wit: Alex. Dunlap, John Underwood, Ann Crane.

JOHNSTON, THOMAS. Aug. 24, 1792. Oct. 1792. Wife: Elizabeth. Children: David, Silas, Mary, Anna, Betsy, Sally. Ex: wife, Joseph Hughes, Thomas Reed. Wit: Daniel Veatch, Jeremiah Veatch, Arthur Ingram.

MAJOR, WILLIAM. April 12, 1790. March 1795. Father John Major. Ex: bro. John Major. Wit: ---- Hickman, James Dupey Sr., Josiah Woodridge.

MARTIN, WILLIAM. Inventory. Jan. 1796. Apprs: Alex. Dunlap, Samuel Stevenson, John Williams.

MCBRIDE, JAMES. April 3, 1783. Nov. 1790. From Cumberland Co., Penn. Sister Mary's sons James and Henry Mc Bride, sisters Jane Childress and Hannah. Ex: James Tree of Cumberland Co. Wit: Joseph Mc Clean, John Maxwell.

MC CRACKEN, CYRUS. Sept. 15, 1787. May 1795. Wife: Elizabeth. Children: Cyrus, Ovid, Virgil, Ruth, Sally, adopted son John Shepherd. Ex: John Williams, bro. Ovid. Wit: John Long, James Hayden, William Branham.

MC CUMPSEY, ROBERT. Inventory. Sept. 1789. Appr: Matt Barkley, William Stevenson, James Dupey, Sr.

MC HARG, ROBERT. Inventory. July 1791. Apprs: Daniel Peak, Benjamin Craig, Joseph Bledsoe.

MC NIEL, THOMAS. May 27, 1790. Dec. 1790. Wife: Elizabeth. Children: Daniel, John. Daus not named. Ex: wife, brother Jonathan. Wit: William Scott, James Milligan.

MOSS, ELIZABETH. Dower.

PROCTOR, JOHN. Jan. 23, 1790. Feb. 1790. (Woodford Co., Va. Wife: Sukey, Children not named. Ex: wife, John Ellis. Wit: Richard Young, John Arnold, Sowyel Woolfolk.

PEMBERTON, CHARLES. Jan. 11, 1790. April 1792. Woodford, Va. Wife: Sarah. Children: Delph Gatewood, Elizabeth Edwards, Bennett, Nancy Owen. Ex: son Bennett. Wit: Sam Cox, John Price, Jr., William Tureman.

RICE, GEORGE. Aug. 4, 1792. Oct. 1792. Late of Fredrick Co., Va. Wife: Elizabeth. Children: six, not named. Father, bro. John, nieces Mary Rice, Elizabeth Boyd, Jean Sullivan. Bro. Edward. Ex: wife, James Mc Donald, Andrew Waggoner.

RICHARDS, PHIL. May 19, 1794. Oct. 1794. Wife: not named. Children: Sarah James and her two children Lucy and Sipio, Anne Chapman, Lucy Christian, Lewis, Philemon, William, Benjamin. Son-in-law: Gilbert Christian. Ex: son Philemon, Daniel Jones, Gilbert Christian. Wit: Turner Richardson, Matt Christian, Benjamin Chapman.

ROBERTS, WILLIAM. Dec. 1791. Cave Johnson. (C. C. C.)

SAMPLE, JOHN. Inventory. Dec. 1793. Isaac Wilson, Admr.

SEARCY, BARTLETT. Sept. 4, 1784. Sept. 1790. of Fen. Co., Va. Wife: Ann. Children: John Morgan, Elizabeth. Ex: wife, Col. Daniel Boone, Flanders Calloway. Wit: Andrew Paull, Squire Boone, Jesse Buzan.

SNEED, FIELDING. Dec. 20, 1794. March 1795. Wife: Elizabeth. Bro. John and sister Elizabeth Sneed. Ex: wife, Samuel Ayers. Wit: Thomas Ayers, Thomas Sneed, Samuel Sneed.

SULLINGER, THOMAS. Oct. 29, 1795. Jan. 1796. Wife: Fanny. Children: Betsy, Nancy, Maria, Reuben, Gabriel, Thomas, John, Mother, Mary Sullinger. Ex: wife, James Stapp, James Garnett. Wit: John Brooking, John Long, James Ford.

THOMSON, ANTHONY. May 7, 1794. Oct. 1794. Children: Eleanor, Judith Bell, Susannah, Robert, Anthony, Nathaniel, Sarah, Mary, Betsy, Henry. Wife: Ann. Ex: wife, David Thomson. Wit: Thomas Bell, David Thomson, Nathaniel Thomson, Moses Ogden, John Blanton, William Blanton.

TODD, ROBERT. Jan. 20, 1792. June 1792. Wife: Jane. Children: William, unborn child. John Parker. Ex: wife, Richard Steele, John Parker, Wit: Nancy Lotte.

WOODFORD COUNTY
BOOK B

A. none.

BLACK, JOSEPH. April 12, 1794. Aug. 2, 1796. Children: Margaret (hus. Timothy Shearer), Elizabeth (hus. William Garrett), Martha (hus. Thomas Woods), Mary (hus. Alex. Blair), Jennet, Jean. Ex: Jean and Jennet Black, William Garrett. Wit: William Scott, William Young, Hugh Garrett.

BROMLEY, DANIEL. Feb. 21, 1796. Oct. 1796. Wife: Susannah. Children: William, Samuel, Betsy and her three children: Hester, Oliver and Betsy; Ellis, Jenny, Daniel, John. Ex: wife, William Christopher. Wit: William Warren, William Alloway.

CAVENDER, DANIEL. July 1796. Apprs: Isaac Dale, Robert Dale, James Rucker.

CLAY, PORTER. May 10, 1797. Guardian to Henry Watkins.

CRAIG, TOLIVER. Dec. 15, 1790. Aug. 1799. Wife: Mary. Children; John, Toliver, Lewis, Elijah, Joseph, Benjamin, Jeremiah, Jane, Faulkner, Elizabeth Cave, John Sander, Sarah Singleton. Ex: John, Toliver and Lewis Craig. Wit: John Cook, Daniel Baldwin, Anthony Lindsay.

CRAMER, HENRY. Inventory. Sept. 11, 1797. Robert Black, Admr.

DALE, ELIZABETH. Dower. Sept. 1799. Formerly widow of Dozier Cavender. James Rucker, William Taylor, R. Hudson.

DALES, ALICE. Dec. 16, 1802. Henry Watkins, John Moss, Abraham Dale.

DICKERSON, WILLIAM. Nov. 18, 1796. June 1797. Wife: not named. Children: Judy, Polly, William, John, Patty, Milley. Ex: wife, Archer Dickerson, James Shropsher. Wit: Richard Bohannon, Joseph Wilson, Benjamin Wilson, Hugh Davison.

DUPREY, BARTHOLOMEW. June 5, 1790. Oct. 1796. Wife: Mary. Children: John, James, Joseph, Joel, Susannah, Elizabeth, Sarah, Martha, Anne, Judity, Aasah. Ex: sons Joseph and Joel. Wit: Daniel Rowharrd, Obediah Hancock, Henry and Richard Rowland.

ELLIOTT, ROBERT. Oct. 1802. Inventory. George Brooks, C. C.

FIELD, HENRY. Sept. 17, 1799. Oct. 1799. Wife: ----. Children: Polly, Laura, Sally, Elizabeth. Wit: Henry Bowman, Charles Railey, Benjamin Berry. Ex: Thomas Mc Clanahan Jr., Field and Richard Fox.

GROOM, ZACHARIAH. Feb. 28, 1799. Apprs: Elliot Bohannon, Mordecai Redd, John Redd.

HAMILTON, SAMUEL. July 30, 1798. Wife: Elizabeth. Children: Jean Smith, Agner Phillips, Margaret Thomson. Gr.dau: Jean Smith. Ex: wife, John Williams.

HOBLETT, MICHAEL. Inventory. May 1796.

HOLLINGSWORTH, -----. Feb. 12, 1807. Apprs: Welham Warren, Samuel Woodford, Leroy Howard.

JOHNSON, JOSEPH. Sale. Nov. 1790. Admr: Robert Dale. Apprs: William Christopher, John Rucker, William Strother.

MC KIRTLEY, ----. Inventory. March 1, 1804. Apprs: John Blackmore, James Coleman.

LEE, JOHN. Dec. 18, 1801. Feb. 1802. Wife: Elizabeth. Children: John, Thomas, Lewis, Mary, Sarah, Elizabeth, Lucinda, Matilda. Wife Elizabeth guardian of children. Ex: wife, Caleb Wallace. Wit: Isarel Pierson, Thomas Hill, Peggy Bell, Robert Alexander.

LONG, JOHN. April 17, 1797. ----1803. Wife: Molly, Children: Sukey, Jane, William, Thomas, Willis, Sally. Ex: wife and Richard Long. Wit: Samuel Brooking, Sally Long.

MOORE, JOHN. Inventory. April 1798.

PRYOR, LUKE. Feb. 14, 1800. June 1800. Bros: Edward and Joseph. Uncle Luke, Aunt Susanna. Ex: Bro. Joseph. Wit: Lewis Craig, James Paxton, Elisha Woolridge.

RATLIFF, THOMAS. Aug. 18, 1796. June 1797. Wife: Mary. Children: Samuel, Isbel, Mary, Betsy, William, Thomas, Joseph, Isaih, Alex., Elisha. Ex: son Samuel, Alex. Mc Clure.

RUDDLES, STEPHEN. June 10, 1799. Sept. 1800. Wife: Sarah. Children: Stephen R., Isaac, Cornelius, Sarah. Ex: wife, son Cornelius. Wit: Elliot Bohannon, Mordecai Redd.

SMITH, ELIJAH. July 12, 1796. Feb. 1801. Children not named. Wife: Hannah. Ex: wife, John Parker, Levi Todd. Wit: Thomas Cox, Leonard Leland, John Armstrong, Robert Todd.

STEVENSON, JOHN. May 18, 1802. Aug. 1802. Wife: Margaret. Children: John, James, Robert, Thomas, Elizabeth. Gr.son, Hugh Stevenson (son of Robert). Ex: sons Robert and James. Wit: Preston Brown, William Elliot, Samuel Stevenson.

STRANGE, JOHN. -------. --------. Children: Sally, David, Nancy, Jesse. Ex: Peyton Short, Tunstal Quarles, Abner A. Frange.

SULLINGER, THOMAS. Jan. 1, 1802. ------. Turpin app. guardian for Thomas, Betty, John, Maria and Nancy Sullinger.

THOMPSON, SARAH. Aug. 2, 1800. Dec. 1800. Sister Susannah, bro. Henry. Ex: William Todd, John Blanton. Wit: Reuben Fox, George Turpin, Thomas Ball.

WHITTIKER, JOHN. Jan. 27, 1797. Received of John Whittkier full satisfaction as guardian of estate of dec'd. Joseph Wilson. Isaac Wilson. Wit: Richard and James Hainds, F. Furpin clk.

WILSON, JOSEPH. Jan. 13, 1800. ------. Wife: Sarah. Chld: John and Samuel. Step dau. Peggy Sterret alias Peggy Mc Cleland, Polly McCleland. Gr.chld: (son Samuel's) Joseph, Peggy, John, Samuel, Sarah. Ex: wife, son-in-law John Sterrett. Wit: Samuel Wilson, Adam Mc Connell, Samuel Logan, Leonard Fleming.

INDEX

Abell: 181, 187, 213, 231, 233
Abett: 69
Abott: 123, 177
Acock:
Adams: 12, 28, 29, 35, 38, 41, 45, 51, 57, 74, 94, 96, 114, 119, 121, 123, 124, 165, 170, 171, 173, 181, 191, 201, 209, 212, 236, 143.
Adamson: 31
Aden: 225
Adkerson: 121
Admine: 113
Adyelott: 181
Agnew: 92, 192
Aikman: 142
Akers: 85
Akin: 139, 154, 158
Aldridge: 39, 41, 141
Alcock: 170, 171
Alexander: 33, 41, 61, 96, 119, 135, 213, 225, 249
Alford: 1
Algee: 23
Alkire: 11
Allen (Allin): 51, 54, 58, 105, 155, 162, 163, 165, 171, 174, 184, 196, 201, 207, 213, 215, 235.
Allentharp: 205
Alleward: 4
Allison: 9, 15, 19, 39, 85, 135, 141, 181, 191, 197, 207, 221, 223, 245.
Allmon: 37
Allon: 35, 58
Alloway: 248
Allnutt: 158
Alves:
Allvey (Allevey): 231, 235
Ambrose: 183
Amelia: 101
Ammon: 191
Anders: 123
Anderson: 2, 3, 4, 13, 23, 26, 28, 29, 43, 51, 71, 84, 101, 102, 119, 135, 141, 151, 165, 167, 171, 177, 181, 187, 193, 195, 203, 208, 214, 221, 223, 155, 161.
Apperson: 101
Applegate: 123, 201, 210, 211.
Arbuckle: 69, 208
Archibald: 52

Archer: 193, 245, 246
Ardrey: 191
Armstrong: 23, 24, 25, 27, 32, 35, 45, 69, 75, 91, 103, 139, 167, 173, 175, 186, 215, 221.
Arnold: 69, 71, 173, 225
Arrington: 155
Arthur: 141, 143, 145
Ash: 181
Ashbaugh: 17
Asberry: 192
Ashbaugh: 17
Ashbrook: 95
Ashburn: 42
Ashby: 195
Ashcraft: 193
Ashcroft: 81
Asher: 132, 142
Ashley: 89, 119, 121, 122
Ashmore: 157
Askew: 123
Askin: 231
Asturgus: 123
Atherton: 182, 184, 195
Attaberry: 89
Atlin: 222
Austin: 1, 3, 195, 197, 235
Autry: 195
Aud: 53
Avery: 193
Avers: 57, 225, 247
Azby: 91

Babbitts: 222
Babcock: 36
Baggs: 132
Bagsby: 2
Bailey (Baley): 96, 155, 197, 207, 215, 237, 245
Baird: 181
Bain: 131, 246
Bainbridge: 209
Baker: 23, 41, 44, 46, 70, 151, 155, 191, 192, 194, 212
Balch: 155, 164
Ball: 101, 113, 138, 147, 234, 249
Ballard: 46, 209, 214, 215
Ballinger: 145
Ballingul: 144
Balts: 124
Baltzelt: 23, 73

Banfield: 174
Banks: 51, 71,
Bannister: 23, 192
Barber (Barbour): 6, 102, 103, 132, 141
Barclay: 225, 227
Barker: 51
Barley: 225
Barlow: 2, 169, 191, 193, 194, 238
Barkley: 217, 247
Barnard: 23, 192
Barnes: 35, 57, 91, 156, 166, 181, 195, 196, 231
Barnett (Barnet): 33, 35, 51, 52, 94, 101, 135, 140, 155, 163, 165, 195, 196, 197
Barnor: 41
Barr: 135
Barrell: 23
Barrings: 191
Barry: 140
Barten: 225
Barton: 33, 141, 145, 155, 181, 192, 204
Basey: 113
Baskette: 191, 193, 194, 215
Bate: 123, 195
Battershell: 43
Batise: 210
Batton: 173
Batson: 192
Bay: 155, 193
Bayles: 169
Baylor: 157
Bayne: 15
Bayman: 92
Baxter: 38, 137
Beadle: 209, 212
Bealle (Beall): 175, 195, 231
Bean:
Bear: 23
Beard: 57, 81, 123, 127, 141, 155, 191, 213, 225
Bearcy: 212
Bearden: 23, 30
Beasland: 231
Beasley: 57, 245
Beathy: 185, 201, 221
Beaty: 141
Beatty: 69, 73, 130
Beauchamp: 2, 3, 63, 204
Beauvis: 130
Beaver: 233
Beavin: 236

Beene: 210
Beggs: 12, 13
Bell: 35, 43, 55, 72, 74, 75, 84, 119, 150, 181, 191, 195, 245, 247, 249
Belew: 142
Belt: 75, 195, 196
Bemis: 54
Benham: 1, 38, 70
Benners: 69
Bennett: 1, 28, 93, 103, 104, 107, 165, 166, 170, 176, 181, 196, 217, 218
Benton: 28, 197
Bensten: 41
Bergen (Bergin): 123, 212, 213
Bornard: 155
Berry: 41, 81, 94, 120, 121, 147, 150, 151, 173, 231, 233, 234
Berryman: 201, 225
Best: 166, 171, 172
Bice: 213
Bidford: 181
Bidwell: 184
Biggar (Bigger): 193, 195
Biggerstaff: 177
Bigham: 23
Bilbo: 231
Billingsley: 155
Binman: 187
Birdwell: 217
Bishop: 1, 120
Bishong: 175
Bissell: 181
Black: 30, 32, 35, 65, 69, 77, 141, 163, 181, 212, 222, 227, 248
Blackbirn: 41, 91, 246
Blackley: 161
Blackford: 123, 225
Blacklock: 196
Blalock: 222
Blackman: 249
Blackwell: 69, 70, 73, 74, 102, 133, 227
Blanchard: 132
Blanford: 53
Blain: 131
Blake: 141
Blakey: 141, 158
Blakely: 135
Blair: 2, 3, 55, 95, 193
Blare: 192
Bland: 38, 182, 187
Blandsford: 181, 231

Blankenbuker: 123
Blanton: 247
Bledsoe: 41, 69, 165, 249
Blythe: 161, 177
Boarman: 182
Bobo: 39
Bobin: 128
Bodine: 85
Bodkin: 41
Bogarth: 182
Boggs: 66
Bohannon: 75, 124, 248
Bolden: 188
Bompay: 30
Bone: 121, 120, 163, 166, 171, 197
Booker: 209, 213
Boone: 41, 115, 212, 214, 247
Boren: 22, 172, 228
Borseau: 2
Boonwell: 61
Booth: 231, 232
Boston: 217
Bostwick: 124, 129
Boswell: 50, 93, 103, 171
Bosworth: 237
Bots: 217
Bourn: 69, 72, 135
Bourland: 119, 120, 121
Bowdery: 147
Bowie: 155
Bowlin: 104, 155
Bowling: 207
Bowlding: 222
Bowland: 23, 24
Bowman: 65, 147, 150, 175
Boulare: 41, 57, 61, 69, 74
Bowles: 1
Bowdery: 147
Bowyer: 38
Boyd: 1, 24, 33, 35, 53, 56, 94, 156, 191, 193, 208, 217, 218, 231, 247
Boyle: 13, 41, 78, 102, 141, 166, 207
Boxwell: 92
Bozell: 212
Bractten: 167
Bradey: 15
Bradenbury: 191
Bradford: 42, 63, 64, 177, 201, 204
Bradley: 37, 57, 64, 65, 66, 75, 81
Braffield: 44
Bradshaw: 57, 212, 226
Brady: 77
Brakes: 182

Brauham: 124, 201, 207, 246
Braut: 215
Bray: 182, 185
Brainou: 119
Brandon: 9, 10
Braikenage: 175
Brashear: 15, 19, 24, 35, 39, 81, 124
Brayer: 69
Breckinridge: 9, 124, 128, 133
Brendlinger: 124
Breed: 1
Breeding: 207
Brengman: 131
Brenham: 71, 75
Brent: 64, 102, 201
Brewer: 232
Brekenary: 102
Bridges: 1, 6, 28, 35, 153, 161
Bridgeford: 128
Bridgewater: 208
Briggs: 52, 182, 229
Brink: 58
Brite: 212
Bright: 57, 66, 113, 209
Brinson: 96
Briscoe: 15, 151, 161
Briston: 17
Brittain: 38
Britton: 191
Bronaugh: 221
Brooks: 2, 24, 35, 36, 52, 73, 161, 201, 207, 221, 248
Brothers: 2, 232
Brower: 173
Browder: 119, 121
Brown: 1, 3, 9, 15, 17, 24, 26, 28, 29, 32, 35, 39, 69, 70, 74, 77, 82, 85, 89, 95, 124, 128, 156, 165,177, 182, 188, 191, 204, 207, 218, 221, 231, 233, 234, 235, 237, 245, 249
Brownfield: 2, 45, 46, 231, 232, 233
Brownell: 172
Browning: 2, 45, 46
Bruce: 57, 197
Bruner: 124, 188
Brunk: 38
Brunneley: 2
Brumfield: 173, 196
Bruster: 135
Bryan: 39, 52, 59, 81, 124, 136, 175, 223
Bryant: 57, 63, 150, 165, 202,

254

Bryant (Cont'd): 204, 209, 234
Bryand: 57
Buckner (Bucknor): 130, 191, 217
Buchanan (Buckhannon): 70, 191, 207
Bucey: 216
Buckler: 172
Buckman: 233
Buckhyn: 32
Buckley: 59
Buggs: 227
Buidusell: 15
Buit: 82
Bulger: 147
Bulgler: 150
Bull: 212
Bullitt: 41, 124, 133
Bullock: 43, 45, 66, 115, 207, 236
Bunton: 173
Bunch: 42, 225
Bunn: 51, 56
Bunton: 173
Burbridge: 46, 64, 201, 204
Burch: 186
Burcham: 185
Burdet (Burdette): 78, 201, 217
Burdin: 35, 191
Burger: 61
Burnetto: 217
Burchfield: 69
Burgess: 151, 222
Burgin: 161
Burkhead: 186
Burn: 57, 81, 182, 186
Burnet: 161, 164, 167, 203
Burnside: 165
Burris: 41, 222
Burton: 29, 45, 52, 53, 54, 61, 137, 151, 246
Buster: 2
Bush: 41, 42, 43, 66, 75, 90, 161, 163, 226
Butler: 10, 73, 75, 139, 167, 177, 207, 208
Buzan: 207, 247
Bybee: 2
Byers: 192, 193, 194

Cabandess:
Cabell: 171
Caddin: 237
Cade: 57
Cain: 39, 42, 141

Caldwell (Coldwell): 17, 25, 27, 36, 58, 59, 61, 91, 95, 138, 156, 157, 162, 169, 174, 184, 192, 193, 213, 214, 227, 228, 229, 233, 238, 239
Calhoun (Caldhoon): 11, 52, 64, 81
Calk: 163
Call: 139, 155
Callico: 233
Calloway: 41, 44, 19
Calterson: 136
Calvin: 35
Calvert: 12, 239
Cameron: 35, 208
Campbell: 1, 3, 24, 32, 36, 38, 39, 42, 61, 74, 101, 121, 127, 135, 139, 141, 161, 163, 164, 167, 177, 225.
Camper: 58
Can: 212
Canady: 173
Candogriff: 103
Caney: 210
Cannado: 105
Caperton: 162
Caraway: 29
Crackman (Carckwell): 204
Card: 141
Cardwell: 45
Care: 133
Cargill: 121
Carly: 31
Carmack (Carmick): 31, 74, 82
Carmole: 127
Carnagy: 203
Carnall: 231
Carnaugh: 222
Carneal: 70
Carnes: 69, 135
Carney: 35, 222
Carnahan: 104
Carpenter: 2, 15, 16, 18, 77, 147, 161, 221
Carr: 38, 52, 81, 94, 135
Carry: 58
Carrick: 24
Carson: 46, 70, 136, 169, 202, 215, 226, 233
Carter: 3, 37, 177, 188, 196
Cartmel: 15
Carver: 225
Carruthers: 171, 194

Cartwell: 91
Cartwright: 24, 27, 34
Cary: 133
Cassady: 191, 194
Cassebier: 177, 179
Casey: 182
Cash: 162
Cassey: 147, 175
Cassell: 137
Cassidy: 27, 52
Catchings: 142
Cather: 142, 148
Catlett: 58, 74, 86, 124, 136
Cave: 65, 169, 203, 246
Cavendar: 205
Cavender: 248
Cavins: 65
Cavinston: 208
Cawley: 152
Cecil: 124
Chaffery: 161
Chambers: 29, 32, 63, 84, 130, 136
Champ: 12
Champlin: 144
Chandler: 26, 29, 33, 39, 91
Chane: 102
Chapman: 147, 225, 227, 247
Chapline: 225
Chasten (Chastian): 225, 226
Chasan (Cheatham): 42, 102, 225
Cherto: 28
Chesnut: 36, 142
Chew: 202
Chich: 142
Childress: 212
Chiles: 75, 135, 174, 175, 212
Chilton: 166
Chinn: 58, 91, 92, 95, 182, 186
Christian: 104, 119, 124, 247
Christopher: 248
Christy: 42, 214
Chizum: 161, 167
Church: 101, 105
Churchill: 89, 124, 130, 132, 169, 185, 213
Cipele (Cisele): 236
Citley: 43
Claggett: 58
Clain: 66
Clair: 58
Clannoh: 172
Clanson: 44
Clanton: 155, 172

Clark: 33, 36, 37, 38, 39, 42, 58, 59, 62, 113, 119, 124, 126, 130, 169, 174, 182, 191, 203, 207, 213
Clarke: 45, 58
Clarkson: 237
Clarl: 124
Clarvo: 201
Clasc: 28
Clay: 59, 60, 62, 102, 103, 164
Cleaver: 182
Cleery: 148
Cleland: 233
Clemens (Clemmens): 86, 152
Clement: 44, 82, 182
Clerm: 113
Clifford: 9
Clifton: 42, 233
Clini: 208
Close: 135
Cloyd: 162, 167
Coats: 42, 81
Cobb: 27, 142
Coburn: 30, 64, 175, 212
Cochran (Cochrane, Cockrum): 52, 139, 162, 215, 217, 218, 177
Cooke: 127
Cookrill: 221
Coe: 84
Coffey: 162
Coffert: 143
Coffuth: 151
Coker: 36
Connell: 31
Connelly: 207
Conley: 2
Colbard: 57
Colbert: 63
Cole: 24, 93, 163, 191, 225, 226
Coleman: 2, 36, 95, 124, 134, 195, 196, 216, 222, 249
Calgahoon: 132
Colgan: 208
Collett: 215
Collier: 78, 162, 194, 213
Collins: 35, 36, 41, 43, 61, 131, 133, 170, 184, 193, 203, 204, 210, 213, 214, 227
Collings: 15, 218
Coon: 70, 91
Cooley: 171
Colton: 186
Colvin: 187
Comason: 202

Combs (Coombs): 53, 81, 82, 177, 183
Comer: 2, 52
Compton: 29, 39, 55, 183, 184, 225
Conchran: 163
Conder: 233
Condit (Condict): 128, 196
Condray: 2
Conley: 2
Conner: 156
Constant: 42, 235
Conway: 52, 151, 187
Conwell: 228
Cook: 30, 41, 70, 84, 136, 161, 169, 191, 205, 245, 248
Cooksey: 27
Cope: 6, 16
Coppage: 201, 204
Coppedge: 147
Copeland: 183
Copell: 136, 233
Corbin: 46, 191
Corby: 184
Corlew: 24
Corn: 233
Cornell: 15, 16
Cornelius: 127
Cosgrove: 239
Couchman: 45, 70, 187
Cozine: 173
Cough: 235, 236
Coulson: 70
Coulter: 162
Courtney: 77
Coverton: 127
Cowan: 103, 127, 193
Cowles: 124, 225, 228
Cowling: 169
Cox (Coxe): 72, 75, 130, 142, 143, 144, 169, 186, 197, 217, 223, 227, 245, 249
Cozine: 173
Crabbe: 209
Crabtree: 39, 226
Craddock: 2
Cradis: 89
Crafton: 81, 86
Craford (Crawford): 2, 45, 51, 81, 83, 127, 165, 188, 191, 196, 226, 229.
Craig: 28, 30, 44, 46, 61, 64, 72, 77, 78, 94, 133, 142, 175, 201, 202, 205, 208, 247, 248, 249
Craik: 170

Cramer: 248
Crane: 246
Crather: 218
Craven: 36, 85, 183
Creath: 162, 163
Creerenstan: 213
Crenshaw: 6, 19, 91, 213
Crews: 139, 162, 165
Crigler: 55
Crines: 245
Crisp: 185
Criswell: 145, 194
Crockett: 58, 69, 75, 193
Croft: 120
Croghan: 132
Crook: 165, 214
Cross: 91, 113, 158, 179, 25
Crosthwait: 42, 44
Croucher: 78
Crow: 2, 16, 27, 147, 174, 175, 195, 197, 214
Crume: 183, 186
Cruse: 104, 151
Crump: 44, 225
Crutcher: 70, 89, 185, 187
Crutchfield: 75, 132
Cubbage: 12
Culhoon: 70
Cullam: 45
Cullen: 228
Culberson: 169, 201
Culbertson: 201, 202
Culton: 145
Culver: 16
Cutting: 147
Custer: 12, 13
Cutright: 136
Cummins: 127, 142
Cumprey: 202
Cumstalk: 142, 144
Cundiff: 196
Cunningham: 17, 136, 218, 222, 233
Curd: 65, 139, 156, 226, 227
Curry: 92, 173, 245
Curts: 183
Curtis: 144
Curtsinger: 233, 238
Cushenberry: 9

Daharen: 204
Daily (Daly): 44, 174, 191
Dairy: 195
Dale: 245
Dallam: 25, 27, 136, 139

Dallas: 192
Dampeer: 192
Dance: 94
Daniel: 43, 52, 150
Dale: 218
Danley: 129
Danner: 153
Dant: 233
Daret: 246
Darnaby: 148
Darne: 218
Darnall: 169
Darrah: 25
Daugherty (Dougherty): 147, 5, 89, 124, 131
Daumes: 43
Davenport: 23, 43, 136, 138
Davis: 5, 25, 26, 33, 36, 43, 52, 58, 101, 102, 104, 142, 148, 167, 170, 173, 177, 179, 180, 181, 182, 183, 185, 186, 191, 192, 197, 212, 218, 221, 222, 226
Davidson: 2, 3, 12, 25, 191, 194, 245
Davidge: 177, 195
Dawson: 13, 234
Day: 15, 91, 175, 183, 218, 226, 228
Deacon: 25, 132, 183, 186
Deal: 43, 151
Deats: 16
Deaver: 89
Dell: 229
Decker: 52, 77, 188
Deen: 84
Dehoney: 33
Delaney: 142, 153
Demaree: 173, 210, 213
Dement: 132
Dennings: 222
Denny: 12
Dennis: 102, 133
Dent: 170
Depp: 5
Derby: 226
De Rohan: 232
Desha: 91
Dervan: 235
Dever: 162
Devine: 175
DeWeese: 246
Dewit: 42
Dial: 92
Dickens: 173, 175

Dickey: 59, 142, 202, 203
Dickenson: 6
Dickerson: 4, 25, 36, 140
Dickinson: 5, 127, 131, 142, 169, 214.
Dicky: 64
Didlake: 43
Dillingham: 36, 37
Dills: 92, 222
Dillins: 136
Dilson: 62
Dinchman: 58
Dilworth: 26
Dingle 58
Dinwiddie: 202
Dixon: 25, 36, 64, 73, 101, 102 103, 228.
Dizney: 142
Ditto: 85
Doak: 135
Doan: 95
Dobbin (Dobyns): 25, 33, 120, 151, 153, 177, 178.
Dobson: 226, 229
Dodd: 3, 5, 30, 32, 70, 153, 210
Dodge: 82, 95
Dodson: 1, 4, 174
Dogge: 121
Doherty: 82
Donaldson: 162, 174
Donden: 9
Donley: 55
Donner: 222
Donohoe: 132
Donoho: 166
Dooley: 16
Dooling: 59
Doom: 25, 31
Doran: 234
Dornan: 207
Dorne: 218
Dorsey: 82, 89, 104, 114, 127, 182, 188.
Dorty: 85
Dosey: 161
Dotson: 191
Douglas: 2, 9, 11, 13, 92, 93, 141, 149, 162, 165, 172, 196, 221.
Doughty: 227
Douitt: 74
Doughet: 74
Dougherty: 131
Douner: 35
Dowdall: 234

Downey: 43, 192
Downing: 3, 11, 42, 58
Downs: 170, 183, 222
Doyle (Doyal): 169, 226, 228, 239
Dozier: 17, 141, 162
Draper: 25
Drake: 15, 135, 147, 171, 180, 183, 184, 195, 228.
Dreskill (Dreskell): 35, 223, 245
Drever: 4
Drewett: 23
Dryden: 92, 96
Drummond: 63, 192
Drury: 236
Dubberly: 132
Duberg: 229
Ducker: 183
Dudley: 59, 60, 155
Duff: 3, 24, 151
Duffy: 89, 169, 172
Dugan: 96, 213
Dugger: 142
Duhamel: 59
Dulaney: 52
Duly: 202
Dunbar: 73, 130
Duncan: 10, 23, 25, 52, 56, 70, 89, 96, 113, 120, 128, 135, 147, 162, 169, 182, 193, 195, 208.
Dunham: 3
Dunkin: 41
Dunlap: 9, 58, 65
Dulin: 218, 246
Dunkin: 41
Dunniman: 27
Dunman: 42
Dunscomb: 222
Dunsmore: 192
Dunwidie: 137
Dupey: 247
Dupree: 194
Dupuy: 114, 113
Durall (Durelle): 178
Durbin: 9
Durett: 115
Durmon: 41
Durley: 27, 147
Duvall: 15, 16, 18, 95, 151, 202, 222
Dye: 62, 82, 226
Dyer: 36, 226, 233
Dyson: 16

Eades: 13, 228
Eakin: 137, 138, 139, 213

Ealils: 10
Eans: 120
Earham: 221
Earickson: 131
Earkinson: 124, 127, 130
Earle: 37, 120, 121
Early: 142
Earnest: 175
Earvin: 58
East: 25, 151
Eastin: 9
Easter: 84
Eastin: 129, 167
Eastwood: 102
Eathernton: 195
Echette: 92
Eckler: 92
Edger (Edgar): 70, 93
Edelin: 231
Edler: 236
Edmistoon: 164
Edmonds: 136
Edmunds: 75
Edmonson: 43, 92, 234
Edrington: 70, 121, 223
Edson: 70
Edwards: 11, 13, 35, 37, 70, 93, 123, 127, 128, 130, 133, 142, 182, 184, 208, 222, 245.
Edwon: 75
Egbert: 71
Eggleston: 175
Egneu: 10
Eggleston: 175
Elder: 27, 82, 177, 178, 234, 237.
Eli (Ely): 156
Elkins: 217
Ellenbaugh: 140
Elliott: 38, 58, 93, 127, 142, 145, 165, 195, 209, 210, 213, 233, 235, 249.
Ellett, 162,
Ellis, 3, 13, 54, 58, 66, 93, 132, 208, 245.
Elley, 201
Ellison, 13, 18, 96, 113, 170
Elly, 202
Elmon, 228
Elmetz 54
Elmore, 1, 5, Elrod, 169, 172
Embree, 43, 234
Emison, 202, 205
Emiston 59, 147

Emmett: 43
Emmons: 131
Empson: 136
Endicott: 13, 96, 194
Enslow: 81, 82, 85, 128, 185
Epeson: 191
Epperson: 58
Ermon: 96
Ervin: 1, 135, 196,
Erving: 138
Erwin: 59, 82, 113
Erwing: 158, 202
Eslick: 194
Essery: 170
Estes: 173
Estill: 166
Essex: 89
Etherton: 113
Eubanks: 43, 45, 63, 226, 227
Evans: 33, 43, 102, 136, 139, 170, 181
Eve: 145
Everall: 16
Everly: 174
Evinger: 133
Evins: 167
Ewell: 169, 170
Ewin: 82
Ewing: 71, 75, 85, 156, 157, 158, 173, 183, 223, 228, 234, 238

Fadford: 169
Faith: 53, 234
Fallis: 147
Faquier: 202
Farguson (Ferguson): 148
Farant: 170
Farley: 136, 153, 207
Farlow: 13
Farnsley: 129
Farmer: 28, 89, 115
Farris: 143, 144, 145, 147
Farthing: 161, 163
Fasinger: 5
Faulkner: 202
Fauquor: 45
Fauntlroy: 149
Foland: 233
Felick: 196
Folter: 82, 128
Felts: 155
Felty: 208
Fenster: 59

Fenwick: 53,
Ferguson: 36, 59, 183, 184, 196, 205
Fethringgille: 237
Ficklin: 2,, 202, 210, 226
Fidler: 16, 19
Fields: 16, 19, 42, 129, 174, 175, 196, 202
Finch: 182, 183
Fine: 130
Finley: 10, 33, 33, 39, 81, 91, 92, 155, 205, 213
Finney: 163, 246
Fipps: 133
Fishback: 43, 44, 46
Fisher: 10, 129, 178, 201, 205, 246
Fitch: 183
Fitts: 52
Fitzgerald: 128
Fitzpatrick: 239
Flanagan: 42, 234
Flanary: 39
Flemming: 9, 66, 124, 127, 156, 249
Flemmons: 181
Fletcher: 52, 136, 163, 172, 227
Flicklin: 135
Flicknxn: 12
Flipping: 4
Florah: 43
Floyd: 103, 127, 133, 144, 147, 150, 223, 226
Flournoy: 2, 5, 25, 27, 66, 171, 212
Fogg: 74
Foley: 25, 62, 63, 143
Fontain: 56
Forbes: 41,
Ford: 25, 29, 31, 113, 119, 212, 216, 227, 234, 247
Fordam: 162
Fordan: 103
Foreline: 82
Forker: 178
Forsythe: 62, 192
Fower: 238
Fowler: 31, 33, 92, 151, 163
Fowles: 103
Foster: 57, 136, 174, 226, 180, 185, 192
Fournier: 234, 235
Fox: 63, 226, 228, 249,120

Frakes: 82, 175
Francis: 55, 172
Frange: 249
Franklin: 2, 5, 6, 23, 35
Fraser (Frazier): 58, 65, 91, 95, 102, 105, 106, 193, 226, 246
Frayer: 154
Fredricks: 130, 182
Freeland: 202
Freeman: 25, 26, 150, 227
Freer: 28
French: 147, 163
Froyer: 188, 192
Friends: 83, 170
Frigate: 119
Fristoes: 222
Fristol: 35
Froman: 147, 174, 234
Frost: 135
Fruit: 37
Frunk: 114
Fry: 59, 94, 170
Frye: 188, 192
Fryman: 194
Fulcher: 224
Fulk: 26
Fulkartson: 183
Fulkerson: 136, 174, 196, 197, 226, 228
Fulkeson: 136
Fulkoyson: 188
Fulton: 193, 213
Funk: 124
Fuquay: 16, 104, 169
Furney: 245, 246
Furnish: 92

Gabriel: 95, 123
Gadsberry: 3
Gadsey: 172
Gaffey: 10
Gage: 94, 226
Gailey: 138
Gaines: 73, 221
Gaithers: 231
Galbreath: 148, 191
Gale: 75, 201
Gallaher: 222
Galley: 96
Galloway: 3, 9, 102, 105, 106, 128, 154, 196, 235
Galusha: 32
Gamble: 16, 35
Ganos: 43

Gano: 69, 71, 75
Gannon: 92
Gardner: 59, 63, 188
Gardinier: 188
Garland: 144
Garley: 23
Garner: 171, 196
Garnett: 7, 59, 70, 136, 245, 247, 248
Gerrard: 71, 73, 75, 85, 102
Garrett: 26, 144, 149, 208, 248
Garrison: 226, 227
Garth: 201
Gartin: 221
Garton: 162, 166
Garvin: 37, 38, 164, 178
Gary: 121, 154
Gash: 215
Gass: 161, 163
Gassaway: 208
Gaston: 148
Gates: 135, 170, 173, 178, 234
Gatewood: 62, 65, 114, 128, 136, 204
Gattiway: 202
Gatton: 18
Gee: 214
Geoghan: 89
Geiger: 128
Gentry: 3, 16, 17, 163, 164, 196, 197
George: 25, 26, 33, 35, 95, 133, 163, 182
Gervas: 52
Geshen: 151
Gess: 167
Getz: 131
Gholson: 26
Gibbons: 234
Gibson: 25, 57, 58, 63, 70, 71, 120, 132, 145, 196, 222, 228, 229
Giddings: 42
Gilberts: 9, 137, 138
Giles: 121
Gilliham: 26
Gilham: 101
Gilkey: 26, 152
Gill: 174, 183
Gillespy (Gillespie): 5, 59, 174, 213, 215, 226
Gillian: 55, 101

Gillas: 148
Gillihan: 5
Gillman: 128
Gilmore: 38, 81, 137, 176, 221
Ginkins: 104
Girdner: 144
Gish: 178
Gist (Guist): 1, 75
Givens (Given): 62, 92, 119, 120, 174
Gladingsberg: 10
Glascock: 188
Glasgow: 9, 92
Glass: 18, 25, 181, 203, 209
Glazebrook: 3, 4, 6
Glenn: 16, 22, 26, 27, 28, 29, 30, 32, 152, 165
Glisten: 170
Gloren: 214
Glover: 6, 53
Gorban (Gorbin): 128
Godman: 192
Gonaway: 175
Goodaker: 39
Goode: 37, 113
Gooden: 143
Goodlett: 187
Goodflow: 164
Goldman: 234
Goodman: 59, 178, 226, 235
Golleher: 151
Goodnight: 59
Goodtill: 38, 39
Goodwin: 27, 83, 115, 132, 141, 184
Gooman: 2
Goosey: 46
Goram: 57, 65
Gordon: 21, 26, 43, 52, 72, 153, 175, 148
Gore: 25, 188
Goren (Gorin): 37, 223
Gormany: 91
Gash: 173
Gassett:
Goldbury: 236
Goudy: 246
Gough: 165, 205, 237
Goulding: 164
Grable: 16
Grase: 170
Graham: 24, 37, 57, 71, 73, 191, 193, 202, 222, 223, 224, 229, 233, 234, 235, 225, 174

Grammer: 226
Grant: 10, 57, 59, 102, 196, 202, 246
Grantham: 103
Grasty: 24
Graves: 52, 59, 61, 63, 66, 71, 72, 156, 177, 178, 213, 224, 235
Graw: 13
Gray: 24, 26, 27, 36, 38, 44, 121, 122, 137, 161, 182, 187, 192, 193, 215, 223, 227, 229, 237
Grayson: 187
Greathouse: 16, 115, 181
Green: 2, 3, 10, 28, 46, 54, 73, 81, 102, 113, 128, 145, 163, 183, 202, 208
Greenfield: 221, 222
Greenup: 66, 69, 76, 93
Greenwall: 81, 83
Greenwill: 18, 19, 183, 237
Greenwood: 135
Greer: 26, 28, 152, 184, 196, 226
Gregg: 128
Gregory: 22, 26, 29, 141, 143, 207, 234, 236
Gresham: 71, 246
Grider: 3, 4, 226
Griffen: 38, 102, 137, 138
Griffin: 16, 19, 102, 137
Griffith: 26, 28, 51, 53, 54, 93, 97, 151, 192, 195, 201, 204
Grigsby: 86, 105, 184, 196, 197, 204, 209
Grimes: 58
Grinstead: 4, 207
Gristy: 182
Grinwell: 182
Groghigan: 192
Groom: 25, 248
Grosvenor: 192
Grover: 178, 178
Grubbs: 26, 28, 57, 93, 148, 154
Grundy: 128, 170, 175, 235, 237, 239
Guardian: 196, 231
Guess: 147
Guinn: 196
Gum: 83, 84
Gunterman: 16
Guye: 94
Gwathney(Gwathing): 124, 125
Gwyn(Gurin): 59, 209

Hackett: 44, 70
Hacknday: 43, 164
Haden: 238
Hadden: 246
Hady: 186
Hadley: 224
Hagan: 53, 234
Hagard: 143
Haggard: 45
Hagerty: 63
Hainds: 249
Hainey: 192
Halbert: 17, 44
Hale: 174
Haley: 61, 246
Halin: 120
Hall: 13, 16, 17, 19, 20,
 24, 27, 30, 36, 69, 70, 71,
 72, 92, 93, 94, 96, 113, 114,
 120, 123, 128, 151, 161, 169, 170,
 187, 191, 192, 193, 194, 202, 203,
 207, 208, 214, 226
Hallet: 184
Hallum: 155
Halton: 69, 245, 246
Ham: 155, 210
Hambaugh: 16
Hambleton: 92, 203
Hamette: 228, 234, 235
Hamilton (Hamelton): 4, 23, 25,
 27, 36, 59, 63, 81, 83, 93, 96,
 101, 102, 152, 163, 187, 233,
 234, 236, 246, 248
Hammels: 183
Hammock: 33
Hammond: 27, 29, 30, 31, 50,
 154, 184, 226
Hampton: 41, 43, 45
Hamtutler: 143
Hancock: 59, 66, 69, 105, 115,
 248
Hand: 194, 235
Handley: 55, 66, 93
Handsford: 16, 53
Haniel: 208
Hanley: 27
Hannah (Hanna): 52, 53, 71, 148,
 156, 226
Hanks: 81, 232
Hankins: 166
Hanley: 27
Hansbrough: 158, 173, 208, 213,
 216
Haralson: 53

Harbison: 149, 185
Harcort: 234
Hardeman: 17
Hardin: 1, 25, 71, 102, 151, 152,
 164, 174, 184, 234, 235,
Harding: 93, 128, 192
Hardy: 46, 138
Hargis: 36, 89
Hargow: 82
Hargroves: 223
Harkins: 102, 152
Harland: 38, 148, 223
Harlow: 174
Harmon: 114
Harney: 192, 193
Harpensing: 30
Harper: 15, 27
Harras: 89
Harreld: 147
Harrell: 186
Harriman: 197
Harris: 15, 17, 27, 41, 43, 46,
 51, 71, 83, 113, 120, 124, 135,
 136, 138, 139, 151, 154, 162,
 163, 164, 174, 176, 178, 192,
 195, 212, 226, 227, 246
Harrison: 9, 12, 13, 27, 38, 59,
 60, 61, 56, 70, 95, 129, 170,
 172, 184, 185, 188, 208
Harrod: 174
Harryman: 128
Hart: 17, 44, 60, 61, 85, 102, 103,
 104, 105, 148, 163, 171, 174, 184,
 185, 186, 197
Hartley: 174
Hartman: 208
Harvell: 172
Harvey: 104, 120, 121
Harrow: 44
Hasting: 54, 246
Hatcher: 144
Hatton: 69, 245, 246
Hauser: 3
Hawes: 53
Hawks: 127
Hawkes: 128
Hawkind: 93
Hawkins: 6, 71, 72, 91, 97, 115,
 128, 163, 166, 201, 202, 204
Haworth: 27
Hawthorne: 131, 172
Hay: 57, 148, 157, 163, 225, 227
Hays: 4, 27, 28, 103, 162, 186,
 205, 226, 228, 229

Hayes: 239
Haycraft: 85, 149
Hayden: 53, 69, 114, 137, 139, 232, 234, 235, 236, 238, 246
Haygood: 223
Haynes: 43, 53, 54, 104, 143, 144, 151, 170, 178, 185, 223, 246
Haytel: 62
Hayworth: 27
Hazelwood: 222
Hazlerigg: 44
Head (Hedd): 51, 53, 54, 55, 71, 72, 203, 236, 239
Heading: 96
Heady: 4, 184
Heard: 11
Hearndon: 202
Heath: 202
Hebbs: 103
Hecks: 10
Hedd: 196
Hedges: 196
Heels: 43, 154, 197
Helemon: 229
Helm: 59, 82, 83, 85, 90, 121, 147, 233
Helt: 197
Heltman: 192
Helton: 141
Heltsley: 178
Hemphill: 140
Henderson: 5, 9, 10, 57, 61, 101, 120, 122, 128, 131, 135, 144, 165, 169, 184, 193, 201, 202, 204, 205, 225
Hendricks: 16, 51, 92, 226, 227
Hendrickson: 143
Henry: 33, 36, 93, 103, 137, 170, 175, 203
Hensley: 71, 75, 114, 207
Henson: 26, 27, 29, 170, 178
Henthon: 152
Henton: 82, 151, 227
Herald: 120
Herbert: 210
Herman: 213, 227
Herndon: 66, 143, 145, 202, 204, 206, 216, 222, 246
Herrale: 226
Herrel: 28, 229
Herren: 93, 141, 184
Heth (Heath) : 103, 192, 202
Heuell: 103

Hewett: 101
Hewlett: 120
Heydon: 137
Heyton: 221
Hibbs: 46
Hickerson: 227
Hicks: 33, 36, 140, 152, 169, 201
Hicklin: 71, 119, 205
Hickman: 46, 61, 69, 75, 92, 97, 238, 245, 246
Hide: 142
Hieatt: 97
Higbee: 138
Higdon: 5, 53, 55
Higginbotham: 137
Higgins: 61, 102, 103, 104, 144, 155
Higginson: 103
Highland: 30
Hightower: 135, 138, 227
Hill: 5, 16, 42, 44, 46, 61, 114, 120, 121, 122, 152, 161, 171, 182, 184, 187, 193, 208, 213, 218, 222, 227, 228, 249
Hillock: 61, 193
Hilt: 114
Hilton: 16, 236
Hillyar (Hillyer): 54, 103, 105
Hinch: 83
Hind: 124
Hine: 96
Hinks: 166
Hinkson: 13
Hinton: 2, 89, 149, 212
Hiren (Hiern): 171
Hite: 27, 128, 131, 175,
Hito: 128
Hoagland: 209
Hobb: 4, 184
Hoblet: 57
Hoblett: 248
Hockaday: 46
Hooker: 194, 195, 197
Hookersmith: 71
Hookerway: 164
Hodgens (Hodgen): 15, 81, 82, 83, 84, 89, 185
Hodges: 35, 36, 62, 93, 97, 128, 153, 170, 182, 224, 227
Hoff: 46, 74
Hoffman: 91
Hoffsinger: 9, 178
Hogan (Hogans): 145, 161, 182, 239
Hogg: 93, 196, 237

Hogland: 184, 209
Hoke: 123, 129
Hoko: 123
Holcomb: 31, 225
Holder: 61
Holderberg: 121
Holeman: 85
Holman: 27, 33, 129, 246
Holland: 27, 93, 163, 181, 204
Holley: 46, 61
Hollingsworth: 120, 249
Hollis: 129
Holmes: 46, 57, 58, 63, 76, 136, 152, 204, 209, 213, 214
Holloday: 4, 12, 66, 93
Holloway: 6, 69, 72, 102, 103, 174, 225
Hollowell: 33
Hollyman: 61
Holstead: 91
Holt: 129, 131, 197
Holton: 71, 72
Holtsclaw: 65
Holston: 187
Hollurn: 151
Home: 9
Honey: 43
Hood: 43, 44
Hook: 166
Hooker: 121, 122
Hooper: 103
Hoover: 137, 138, 195
Hopkins: 54, 63, 101, 102, 103, 104, 105, 121, 179
Hopp: 238
Hopper: 141, 143, 165, 224
Hoard: 54
Hord: 46, 63, 127
Horgin: 46
Horn: 143, 201
Hornback: 84, 85
Hornsby: 204, 213
Horseman: 197
Hosidlor: 17
Hoskins: 237
Hostaters: 92
Hosteler: 208
Hostettler: 215
Hough: 17
Houghton: 54
House: 170
Hously: 103
Hovis: 4

Howard: 1, 4, 28, 39, 51, 53, 55, 66, 81, 103, 124, 137, 138, 141, 142, 144, 182, 184, 197, 201, 211, 227, 236, 238, 245, 249
Howe: 5, 9
Howell: 27, 83, 103, 120, 139
Howes: 54
Howland: 226
Hubbard: 17, 182, 184, 229
Huckaby: 6
Huckleberry: 133
Huckwin: 165
Huddleson: 96, 194
Huddleton: 102
Hudgins: 70
Hudspeth: 225, 227, 231
Hudson: 52, 54, 135, 225, 246
Huff: 145
Hufford: 61
Huffman: 95
Hugh: 29, 72
Hughs: 27, 29, 30, 60, 83, 103, 124, 126, 130, 138, 139, 169, 223, 233, 234, 246
Hughlett: 32
Hukell: 44
Hulls: 41, 45
Hulse: 137, 139
Humble: 10, 114, 211
Hume: 93, 128, 129
Humphrey: 55, 184, 196, 208, 238
Hundley: 58
Hungate: 239
Hunsaker: 179, 224
Hunt: 61, 65, 71, 73, 135, 223
Hunsinger: 179, 224
Hunter: 5, 36, 41, 61, 72, 75, 95, 129, 137, 140, 166, 194, 203
Huntsman: 36, 37
Hurst: 106, 239
Husband: 37, 102, 103, 104
Huston: 17, 51, 54, 84, 104, 114, 188, 217
Hutchinson: 11, 30, 58, 203, 205, 245
Hutcherson: 93, 94, 96
Hutson: 143, 148, 184, 188
Huttin: 44
Hutton: 71, 148
Hynes: 83, 181, 184, 185, 246

Ice: 163
Iglehart: 195
Imbler: 177
Ingraham: 104
Ingram: 3, 29, 143, 151, 157,
 203, 246
Innes: 11
Innis: 69, 72, 73
Instone: 69
Ireland: 41, 44
Irvine: 36, 43, 164, 167, 170,
 234, 236
Irwin: 18, 64, 164, 178, 192,
 208, 235
Isaac: 5
Iseenhootz: 73

Jack: 246
Jackman: 150
Jackson: 12, 24, 54, 72, 74,
 84, 85, 93, 119, 120, 121, 136,
 177, 179, 180, 185, 197, 214,
 229, 233
Jacob: 30, 44, 208
Jacoby: 10
Jaggers: 83
James: 17, 19, 43, 66, 72, 74,
 89, 92, 151, 155, 174, 187, 209
Jameson: 3, 10, 93, 96, 97, 144,
 164, 222
Jamison: 13, 69, 70, 96
Janes: 44
January: 32, 61, 136, 152, 246
Jarbo: 185, 236
Jarrell: 154
Jarveson: 246
Jean: 113
Jeffries: 174, 234
Jenkins: 26, 28, 29, 33, 62, 128,
 144, 152, 201, 205, 208, 235, 236
Jennings: 4, 28, 41
Jenny: 227
Jeter: 223
Jott: 74, 107
Jewell: 5, 70, 213
Johnes: 31, 157
Johnson (Jonson): 1, 10, 11, 15,
 29, 37, 39, 44, 46, 51, 52, 54,
 55, 62, 72, 102, 104, 114, 123,
 127, 128, 133, 137, 138, 143, 145,
 150, 151, 202, 203, 214, 216, 221,
 227, 228, 243, 246
Johnston: 6, 24, 28, 29, 52, 90,
 129, 195, 246

Jones: 10, 12, 13, 17, 25, 28, 29, 31,
 37, 51, 52, 58, 59, 72, 92, 93, 113, 114
 120, 127, 129, 131, 145, 156, 163, 185,
 187, 193, 195, 196, 203, 214.
Jordon: 185
Jourdon: 4, 5, 17, 53, 59, 74, 84
Joyes: 74, 129, 133
Judd: 61
Julian: 71
Julianna: 72

Kamp: 186, 187
Kampt: 185
Kanady: 39
Kannada: 35
Kannady: 84, 188
Kannon: 28
Karmady: 187
Karr: 120, 152
Karrick: 61
Kaster: 81
Kavanaugh: 164
Kaw: 152
Kay: 205
Kearn: 201, 203
Kearney: 169
Keene: 203
Keiser: 179
Keisore: 10
Keith: 52, 89, 96, 187, 196
Kelby: 72
Kellam: 31, 84
Kellar: 128, 137
Kelso: 91
Kelly: 5, 6, 41, 51, 54, 62, 91, 196,
 197
Kelley: 132, 204
Kemp: 24
Kemper: 92, 96, 143, 145
Kenedy(Kenndy, Kanady): 10
Kennedy: 35, 39, 51, 53, 71, 83, 95,
 138, 148, 175, 176, 186, 188, 203, 215
Kennels: 166
Kenneth: 11
Kenningham: 141
Kennison: 129
Kenny: 9, 10, 11
Kenslow: 2
Kerlin: 113
Kermikle: 83
Kerns: 203
Kerr: 4, 137, 147
Kersie: 207
Kersey: 138

Kersiles: 145
Kersner: 62
Kester: 185
Kesterson: 26
Keston: 213
Ketcham: 207, 209
Kevil: 28, 153, 154
Keys: 4, 97, 156, 227
Kibbie: 131
Kidson: 195
Kidwell: 163
Kilgore: 24, 92, 106, 152
Killian(Killan): 24, 28
Killigan: 102
Killough: 152, 153
Kimberly: 83
Kimble: 170, 171
Kimbrough: 191, 193
Kincaid: 10, 162, 164, 166
Kinchloe: 177, 179, 185, 217
Kinder: 164
Kindle: 237
Kindrece: 43
King: 3, 11, 17, 18, 22, 31, 37, 39, 42, 66, 77, 91, 93, 94, 96, 97, 101, 103, 106, 185, 186, 191, 207, 223, 227, 236
Kinhart: 193
Kinningham: 143
Kinsler: 93
Kirk: 153
Kirkland: 229
Kirby: 4, 5, 129, 131, 227
Kirkpatrick: 10, 84, 85, 94, 96, 153
Kirtley: 6
Kiser: 15, 57
Kivel: 27
Knight: 213
Knot: 42, 119, 121
Knott: 54
Konkright: 233
Kuykindale(Keykindale): 28, 84
Kuturah: 92
Kykendall: 84, 128
Kyle: 245, 246

Lacassagne: 129, 130
Lacefield: 137, 149
Lacklin: 43
Lacky: 24
Lacy(Lacey): 24, 29, 37, 152, 153, 154
Lafferty: 46
Lafoon(Lafon): 69, 121, 122, 139

Laham: 234
Lail: 10
Lair: 3
Lamar: 29, 114
Lamber: 102
Lambert: 104, 143, 203
Lampkin: 37
Lampton: 124
Lamy: 10
Lancaster: 185, 216, 233, 235, 236, 238
Landon: 46
Landers: 15, 32
Landes: 205
Landis: 178, 228
Lane: 43, 154, 208, 215
Lang: 156
Langley: 180, 187
Langston: 27, 156
Lanier: 225
Lanham: 197
Lankston: 9, 29
Lansdale: 184
Lantaman: 201
Lapley: 181
Lark: 5
Larue: 83, 89, 182, 185
Lash: 104
Lashbrook: 54
Latan(Laton): 204
Latham: 36, 156, 188, 222
Latimore: 2, 173
Laughlin: 10, 32, 33, 62
Laughten: 29
Laurence(Lawerence): 35, 36, 72, 104, 127, 173, 174, 185, 208, 214
Lawless: 233
Lawry: 95, 96, 222
Lewson: 113, 115, 209
Lay: 58, 171
Layton: 205
Looften: 37
Leach(Leech): 25, 28, 29, 30, 197, 204
Leash: 141
Leatherman: 129, 130, 208, 229
Leavel: 3
Ledgerwood: 44, 71, 75
Lee: 121, 141, 143, 185, 195, 213, 214, 227, 249
Leeper(Leiper): 3, 31, 105, 121
Lefollett: 89
Leforce: 64
Leman: 54, 201

Lemare: 37
Lemaster: 17
Lemen: 130
Lemon: 19, 94, 202
Lemone: 19
Lemorrison: 195
Lend: 157
Lender: 85
Lendram: 54
Lepensberry: 4
Lerue: 185
Lesley: 178
Lest: 213
Lester: 39
Letcher: 74
Letchworth: 225
Levington: 128
Lewallen: 227
Lewellyn: 124, 196
Lewis: 2, 4, 6, 29, 44, 69, 70, 84, 86, 92, 104, 138, 141, 152, 153, 162, 166, 177, 185, 208, 213, 214, 216, 226, 227, 228, 234
Liggett: 29, 203, 226
Lightfoot: 70, 74, 227
Lillard: 70, 73, 75, 174
Lilly: 91, 193, 217
Lincoln: 85, 232
Linden: 82
Lindley: 196
Lindsay: 63, 148, 201, 202, 203, 205, 248
Lingerfelter: 62, 92
Linn(Lyne, Lynn): 11, 35, 39, 72, 97, 104, 121, 129, 130, 171
Linnelle: 193
Lisk: 122
Litching: 185
Liter: 130, 147
Litsen: 185
Litten: 227
Little: 66, 174
Littlepage: 178
Lively: 209, 223
Lloyd(Loyd): 54, 72, 75, 167, 227, 228
Lock: 128, 130
Lockett: 136
Lockhart: 37, 44, 52, 96, 137, 156, 209
Lodge: 156
Lofter: 19
Lofton: 29, 138, 152

Loftus: 72
Logan: 11, 38, 58, 61, 63, 66, 72, 74, 75, 101, 138, 145, 147, 148, 210, 249
Logsdon: 4, 81, 163
Lomax: 223
Long: 25, 26, 28, 29, 32, 75, 95, 129, 152, 176, 215, 227, 246, 247, 249
Looflourrows: 74
Lotte: 247
Lovas: 147
Love: 147, 153
Lovelace: 171
Lovell: 128
Lovely: 170
Loving: 227
Lowden(Lowdon): 210
Lowe: 194, 217
Lowen: 135
Lowhorn: 166
Lowrie: 149
Lowry(Lowrye, Lowery): 62, 72, 94, 95, 96, 133, 135, 136, 138, 139, 149, 152, 164, 174, 201, 203, 222, 227
Loyalless: 36
Lucas(Lucuss): 62, 82, 83, 179, 228, 232
Luckett: 127, 130
Lunner: 179
Lunnsden: 222
Lusk: 44, 86, 152, 153
Lutteral: 216
Lynch: 164
Lyle: 37, 62, 66, 228
Lyon: 21, 29, 32

Machen: 25, 28
Mack: 82
Mackay: 102
Macklin: 43
Mackerson: 133
Maclin: 74
Madduk (Maddox): 37, 147, 210, 212
Madison: 75, 137, 157, 228
Magoe: 91
Maggart: 3
Magner: 172
Magill: 147
Magnis: 228
Magruder: 57, 135, 156
Mahon: 94
Mahak: 171
Maidis: 129

Main: 148
Mais: 94
Major: 246
Makey: 4, 164
Malden: 106, 121
Malin: 186
Malone: 1, 214
Mallory: 25
Malott: 123
Man: 38
Manning: 38, 70
Manor: 123
Maupin: 142
Marden: 130
Mark (Marks): 51, 55, 104, 236
Marmen: 228
Marrick: 23
Marrs: 3, 135
Marsh: 27, 91, 93, 94
Marshall: 17, 28, 58, 59, 61, 62, 73, 114, 147, 186, 204, 216, 228, 246
Marshay: 162
Martin: 2, 6, 11, 29, 30, 36, 37, 43, 44, 45, 46, 54, 59, 66, 72, 73, 75, 81, 82, 85, 93, 96, 114, 120, 129, 158, 161, 163, 169, 171, 197, 203, 207, 213, 215, 245, 246
Martinie: 70
Marx: 171
Mash: 188
Mason: 11, 51, 56, 62, 104, 124, 131, 164, 221
Massey: 92, 95, 143, 207
Masters: 152
Masterson: 182
Mater: 238
Mathew: 119, 121
Matthews (Mathews): 3, 4, 121
Mathis: 35, 103, 104, 177
Matire: 46
Matlock: 31
Matson: 12
Mattingly: 187, 232, 236, 238
Maum: 104
Maupin: 121, 164
May: 55, 84, 186, 187
Mayfield: 3, 4, 77
Mayo: 171
Maxwell: 11, 24, 29, 153, 161, 164, 166, 238, 246
Maxey: 5
Mazfield: 62

McAchron: 212
McAdams: 246
McAdoe: 4
McAfee: 73, 175, 176
McAllister: 153
McAlroy: 35
McAnmulty (McAnulty): 193
McAter: 186
McBrayer: 73
McBrayne (McBrayner): 73, 74
McBride: 101, 105, 148, 149, 246
McCaa: 25
McCabe: 136, 156
McCachrow: 174
McCaffric: 44
McCager: 36
McCakin: 33
McCalla: 65
McCalley: 228
McCallister: 73
McCampbell: 137, 209, 214
McCan (McCaun): 11, 63, 92, 201
McCanley: 74
McCannico: 91
McCargo: 45
McCarol: 121
McCarter: 235
McCartney: 178
McCarty: 30, 37, 89, 211
McCaryl: 121
McCasland: 129
McCaulis: 179
McCawley: 152
McCawlin: 233
McCornay: 103
McClanohan (McClanahan): 11, 12, 93, 248
McClames: 104
McClain: 1, 128, 209, 214
McClaskey: 188
McClaughton: 239
McClean: 246
McClelland: 39, 63, 114, 130, 187, 249
McClenachan: 58
McClender: 104
McClintock: 11
McCloud: 36
McClough: 155
McCloughlin: 236
McClure: 10, 11, 13, 29, 73, 92, 94, 96, 123, 136, 143, 173, 191, 197, 203, 205, 249

McColl: 46
McColly: 26
McColoman: 186
McComas: 84
McConless: 6
McConnell: 131
McCoombs: 157
McCord: 105
McCormack (McCormick): 54, 193, 203
McCornell: 135
McCoun: 57, 175, 176
McCown: 36, 185
McCoy: 9, 95, 213
McCracken: 156, 246
McCracklen (McCracklin): 72, 214
McCrary: 10
McCrosky: 57, 210, 215
McCroy: 207
McCrury: 38
McCullough: 63, 149
McCumpsey: 247
McCurry: 228
McCutcher: 9
McDaniel: 6, 37, 45, 92, 95, 96, 106, 153, 186
McDavitt: 208, 214
McDonald: 35, 37, 39, 58, 66, 136, 193, 247
McDonell: 41
McDow: 12
McDowell: 29, 57, 58, 59, 63, 65, 73, 84, 93, 94, 103, 136, 137, 138, 139, 158, 191, 214
McDufee: 37, 93, 94, 96
McDougal: 202
McElhaney: 138
McElroy: 27, 28, 30, 236
McElya: 170
McEnney: 151
McFadden: 36, 37, 38, 157
McFadin: 226, 228
McFall: 214
McFarin: 223
McFarland: 37, 38, 51, 52, 54, 63, 94, 177, 191, 196
McFarley: 41
McFarlin: 39
McFranks: 63
McGarrick: 204
McGarvey: 181
McGary: 122
McGaughey: 71, 207, 209, 210, 214
McGee: 181, 217,
McGill: 174

McGinnis: 228
McGlathon: 233
McGoveran: 84
McGowand: 143
McGowens: 174
McGown: 57
McGrath: 96
McGready (McGrady): 104, 195, 197
McGrew: 73, 196, 212, 215
McGuire: 36, 114, 161, 163, 164
McGunnis: 193
McHarg: 247
McHenry: 75
McIlean: 65
McIllvan (McIllvain): 35, 93, 96
McIlroy: 232
McIntore: 84
McIntire: 89, 91
McIntosh: 157, 172, 229
McIntyre: 73, 82, 127, 191, 194, 238
McIsaac: 61
McJunklin: 37
McKee: 41, 45, 73, 91, 142, 175, 221, 222
McKensey: 84
McKime: 187
McKinney: 92, 136, 137, 138, 139, 147, 164, 178, 202, 214, 221
McKinley: 113, 207, 207, 208, 213
McKitrick: 93, 94
McKnigh: 166
McKnight: 135
McKnown: 157
McKnutt: 94
McKonky: 176
McLain: 5, 84
McLahlan: 128
McLanathan: 122
McLane: 215
McLaughlin: 10, 173
McLaurine: 144
McLean: 157, 177, 178, 186
McLeod: 30
McMahan: 128
McMannis: 130
McMeeter: 53
McMichel: 73, 130
McMillion: 11, 12, 38, 43, 45, 94, 95
McMullen: 162
McMunn: 129
McMurry: 36, 44
McMurty: 63, 83, 91, 148, 175

McNabb: 28
McNair: 58
McNary: 178
McNeel: 157
McNeely: 166
McNeer: 52
McNeese: 44
McNeil: 58, 85, 142, 144, 145, 247
McNey: 11
McNutt: 132
McPicking: 202
McPhail: 157
McPheeters: 45
McPherson: 157
McQuade: 72, 208, 214
McQuillion: 179
McReynolds (McReynold): 156, 157, 223, 227
McSpadden: 141
McVay: 30
McVey: 222
McWade: 214
McWard: 214
McWilliams: 44, 162, 225
McWorthy: 171
McWortors: 171
Means: 1, 37, 38
Medcalf: 186
Medley: 237
Meeks: 32, 89, 147, 195, 209
Meglemmery: 94
Megonan: 63
Menefee: 216
Melinger: 84
Mennet: 154
Meper: 144
Menser: 121
Mercer: 25, 26, 30
Merchant: 92
Meredith: 234
Merino: 229
Merner: 153
Merriwether: 130, 207
Merry: 65, 156, 226
Merryman: 9
Metcalf: 13, 135, 137, 138, 209, 212, 213, 215
Meter: 45
Methenly: 11
Metzel: 17
Mickie: 203
Michir: 175
Middleton: 15

Migill: 59
Milam: 72, 75, 203
Miles: 17, 53, 70, 152, 153, 174, 214, 231, 236
Miley: 55
Miller: 6, 10, 23, 27, 30, 35, 36, 38, 45, 54, 63, 69, 71, 72, 84, 89, 91, 92, 93, 95, 114, 115, 123, 124, 129, 130, 131, 132, 137, 139, 141, 143, 144, 145, 147, 148, 152, 153, 154, 157, 162, 165, 175, 186, 194, 197, 203, 208, 222, 223, 226, 228
Millholland: 45
Milligan: 247
Mills: 25, 39, 94, 103, 130, 162, 164, 144, 233, 236, 237
Milton: 185, 186, 187, 196, 227
Miner: 136, 138, 182
Milyer: 58
Minter: 95, 96, 128
Minton: 55
Mintur: 194
Mitchell: 30, 36, 55, 65, 69, 71, 101, 113, 130, 151, 154, 155, 157, 143, 163, 173, 192, 193, 205, 209, 212, 214, 215, 223, 226, 227, 245
Mitcheltree: 153
Mitcheson: 153
Mitchelson: 30, 31
Mitchenson: 31
Mitchum: 245
Moberly: 228
Moffett: 51, 63, 148
Molohan: 236, 238
Molohane: 236, 238
Moncrieff: 193
Money (Mooney): 63, 114
Monfort: 173, 174
Monroe: 6, 201
Montage: 2, 4
Monteith: 203
Montgomery: 24, 37, 55, 59, 63, 64, 69, 72, 73, 114, 119, 148, 153, 162, 207, 231, 236, 237, 245
Montjoy: 15
Moody: 165
Moon: 163, 181, 226
Moore: 4, 11, 12, 27, 30, 35, 36, 41, 56, 57, 59, 62, 65, 69, 91, 95, 114, 123, 124, 126, 127, 130, 131, 132, 136, 138, 142, 148, 149, 161, 163, 164, 165, 170, 174, 178, 186, 207, 214, 215, 223, 226, 236, 238, 249
Morehead: 156, 179

Moreland: 230
Moreman: 85, 89
Morgan: 10, 29, 41, 42, 44, 45, 91, 96, 127, 131, 186, 193, 247
Moorman: 51, 55
Morris: 41, 63, 72, 177, 184, 203, 204, 207, 228
Morrison: 4, 57, 63, 84, 85, 91, 95, 104, 138, 151, 161, 164, 165, 166, 186, 220
Morrow: 42, 93
Morse: 23, 30, 33, 171
Morton: 33, 44, 45, 46, 52, 102, 188
Mosby: 6, 171, 174
Mosely: 38, 51, 81, 85, 97, 121, 130, 139, 202, 245
Moss: 2, 74, 102, 132, 145, 169, 247, 248
Mossey: 103
Motley: 155, 228
Mouide: 192
Mow: 175
Moxley: 69, 70, 71, 72, 73
Moylan: 133
Mudd: 236, 238
Mulberry: 202
Muldrough: 234
Mullenberging: 192
Mullins: 94, 164
Mumsford: 5
Mumfore: 193
Mundle: 132
Murdah: 205
Murphy: 2, 5, 42, 63, 70, 121, 177, 208
Murrain: 138
Murrel: 2, 4, 5,
Murry: 5, 6, 53, 73, 104, 186, 202, 238
Musgrove: 18, 27
Musset: 192
Musick: 1, 6, 72
Muter: 149
Myers: 18, 51, 129
Myriack: 38
Myles: 156
Myrtle (Mirtle): 131

Nain: 18
Nall (Nalle): 148, 237
Nances: 236
Nanhook: 193

Naper: 59
Nash: 204
Nation: 122
Naught (Vaught): 179
Naylor: 170, 174
Neale (Neal): 11, 17, 63, 95, 102, 113, 128, 131, 204, 205
Nealy: 225
Neeld: 175
Neeley (Neely): 26, 95, 186
Neese: 4
Neil: 44, 143, 218
Neilson: 233
Nelson: 44, 73, 89, 115, 137
Nesbit: 10, 95, 193
Nestor: 225, 228
Netherland: 28, 138
Newbery: 26
Newbelt: 55
Newbout: 185
Nowingham: 204
Newell: 94
Newitt: 186
Newland: 130, 133, 209
Newlin: 24
Nevill (Neville): 4, 14
Newman: 103, 104, 171, 208
Newton: 53, 121, 228, 233
Nicholas: 213
Nichols: 23, 26, 53, 61, 75, 165
Nicholson: 169
Nickolls: 203
Nickson: 203
Niel: 188
Nighmyoir: 179
Nisbitt: 96
Nixon: 121, 128
Noble: 104
Noe: 45, 63
Noel: 57, 175, 176
Noland: 165, 231
Noftzinger: 179
Noobs (Nobbs): 17, 122
Noonan: 138
Norris: 11, 24, 26, 181
North: 222
Nourse: 83, 84, 183, 186
Nottingham: 237
Nuckols: 5
Nukam: 192
Nulton: 204
Nuttell: 63

Oats: 122, 179
O'Bannon: 172
Oberby: 52
Odaniel: 81
O'Fallon: 124, 125, 126, 169
Ogden: 13, 24, 30, 247
Ogle: 11
Oglesby: 127, 131, 213
Oglive: 172
O'Harrow: 45
O'Higgins: 62
Oldfield: 44
Oldham: 41, 43, 131, 164, 203
Oliver: 30, 44, 45, 69, 136, 193, 229
Olynin: 121
O'Nail: 185
Onan: 214
Orear: 163, 165
Ormsby: 101, 130, 183
Orr: 2, 11, 30, 54, 133
Orton: 121
Osborn (Osborne): 30, 236
Osburn (Osburne): 19, 204, 212
Overall: 16, 18, 52, 83, 216
Oversake: 92
Overstreet: 135
Overton: 58, 175, 236, 237
Owen: 16, 24, 25, 29, 33, 44, 52, 53, 72, 73, 119, 120, 139, 144, 152, 166, 172, 175, 209, 211, 215, 226, 234, 247
Owing: 38
Owsley: 165
Oxbury: 232

Padget: 172
Pairleigh: 83
Palmer: 75
Palkner: 63
Parant: 75
Paret: 25
Pareman: 81
Parham: 164
Parher: 64
Paris: 19
Parish: 11, 43, 58, 59, 63, 64, 82, 131, 166
Parker: 13, 57, 61, 62, 63, 64, 73, 121, 122, 124, 132, 144, 197, 237, 247, 249
Parkinson: 86
Parkhurst: 115
Parks: 71, 193, 210

Parman: 144
Parmer: 92
Parsell: 166
Parsley: 131
Parsons: 141, 144
Parpoint (Pearpoint): 81, 84
Partin: 164
Pasley: 181
Passmore: 175
Pate: 53, 197
Patric: 164
Patto: 101
Patterson: 15, 59, 62, 64, 65, 73, 95, 152
Patton: 11, 36, 41, 93, 132, 137, 138, 144, 145, 161, 187, 204, 207, 233
Paul: 131, 247
Paxton: 236
Payne: 11, 18, 55, 58, 60, 61, 64, 65, 69, 74, 75, 93, 129, 144, 151, 201, 208, 223, 234
Payton: 187, 214, 249
Peacock: 119, 120
Peak: 71, 72, 75, 197, 247
Peebles: 83
Pemberton: 26, 27, 28, 39, 57, 69, 70, 74, 114, 245, 247
Pendall: 95
Pendergrass: 131
Pendergart: 192
Pendleton: 95, 132, 181, 222
Penn: 91, 131
Pennebaker: 187
Pennington (Penningston): 178, 209, 221
Pennland: 24
Penny: 74
Penrod: 170, 179
Periar (Perrin): 91, 94
Perkins: 31, 32, 92, 93, 115, 128, 153, 209
Perry: 74, 114, 131, 140, 215
Persons: 152
Peterson: 55, 232
Pettinger: 188
Pettit: 63
Pettus: 175
Petty: 10, 174
Peyton: 12, 16, 18, 69
Pharis: 17
Philes: 201
Phelps: 23, 24, 28, 29, 30, 124, 144, 229
Philley: 31

Phillips: 73, 81, 83, 95, 127, 151, 152, 153, 169, 172, 185, 187, 193, 234, 248
Phyle: 213
Pickett: 43, 93, 95
Pierson: 249
Piety: 81
Piggott: 147, 161
Pigman: 138
Piles: 227, 234
Pinacer: 28
Pindell: 60, 61
Pitman: 144, 166, 173, 177
Pittinger: 18
Pitts: 201
Plasters: 129
Pleasants: 101, 103
Plough: 245
Plummer: 41, 172, 181
Plunkett: 204
Poage: 57, 63
Poffe: 175
Pogue: 144, 176, 215
Poindexter: 69, 74, 77, 135
Pollard: 136, 210, 211, 215
Polke: 63, 89, 187, 212, 214
Pollock: 58, 138
Pomeroy: 127, 128
Pool: 64
Pope: 17, 60, 96, 124, 127, 129, 131, 144, 145, 171, 225
Porkypee: 38
Porter: 17, 70, 96, 133, 153, 156, 157, 158, 177, 227
Portwood: 165
Posey (Posy): 103, 119
Potter: 101, 105, 119, 157
Price: 43, 57, 60, 62, 64, 65, 66, 72, 74, 91, 93, 96, 138, 157, 172, 203, 247
Pottonger: 187
Pottorf: 129
Potts: 147
Poulter: 130
Powell: 96, 105, 192, 209, 233
Powers: 55, 74, 93, 171, 197
Poynter (Pointer): 51, 52, 104
Pratt: 31, 38
Prater: 193
Prather (Prayther): 43, 64, 119, 121, 175, 187, 208
Pressley: 132, 217, 222
Preston: 64, 169

Prewitt (Pruitt): 58, 63, 132, 138, 139, 156, 173, 209, 213, 215
Prichard (Pritchard): 144, 145, 207
Priest: 55
Prince: 31, 130, 131, 132, 153, 154
Pringle: 114
Pritchett: 156
Pritty: 51
Proctor: 66, 247
Profit: 38, 141
Profith (Proffitt): 164
Province: 165
Prawitt: 141
Prowse: 179
Prowett: 105
Pruate (Prewett): 7
Pruden: 52, 197
Pryor: 127, 207, 249
Puckett: 41, 153
Puckrill: 232
Pugh: 31
Pulliam: 226
Pullian: 226
Purtian: 163
Purnell: 53, 55
Pursley: 93, 185
Purtle (Pirtle): 25, 28, 31, 153, 233
Pyle: 35

Quarles: 249
Quartermous: 132
Query: 127
Quidy: 75
Quinn: 16, 167, 202, 204, 245
Quisenberry: 43

Rabourn: 165
Radford: 211
Radley: 90
Rafferty: 51
Ragland (Raglin): 6, 246
Ragsdale: 157
Railey: 74, 248
Rains: 138, 145
Raitton: 69
Rall: 191
Ralston: 2, 4, 62, 97
Ramages: 151
Ramey: 121
Ramon: 18

Ramsey: 27, 42, 43, 44, 45,
  101, 152, 194
Randall(Randle): 63, 114, 223
Randolph: 59, 62, 187
Rankin: 33, 61, 64, 95, 101, 102,
  104
Ransdale: 203
Ransom: 5
Rapier: 235
Ratliffe: 31, 75, 149, 170, 201,
  249
Rawleigh: 11
Rawlings: 83, 84, 85, 184
Rawlins: 226, 229
Rawson: 188
Ray: 45, 70, 145, 148, 153,
  164, 226, 228, 229
Raymon: 96, 97
Read: 38, 52
Reading (Redding): 11, 12, 69, 71,
  93, 194, 209, 215
Readman: 217
Reagan: 38
Reager: 132
Reason: 217
Reaugh: 127
Reaves: 170
Reburn: 187
Redmon (Redman): 12, 44, 64
Reece: 9
Reed: 3, 25, 43, 74, 81, 84,
  103, 105, 127, 131, 132, 135,
  147, 152, 153, 157, 163, 165,
  167, 181, 204, 208, 209, 210,
  215, 229, 235, 248, 249
Reede: 187
Reeder: 38
Rees: 210
Reeves: 38, 177, 227
Reid: 96, 215
Rendon (Render): 195, 197
Renfro: 145, 228
Renner: 227
Rennick: 63, 74
Reno: 179
Reyburn: 64
Reynolds: 31, 36, 37, 38,
  165, 178
Rhoads: 179
Rice: 114, 115, 139, 141,
  153, 157, 173, 174, 179,
  216, 247
Rich: 115

Richards: 18, 41, 121, 165,
  194, 236, 237, 247
Richardson: 45, 57, 70, 71,
  75, 127, 166, 170, 172, 247
Richetts: 15
Rickets: 18
Rickey: 192
Rickman: 234
Ricks: 187
Ride: 105
Riddle: 36, 192, 222
Ridge: 237
Ridway: 215
Riggs: 38, 233, 235, 237
Right (Wright): 179
Riley: 55, 96, 174
Rimbrough: 194
Riney: 232, 235, 237, 239
Ring: 222
Ringe: 2
Rise: 156
Risk: 136, 186, 204, 245
Ritchey (Ritchie, Richey): 6, 31,
  45, 132, 151, 156
Ritter: 5, 96
Roach: 26
Robards: 18
Robbs: 57, 62, 95, 132, 232
Roberts (Robert): 24, 25, 36, 37,
  38, 44, 54, 69, 115, 122, 137,
  152, 157, 165, 166, 181, 191,
  237, 247
Robertson: 1, 31, 36, 104, 105,
  113, 120, 162, 166, 180, 186,
  187, 207, 235, 239
Robeson: 27, 105, 175
Robins: 209, 237
Robinson: 10, 24, 25, 27, 31,
  36, 58, 64, 73, 74, 95, 144,
  161, 166, 173, 175, 194, 201,
  209, 214, 215, 229, 235
Roby: 18
Rocken: 32
Rodes: 201, 204
Rodman: 54, 127
Roe: 228
Roger: 38
Rogers: 13, 18, 31, 38, 39,
  55, 64, 65, 95, 124, 125,
  137, 153, 188
Rodez: 161
Rohan: 235
Roland: 44

Rolling: 63
Rollins: 157
Rony: 234
Roon: 121
Roror: 25
Rose: 27, 143, 179
Rosell: 204, 228
Ross: 5, 29, 121, 145, 204, 223, 229
Rountree: 226
Routh: 35
Rowan: 183
Rowe (Row): 171, 239
Rowharrd: 248
Rowland: 31, 152, 165, 229, 246, 248
Rowling: 149
Rowzee: 74
Roy: 143
Royster: 101
Rozer: 96
Ruby: 16, 119
Rucker: 24, 25, 31, 33, 248, 249
Rudd: 15
Ruddell: 33
Ruddle: 147, 245, 249
Rudo: 105
Rudy: 3
Ruland: 201
Rule: 11
Rulon: 45
Rupard: 43
Ruppert: 92
Rush: 181
Rusk: 137
Rutherford: 65
Rutledge: 212, 215
Rutter: 72, 153
Russell: 15, 57, 96, 177, 188, 218, 237
Ryan: 39, 232, 234
Ryker: 209, 210
Ryland: 10, 138

Sacra: 70
Sacrey: 74
Saddler: 191
Sadler: 153, 194
Salee: 137
Sallie: 135, 136
Sample: 228, 247
Sampson: 65
Samuels: 16, 69, 71, 73, 74, 75, 115, 132, 187
Sandefer: 104, 105
Sanders: 45, 115, 174, 201, 224, 245
Sanderson: 166
Sandifor: 212
Sands: 185
Sandusky (Sodusky): 136, 137, 232, 237, 239
Sanford: 42
Sansberry: 236, 238
Sapp: 166
Sappington: 161, 163
Satterfield: 31, 32
Saunders: 5, 16, 65, 71, 72, 74, 132, 204, 223
Save: 144
Savilla: 51
Sawyer: 81, 82, 141, 215
Saxon: 28, 29, 32
Sayberd: 89
Scantlan (Scantlen): 64
Scatterfield: 225
Schooler: 94, 96, 163, 167
Scholl: 46
Scone: 12
Scott: 23, 25, 26, 29, 37, 41, 43, 45, 46, 58, 62, 70, 71, 73, 91, 96, 105, 113, 114, 124, 127, 135, 136, 138, 148, 149, 152, 153, 158, 162, 164, 171, 187, 194, 202, 248
Scraghan: 62
Scrivner: 166
Scroggins: 227
Scearcy: 166
Seaton: 55, 129, 132
Sebastian: 124, 126, 129, 130
Sebree: 167
Segler: 133
Sellars: 153
Sellers: 91, 96, 104
Seslee: 184
Settle: 71, 75, 245
Severs: 179
Shackleford: 115, 166, 208
Shadmore: 166
Shain (Shane): 18, 132
Shaker: 132
Shalley (Shall): 83, 187
Shaneey: 188
Shanhan: 12
Shankland: 135
Shanklin: 37, 138, 224

Shanly: 96
Shannon: 65, 133, 155, 209, 210, 213, 229, 245, 246
Sharp: 36, 46, 194, 229
Shaw: 32, 38, 65, 82, 115, 127, 133, 149
Shavor: 103, 211
Shearcliffe: 233
Shearly: 181
Sheave: 140
Sheeths: 195
Sheets: 69
Shell: 41
Shelly: 39, 141
Shelton: 96, 162, 223
Shepherd: 18, 133, 201, 202, 215, 246
Shepman: 32
Sherman: 96, 131, 225, 226
Sherrill: 240
Sherwood: 135
Shields: 154
Shiell: 72
Shildrey: 174
Shimor: 165
Shipp: 72, 202
Shirley: 51, 204
Shook: 11
Shoemaker: 55, 142, 237
Shoemate (Shumate): 55, 121, 187
Shorpe: 61
Shorp: 46
Short: 2, 121, 249, 167
Shropshire: 95
Shortridge: 65
Showmaker: 119
Shreador: 132
Shuck: 210
Shurliffe: 187
Shutts: 226
Shyrock: 58
Sigg: 28
Skelter: 61
Skiles: 227
Skinner: 32, 44
Skire: 11
Sibley: 105
Sidmer: 65
Silkwood: 126, 184
Simes: 132
Simeton: 4
Simmons: 17, 18, 19, 97, 187, 238
Simolt: 10

Simons: 33, 229
Simpson: 29, 42, 57, 137, 138, 212, 215, 221, 238
Simrall: 214
Sims: 27, 142, 238
Simson: 5
Sinclair: 203
Singleton: 52, 147, 223
Sisk: 121
Sissel: 238
Slack: 12, 82, 119, 237, 238
Slade: 149
Sladon: 101
Slagle: 11
Slater: 105
Slaton: 119
Slaughter: 74, 129, 130, 132, 142, 188
Slayton: 225, 235
Sloane: 12
Slocum: 155, 156
Slute: 9
Smallwood: 12, 42, 90
Smart: 74
Smathers: 55
Smeathers: 195
Smedley: 171, 172
Smelzer: 12
Smieser: 91
Smiley: 211
Smith: 5, 12, 23, 24, 26, 28, 29, 30, 32, 33, 35, 36, 42, 46, 65, 66, 69, 70, 71, 73, 74, 81, 86, 93, 94, 96, 103, 105, 113, 115, 119, 120, 127, 132, 135, 136, 137, 139, 141, 145, 149, 152, 153, 166, 169, 172, 175, 176, 179, 180, 182, 183, 188, 194, 195, 196, 201, 202, 203, 204, 207, 208, 211, 222, 224, 226, 227, 229, 237, 238, 248, 245
Smithers: 187
Smock: 232, 236, 237
Snap: 194
Snead: 245
Sneed: 247
Snell: 10, 204
Snider: 74, 97
Snithah: 77
Snoddy: 162, 163
Snoden: 39, 223
Snodgrass: 94, 95, 236
Snyder: 188, 215,
Solomon: 186

South: 162, 163
Southland: 42
Soverains: 129
Spalding: 217, 231, 234, 236, 237, 238
Sparker: 72
Sparks: 10, 231
Spears: 13, 28, 136, 138, 139
Speed: 136
Spencer: 29, 83, 103, 105, 153
Sperlin: 222
Spillman: 42, 52,
Spillard: 25
Spink: 154
Springer: 3, 231, 237, 238
Sprinkle: 66, 101, 102, 104
Spurgin: 45
Spurr: 57, 65
Spurrier: 184
Squires: 37, 82, 210
Stafford: 130
Stalcup: 238
Stalion: 23
Stallard: 213
Stallings: 17, 19
Stamfer: 42
Standiford: 132, 209
Stanislaw: 235
Stanfield: 23
Stanley: 32, 105, 172
Stanton: 169
Stapleton: 186
Stapp: 166, 204
Stator: 85
Stateler: 195
Stayton: 170, 231
Steadycorn: 96
Stearns: 194
Stears: 93
Steel: 19, 43, 61, 65, 123, 135, 138, 140, 173, 174, 192, 194, 210
Steen: 175
Stephens: 16, 32, 70, 75, 92, 105, 136, 147, 164, 177, 182, 202
Stephenson: 96, 120, 157, 166, 175, 203, 205, 223
Sterling: 217
Sterrett: 204
Stewart: 25, 38, 95, 114, 124, 129, 132, 141, 145, 149, 150, 151, 154, 173, 194, 218, 222, 229, 246

Stevall: 171
Stevens: 23, 32, 42
Stevenson: 10, 32, 38, 43, 92, 93, 95, 96 196, 245, 246, 248, 249
Stigler: 188
Stiles: 69, 203
Stillwell: 210, 237
Stinson: 131
Stoats: 51
Stockton: 5
Stoker: 192
Stokes: 32, 121, 122, 192
Stollard: 182
Stone: 30, 33, 59, 63, 65, 166, 215, 217
Stoner: 43, 131, 188
Stonestreet: 133, 136, 138, 139
Stovall: 81, 172
Stout: 209, 210
Stoval: 226, 229
Strange: 249
Strader: 84
Strain: 105
Strawhen: 161
Strawmatt: 30, 33
Stringer: 19
Stripling: 46
Strode: 11, 13, 44, 45, 46
Stromat: 27
Strothers: 229, 249
Stroud: 35, 132
Stuart: 64, 65, 83, 85, 96, 132, 179
Stubbs: 115
Stubblefield: 223
Stucker: 163
Stumberger: 2
Stump: 97, 179
Sturdivant: 55
Sturgeon: 122, 124, 129, 184
Stutts: 120, 203
Suddeth: 42, 44, 46
Suffrett: 140
Suggs: 103, 105, 106
Suggett: 65
Sullinger: 75, 247, 249
Sullivan: 132
Summers: 42, 46, 139, 157, 231
Sumner: 145
Summit: 192
Sutton: 114, 175
Swan: 64, 149
Swank: 85

Swaney: 46
Swasick: 10
Sweargen: 15
Swinford: 95
Swinney: 46

Taggart: 127
Talbert: 179
Talbot (Talbott): 51, 127, 138, 148, 157, 215,
Taliaferrio: 127, 223
Tamor: 65
Tandy: 57, 222
Tannahill: 188
Tanner: 33, 54, 195
Tapp: 139
Tapscott: 55
Tate: 72
Tatum: 167
Taul: 45, 58
Taylor: 9, 11, 46, 51, 53, 55, 71, 91, 94, 97, 131, 133, 139, 145, 148, 170, 186, 195, 197, 209, 212, 237, 238, 245, 248
Teagarden: 212
Templemore: 139
Templen: 13
Templeton: 143
Terment: 132
Terrill: 33, 215
Terry: 24, 104, 154, 223
Tevis (Tivis): 165, 167, 215
Thacker: 5
Tharp: 33, 85, 205
Thomas: 8, 12, 27, 33, 35, 38, 75, 81, 84, 85, 92, 136, 137, 139, 173, 174, 202, 208
Thomason: 18, 55, 204, 205, 248
Thompkins: 177
Thompson: 1, 12, 18, 26, 27, 33, 35, 39, 54, 75, 96, 103, 105, 120, 130, 156, 169, 174, 176, 192, 193, 194, 195, 196, 203, 205, 210, 222, 223, 236, 238, 247, 249
Thomson: 247, 248
Thornburg: 174, 182
Thornton: 24, 132
Threkeld: 176, 201, 215
Thruston: 124, 125, 126, 130, 131, 133
Throckmorton: 194
Thurman: 13,
Thurston: 115, 130, 132

Tichner (Tichenor): 54, 188
Tigert: 229
Tilford: 65, 176
Tilley: 214
Tilton: 192
Timberlake: 91, 94, 167
Timmons: 23
Tinnon: 119, 120, 122
Tinsley: 46, 207
Tipping: 75
Titsworth: 169
Todd: 13, 59, 62, 63, 64, 65, 66, 75, 133, 174, 247, 249
Todhunter: 139
Toland: 165
Tomlinson: 65
Tothers: 174
Towles: 101
Town: 103, 105
Townoon: 165
Townsend: 156, 157
Townsin: 46
Toy: 239
Trabue: 75
Tracy (Tracey): 6, 45, 75
Trant: 133
Travis (Trvis): 161
Tredway: 39
Tresper (Trosper): 141, 144
Tribble (Trible): 3, 41, 51
Trigg: 41, 69, 70
Trimble: 12, 13, 154
Triplett: 51, 53, 55, 58
Trotter: 6, 57, 62, 205
Trousdale (Trusdale): 194
Troutman: 19
Truman: 85
Trunk: 85
Tucker: 13, 41, 84, 95, 96, 115, 143, 163
Tuder: 6
Tuggle: 142, 144, 145
Tully: 133
Tumery: 65
Tunstall: 4, 75, 163
Turemah: 247
Turner: 139, 225, 229
Turney: 96
Turpin: 55, 133, 238, 249
Turvey: 96, 97
Twyman: 201
Tyler: 46, 131, 180, 208, 216
Tyree: 96
Tyson: 131

Underwood: 13, 29, 71, 114, 173, 177, 208, 246
Unsell: 179
Utter: 205
Utterback: 215

Vain: 236
Valendingham: 66
Vanarsdal: 173
Van Cleve: 173
Vankerk: 105
Van Matra (Van Matre): 82, 149
Van Meter: 128, 179
Vannada: 197
Vansdal: 212
Van Swoargen: 9
Vantrees: 174
Van Zandt: 203
Vardaman: 216
Varmay: 223
Vaughn: 19, 29, 70, 94, 124, 133, 205, 239
Vaught: 179, 180
Vawter: 167
Veatch: 246
Veech: 217
Venable: 139
Verkenny: 104
Vessels: 236
Vertrees: 81
Vier: 45
Vinard: 92
Vincent: 167
Viterow: 82
Vivion: 66
Vorhees (Vorhis): 72, 173, 210, 212

Wade: 24, 25, 133, 172
Waddell: 43
Waddle: 46
Wadill: 223
Wadington: 30
Wadlington: 25, 26, 28, 31, 33, 36, 39, 154
Waggoner: 6, 102, 123, 228, 247
Wainscott: 113
Wait: 194
Walden: 102
Walding: 167
Walker: 1, 2, 18, 35, 37, 43, 54, 64, 130, 135, 136, 137, 138, 139, 140, 151, 157, 178, 205, 210, 217, 223, 229, 235, 246

Wall: 23, 62, 201
Wallace: 11, 57, 66, 75, 131, 137, 197, 223, 226
Waller: 13, 231
Walters: 5, 15, 139, 140
Walton: 37, 92, 149, 151, 205, 234
Wamick: 205
Wammeter: 192
Warble: 113
Ward: 13, 41, 45, 66, 75, 91, 94, 115, 120, 128, 145, 158, 171, 180, 201, 204, 205
Wardlaw: 45, 104, 105
Ware: 46, 69, 70, 75, 148, 214, 245
Warren: 18, 46, 55, 71, 75, 203, 231, 239, 248, 249
Warfield: 91, 124, 143, 158
Warford: 185, 207
Warmock: 210
Warwick: 127
Washbough: 179
Washburn: 52, 237
Washington: 131
Watham: 231
Wathan (Wathen): 239
Watkins: 55, 132, 133, 202, 203, 221, 248
Watson: 12, 33, 46, 62, 97, 133, 154, 158, 167, 172
Watts: 81, 133, 167, 209, 215, 239
Waugh: 194, 246
Way: 239
Wayman: 44
Weaklin: 13.
Wear: 38, 39, 172
Weaver: 55, 216
Weathers: 18, 66, 135
Weatherspoon: 24, 228
Webb (Web): 13, 177
Webber: 138, 139, 213
Weeks: 29
Webster: 64, 66, 75
Weiger: 69, 72, 73, 75
Weir: 105, 120, 177, 179, 213
Weldon: 36
Wells: 19, 93, 131, 133, 155, 178, 180, 185, 194, 213, 234
Welsh (Welch): 63, 130, 136, 194

West: 13, 16, 70, 73, 114, 136, 139, 158, 191, 194
Westerfield: 51
Whaley: 57, 58, 62, 65
Wharton: 46, 204, 205
Whayne: 54, 55, 132
Wheeler: 3, 124, 161, 166, 167
Whicks: 115
Whips: 127
Whitaker (Whittaker, Whitker): 11, 92, 94, 156, 158, 197, 207, 209, 210, 211, 212, 214, 249
White: 6, 10, 29, 33, 46, 51, 55, 56, 70, 73, 113, 114, 115, 120, 135, 145, 147, 158, 167, 197, 216, 228
Whiteside: 35, 66, 122
Whitledge: 13
Whitley: 93
Whitnel: 30, 33
Whitney: 35
Whitsette: 158, 226, 227
Whitson: 114
Whitten: 229
Whitting: 133
Whittock: 133
Whyte: 157, 158
Wickersham: 13
Wicliff: 63, 122, 233
Wiett: 158
Wiggins: 194
Wigginton: 101
Wiglesworth (Wigglesworth): 91, 205
Wilborn: 6
Wilcox: 28, 158, 172, 210, 214, 216
Wilcoxson: 176
Wiley: 114, 193, 194
Wilhoit: 18
Wilhite: 181
Wilkey: 38
Wilkerson: 139
Wilkins (Wilkinson): 158, 224
Wilkinson: 61, 187, 225
Willbanks: 39
Willett: 187
Williams: 1, 5, 6, 24, 33, 41, 52, 71, 77, 82, 84, 86, 91, 94, 102, 103, 105, 128, 131, 135, 140, 152, 161, 172, 179, 186, 191, 193, 196, 213, 227, 246, 248
Williamson: 130, 140
Willing: 29
Willingham: 106
Willis: 140, 175
Willoughby: 225

Wills: 10, 46
Wilmouth: 128
Wilson: 1, 6, 11, 13, 23, 25, 46, 59, 62, 75, 84, 95, 105, 120, 121, 122, 135, 140, 145, 153, 157, 173, 177, 180, 181, 182, 192, 194, 195, 201, 293, 204, 205, 210, 212, 217, 226, 232, 239, 248, 249
Winchester: 81, 82, 85, 89
Winfield: 235
Wing: 53, 177
Wingate: 71, 75, 237
Winlock: 207, 212, 213
Winn: 6, 13, 46, 64, 65, 66, 174
Winten: 86
Winstead: 52
Winston: 54
Wise: 16, 41
Witherow: 29, 33, 69
Withers: 16, 71, 86, 89, 202
Wolf: 16
Womax: 28
Wood: 18, 25, 136, 152, 153, 158, 162, 164, 165, 170, 197, 201, 203, 216
Woodberry: 133
Woodford: 249
Woodman: 186
Woodridge: 75, 246
Woods: 38, 59, 66, 77, 144, 145, 162, 176, 248
Woodson: 2, 43, 92, 121, 122, 141
Woodward: 105, 196, 197
Wooley: 78, 239
Woolfolk: 53, 113, 169, 172, 247
Woolman: 46, 148
Woolridge: 13, 249
Woolscale: 167
Woolsey: 41
Wootton: 180
Worland: 233
Workman: 63, 191
Wortham: 188
Worthing: 182
Worthington: 52
Wray: 4
Wren: 173, 174, 229
Wright: 10, 15, 94, 133, 147, 175, 179, 185, 186, 228, 234
Wroton: 6
Wyatt: 145
Wyley (Wylie): 86, 148
Wymore: 62

Yancy: 4, 224
Yardley: 45
Yarnell: 97
Yates: 192, 193, 218, 233, 238
Yatsler: 83
Yenowine: 133
Yewell: 52
Yoder: 183, 188, 234
York: 39
Young: 1, 6, 13, 33, 39, 41, 44, 45,
 46, 57, 58, 59, 60, 61, 65, 66, 83,
 86, 114, 115, 135, 136, 138, 139, 148,
 154, 174, 177, 180, 181, 185, 187, 211,
 212, 223, 227, 245, 247, 248
Younger: 69, 70, 76

Zimmerman: 140, 179
Zook: 76
Zummutt: 97

APPENDIX.

INDEX TO WILLS AND INVENTORIES OF GALLATIN COUNTY AND GREEN COUNTY.

Abney John ---- 285	Hutcherson Anney ------- 287
Adams Richard --- 285	Hopkins John -----------287
Ayers Thomas --- 295	Jennings Jonathan ------ 295
Black Robert ----- 285	Jones William ----------287
Black Hugh ------ 285	Kelly Samuel ----------- 296
Bass Thomas ---- 285	King John -------------- 296
Blanton James --- 295	King William ---------- 296
Bledsoe Joseph -- 295	Lee Gresham ---------- 296
Bledsoe Rice ----- 295	Loyall Alex. ---------- 285
Bledsoe William ---295	Maddox James --------- 296
Bledsoe Zachariah 295	Martin John ------------ 287
Bloide William ----285	Marshall Joseph -------- 287
Bottom Robert ---- 285	Mathis William --------- 287
Bruce James ------ 295	Moore Robert ----------- 287
Buchannan James ---285	Munford James --------- 288
Buckner Horace -- 285	McCleland Joseph --------297
Calvert Philip -- 295	McMair Chris. -------- 297
Campbell Arch. -- 295	Peter Thomas --------- 288
Charlton Thomas -- 285	Peter William ---- 286
Chisholm William 285	Plummer Robert -------- 297
Clark Barnes ---- 285	Preeees David --------- 288
Clayton Jacob ---- 295	Rhea Alexander --------- 288
Colgan Henry ---- 285	Rice John -------------- 286
Cook Benjamin ---- 285	Rilley Mathew ---------- 297
Crawford John ---- 295	Russell George -------- 297
Dobson Joseph --- 286	Sanders------------ 288,297
Durrett Joel ----- 286	Scott John ------------- 297
Eaton William ---- 296	Sidebottom Charles ----- 268
Edmonson Philip-- 296	Simpson Elizabeth ----- 286
Farmer --- 286	Sizzer Will --------- 286
Forbis --- -----286	Skaggs Chas.,Henry -286, 289
Gardner John ------296	Smith Jas.-289,George ---- 297
Gaunt Sarah ------ 296	Spencer John -------- 297
Gills William ---- 286	Spillman William ---- 297
Glimblen Daniel -- 286	Stafford Henry -------- 297
Graves Benjamin -- 286	Sublett Valentine ------ 289
Gray Drakeford --- 296	Tandy John ----------- 297
Gullion Jeremiah --296	Tanner Joel ------------ 289
Gullion Thomas -- 296	Tibbs Daniel ----------- 289
Gum Jacob ------- 286	Vance Alexander --------289
Hait John --- -- 296	Vanpelt John -----------296
Harding Steven -- 286	Walker John, William --- 289
Harper James ---- 287	Ward David ----------- 289
Harris James ----- 287	White Samuel ----------- 289
Harris Vincent ----296	Wilson Spencer -------- 289
Hicks Thomas ---- 295	Whitaker R. ----------- 290
Hogeland William --287	Whitehead William ------ 290
Holloway Hugh --- 296	Williamson Joseph ------ 290
Hutcherson ----- 287	Williams William ------- 290
Hutcherson Nancy - 287	
Hutcherson David --287	

GREEN COUNTY

BOOK "A"

ABNEY, JOHN. June 14, 1788. Sept. 16, 1788. Wife: Isabella. Children: John, William. Ex: wife. Wit: William Chambers, Albert Humphreys.

ADAMS, RICHARD. Jan. 30, 1800. Nov. 10, 1800. Wife: Elizabeth. Children: John Griffen Adams, Samuel, Tabitha, Elizabeth Griffin, Ann, Sarah, Alice, Richard. Ex: Charles Carter, Peter Lyons, William Marshall, George W. Smith, sons Richard, Samuel and John. Wit: William Smith, Bowler Coche, William Danridge.

BASS, THOMAS. ------- 1812. ---------. Wife: Susanna. Children: Mosly, Judah, Robinson, Elizabeth, Thomas, Archibald, Peter, Therisa. Ex: Susanna and Peter Bass. Wit: George Moody, Josiah Bass, Lawerence Snapp.

BLACK, ROBERT. Feb. 1, 1805. ----------. Wife: Sarah. Children: John, Jane. Ex: John Black, John White. Wit: Robert Cox, Samuel Workman, John Moore.

BLACK, HUGH. Feb. 29, 1808. August Court, 1810. Children: Jeremiah Black, Sarah B-----a. Wit: Henry Clendenneu, William Simpson.

BLOIDE, WILLIAM. March 30, 1809. April 24, 1809. Wife: Keziah. Children: Ely, William, Esther McMurty, Prunett, Martha, Barsheba, Jacob, Steven, Tubby. Ex: wife. Wit: James Aiken, John Blyath.

BOTTOM, ROBERT. Nov. 14, 1814. July 24, 1815. Wife: Polly. No children. Wit: Will Buchner, William Mahan.

BUCHANNAN, JAMES. July 14, 1809. April 25, 1814. Sisters: Mary and Catharine Buchannan. Ex: Pouncy Anderson, Isaac Tate, Andrew Campbell. Wit: James Buchannan, John Murphy, Alexander Buchannan.

BUCKNER, AYLETT. May 25, 1805. ---------------, Children: Thornton, Caty J. Taylor, Louisa, Elizabeth, John. John Y. Taylor (son-in-law) guardian for John Buckner, infant heir. Wit: Anthony Thornton, Andrew Chaudowin, David Chaudowin, John B. Smith.

BUCKNER, HORACE. Dec. 10, 1810. ----- 1810. Sons: William, John. Ex: William Buckner, John Y. Taylor. Wit: Isaac Gibbons, John Buckner, Eliza A. Gibbons.

CASEY, MICAJAH. Nov. 9, 1806. ---------, Wife: Nansey. Bro. John Casey. Ex: Samuel Durham, John Chandler. Wit: Ben Chisholm, Granville Chisholm, Thomas Smith.

CHARLTON, THOMAS. Dec. 20, 1804. -----. Legatees: Peggy Polly, Jincy Mourning, John Mourning, Sally Niffly, James Mourning, Daniel Mourning, Samuel Mourning, Nansie Mourning. Ex: Roger and John Mourning. Wit: James Craig, Ben Ball.

CHISHOLM, WILLIAM. Sept. 9, 1795. ---------. Wife: Ann. Children: not named. Ex: John Brents, Samuel Brown, Benjamin Chisholm, Ann Chisholm. Wit: Samuel Brown, John Brents, Benjamin Chisholm.

CLARK, BARNES. Oct. 18, 1796. Dec. 13, 1796. Wife: Elizabeth. Children: William, Tabby, Chandler, Eliza. Ex: Elizabeth Clark, John Brents, Samuel Brents. Wit: John J. Walker, Peter Bass, John J. Brents.

COLGAN, HENRY. Feb. 15, 1816. March 25, 1816. Wife: Susanna. Children: mentioned but not named. Ex: wife. Wit: Joseph Cogseal, William Gouch, William Ralston.

COOK, BENJAMIN. March 20, 1806. April 7, 1806. Wife: Catharine. Children: William B. Cook, Steven Cook (son-in-law). Other children mentioned but not named. Ex: Catharine, William B. and Steven Cook. Wit: Thomas Elliotte, James Daniel, Joseph Wyatte.

DOBSON, JOSEPH. Dec. 18, 1813. March 28, 1814. Wife: Elizabeth. Children: mentioned but not named. Ex: wife. Wit: Thomas Bell, Edward Lewis, William Mathurson.

DURRETT, JOEL. Aug. 5, 1813. Sept. 26, 1814. Wife: Sarah Durett. Children: John, Larkin, Nansie, Betsie, Fanny, Milly, Dinah, heirs of son Achilles. Ex: Sarah Durrett, John Chandler, John Smith. Wit: Thomas Smith, Lucy Smith, Richard Hord, Josiah Bass.

FARMER, WILLIAM. May 17, 1816. Sept. 25, 1815. Wife: Mary. Children: Labam, others mentioned but not named. Ex: wife. Wit: James Craig, Robert Craig, Henry Moore.

FORBIS, ROBERT. --- 1808. June 28, 1813. Wife: Mary. Children: Juliet, Mariah, Patsy, Eliza, Yeats, Richard, David. Ex: wife. Wit: Fredrick Moss, J. Blane, Will Brownlee.

GIMBLEN, DANIEL. Sept. 12, 1806. Nov. 6, 1806. Wife: Ann. Ex: wife. Wit: Joseph Benton, Samuel Marshall, John Cannon.

GRAVES, BENJAMIN. Jan. 6, 1803. -----------. Wife: Mary. Children: Betsy Burks (wife of Silas Burks), Polly Price (wife of Eilam Price). Ex: wife. Wit: James Allen, John Emerson, Joshua Hall.

GUM, JACOB. Oct. 9, 1792. Nov. 20, 1792. Wife: Margaret. Children: Jacob, Eleanor Bell, Sarah Montgomery, Lydia Skaggs, Charles, Jihu, Jessie, Henry Bell, Elijah, Mary, Nansie. Ex: James Shields, Samuel Watt. Wit: Zephenias Bell, Rhoda Gum.

HARDING, STEVEN. Feb. 25, 1815. March 25, 1816. Wife: Elizabeth. Children: Asa, Steven, John, Margaret, Prudence, Elizabeth, Mary, Rebecca. Gr. daus: Elizabeth, Nancy and Susanna Hoves, children of son Abraham, decd. Ex: John C. Harding, Asa Harding. Wit: Lewis Webb, Aaron Harding.

HARPER, JAMES. March 9, 1814. July 25, 1814. Wife: Agnes. Children: Lucy, Agnes, Major, Francis. Ex: wife, James White, John Moore. Wit: Major Parson,

Jonathan Peterson.

HARRIS, JAMES. March 17, 1798. -----. Wife: Ann. Children: Josiah, Alexander, James, William, Samuel, Sally, Susanna, Mary. Wit: Jesse Gray, John Moore, John Bunton, Will Bunton.

HOGELAND, WILLIAM. Jan. 13, 1799. --------. Wife: Elizabeth. Children: Abraham, James, Ann. Ex: Elizabeth Hogeland. Wit: Isaac Hogeland, Ben Bruster, Deerskin Tibbs.

HUTCHERSON, WILLIAM. Nov. 9, 1805. Jan. 1806. Wife: Nancy. Ex: wife, Hut. B. Hutcherson. Wit: W. Barnett, David Hutcherson, Jr.

HUTCHERSON, NANCY. March 4, 1808. May 23, 1808. Brother: Samuel Hutcherson. Niece: Nancy Mason. Father: David Hutcherson. Ex: David Hutcherson. Wit: W. Barnet, John McKinney, John Biggs.

HUTCHERSON, DAVID. Sept. 23, 1811. 4th Monday, Nov., 1811. Wife: Hannah. Children: John, William, Mathew, Joseph, Hatty, Thomas, Samuel, Hannah Mason, Christopher Brooks (son-in-law), Ann Hutcherson (dau.-in-law). Ex: Hannah Hutcherson, son Mathew. Wit: William Barnett, James Wyatt, John Atwell.

HUTCHERSON, DAVID. Dec. 7, 1809. Jan. 22, 1810. Wife: Anne. Dau: Elizabeth. Ex: Anne Hutcherson, Hutty B. Hutcherson. Wit: William Rhea, David Hutcherson, Sr., Richard Atwell.

HUTCHERSON, ANNEY. May 26, 1809. July 27, 1812. Dau: Elizabeth Hutcherson. Bros: William, Alexander and John Rhea. Ex: William Rhea. Wit: W. Barnet, Belfield Henry, Alexander Brownlee.

HOPKINS, JOHN. Oct. 12, 1813. Oct. 25, 1813. Wife: Martha. Children: Washington, Polly Moore (stepdaughter). Ex: Martha Hopkins, William McNabb, Aaron Blakeman. Wit: John Chinault, John Emerson, D. McDaniel.

JONES, WILLIAM. April 28, 1804. ---------. Wife: Nancy. Children: mentioned but not named. Ex: wife. Wit: David Vance, Thomas Smith, Robert Forbis.

LOYALL, ALEXANDER. March 6, 1805. ---------. Wife: Elizabeth. Ex: wife. Wit: Holman Rice, Peter Loyall, Sarah Blevens, Nancy Loyall, Sally Moran, Abraham Mayes.

MARTIN, JOHN. Nov. 13, 1807. May 1808. Wife: Peggy. Children: John, Francis, Charles, Peggy, Mariah, Letty, Jinney, James, Noal. Ex: Ely C. Murray, James McGill.

MARSHALL, JOSEPH. Jan. 6, 1811. Codcil. Jan. 17, 1811. County Court, 1811. Wife: Frances. Dau: Patsy Marshall. Ex: John Marshall, Robert Jarboe. Wit: Samuel Brents, Samuel Marshall, Jr.

MATHIS, WILLIAM. August 17, 1814. Sept. 26, 1814. Wife: Jeminah. Children: Mentioned but not named. Ex: Edward Lewis, assisted by Johnson Graham and

Joel Gordon. Wit: Eliphaet Jarves, Henry Bonnar, William Graham, Patrick Deshay, James Goldsby, Jr.

MOORE, ROBERT. July 28, 1808. -----. Wife: Susannah. Children: Thomas, John, others but not named. Ex: Thomas and John Moore. Wit: Richard Walker, William Moore, Gunthry Moore.

MUNFORD, JAMES. April 13, 1808. -----. Wife: Martha Williams Munford. Children: Jane Watsin, Alethea Scott. Ex: wife, William Munford. Wit: Richard Munford, Robert Carter, James Munford.

PREECES, DAVID. Feb. 11, 1811. March 25, 1811. Wife: Ann. Children: Levicey, Eleanor Scott, William Powell Preeces, John, Jonathan, Mary Pepper, Priscilla Perry, Lydia Money, Daniel, Susannah Mears. Ex: none. Wit: Elias Barbee, James Money, Zachariah Nance.

PETERS, THOMAS. Feb. 25, 1814. Oct. 24, 1814. Wife: Rhody. Children: Betsie, others not named. Ex: none. Wit: Daniel White, John Carlile, Sarah Carlile.

PRICE, WILLIAM. June 10, 1813. March 28, 1814. Wife: Elizabeth. Children: William(inheritance to go to his wife, Nancy, at death), Sally Moss(wife of William Moss), ----- Allen(wife of David Allen). Gr. child: William Price Allen, Robert Price, Mary Price. Ex: William, Robert and William H. Price. Wit: Josiah Moss, John Biggs, James Allen.

RHEA, ALEXANDER. March 9, 1815. March 27, 1815. Wife: Polly. Ex: wife, Daniel Brown. Wit: William Gray, James Allen.

RICE, JOHN. March 23, 1815. Sept. 15, 1815. Wife: Laruhaney. Children: seven mentioned but not named. Ex: wife, David Rice. Wit: Samuel Harding, Aaron Harding.

SANDERS, SAMUEL. Sept. 20, 1807. -----. Wife: Anna. Children: mentioned but not named. Ex: James Munford, Richard Munford. Wit: John Whitlow, Elizabeth McCubbin.

SIDEBOTTOM, CHARLES. Feb. 11, 1806. --------. Wife: Susannah. Children: mentioned but not named. Wit: William Roundtree, William Miller, Thomas Roundtree, Charles Sidebottom.

SIMPSON, ELIZABETH. Aug. 3, 1815. Jan. 22, 1816. Children: Sarah Patton, William Simpson, David Simpson, Elizabeth Patton, Laura Joan, Polly Patton. Gr. child: 4 mentioned but not named. Ex: Edward Lowis, Richard Munford. Wit: Thomas Bell, M., Gibson, Britton and Robert Carter, Jr.

SIZZER, WILL. Feb. 18, 1808. --------. This estate was bequeathed to needy poor children. Ex: William Simpson. Wit: John Moore, Dempsey Guthria, Michael Simpson.

SKAGGS, CHARLES. Feb. 9, 1815. March 28, 1816. Wife: Lucy. Children: Moses, Archibald, Rachel Blevons, Nancy Meredith, Fredrick, Polly Gray, Sally, Robertson, Thomas, Tompy Bolcher(wife of Berry Bolcher). Ex: Thomas Skaggs.

Wit: James Akin, Charles Blevens, Charity Howell, William G. Owens, Zachariah Nance.

SKAGGS, HENRY. April 15, 1809. Dec., 1810. Children: Sarah, Stephen, Soloman, Lucy Stacey, Rachel Ray, Nancy De Spain, Polly Combs, James Skaggs (son-in-law). Ex: James Skaggs, Elias Barbee. Wit: Elias Barbee, John Barbee, Larkin Durrett, James Rafity, William Barbee.

SMITH, JAMES. April 22, 1810. April 22, 1811. Wife: Elizabeth. Children: George, John, Betie, Susannah, two daughters mentioned but not named. Ex: Elizabeth, John and George Smith. Wit: B. Chisholm, William Durrett, Richard Hord.

SUBLETT, VALENTINE. Feb. 11, 1809. -------. Wife: Margaret. Children: Allen Branch, Field, William. Ex: Liberty Green, Daniel Henry. Wit: James Craig, John Buchannan.

TANNER, JOEL. June 9, 1811. July 27, 1812. Wife: Mary. " If Mary Tanner should have a child nine months after my death let it be either a boy or girl, I give to it half of my estate." Ex: Mary Tanner, George Tibbs. Wit: Deerskin Tibbs, Margaret Tibbs, John Tibbs.

TIBBS, DANIEL. Nov. 25, 1814. July 24, 1815. Legatees: Lenah Tibbs(mother), Elizabeth Tibbs, Sarah Edrington(sisters), Joshua Tibbs(brother). Ex: George Tibbs, John Johnson. Wit: Isham Ready, William Rhea, Jr.

VANCE, ALEXANDER. March 30, 1805. Dec. 24, 1810. Wife: Jane. Legatees: son William, Jeremiah Cleatheron, Ruth Trent, William Vance, Clerasy, Belchex and Ann Skaggs. Ex: William Vance, Britton Trent(son-in-law). Wit: Thomas Hall, John M. Daniel, William Downing.

WALKER, JOHN. April 27, 1799. ---------. Son: Francis. Ex: William Buckner, John Helm. Wit: Henry Sanders, Sr., Henry Sanders, Marshall Reed.

WALKER, WILLIAM. Nov. 30, 1801. May 7, 1802. Wife: Elizabeth. Children: Thomas, Jeremiah, Nancy. Provisions heretofore made to John Jones Walker, James Walker, Martha Tolbert Bond. Ex: Elizabeth Walker, Luke Ford. Wit: John J. Brents, David Acre, Joshua Brents.

WARD, DAVID. Oct. 12, 1815. Oct. 23, 1815. Wife: Polly. Father: William. Ex: Ignatus Hazell. Wit: Benett Lucuss, Jedson Hazell.

WHITE, SAMUEL. Nov. 12, 1814. Jan. 22, 1816. Wife: Jane White. Children: Samuel, Jane, Nancy Carden, Betsy Cox. Ex: Jane R. White, Benjamin T. Moss, Francis C. Drake. Wit: Joseph Ellison, William Phillips.

WILSON, SPENCER. ------- 1799. --------. Wife: Lucy. Children: Mentioned but not named. Nuncupative will.

(These wills and inventories were copied by Mr. Rhea H. Tucker, Greenburg, Kentucky.)

WILL BOOK "A"

The following are the names of those of whom an inventory has been filed for Record, in the office of the Clerk of the Green County Court.

Allen, John C.   April 24, 1810.
Andrew, William   June 29, 1810.

Bartlett, John   ------------
Bass, Josiah   Oct. 22, 1812.
Bernard, Valentine   April 30, 1808.
Black, Robert   Aug., 1805.
Bloide, William   May 20, 1809.
Brown, Ignacious   April 22, 1811.
Buckner, Horace   March 20, 1811

Cantril, Zebulon   Jan. 9, 1808.
Caulks, James   Jan. 21, 1813.
Carey, John   ----- 1806.
Charlton, Thomas   Oct. 3, 1805.
Chisholm, Ann   April, 1811.
Clark, Barnes   ------------
Cook, Thomas   Feb. 5, 1812.

Damron, George   August 13, 1801.
Davis, George   Dec. 2, 1806.
Dobson, Robert   April 5, 1806.
Downing, Benjamin   Oct. 28, 1803

Frazier, Martin   July 16, 1798.
Ford, Luke   ---------------

Gills, William   1804 & 1805
Goldsby, William   Nov. 22, 1803.
Gumpton, Stephen   Sept. 20, 1804.
Gum, Jacob   ----- 1804.

Harris, James   July 3, 1798.
Hazell, Hanson   April 24, 1812.
Hicks, Thomas   Jan. 9, 1810.
Hovice, George   June 26, 1801.
Howerton, John   April 15, 1805.
Hutcherson, Anney   Aug. 25, 1812.

Hutcherson, Benj.   March 30, 1807.
Hutcherson, David   Feb. 8, 1810.
Hutcherson, David   Jan. 27, 1812.

Jones, William   April 30, 1808.

Martin, John   Feb. 24, 1808.
Marshall, Joseph   Jan. 29, 1811.
McCandles, William   Dec. 25, 1799.
McQueen, Benj.   Feb. 16, 1801.
Miller, Thomas   July 24, 1809.
Moore, Samuel   --------------
Moore, John   ----------------
Moore, William   -------------
Moore, Robert   August 1808.

Patterson, Jonathan   May 13, 1808.
Pimberton, George   ----------
Piper, Benjamin   Feb. 1802.
Price, David   Jan., 1812.

Simpson, Michael   ---------
Sizzer, William   Jan. 9, 1809.
Skaggs, Henry   Jan. 27, 1812.
Skaggs, Chadrack   -----------
Smith, Charles   May 1802.
Smith, James   Oct. 28, 1811.
Speaks, Jane   ---------------
Sublett, Littleberry   July, 1800.

Vance, Alexander   Dec., 1810.

Walker, John   ----------
Walker, William   Jan. 26, 1803.
Wakefield, Allen M.   Jan. 23, 1809.
Whitlock, Benjamin   -------------
Withers, Hollingsworth   Jan. 2, 1804.
Winlock, William   June 28, 1810.

Inventory: ------- Thomas Hicks, Deceased.

Agreeable to an order of the Green County Court We the undersigned Appraisers have proceeded this 9th day of January, 1812, after first being duly sworn for the purpose to view and appraise all the personal estate od Thomas Hicks, Decd., that were unto us produced. An inventory and appraisal is as follows, towit:-

2 Kettles, 2 pots, 2 ovens, 5 pr. hooks, 1 wire sieve, 1 loom	$ 20.50
2 Pot racks, ladle, flesh fork, 4 bells, 1 churn, pigging etc.	6.25
5 Axes $ 4.50, 1 set waggon boxes, 2 iron wedges, 1 joiner	8.25
3 Brasheer plows, 1 shovel plow & irons, 4 pr. cotton cards	15.00
1 Basket containing sundry tools, 1 halter chain	4.00
Sundry coopers tools, drawing knife & chisel, 1 bridle	2.75
1 Sythe, 1 rifle gun, 1 shot pouch, 2 pr. giers	16.50
1 Hand saw, 3 weeding hoes, 1 grubbing hoe, 1 womans saddle	7.50
1 Spinning wheel, reel, coffee mill, 2 mens saddles and bridles	7.50
1 Pr. sad irons, 6 butter plates, 7 d jars	5.00
2 Keggs 1.75, 3 basons, 3 plates, coffee pot $ 3.50	5.25
2 Stone butter pots, 4 earthen dishes, 6 plates, 1 bowl and pitcher	8.00
1 Tea pot, set of spoons, tea cup and saucers, tumblers, 3 canesters	4.25
1 Set knives and forks, tin pans, spoons etc., 1 bottle and mugg	5.50
1 Cupboard $ 12.00, 1 do $ 14.00, 1 bureau $ 12.00	38.00
1 Case of razors, box, sundry books, 1 looking glass	4.25
1 Iron tea kettle, trunk, 2 half round tables, 2 common tables	20.25
1 Dozen chairs $ 7.00, 1 cloathes brush, candle sticks, snuffers	1.75
1 Small wheel, 2 tubs, 1 hackle and 2 slays, 1 kegg, 3 chests	11.75
4 Beds and furniture A	246.00
1 Trundle bed, 1 cotton wheel and cards	4.75
1 Negro woman, Dinah	75.00
1 Negro child	50.00
1 Negro woman (50 years old)	140.00
1 Negro fellor for 1 year	55.00
1 Black mare & colt $ 20.00, 1 sorrel filly $ 40.00	60.00
1 Black and bay filly $ 40.00, 10 sheep $ 15.00, 13 cattle	107.00
1 Cart and steers	60.00
Sundry hogs	50.75
	1098.50

John Sandidge
James Mitchell   Appraisers
Benjamin Rice

HARRISON COUNTY INVENTORIES.

BOOK "A"

Rankin David. June 6, 1796.
Graham Jarett. July - 1797.
Furnace Samuel. April, 1796.
Tittle Peter. August, 1797.
Thompson William. " 1796.
Garnett May. October, 1796.
Jones Benjamin. August, 1798.
Doyle Edward. March, 1797.
Campbell Joseph. October, 1797.
Moore John. January, 1798.
Nealey Benj. July 1798.
Lemmon Jacob. Jaunry, 1799.
Gilbreath Evan. " "
Thompson Robert. Jan. 6, 1799.
Scott Archibald. August, 1799.
Hicks Nathaniel. May, 1799.
Laughland James. August, 1799.
Shaw James. January, 1800.
Jameson George. March, 1800.
McPheters James. March, 1800.
Vanderson Bernard. May, 1800.
Anderson John. May, 1800.
McFall John. August, 1800.
Clayton James. August 1800.
Moore Samuel. January, 1801.
Vance John. July, 1801.
Langley Abrm. and Margaret. Aug. 1801.
Stephenson John. December, 1801.
Clough John. December, 1801.
Frazier George. January, 1802.
Coonrod Henry. March, 1802.
Thornley Epaphroditus. June, 1802.
Henderstrot Jacob. January, 1803.
King Joshua. October, 1802.
Snodgrass Sam'l. Jan. 1803.
Hale Robert. December, 1802.
Tittle James. Oct. 1803.
Dryden Thomas. Jan. 1804.
Stephenson Joseph. Jan. 1804.
Mitts John. April, 1804.
Dryden David. May 1804.
Safford Henry. July, 1804.
Hutchison Elizabeth. March, 1805.
McNees John. May, 1805.
Hutcherson John. October, 1805.
Frye Jacob. January, 1806.
Scott James. Feb. 1806.
McMillen James. May, 1806.
Eads Jonathan. May, 1806.
Ross James. October, 1806.
McIllvain John. October, 1807.

Dunn Samuel. January, 1807.
Carrick John. January, 1807.
Adams Chas. W. Feb. 1807.
Richey Stuart. April, 1807.
Dills David. May 1807.
McKee William. August, 1807.
Naylor Thomas. October, 1807.
Smith John. November, 1807.
Loan Isaac. Nov. 6, 1807.
Hawkins Alex. H. January, 1808.
Shields David. April, 1808.
Turvy William. April, 1808.
Slade Ezekiel. April, 1808.
Coleman Henry. August, 1808.
Green Thomas. July, 1808.
Hutcherson John. July, 1808.
Angell John. October, 1808.
Hutcherson Mary. Dec. 1808.
Ralston David. January, 1809.
McCadycorn David. January, 1809.
Pickett John. February, 1809.
Hamilton George. " "
Ross Alexander. Jan. 1809.
Wells John. July, 1809.
Jones John. July 1809.
Yarnall Jep. August 1809.

Stevenson Joseph. August, 1809.
Lewis William. Nov. 1809.
Shearman John. Jan. 1809.
Doan Hezekiah. January, 1810.
Miller Hugh. March, 1810.
Coonrod Joseph. March, 1810.
McMillen James. July, 1810.
Colvill James. November, 1810.
Gilliam Charles. December, 1810.
Henson George. March, 1811.
Page Elijah. March, 1811.
Hopkin Thomas. April, 1811.
Snood Richard. April, 1811.
Hannon James M. March, 1811.
Thompson Robert. July, 1811.
Pendleton Philip. July, 1811.
Lowell Andrew. August, 1811.
Claypole Jonathan. October, 1811.
Schofield John. November, 1811.
Stevenson Thomas. May, 1812.
Carnagy John. July, 1812.
Holiday William. May, 1812.
Stevenson William. May, 1812.
Ritter Michael. August, 1812.

Brownfield Nancy. August, 1812.
Galloway William. August, 1812.
Coleman Frances. November, 1812.
Blackburn James. December, 1812.
Jaquess Isaac. January, 1813.
Edwards Henry. April, 1813.
Swanson John. April 1813.
Gordon James. May, 1813.
Hall Joshua. July, 1813.
Swinford Elisha. " "
Ellis William. " "
Hinston George. " "
Abner George. " "
Artle Sophia. August, 1813.
Hannon James M. " "
Norman Caleb. " "
Lilly Joshua. November, 1813.
Campbell Lindsey. " "
Dunn Hugh S. " "
Scott Robert. December, 1813.
Hall William. May, 1814.
Endicott William. " "
Givens George. February, 1814.
Johnson Emanuel. April, 1814.
Spindle Edmond. January, 1814.
Marsh Samuel. July, 1814.
Logan Samuel. December, 1813.
Clements Benjamin. " "
Herring William. July, 1814.
Herring William. July, 1814.
Hamilton David. July 1814.
Whitsit Joseph. October, 1814.
Pickens James. " "
Holland William. August, 1814.
Nesbitt Samuel. November, 1814.
Horning Jonathan. July, 1814.
Wall John. November, 1814.
Phillips William. " "
Blair Joseph. December, 1814.
Chambers James. January, 1815.
Ward William. October, 1814.
Godman William B. February, 1815.
Brown Samuel. October, 1814.
Laughland Robert. January, 1815.
Rolland John. October, 1814.
Mahan Thomas. January, 1815.
Spindle Edmond. " "
Hutcherson George. April, 1815.
Hamilton David. " "
Rankin Simeon. " "
Walton Thomas. May, 1815.
King Joseph. August, 1815.
Griffith Robert. October, 1815.

Tucker William. July, 1815.
Woods Archibald. August, 1815.
Crutchlow James. " "
Denny Thomas. October, 1815.
Madison Henry. " "
Jackson Joshua. January, 1816.
Bell Joseph. February, 1816.
Henry John. " "
Zumwalt George. April, 1816.
Miller John. May, 1816.
McClain Robert. April, 1816.
Arbry Linsey. August, 1816.
Wells William. July, 1816.
Forest Memorial. November, 1816.
Robb James. May, 1816.
Picket Wilson. Jan. 1817.
Jones George. July, 1816.
Simmons Mark. August, 1816.
Galbreath John. October, 1816.
Martin Ralph. December, 1816.
Coppage Charles. August, 1816.
Grig Daniel. October, 1816.
Tizdale Richard. February, 1817.
Boyd Thomas. October, 1817.
Perrin William C. November, 1817.
Watson James. " "
McClain Samuel. October, 1817.
Patton Joseph. February, 1817.
Eckler Samuel. August, 1817.
McMillin Sam'l. February, 1817.
Harden John. August, 1817.
Phillips Thomas. December, 1817.
Taylor Samuel. November, 1817.
Story Asa. January, 1818.
Pock Gasper. Feruary, 1818.
Henry John. April, 1818.
Cox Charles M. " "
Neale Benj. " "
Barns John. " "
Lewis William. August, 1818.
Perrin Joseph L. " "
Finley George. " "
Turner George. October, 1818.

GALLATIN COUNTY

BOOK A

AYERS, THOMAS. Nov. II, I8II. May II, 1812. Wife: Mary. Legatees: children of son Thomas Cornelius, sons Daniel C. and Lewis. Wit: John Scott, Sallie Jones. Apprs: John Scott, James Jones, William Blanton, Allen A. Hamilton.

BLANTON, JAMES. Sept. 18, 1814. Feb. 1815. Wife: Jane. Twelve Children. Ex: Jane Blanton, John Scott. Wit: John Barnard, Danc Gambrial, Mose Jackson.

BLEDSOE, JOSEPH. Inventory. Oct. 24, 1812. March 1813.

BLEDSOE, JOSEPH. July 12, 1812. Sept. II, 1812. Wife: Nancy. Children: John, Moses, Bob, Gilbert. Admr: Isaac Bledsoe, Moses Jackson. Wit: Isaac Ellis, Abraham Bledsoe, James Blanton, Robert Scanland.

BLEDSOE, RICE. Inventory. Sept. 9, 1811. Sept. II, 1811. Apprs: John Tandy, Samuel Sanders, Pierce Butler.

BLEDSOE, WILLIAM. Feb. 26, 1817. Oct. 14, 1817. Wife and children mentioned but not named. Admr: John Brock. Wit: Henry Yates, Robert Yates, Robert Guinea.

BLEDSOE, ZACHARIAH. Feb. I, 1815. March 1815. Wife: Anne. Admrs: John and Mose Bledsoe. Wit: Alex. Darter, Samuel Sanders, John B. Shelton.

BRUCE, JAMES. Inventory. Dec. 4, 1813. Apprs: Robert Sale, John Elliston, John Steger.

CALVERT, PHILIP. Inventory. March 22, 1800. March 1802. Apprs: Thomas Ayers, Joshua Baker, John Ray, Samuel Snow.

CAMPBELL, ARCHIBALD. Inventory. Oct. 6, 1806. Apprs: William Boling, William Blanton, James Coghill.

CLAYTON, JACOB. Inventory. Jan. 8, 1807. Admr: Margaret Clayton. Apprs: John M. Price, Thomas Craig, David Owens. Wit: Cornelius Coghil, Dutton Lane.

CLAYTON, JACOB. Oct. 12, 1808. June 1809. Apprs: James Wilson, J. Searce, Edward Holman.

CRAWFORD, JOHN. Inventory. May 27, 1805. Admr: Sarah Crawford. Apprs: Alfred Vivlett, Richard Masterson, William Ellis, Mose Ray.

CRAWFORD, JOHN. Inventory. Jan. 10, 1806. Apprs: John Vivlett, Thomas Lewis.

EATON, WILLIAM. Sept. 1, 1817. Wife: Anne. Apprs: John McNeal, Green W. Shelton, John D. Alexander. Admrs: Wife Anne, Samuel Todd.

EDMONSON, PHILIP. Feb. 27, 1805. March 1805. Wife: Susana. Legatees: son Robert and his heirs. Ex: Robert Sale, William Blanton. Wit: Moses Ray, Moses Jackson, James Furnish. Inventory, April 25, 1805. Apprs: William Ellis, Robert Sale.

GARDNER, JOHN. April 29, 1806. Aug. 1806. Wife: Nancy. Wife to have estate as long as she remains his widow. Mentions children. Wit: Robert King, John Conway, John Taylor.

GAUNT, SARAH. Dec. 9, 1800. April 10, 1801. Legatee: Daughter. Wit: Sally Sullinger.

GRAY, DRAKEFORD. Inventory. Sept. 1804. Aprs: Hugh Gatewood, Joseph Bledsoe, John Wood. Ex: Jesse Gray.

GULLION, JEREMIAH. Inventory. Sept. 1, 1816. Admr: Belle Gullion. Apprs: John Brown, Jerry Gullion, John Gullion.

GULLION, THOMAS. Inventory. May 11, 1810. Admr: Jeremiah Gullion. Wit: Jeremiah Gullion, Janet Dement.

HAIT, JOHN. June 15, 1814. June 30, 1814. Wife: Margaret. Children: mentioned but not named. Ex: wife. Apprs: Dane Owens, Thomas Carraco, Samuel Sanders.

HARRIS, VINCENT. Inventory. June 23, 1806. Apprs: John Lister, James Coghill, Daniel Owens.

HOLLOWAY, HUGH. July 1817. Sept. 1817. Heirs but not named.

JENNINGS, JONATHAN. Dec. 23, 1810. Sept. 1816. Wit: John Bond, Joseph Gray, Moses Baker. Admr: Samuel Todd.

JENNINGS, JONATHAN. Jan. 14, 1800. March 1817. Wife: Elizabeth. Admr: wife. Wit: John Gatewood.

KELLY, SAMUEL. Jan. 11, 1813. Feb. 8, 1813. Wife: Mary. Wit: Robert King, John Thomas, Osbourne King. Admr: Mary King.

KING, JOHN. Dec. 23, 1805. Admr: Robert King.

KING, WILLIAM. Inventory. Jan. 1, 1806. Wit: P. B. Butler.

KING, WILLIAM. Jan. 18, 1800. Wife: Elizabeth. Wit: Prisley Gray, Jesse Connell, George Lewis.

LEE, GRESHAM. Feb. 10, 1803. March 1, 1803. Heirs but not named. Wit: Martin Hawkin, Percival Butler, Robert Scanland.

MADDOX, JAMES. Inventory. Oct. 6, 1806. Apprs: Samuel Owens, William Blanton,

Isaac Jones.

McCLELAND, JOSEPH. July 14, 1817. Sept. 1817. Wife: Mary Mills. Son: Andrew H. Ex: Wife, Henry Winslow, ---- Gatewood. Wit: James R. Lowe, Jas. Tarbitt, J. B. Bernard.

McMAIR, CHRISTIAN. June 15, 1801. May 10, 1803. Dau: Margaret. Gr. Child: Robert and Christian. Wit: Margaret Hawkins, Mary Plummer, Mary Clany.

McMAIR, CHRISTIAN. Inventory. Aug. 27, 1805. Apprs: Gresham Lee, George Boling, James Coghill.

PLUMMER, ROBERT. Feb. 8, 1817. March 10, 1817. Wife: Mary. Children: William, Robert, James, Blair, John, Dudley, Mary Whitman. Ex: wife.

RILLEY, MATHEW. Inventory. Feb. 7, 1809. May 4, 1810. Apprs: Daniel Barbie, George Mayfield, Presly Gray. Admr: Elijah Craig.

RUSSELL, GEORGE. May 29, 1807. March 15, 1815. Legatee: Sister Sarah Stewart Roote. Wit: Robert Plummer, Ashford Vivlet, Richard Butler.

SANDERS, JOHN. Jan. 2, 1804. Jan. 10, 1804. Wife: Nancy. Son: Samuel. Ex: James Smith, Thomas Samuel. Wit: John M. Price, David Owen, Benjamin Craig, Lewis Craig. Apprs: Hugh S. Gatewood, John Wood, Joseph Bledsoe.

SCOTT, JOHN. March 11, 1800. Estate to heirs but names not given. Wit: Percival Butler, John Ray.

SMITH, GEORGE. Oct. 11, 1801. Jan. 10, 1802. Wife: Elizabeth. Ex: Wm. Ellis, Wm. Roswell. Wit: Hugh Gatewood, John Sandon(?), John Sandin,jun.

SMITH, JONATHAN. Inventory. Jan. 1, 1812. Admx: Sarah Smith. Apprs: Joseph Vanpelt, Samuel Simpson, John Vanpelt.

SPENCER, JOHN. Inventory. June 23, 1819. Apprs: John Bond, William Sale, John Adams.

SPILLMAN, WILLIAM. May 4, 1808. ---------. Wife: Mary. Son: Thomas. Gr. son: William. Daughters: Sarah Bristos, Nancy Hensley. Children of Nancy Hensley: Charles, James, Michael, Wesley, Phoebe, Zachariah, Fielding, Ezecle, Martha, Frank, Elizabeth Browning, Spillman. Wit: David Barbee, Michael Miller, Pete Roberts, Henry Brintos.

STAFFORD, HENRY. Aug. 5, 1803. Sept. 1803. Wife: Mary. Daus: Cinthia, Vimah. Ex: John Vanpelt, John Vivlet. Apprs: John Vivlet, William Thomas, Ashford Vivlet.

TANDY, JOHN. Dec. 20, 1813. Legatees: not named.

TANDY, JOHN, Sr. Jan. 13, 1817. Wife and children mentioned but not named. Wit: William Whitehead, Wesley Wayland, Joshua Wayland.

TANDY, JOHN, Jr. June 1, 1817. Inventory. Admrs: Mose Tandy, Rodger Tandy,

Apprs: Daniel Barrol, Henry Ramey, Ephiram Yager, William Whitehead.

VANPELT, JOHN, Sr. Dec. 13, 1813. Wife and heirs mentioned but not named. Apprs: Benjamin Waller, Ligo Cox, Rice Bledsoe. Admr: John Vanpelt Jr.

WHITAKER, R. Inventory. Nov. 25, 1805. Ex: John Davis. Apprs: Wyant James, Alexander Latty, George Bowling.

WHITEHEAD, WILLIAM. March 1, 1819. --------. Legatees: Wife, children and brother Richard. Ex: Richard Whitehead. Wit: William Tandy, John Whitehead, Thomas Hanks.

WILLIAMSON, JOSEPH. Nov. 2, 1807. Legatees: Nephew Joseph Williamson, and brothers(sons of brother John Williamson), Elizabeth King. Ex: Daniel Farley. Wit: George Strother, Daniel Mattox. Apprs: Daniel Farley, Thomas King, Thomas Chagent(?).

WILLIAMS, WILLIAM. Inventory. March 23, 1807. Admr: wife Molly. Apprs: Robert Coleman, William Doan, James Dement, John Hammons.

An inventory and appraisement of the personal estate of George Smith, Decd., which is as follows, towit:-

1 negro man	80:00:00	
1 " "	80:50:00	
1 negro girl	50:00:00	
1 negro boy	40:00:00	
1 " "	40:00:00	
1 negro man	50:60:00	
1 negro woman	50:10:00	
1 negro girl	36:10:00	
1 negro girl	42:60:00	
1 negro boy	70:00:00	
1 negro boy	54:13:00	
1 negro woman	57:10:06	
1 saw	06:18:00	
1 gray horse	06:18:00	
1 whipsaw	01:00:00	
1 gray horse	07:10:00	
1 tea pot	00:10:00	
1 sorrel mare	12:12:00	
1 hoe	00:17:00	
1 "	00:16:00	
1 ax	00:07:06	
1 ax	00:13:00	
1 ax	00:12:00	
1 foot adz	00:06:00	
1 gray mare	09:00:00	
1 barshear plow	01:16:00	
1 log chain	02:04:00	
1 broad ax	00:07:00	
1 grubbing hoe	00:05:06	
1 fan hoop	00:04:06	
Sundries irons etc.	00:16:00	
1 briar sythe	01:00:00	
1 fish gig	00:13:00	
1 pitch fork	00:02:03	
5 earthern ware	02:04:00	
1 smoothing iron	00:10:06	
1 hackles	00:16:00	
Bed furniture	09:12:00	
Spoons, glass tumblers	00:09:06	
Pewter	00:14:00	
Bed and furniture	10:04:00	
Pewter	00:17:00	
1 sugar box	00:15:00	
1 wagon	12:06:00	
1 rifle gun, shot gun	04:26:00	
1 candle mole, 1 urn	00:08:00	
Saddle 1:16:00, wheel	01:12:00	
Chairs 00:18:00, bureau	00:09:00	
1 cow hide	00:08:00	
1 chaise	02:04:00	
saddle bags	06:06:00	
cow and calf	15:00:00	

This list of sale of the estate of George Smith, dec'd., returned to the Court of Gallatin County and ordered recorded, March 1806.
P.B. Butler, Clerk.

www.ingramcontent.com/pod-product-compliance
Lightning Source LLC
Chambersburg PA
CBHW020057020526
44112CB00031B/206